EAST ASIAN LABOR MARKETS

AND THE ECONOMIC CRISIS

IMPACTS

RESPONSES

& LESSONS

Edited by:
Gordon Betcherman
Rizwanul Islam

The World Bank, Washington, D.C.
The International Labour Office, Geneva

Cover design by Design Studio Grafik, Herndon, VA.

Library of Congress Cataloging-in-Publication Data

East Asian labor markets and the economic crisis : impacts, responses, and lessons / edited by
    Gordon Betcherman, Rizwanul Islam.
      p. cm.
    Includes index.
    ISBN 0-8213-4478-1
    ISBN 92-2 112274-3 (ILO)
    1. Labor market—East Asia.   2. Labor market—Asia, Southeastern.   3. East Asia—
Economic conditions.   4. Asia, Southeastern—Economic conditions.   I. Betcherman,
Gordon.   II. Islam, Rizwanul.

HD5826.A6 E37 2000
331.12'095—dc21   00-066782

Contents

TABLES

BOXES

NA

Foreword

AFTER YEARS of remarkable progress in the region, the financial crisis in East and Southeast Asia had sudden and often painful consequences for millions of workers. With disappearing employment and earning opportunities in the formal sector, affected employees and their families had little option but to survive on reduced incomes, informal activities, meager social assistance, and support from others. As the effects of the crisis worsened in late 1997 and 1998, the World Bank and the International Labour Office (ILO) began to explore ways in which they could collaborate with the region's governments, employers, and workers in their response to the difficult social and economic situation.

The two organizations agreed that one important contribution they could jointly make would be to create an opportunity for the affected countries to share their experiences regarding the crisis, its labor market impacts, and the policy lessons that have emerged. With substantial financial support from the Asia-European Meeting (ASEM) fund, the World Bank and the ILO sponsored a regional labor market project covering the Republic of Korea, Indonesia, Malaysia, the Philippines, and Thailand. This included the preparation of five country papers analyzing the labor market aspects of the crisis. The difficult events of the late 1990s also raised important questions for these countries regarding needed labor policy reforms for the longer run. Accordingly, the World Bank and the ILO also sponsored a series of papers by international experts on policy options in key areas including unemployment benefits, active labor market programs, support for vulnerable groups, and social dialogue.

In October 1999, these papers provided the basis for a workshop in Tokyo organized and hosted by the Japanese Ministry of Labor and the Japan Institute of Labor. This workshop involved tripartite delegations from the five Asian countries as well as Japan, academic specialists, and officials from international organizations including the Organisation for Economic Co-operation and Development and the European Union, as well as the World Bank and the ILO.

This book includes the country reports and the international policy papers prepared for the Tokyo workshop, revised to reflect the discussions at that seminar. It describes how the labor markets in the region were affected by the financial crisis and how governments and communities responded. It also looks forward in setting out the labor policy options for the future, based on international experience. We hope that these chapters will be of interest for the countries in East and Southeast Asia in their quest to understand the crisis and to move forward from it. We also hope the book will be a valuable resource more broadly in a world where economic crises seem to occur too frequently and where developing countries are grappling with a range of labor market challenges.

We are pleased that the World Bank and the ILO, with ongoing support from the Japanese government, will continue to collaborate with governments in the region in exploring labor policy options. A follow-up project now under way focuses on the application of active and passive labor programs. With the cooperation of the Philippine government, we will discuss these issues at a regional seminar in Manila in early 2001.

Robert Holzmann
DIRECTOR
SOCIAL PROTECTION UNIT
WORLD BANK

Göran Hultin
EXECUTIVE DIRECTOR
EMPLOYMENT SECTOR
INTERNATIONAL LABOUR OFFICE

Acknowledgments

THIS PROJECT could not have been successfully under-
taken without a number of partner organizations and the contributions of
many individuals. The Asia-European Meeting (ASEM) fund provided
substantial financial support for the research, the Tokyo workshop, and
the publication of this volume. We also want to acknowledge the major
contribution of the Japanese Ministry of Labor (JMOL) and the Japan Institute of Labor (JIL) in organizing and co-hosting the Tokyo workshop.
We would especially like to thank Kimie Iwata (JMOL) and Kunihiko
Saito (JIL) in this regard. Robert Holzmann of the World Bank's Social
Protection Unit was instrumental in the initiation of the project and continued support throughout. From the ILO, Katherine Hagen provided
encouragement in launching the project; Samir Radwan and Mitsuko Ho-
riuchi provided active and ongoing support throughout the project; and
Stanley Taylor coordinated ILO involvement. In addition to their sub-
stantive contributions, Amit Dar, Makoto Ogawa, and Amy Luinstra of
the World Bank flawlessly assumed responsibility for virtually all aspects
of the project's coordination. Mr. Ogawa deserves special mention for initiating the involvement of the government of Japan and coordinating the
workshop arrangements with the Japanese Ministry of Labor and the Japan
Institute of Labor. Melvina Clarke provided excellent administrative support throughout the project. Emily Chalmers expertly edited the volume
in an efficient manner. Studio Grafik designed the volume cover. Finally,
we are grateful to Nicola Marrian, Sheila Queano-Colletta, and Carlos
Rossel of the World Bank's Office of the Publisher for their wise advice
and for guiding us through the entire publication process.

Labor Market Experiences in the Crisis Countries

ōΙ5 J3| J22 3-37
ōΙ5 J24 J23 J68

1 East Asian Labor Markets and the Economic Crisis: An Overview

GORDON BETCHERMAN AND RIZWANUL ISLAM

THE EAST ASIAN crisis has had serious consequences for workers throughout the region. Unemployment has risen, earnings have fallen, and workers' rights have been endangered. The resulting poverty, declines in living standards, and social tensions have threatened the gains made during the unparalleled growth of the 1980s and most of the 1990s. The negative effects of the crisis have also raised difficult questions about development in East and Southeast Asia and, in particular, about the social protections it has afforded. More than three years after the onset of the crisis, evidence suggests that macroeconomic stabilization and recovery are beginning to take hold. But for millions of workers, social and economic hardship continues. Important challenges remain for governments as they work to alleviate the hardship the crisis has caused and to build a sustainable path toward future prosperity.

In 1998 the World Bank and the International Labour Organization (ILO) initiated a project on labor markets and the East Asian crisis. This project was one element in a larger collaboration between these two institutions aimed at providing support as the region responds to the social dimensions of the crisis. The labor market project covers the five countries that received the brunt of the impact—Indonesia, the Republic of Korea, Malaysia, the Philippines, and Thailand—and is designed to stimulate analysis and policy dialogue in the context of international experience.

The project is concerned with both the immediate crisis and long-term policy issues. The crisis has generated a pressing need for an accurate, em-

3

pirically based picture of the impact on employment. How are the labor markets adjusting to the economic contraction? What groups are especially vulnerable to unemployment, underemployment, and wage cuts? And what actions have governments taken to mitigate the hardships workers face and to help those affected cope with the downturn? Understanding the immediate labor market and labor policy as it relates to the crisis is essential for the countries discussed here. But such a study also has wider relevance. Serious economic shocks are occurring with increasing frequency. Policymakers everywhere are eager to learn from the Asian experience in order to improve their understanding of the ways shocks are transmitted to the labor market and to identify measures governments can take to minimize the impacts.

The Asian countries need to begin building on their experiences with the crisis in order to develop long-term labor market policies. With the exception of Korea, the region has seen little policy development in this area. The high rates of economic growth of the 1980s and early 1990s meant that unemployment was not a serious problem, and workers' incomes were rising. Even before the crisis, however, questions were being raised about the adequacy of existing arrangements in areas such as support for unemployed workers, vocational education and training, employment services, and industrial relations. The crisis has underscored the need for careful analysis and consideration of labor policy options.

These issues—some immediate, others long-term—have been at the center of the Asian labor market project. To inform the dialogue, analysts prepared papers on recent labor market developments in each of the five countries. A second series of papers placed the developments in the context of international experience and identified best practices in labor policy. Together these papers formed the basis for a three-day workshop sponsored by the Japanese Ministry of Labor and the Japan Institute of Labor. The workshop, held in Tokyo in October 1999, included tripartite delegations from Indonesia, Korea, Malaysia, the Philippines, and Thailand, as well as specialists from international organizations and the research community.[1]

This volume is based on the papers and discussions that took place in Tokyo. Part I includes chapters on each of the five countries under discussion. Each chapter presents an empirical overview of recent labor market trends in the country and then reviews current policies in employment creation and maintenance, income support for unemployed workers, employment services, and vocational education and training. The chapters in part II place the experiences of these countries in an international context by drawing on the experiences of other countries. The chapters cover active labor market programs, unemployment benefits, vulnerable populations, the relationship between social dialogue and labor market adjustment, and the Japanese experience with employment policy.

The Impact of the Crisis on Labor Markets

In the 15 years before the crisis, Southeast Asia enjoyed dramatic growth. Basic indicators for the five countries under discussion show the region's remarkable growth path (table 1.1). Except for the Philippines, annual GDP (gross domestic product) growth in 1980–95 was more than 6 percent. A key element in this success was the region's openness to international trade and investment. Export growth reached as high as 16 and 22 percent (for Korea and Thailand, respectively) in 1980–96. Net capital inflows were more than 9 percent in Malaysia, the Philippines, and Thailand in the mid-1990s. By 1997 the region, one of the world's poorest a generation earlier, had risen to middle-income level. Korea was moving toward the level of development seen in countries of the Organization for Economic Cooperation and Development (OECD).

This rapid development led to significant changes in the region's labor markets. For the most part, these changes brought improved outcomes for workers. In the 1990s real wages increased significantly in all of the countries except the Philippines.[2] At the same time strong job growth kept unemployment at very low levels (typically well below 5 percent) in all countries but the Philippines. The structure of employment changed as well, with major shifts out of agriculture and into industry and service employment in urban areas. By the onset of the crisis in 1997, at least half of all jobs in each of the five countries were in nonagricultural sectors. Important developments also occurred in the region's labor force: educational levels rose, and female participation increased in every country but Thailand.

The financial crisis began in July 1997 in Thailand and quickly spread throughout the region. The timing and magnitude of the economic contraction varied across countries (figure 1.1). GDP began declining in Thailand in the third quarter of 1997. In the other countries economic growth slowed but remained positive until the beginning of 1998. GDP decreased in 1998 by 0.4 percent in the Philippines, 5.8 percent in Korea, 7.5 percent in Malaysia, 10.0 percent in Thailand, and 13.7 percent in Indonesia. The decline in each country bottomed out sometime between the second and fourth quarters of 1998, and all five countries were growing

demand for labor results in lower employment levels or lower wages. Under perfectly competitive market conditions, adjustment occurs in prices (wages) but not in quantity (employment). But a range of behavioral and institutional factors can generate both types of responses. In developing countries that are undergoing structural adjustment, economic contraction, or both, adjustment occurs primarily through wage declines, which are often greater than declines in GDP (Horton, Kanbur, and Mazumdar 1994; Fallon and Lucas 2000). However the studies also show evidence of adjustment through decreasing employment and rising unemployment.[5]

Important adjustments also occur on the supply side. Labor supply decisions made when demand for labor is weak can lead to either higher or lower participation rates, depending on the relative importance of the discouraged worker and added worker effects. The case studies reported in Horton, Kanbur, and Mazumdar (1994) show that both effects can be important. Similarly, workers faced with a weak labor market may decide to relocate. In Southeast Asia both internal and international migration are important supply-side responses. Workers move between rural and urban areas in response to changes in economic opportunities. Workers also migrate across borders, moving in and out of countries, although such movements are often constrained by policy.

A final aspect of adjustment involves the interaction among segmented labor markets. When labor demand decreases in the formal market, displaced workers have the option of moving to the informal sector, which often expands during economic contractions (Horton, Kanbur, and Mazumdar 1994). This sector includes both rural agricultural employment and informal urban activities. Involuntary open unemployment is essentially nonexistent in informal sectors. But when the labor supply expands because formal-sector workers are displaced, we can expect to observe downward pressure on earnings.

Labor market adjustment to shocks such as the Asian financial crisis, then, involves a number of dimensions: open unemployment, underemployment, declining wages and earnings, changes in labor force participation and migration, and informalization. The importance of each of these aspects depends on various factors, including the magnitude of the economic shock, the structure of the economy, the composition of the labor force, and labor market policies and institutions.

THE MAGNITUDE OF THE SHOCK. The severity of a macroeconomic crisis affects both the scale of labor adjustment and the forms adjustment takes. As we have noted the magnitude of the shock differed across countries in Southeast Asia. Indonesia experienced the largest contraction and the Philippines the smallest, with the other three countries falling somewhere between these extremes.

THE ECONOMIC STRUCTURE. Reduced demand is most likely to be transmitted to the labor market through quantity rather than price adjustments in countries with a relatively high proportion of employment in nonagricultural industries and the formal urban sector. Over the past two decades, major structural shifts away from agriculture and into industry and services occurred throughout the region. But in the late 1990s the five crisis countries were at different stages of development and had different economic structures. According to indicators such as industrial composition and urbanization, Korea was the most developed, followed by Malaysia. Indonesia, the Philippines, and Thailand still had large agricultural sectors, and Indonesia and Thailand had low rates of urbanization.[6]

THE LABOR FORCE. The composition of the labor force can also affect responses to reduced labor demand. Characteristics such as gender, age, and level of education are likely to affect a number of variables, including workers' reservation wage and willingness to move to the informal sector. We have already noted the potential role of migration.[7]

LABOR INSTITUTIONS. Because they affect the decisions of both employers and workers, labor institutions and policies affect labor adjustment in many ways.[8] In Southeast Asia wage setting is generally decentralized and collective bargaining is relatively uncommon, except in the Philippines and Korea (table 1.2). There are certain restrictions on hiring and firing in some countries, although enforcement is often weak. Social protection for unemployed workers is minimal. Only Korea has an unemployment insurance scheme (introduced in 1995), but coverage is low. In the other countries some unemployed workers (usually older workers) have certain drawing rights on provident funds, but these funds tend to offer only minimal support. Severance exists in all countries, although again enforcement is weak. And none of the existing institutions offers protection directly to the informal sector.

Evidence from Southeast Asia

The chapters that constitute the first part of this volume describe the labor market impacts of the economic shock in each of the five crisis countries.

TABLE 1.2

Summary of Labor Market Institutions, late 1990s, Crisis Countries

	Indonesia	Korea	Malaysia	Philippines	Thailand
Minimum wage	Yes	Yes	No	Yes	Yes
Unionization rate	Around 5%	12.6% (1998)	8.4% (1996)	27.0% (1997)	1.7%
Level of wage determination	Company level	Company level	Company level	Company level	Company level
Restriction on hiring	Fixed term contract approved in certain cases	Fixed term contract more than one year prohibited	No restriction	No restriction	No restriction
Restriction on dismissal	Dismissals require tripartite committee approval	Dismissal article will be enforced from 1999 Dismissal article was enacted on Feb. 1998	Advance notice required	Advance notice required	Advance notice required
Severance payment	Mandatory severance payment	Mandatory severance payment	Mandatory severance payment (83% paid in 1998)	Mandatory severance payment	Mandatory severance payment (compliance is noted to be low)

Social protection for unemployed	Employees with more than 5 year service can withdraw accumulated fund from JAMSOSTEK.	UI introduced in 1995. Covering more than 30 employees' firms. Coverage of UI was expanded to all since Jul. 1998	Employees age 50+ can withdraw part of provident fund.	Emergency loan for displaced workers (introduced in March 1998)	Employees have some drawing rights from provident fund
Public Employment Service	1.5 million job applicants (37% of unemployed) registered with PES (1997)	2.1 million job applicants (140% of unemployed) registered with PES (1998)	1.2 million job applicants (30% of unemployed) registered with PES (1998)	0.4 million job applicants (10% of unemployed) registered with PES (1998)	0.7 million job applicants (40% of unemployed) registered with PES (1998)

Source: Based on country papers (this volume).

These chapters focus on the first full year of the crisis. Cross-country empirical analysis tends to be complicated by data comparability issues, and the discussions therefore take into account definitional differences and series breaks. We look here at the major points covered in the chapters.

ADJUSTMENTS IN THE DEMAND FOR LABOR. Quantity-related adjustments varied across the region but were most pronounced in Korea and Thailand (table 1.3). Between 1997 and 1998 open unemployment more than doubled in these two countries, although previous levels had been relatively low. Increases in unemployment were relatively small in Indonesia and the Philippines. The modest increase in the Philippines reflects the equally modest impact of the crisis there. But unemployment rose only 0.7 percentage points in 1998 in Indonesia, despite the fact that GDP declined by 13.7 percent. Similar results emerge for underemployment.[9]

Employment trends repeat this pattern. The largest absolute declines in 1998 occurred in Korea, Thailand, and Malaysia (in that order). Indonesia and the Philippines recorded employment gains, despite the effects of El Niño and despite Indonesia's substantial decline in output. In Indonesia the increase was the result of a gain of 5.4 percent in agricultural employment (table 1.4). In contrast the other countries in the region experienced either no growth or declines in agricultural employment. All countries, including Indonesia, experienced employment losses in industry (manufacturing and mining). Losses in this sector were particularly large in Korea, the most industrialized country in the region.

The crisis also resulted in real wage decreases in all countries (table 1.5).[10] The decline was particularly dramatic in Indonesia, where real wages fell an estimated 41 percent, reflecting the intensity of the impact there. But in comparison with the other countries, Indonesia's labor market response involved mainly prices rather than quantity. Downward pressure on wages was also significant in Korea (9.3 percent) and Thailand (7.4 percent).

ADJUSTMENTS IN THE SUPPLY OF LABOR. Labor force participation rates vary for the five countries we discuss (table 1.6). In three countries (Korea, Malaysia and to a small extent Thailand), the participation rate fell between 1997 and 1998, suggesting that many workers became discouraged and stopped looking for work. In Indonesia and the Philippines, participation increased as more workers joined the labor force (the added worker effect). The labor supply response was generally greater among women than men. In countries where aggregate participation rates fell (Korea and

TABLE 1.3

Summary of Unemployment, Underemployment, and Employment Trends, Crisis Countries, 1996–98[a]

	Unemployment				Underemployment[b]				Employment
	1996	1997	1998	% Change 1997–98	1997	1998	% Change 1997–98		% Change 1997–98
Indonesia	4.9	4.7	5.4	14.9	35.8	39.1	9.2		2.7
Korea	2.0	2.6	6.8	161.5	7.3	9.3	29.2		-5.3
Malaysia	2.6	2.6	4.0	53.8	7.3	7.9	8.2		-2.7
Philippines	8.6	8.7	10.1	16.1	11.3	11.9	5.3		5.8
Thailand[c]	2.0	2.2	5.2	136.4	0.9	1.2	33.3		-2.8

a. Thailand figures for February; Indonesia for August; Korea and the Philippines are averages of quarterly estimates.

b. Underemployment (as % of employed population) defined as: Malaysia, less than 30 hours per week; Korea, 35 hours or less per week; Indonesia, less than 35 hours per week; Thailand and the Philippines, less than 40 hours per week and available for more hours.

c. Working age population in Thailand defined as 13 years of age and older.

Sources: Country papers with updates (this volume); Kakwani (1998); World Bank, *Thailand Economic Monitor*, January 2000.

TABLE 1.7
Employment Status Trends, Crisis Countries, 1997–99

	Indonesia			Korea			Malaysia			Philippines			Thailand		
	% Distribution		% Change	% Distribution		% Change	% Distribution		% Change	% Distribution		% Change	% Distribution		% Change
	1997	1998	1997–98	1997	1998[a]	1997–98	1997	1998	1997–98	1997	1998	1997–98	1997[b]	1998[b]	1997–98
Employer	1.7	1.7	3.4				2.6	2.9	13.5				2.5	2.7	1.3
Self-employed	43.7	45.2	6.3	28.1	29.2	-2.3	16.9	17.7	5.0	37.5	37.6	2.5	30.7	32.2	1.9
Unpaid family worker	19.6	20.6	8.1	8.8	9.5	1.2	6.0	6.0	0.3	14.8	13.4	-7.4	20.3	19.7	-5.5
Employee	35.0	32.4	-4.9	63.1	61.3	-8.3	74.5	73.4	-1.1	47.7	49.0	5.0	46.4	45.4	-5.0
Total	100	100		100	100					100	100		100	100	

a. Figures are for fourth quarter.
b. Figures are for February.
Sources: Country papers and updates and Horton and Mazumdar (this volume).

migrant laborers. Data for the latter two groups are particularly difficult to obtain. Even for women and youth information is generally available for unemployment and labor force participation, but not for other important indicators such as wages and hours.

Have female workers been especially hard hit by the crisis in Asia?[13] The available evidence offers only a partial picture. Differentials in unemployment rates between men and women are not strong. In Korea the unemployment rate for men increased more than the unemployment rate for women, but the other countries show no significant differences in male and female unemployment rates. And as we have already noted, female participation rates rose in Indonesia.

Young workers tend to be particularly vulnerable during an economic crisis, not only because of their lack of experience and low productivity, but also because of hiring slowdowns and seniority practices. The crisis did not substantially affect the traditionally high ratio of youth unemployment to aggregate unemployment. But with the increasingly slack labor market, youth unemployment rose to very high levels. For young males (15–24 years old), 1998 unemployment rates ranged from 11.2 percent in Thailand to 20.8 percent in Korea. For females the range was 8.6 percent in Thailand to 22.1 percent in the Philippines. Participation rates for youth decreased substantially in Korea and Thailand and slightly in Indonesia, but they increased somewhat in the Philippines.

Interpreting the Evidence

In the first year of the crisis, the Korean, Malaysian, and Thai labor markets seem to have responded in broadly comparable ways (table 1.8). All experienced downward pressure on both employment and wages, declining labor force participation, and a shift in employment from the formal to the informal sector. But the magnitude of these adjustments was much more severe in Korea, despite the fact that the scope of the economic shock was slightly smaller there than it was in Malaysia or Thailand. Korea had the region's biggest increase in the region in unemployment (4.2 percentage points) and the largest decline in employment (5.3 percent). Similarly employment declines in the industrial sector (13.2 percent) and in wage employment (8.3 percent) were considerably larger than in the other four countries. Real wages also declined substantially (9.3 percent).

The overall pattern was much the same in Malaysia and Thailand, although adjustments were more moderate, especially in Malaysia. In each country unemployment rose in the first year of the crisis (3.0 percentage

TABLE 1.8
Summary of Labor Adjustment in the Crisis Countries

| | Panel A | | | | Panel B | | | |
| | Severity of crisis (% change in GDP 1998) | Industrial structure (% of employment in agriculture) | Labor market institutions | | Quantity adjustment | Price adjustment | Labor supply adjustment | Informal adjustment |
			Regulation	Unemployment benefits				
Indonesia	−13.7	44	Medium	No	Low	Very high	Small increase	Large
Korea	−5.8	12	High	Yes	High	Medium	Decrease	Medium
Malaysia	−7.5	20	Low	No	Medium	Low	Decrease	n/a
Philippines	−0.4	42	Medium	No	Low	Low	Small increase	Small
Thailand	−10.0	50	Low	No	High	Medium	Small decrease	Medium

Source: Assessments by the authors based on country papers.

points in Thailand and 1.4 percentage points in Malaysia), and employment fell (2.8 percent in Thailand and 2.7 percent in Malaysia). In both countries wage employment declined (5.0 percent in Thailand and 1.1 percent in Malaysia). Migration was also an important adjustment mechanism in Thailand, which saw extensive urban-to-rural flows, and in Malaysia, where the number of foreign workers fell. The major difference in the Thai and Malaysia experiences was the larger decline in real wages in Thailand—7.4 percent, compared with 1.1 percent.[14]

Compared with the other countries, labor adjustment in the Philippines was moderate in all ways. This moderation reflects the much smaller output shock (a 0.4 percent decline in GDP in 1998) caused by the crisis. The labor market experience in Indonesia was also unique, with huge downward wage adjustments and a significant shift in employment to the informal sector. Real wages declined by an astounding 41 percent, with all sectors experiencing similar downward pressures. Workers displaced from the wage sector and new entrants went into informal employment in large numbers. In 1998 agricultural employment increased by over 5 percent, and self-employment and unpaid family work grew by 6.3 and 8.1 percent, respectively. Despite the fact that the output shock was greatest in Indonesia, however, the unemployment rate rose less than 1 percentage point, and employment actually increased by almost 3 percent in the first year of the crisis. The labor force participation rate also rose slightly.

Many aspects of the experience in Southeast Asia—the decline in real wages, labor displacement in the industrial sector, and a shift from wage to nonwage employment—are common across countries in the region. But the way the labor markets have adjusted also differ in important ways. As we have seen Korea saw significant reductions in employment, while Indonesia saw informal sector expansion and extremely high wage reductions. These patterns are not surprising, given the differences between the two countries in level of development, labor regulation, and formal social protection and in the severity of the economic shock.[15]

In the final analysis, evaluating how differences in the adjustment process affected the welfare of workers will be of the utmost importance. Economists often argue that adjusting to reduced labor demand through downward wages is preferable to quantity adjustments that result in open unemployment. But as Horton, Kanbur, and Mazumdar (1994) point out, the net welfare effects of these different adjustment paths are not so clear. Unfortunately assembling the evidence necessary to compare outcomes is not straightforward. Poverty rates are one potentially important indicator, and these rates rose significantly in both Korea and Indonesia.

In Korea the urban poverty head count went from 9 percent in 1997 to 19 percent in 1998 (World Bank 2000a).[16] In Indonesia the rate rose from 11 percent in 1996 to 20 percent in late 1998 (World Bank 2000b). But these data are spotty and not generally comparable across countries, and their links to labor market experiences are difficult to establish. More detailed analysis will be required to identify the full labor market impacts of the Asian crisis.

Government Responses to the Crisis

Governments in Southeast Asia have responded to the crisis with two types of interventions: active labor market programs, and measures designed to support incomes. Before the crisis experience with active labor market interventions (especially the kind found in industrial economies) in the region was limited, except in Korea. Since the crisis Indonesia, the Philippines, and Thailand have instituted direct employment creation schemes, including labor-intensive infrastructure construction programs and credit schemes to promote self-employment and enterprise development.[17] All five countries have functioning institutions that provide vocational training and employment services, and their responses to the crisis have included interventions in skill training and job search services specifically for displaced workers.

Job Creation Measures

All five countries discussed in this volume have introduced or revived public works programs, in part because introducing such schemes as an emergency measure was a natural response to the crisis. In addition to these programs, and as a longer-term measure, governments have put in place or stepped up programs that support (mainly in the form of credit) self-employment and enterprise development.

PUBLIC WORKS PROGRAMS. Governments introduced a variety of public works programs in Southeast Asia (table 1.9). Indonesia reintroduced the labor-intensive infrastructure construction programs (*padat karya*) that had been phased out in the early 1990s as the labor market tightened. The programs started in 1997 with four-month projects and were followed in 1998 by large-scale programs covering the entire country. The programs were expected to generate 300 million person-days of work. In Korea public works programs generated 440,000 jobs in 1998 and nearly 1.2 million jobs in 1999, providing work for around 70 percent of the country's 1.7 million unemployed in 1999. The Thai government also launched massive programs using both government and donor funds.

In the absence of unemployment insurance schemes (except in Korea), public works programs provided unemployed workers with much-needed income. These schemes have also proved more cost-effective than other types of income support, such as subsidies. The Indonesian public works programs, for example, spent less than $4 for each $1 that was transferred to the poorest 15 percent of the population. The cost of rice subsidies was twice as high—$8.20 for each $1 transferred (World Bank 1998).

Despite their positive aspects, all the programs suffered from a number of problems. First, they were not well targeted. In general the best type of targeting for public works programs is self-targeting, but in Southeast Asia this method did not work because wages were set too high. Second, many of the programs were poorly designed, as they were rushed into operation when the crisis hit. And in countries like Indonesia and Thailand, where public works programs had already been phased out, planning and implementation capacity was severely limited.

Third, the programs suffered from poor coordination and a lack of proper monitoring. In Thailand, for example, several programs were launched at once without proper coordination, and the projects were unable to recruit enough workers. Fourth, female participation was low, largely because women often do not participate in construction projects and no programs were targeted specifically to women. Finally, in Indonesia the wage bill as a percentage of total project costs was too low, so that fewer jobs than anticipated were created.

Even with their shortcomings, public works programs in Southeast Asia have demonstrated that carefully designed and implemented schemes can succeed. In Indonesia schemes that involved local communities have performed much better than those planned and implemented without such participation. In Korea women accounted for nearly half of the participants in public works programs in 1999.

PROGRAMS IN SUPPORT OF SELF-EMPLOYMENT AND ENTERPRISE DEVELOPMENT. Many Southeast Asian countries had programs supporting self-employment and the development of small enterprises in place before the crisis. These programs focus mainly on credit, although they also include a variety of technical support services. High interest rates and the credit crunch during the crisis posed problems for some of these initiatives, but

TABLE 1.9

Job Creation through Public Works Programs

Country	Brief description of the public works program	Problems identified	Observations
Indonesia	• A four-month, Rp. 42 billion program targeted retrenched workers from construction and manufacturing (December 1997). • Massive infrastructure construction project with 16 sub-programs covering all provinces (April 1998).	• Poor program design • Poor targeting • Too low a wage bill compared with material costs • Low incidence of female participation • Significant leakages	• Projects with community participation in design and implementation did better
Korea	• Public works programs created 440,000 jobs in 1998 and 1,190,000 jobs in 1999.	• High wage and poor targeting • Poor project design	• High female participation

Malaysia	• Public works program extended	
Philippines	• Public works programs created 476,000 jobs (1997) • Rural works program generated 4,837 jobs	• No geographical targeting • No targeting of vulnerable groups in some projects • Administrative delays • High wages preclude self-targeting
		• Department of Labor and Employment (DOLE) projects did target vulnerable groups
Thailand	• Ministry of Interior projects targeted to create 788,799 jobs (1999) • Various donor-funded projects targeted another 11 million persons-months of jobs	• Lack of information about location of the jobs • Lack of coordination of projects created labor shortage • Low quality of projects

several countries implemented new programs aimed at creating jobs through enterprise development (table 1.10).

In 1998 Korea initiated two programs. This first was designed to provide jobs for unemployed professionals through new ventures and self-employment; the second combined training and start-up loans for small businesses. In 1998 Malaysia launched a fund for small-scale entrepreneurs aimed at creating self-employment opportunities and a second fund for small and medium-size industries. The Philippines already had over 100 "livelihood programs" covering nearly 90,000 beneficiaries when the crisis struck in 1997, but high interest rates and reduced funding limited these programs during the crisis. Thailand also launched several programs to promote self-employment, but they were small in both size and coverage. The government and some commercial banks introduced credit programs for small and medium-size enterprises (SMEs) in 1999.

The Indonesian government requires commercial banks to set aside a percentage of their loans for small borrowers. Cooperatives offer subsidized credit, and at least 24 government programs offer credit to microentrepreneurs and SMEs, particularly farmers, transmigrants, and women. Despite the plethora of programs, most require collateral and thus are not available to borrowers without assets. Only a few offer collateral-free credit—far fewer than are needed—and many have been constrained during the crisis by high interest rates and the credit crunch.

Skill Training Interventions

All five countries discussed here had national systems of vocational training in place when the crisis hit, but the governments made special efforts to respond to crisis-related training needs (table 1.11). In Indonesia and the Philippines, the skill training programs undertaken in response to the crisis were small compared with the number of displaced workers. Indonesia's programs also suffered from design and targeting problems. Korea's training program, however, covered nearly a quarter of the unemployed in 1998, and in 1999 the government increased the training budget by 19 percent. Preliminary assessments indicate that the program in Korea did help increase employability, despite inadequate labor market information and management problems. Malaysia also launched several programs, including a retraining scheme for retrenched workers and a graduate entrepreneur scheme. Thailand initiated several government- and donor-funded skill training programs, but they have not yet been assessed.

TABLE 1.10
Job Creation through Support of SMEs and Self-employment

Country	Support for self-employment and SMEs	Observations
Indonesia	• Government required percentage of commercial lending to small borrowers • Subsidized credit for cooperatives • 24 government micro and SME credit programs targeted groups such as farmers, transmigrants, and women	• Most credit programs require collateral • Too few collateral-free microcredit programs • Very high interest rates during the crisis
Korea	• Government allocated 700 billion won and targeted 50,000 persons to support new ventures and self-employment (1998) • Training and start-up loans allocated 300 billion won and targeted 10,000 persons (1998)	• The program targeted unemployed professionals and managers
Malaysia	• Small-scale Entrepreneur Fund allocated 390 million RM (1998) • SMI Fund (RM 1,123.4 million through first quarter of 1999)	• Aimed at creating self-employment opportunities • For small and medium industries in manufacturing

(Table continues on the following page)

TABLE 1.12
Response through Employment Services

Country	Response to the crisis	Observations
Indonesia		• Regional employment service offices registered about 8 million laid-off workers; but no special measures undertaken.
Korea	• Increased number of public employment services agencies and counselors. • Information technology utilized. • One-stop "Employment Security Centers" set up.	• The number of job seekers using the PES increased. • The effectiveness of PES is still a question.
Malaysia	• Registration and placement of retrenched workers introduced in January 1998. • "Job fair"/"job link" programs for retrenched workers.	• New programs achieved some success.
Philippines	• 146 new Public Employment Service Offices (PESOs) were established and 118 were reactivated (1998). Expansion continued in 1999. • Philippine Job Exchange Network launched in 1998. • Jobs/Livelihood fairs conducted.	
Thailand		• No significant new initiatives.

also expanded its public employment service system and launched an Internet-based job-matching system. Malaysia has introduced a program to register and place retrenched workers, and both Malaysia and the Philippines have organized job fairs for retrenched workers. Malaysia has reported success with both its initiatives.

Wage and Employment Subsidies

Incentives for employers—often in the form of wage subsidies—are another active labor market measure that helps maintain existing jobs and create new ones. Such incentives have not been a significant policy tool in the Asian countries affected by the crisis, except for Korea and Malaysia. (The Philippines has two small wage subsidy programs targeting young people.) In Malaysia job-maintenance programs are designed to encourage the private sector to choose pay cuts, temporary layoffs, retraining, flexible work hours, and part-time employment over retrenchment. Korea has introduced an effective program to provide subsidies to firms that agree to maintain their current workforce.

Income-Support Measures

Income support for workers in Southeast Asia is limited (see chapter 8). The only country in the Asian region that had unemployment insurance when the economic crisis hit was Korea, and none of the other countries has instituted an unemployment insurance scheme since the crisis. The Employment Insurance System established in Korea in 1995 was initially limited to workers in firms with more than 30 employees. By October 1998 coverage had been extended to firms with fewer than 5 workers, temporary workers employed at least 1 month, and part-time workers working more than 18 hours a week. The length of time workers can collect benefits was also increased. Despite these reforms only 12 percent of unemployed workers were receiving benefits in mid-1999.

As we saw earlier severance pay is widely used in Southeast Asia, but enforcement is weak. Severance pay varies from two to six months' salary in the countries affected by the crisis. But many bankrupt companies have not met their obligations, and they have not been forced to do so. Special funds have been set up in Korea and Thailand to guarantee that severance is paid (Lee 1999).

A final form of income support available to retrenched workers is money they have saved in the state-run provident funds designed mainly to provide retirement benefits. The proportion of employed workers able to access this benefit varies considerably across countries but is only 12 percent in Indonesia and 16 percent in Thailand. The average balance per worker in the national provident fund of Indonesia in 1997 was the equivalent of $22 and thus could not be regarded as a substantial means of income support.

Emerging Labor Policy Issues in Southeast Asia[18]

For the most part the impact of the Asian economic crisis on labor markets has been similar to the impact of other serious downturns. Workers throughout the region have suffered declines in real earnings, industrial sectors have contracted, and employment has shifted from formal to informal activities. These adjustments have been most dramatic in Indonesia, where the effects of the crisis have been most severe. In parts of the region, most notably Korea, open unemployment has increased as well. With most countries now enjoying some degree of stabilization and recovery, employment is beginning to pick up. However experience from earlier crises suggests that the upswing in labor markets during recoveries progresses more slowly than the downswing during contractions.

The experience of the crisis has been an important one for policymakers, both in terms of responding to major economic downturns and in terms of building a sustainable development path for the future. During the era of rapid development in East and Southeast Asia, labor market policy was put on the back burner. Growth, after all, is the best way to increase employment and raise incomes. When the crisis hit, none of the affected countries (except to a small extent Korea) had policies in place to help workers cope. Governments throughout the region must now work to develop policy instruments to manage labor market risks. As they do so they must address several issues. First, they must find the right mix of policies to promote job growth, improve skills, increase labor productivity, and protect workers against both structural and cyclical shocks. Second, given that traditionally the family and community have served as support structures, governments must find a balance between formal and informal mechanisms. And policymakers in each country must identify the kinds of industrial relation institutions that are appropriate to both the country's culture and its social and economic stage of development.

The Southeast Asian countries will cope with these complex issues in different ways. There is no simple solution to the question of income support for unemployed workers, for instance. As mentioned earlier, unemployment insurance had a limited coverage in precrisis East Asia. Lee (1999), however, makes a strong case for introducing unemployment insurance. While refuting the arguments against this form of income support, he addresses the technical issues of affordability and feasibility from the point of view of a number of countries and concludes that "an average required contribution rate of between 0.3 and 0.4 per cent of payroll from 1991 to 2000 would have made a significant contribution to cushioning the harsh impact of the crisis on modern sector workers"(p. 83).[19]

There is also the view that many countries in the region have relatively few resources and a small formal sector, and in these economies unemployment insurance may not be the most effective means of providing support for the unemployed. Chapter 8 raises a series of questions about unemployment insurance and suggests alternative approaches that merit careful consideration from governments in the region.

Labor market interventions by and large have focused on direct job creation rather than on skill training and job search assistance. One reason for this focus is that in the absence of income-support measures such as unemployment insurance, governments saw job-creation schemes as a quick means of generating much-needed incomes for those in distress.[20] Chapter 7 notes that the effectiveness of skill training as an active labor market measure in industrial countries has been called into question because of the low rates of return associated with training programs. But the social benefits of skill training, especially for disadvantaged groups, also need to be examined, along with cost-cutting measures. And given the fact that job search assistance programs have been found to be relatively cost-effective, countries may want to use them to broaden the range of active labor market policies during the recovery.

Public Works

A number of issues relating to public works have emerged from the experience of the Southeast Asian countries that implemented these programs in response to the crisis. First, there is the question of objectives. While it is possible to think of job creation and income generation as the sole objectives of such programs, experience shows that pursuing other goals— for instance, the provision of much-needed infrastructure and social capital—is possible and indeed desirable. If labor-intensive infrastructure projects are carefully selected and implemented, they can meet the criterion of economic efficiency in low-wage situations. And the main development justification for such programs is their ability to serve a dual function as a social safety net in crisis situations and as a long-term means of creating assets. But the objectives need to be made explicit so that they can be taken into account in designing and evaluating the programs.

Institutional capacity for designing, implementing, and monitoring job creation programs is a second important issue. Countries where labor-intensive public works programs were phased out or had never existed had limited capacity to institute them. Such countries could not realistically be expected to launch projects that would meet the criteria for sound design and quality. The programs they rushed to implement were certainly open to criticism. In some cases low-priority projects that had been discarded earlier were resumed. And the administrative machinery of the governments was also caught unprepared, resulting in inefficient implementation and monitoring. Policymakers must now consider how best to prepare for a crisis situation and then set up the necessary organizational machinery.

A third important issue for direct job creation programs is targeting. While the poor constitute a category that is obviously in need of assistance, the crisis affected vulnerable groups differently, as chapter 9 discusses, and its impact also differed across geographic regions. These differential effects need to be considered in planning and implementing job creation programs. In addition, mechanisms need to be devised that will attract target groups. Self-targeting through wage setting is an effective mechanism for ensuring that public works projects benefit the poor. Wages that are set too far above market levels—especially in the absence of means testing—often attract those with high reservation wages and other nontarget groups. Alternative targeting mechanisms, such as involving communities in the selection of beneficiaries, also need to be explored.

Self-employment and Entrepreneurship Support

Support for self-employment and entrepreneurship, especially programs aimed at microentrepreneurs and small enterprises, can be a promising means of job creation. These programs also involve issues of targeting, as well as the problem of collateral for credit. But two additional issues have emerged from the experience in Southeast Asia. First, in a major economic crisis with soaring interest rates and a severe credit squeeze, promoting and sustaining credit-based programs may be difficult until interest rates fall to reasonable levels. Second, in a deep recession, contractions in demand may add to the challenges microentrepreneurs and small enterprises face.

Vocational Education and Training

The economic crisis has also changed the overall context of skill training. In many countries the crisis has highlighted the lack of institutional capacity to respond to changing situations. The importance of preparing training systems to respond to structural reforms has become increasingly apparent. Even in noncrisis situations growing and dynamic economies undergo structural reforms, and governments must provide the training necessary to meet the ensuing challenges. Doing so will require improving coordination among providers and incorporating a stronger demand-side orientation into the training systems themselves.

Employment Services

A number of issues have emerged in the area of employment services. The key question concerns the effectiveness of publicly provided job search assistance during a period of recession. The crisis has called into question the institutional capacity of Southeast Asian economies to provide effective public employment services. Governments must find ways to extend the geographic reach of employment services and the range of services provided, to ensure that the services offered are in demand, to update technology (particularly computer networks), and to provide training for staff. By offering comprehensive services, including counseling, labor market information, and referrals to skill training, public employment services can make themselves more relevant. And as the economies recover, employment services can play a valuable role in efficiently matching workers with new job opportunities.

Governance and Dialogue

The Asian economic crisis has highlighted the importance of transparency and accountability in governance and the need for dialogue that will involve civil society in the process of change. Even before the crisis many Southeast Asian countries were looking at political reforms that would foster an environment of participation and dialogue. As chapter 10 points out, dialogue has economic as well as social benefits. And Lee (1999) argues that "the strengthening of democratic institutions is central to the post-crisis economic model that is required" (p. 64). Indeed, the economic crisis created situations and opportunities for closer adherence to basic international labor standards and further consolidation of appropriate institutions of social dialogue at the macro level. The experience has not only demonstrated the negative consequences of a relative neglect of labor rights and social protection in the precrisis period, but also the potential as well as actual role of labor standards and social dialogue in ensuring smooth adjustment to structural change and in coping with economic crisis.[21]

But meaningful and effective dialogue in the area of labor policy requires strong labor market institutions as well as an enabling political and social environment, and the economic crisis has weakened many of these institutions. Large-scale retrenchments have resulted in declining union membership. And the national-level tripartite initiatives some countries have instituted are not effective substitutes for established institutions. Governments need to continue working to institutionalize a culture of cooperation and dialogue. The legislative reforms that have been implemented so far represent important steps toward creating such a culture. These efforts must not be abandoned as economies find themselves on the road to recovery.

Notes

1. The project received substantial funding from the Asia-Europe Meeting Trust Fund, which is sponsored by the European Union. The World Bank and the International Labour Organization greatly appreciate the contributions of the European Union, the Japanese Ministry of Labor, and the Japanese Institute of Labor.

2. Real wage growth was 52 percent in Korea (1990–97), 25 percent in Malaysia (1990–96) and Thailand (1990–97), and 13 percent in Indonesia (1990–96) (ILO 1999a). The decline in the Philippines was 5 percent between 1990 and 1995.

3. A caveat should be made concerning the role of economic policy. The particular macroeconomic responses to the financial crisis have not been uniform across the region. For example Korea and Thailand largely adhered to the orthodox prescriptions of the International Monetary Fund, while Malaysia took a dramatically different approach that included instituting capital controls. These differences in economic policy undoubtedly have affected how the crisis has been transmitted to the labor market, but we do not explicitly consider them here.

4. For a conceptual discussion see Layard, Nickell, and Jackman (1994). Also see Horton, Kanbur, and Mazumdar (1994) for a review of these issues based on case studies in developing countries.

5. In terms of quantity adjustments, reduced labor demand can also be manifested in underemployment, or reduced working hours. Unfortunately there is little evidence of such adjustment.

6. The GDP per capita figures shown in table 1.1 support this relative ranking.

7. The participation rates for Thailand in table 1.1 are based on a working-age population defined as 15 and older (ILO 1999b). These rates differ from those cited later in the chapter, which come directly from the Thai Labor Force Survey and are based on a population 13 years and older.

8. The extensive literature on this issue examines the impact of minimum wages, wage determination processes, employment protection laws, active labor market programming, and social insurance on labor market performance. See, for example, OECD (1999); Elmeskov, Martin, and Scarpetta (1998); Nickell and Layard (1997). On labor market adjustment to shocks, see Blanchard and Wolfers (1999). This literature deals largely with labor markets in industrial countries. Much less analysis has been done on developing countries. See, however, Freeman (1992) and Lindauer (1999).

9. The number of hours that constitute underemployment varies across countries (see table 1.5), but in all cases the underemployment rate represents the proportion of the employed labor force that is working less than a full-time standard.

10. Wage earners represent only between one-third and two-thirds of the labor forces in the countries discussed here. Data on labor income for nonwage earners are scarce, so that estimating price adjustments for this group is difficult. Kakwani (1998) has computed labor incomes for different classes of Thai workers. According to these calculations, average wages decreased by 7.1 percent between 1997 and 1998 (February surveys), and average total labor income (both business and farm) decreased by 10.1 percent.

11. ILO (1999a) reviews migration patterns in Indonesia during the crisis.

12. Wage employment also shifted from regular and temporary forms to more informal daily work

13. This volume is directly concerned with the position of women in the labor market. Second-order effects may also exist (such as the intrafamily distribution of income and declines in women's economic position before the crisis, especially for single mothers) that have had negative welfare impacts.

14. These figures relate only to formal (wage sector) employment. Possible inaccuracies exist in nominal wage data, and price deflators are often uncertain. The figures based on the country reports are not always consistent with real wage trends reported elsewhere.

15. The differences across countries are also attributable to the state of the labor markets at the onset of the crisis. For example the chapters on Thailand and Korea argue that even before the crisis, labor competitiveness in these countries had been eroding. These observations are supported by unpublished World Bank estimates, which find that unit labor costs in Korea and, to a lesser degree, in Thailand increased in the late 1980s and early 1990s. But unit labor costs in Indonesia declined during this period. The quantity adjustments observed in Korea and Thailand, but not in Indonesia, reflect trends in competitiveness that predate the crisis. The macroeconomic shock simply provided a stimulus for overdue labor rationalization.

16. This rate seems to be dropping rapidly as the recovery takes hold in Korea. The figure for the first quarter of 1999 was 15 percent (World Bank 2000b).

17. Such schemes are better known by their generic name, *public works*, although this term no longer reflects the nature of such schemes. In many instances the projects are run by private contractors.

18. The Chairman's Summary from the seminar on Economic Crisis, Employment, and the Labor Market in East and Southeast Asia, which is appended at the end of this chapter, provides a good overview of the labor issues that emerged from the recent economic crisis in Asia as well as ideas for possible responses to such issues. This section should, therefore, be read along with the Chairman's Summary appended to the present chapter.

19. Indeed, the ILO Governing Body symposium on the Social Impact of the Asian Financial Crisis held in Geneva on 19–20 March 1999 called for the assignment of high priority to the design and implementation of efficient social insurance systems.

20. In Korea, where some unemployment insurance was available, the government made considerable efforts in the areas of skill training and job search assistance.

21. One of the conclusions of the ILO Governing Body Symposium on the Social Impact of the Asian Financial Crisis referred to earlier statements that social dialogue confers substantial economic and social benefits in terms of its contribution to non-conflictual economic restructuring and to the weathering of economic crisis.

References

Blanchard, Olivier, and Justin Wolfers. 1999. "The Role of Shocks and Institutions in the Rise of European Unemployment: The Aggregate Evidence." Cambridge, Mass: National Bureau of Economic Research. Working Paper 7282.

Elmeskov, Jorgen, John Martin, and Stefano Scarpetta. 1998. "Key Lessons for Labor Market Reform: Evidence from OECD Country Experiences." *Swedish Economic Policy Review* 5(2) pp. 205–58.

Fallon, Peter R., and Robert E. B. Lucas. 2000. "The Impact of Financial Crises on Labor Markets, Household Incomes and Poverty: A Review of Evidence." Washington, D.C.:World Bank. Unpublished paper.

Freeman, Richard. 1992. "Labor Market Institutions and Policies: Help or Hindrance to Economic Development?" *Proceedings of the World Bank Annual Conference on Development Economics*. Washington, D.C.: World Bank, pp. 117–44.

Horton, Susan, Ravi Kanbur, and Dipak Mazumdar. 1994. "Vulnerable Groups and the Labor Market: The Aftermath of the Asian Financial Crisis." Paper prepared for the seminar "Economic Crisis, Employment, and the Labor Market in East and South-east Asia," sponsored by the World Bank, International Labor Organization, and Japanese Ministry of Labor-Japan Institute of Labor, Tokyo.

ILO (International Labour Office). 1999a. *Indonesia: Strategies for Employment-Led Recovery and Reconstruction*. Geneva.

———. 1999b. Key Indicators of the Labor Market. Geneva.

Kakwani, Nanak. 1998. "Impact of the Economic Crisis on Employment, Unemployment, and Real Income." Bangkok: Thailand National Economic and Social Development Board. Conference Paper.

Layard, Richard, Stephen Nickell, and Richard Jackman. 1994. *The Unemployment Crisis*. New York: Oxford University Press.

Lee, Eddy. 1999. *The Asian Financial Crisis: The Challenge for Social Policy*. Geneva: International Labor Office.

Lindauer, David. 1999. "Labor Market Reforms and the Poor." Department of Economics Wellesley College. Wellesley, Mass. Unpublished paper.

Nickell, Stephen, and Richard Layard. 1997. "The Labor Market Consequences of Technical and Structural Change." Discussion Paper Series 23. Oxford: Centre for Economic Performance.

OECD (Organization for Economic Cooperation and Development). 1994. *The Jobs Study*. Paris.

———. 1999. *Employment Outlook*. Paris.

World Bank. 1998. *Indonesia in Crisis: A Macroeconomic Update*. Washington, D.C.

———. 2000a. *Global Economic Prospects and the Developing Countries 2000*. Washington, D.C.

———. 2000b. *East Asia Quarterly Brief*. January. Washington, D.C.

38–41

Chairman's Summary

KENJI TUNEKAWA

THE SEMINAR ON THE Economic Crisis, Employment, and the Labor Market in East and Southeast Asia was held in Tokyo under the sponsorship of the World Bank, the International Labour Organization, the Japanese Ministry of Labor, and the Japan Institute of Labor on October 13–15, 1999.

Tripartite delegations from Indonesia, the Republic of Korea, Malaysia, the Philippines, and Thailand; officials of international organizations; the Japanese government; and academic resource people met to discuss recent labor market trends related to the financial crisis; examine the roles of governments, trade unions, and employers' associations in each nation; and consider policy options both for mitigating the impacts of the crisis and for building strong labor policies in the region.

The discussions were very constructive because of the interaction of the tripartite delegations, the well-prepared documents on which the proceedings were based, and the sharing of experiences across countries.

This was the first time for the World Bank and the ILO to hold such a seminar regarding the Asian financial crisis. The seminar demonstrated the usefulness of collaboration between the World Bank and the ILO in supporting a social development agenda.

The following conclusions emerged from the discussions:

1. Generally, the macroeconomic and labor market conditions in the five Asian countries are improving, although the overall situation remains severe.

2. Wide diversity exists throughout the region in the stage of economic development, the impacts of the financial crisis, and the current status of the recovery. Therefore, countermeasures need to be designed in accordance with each country's situation.

3. The financial crisis has created an opportunity for strengthening democratic mechanisms, particularly social dialogue, in each country. This can enhance the search for solutions to the negative socioeconomic impacts of the crisis, and facilitate recovery by building consensus and securing commitment to decisions made. Therefore, it is important to create an effective tripartite framework to enhance the exchange of ideas and policymaking. This must be accompanied by efforts to strengthen the capacity of trade unions and employers' associations to engage in constructive social dialogue.

4. A strong labor policy framework includes active labor market programs, human resource development, a social safety net for workers, and appropriate labor laws and standards. These components need to be well balanced and integrated. Countries need to consider both growth and social protection objectives and the formal and informal sectors. However, there is no uniform solution: an individual country's strategy will depend on its stage of development and its institutions. More detailed conclusions include:

    (a) Active labor market programs (ALMPs) include employment services such as job search assistance and placement services, training, and employment creation, including wage subsidies and public works. These programs have the potential to reduce unemployment, enhance human resource development, increase the employability of disadvantaged workers, and improve the functioning of the labor market. Evaluations of these programs, however, mainly in OECD countries, show that economic conditions, worker characteristics, and program design have significant impacts on their effectiveness. An effective active labor market program is essential as formal labor markets grow, and a skilled work force becomes increasingly important. East and Southeast Asian countries now need to think about the roles of the public and private sectors and building capacity to design, implement, and evaluate programs. An immediate priority is to develop a strong employment service, since this is the cornerstone of the overall strategy.

    (b) Programs of labor-intensive infrastructure construction, if carefully targeted and properly designed and implemented, can not only provide a valuable safety net for the poor and the unemployed, but also contribute to further economic recovery and development. Efforts should be made, therefore, to overcome the observed deficiencies in designing and implementing such programs. Increased involvement of local communities and private sector participation can contribute to their improvement.

(c) Small and medium enterprises (SMEs) that utilize local resources, are less dependent on imported inputs, and are capable of exploiting export markets have demonstrated a degree of resilience during the current crisis as well as their potential for growth and employment creation during the recovery period. Policies need to be geared toward creating an enabling environment and providing necessary support services for boosting their development.

(d) The fulfillment of employment service systems is one of the most inexpensive and effective policies, but introducing this system during a recession might limit its effect. The development of public employment services during recovery is necessary not only for this crisis, but also for future economic development.

(e) Human resource development is essential for national competitiveness. This includes strong universal basic skills, workers with advanced technological abilities, and personnel with the capacity for creativity and innovation. While human resource development policy is more effective in economic recovery, it is now important to formulate an effective strategy and measures to meet the challenge.

(f) The crisis has underlined the vulnerability of certain groups such as women, children (especially child laborers), the disabled, and foreign workers. Generally, protection for these groups has not been adequate compared with the hardship they have experienced. Appropriate policy responses will differ according to the group and its needs. In any event, policies need to reflect the fact that many vulnerable workers are in the informal sector.

(g) The importance of a safety net for workers, including income support for the unemployed, has been underlined by the impacts of the financial crisis. While it might be difficult in some countries to introduce a well-designed system that would have a significant impact during the current crisis, evaluating the design of new, or improving existing, systems should begin immediately. For formal sector workers, options include unemployment insurance, unemployment assistance, and strengthened severance systems.

There are relative strengths and weaknesses to each approach. Well-designed systems, however, can both limit the social costs of an economic downturn and help to speed recovery. Consideration of options includes financial and political sustainability, administrative capacity, the degree of support offered to the unemployed, and the implications for labor market efficiency and economic restructuring. Policymakers also must recognize the large numbers of informal risk management strategies already in place and how to extend and improve these.

(h) Labor laws affecting hiring, deployment, and dismissal are needed to achieve the twin objectives of economic efficiency and social protection. Both of these objectives need to be considered jointly. Labor standards are also critical for protecting the rights of workers. The core labor standards included in the ILO Declaration on the Fundamental Principles and Rights at Work should be encouraged in each country. The principles embodied in these standards should be promoted, and the ILO Conventions to which they refer should be reviewed by governments and the social partners with a view to their ratification.

5. It is important to strengthen technical cooperation across countries and between countries and the international organizations to cope with both the impacts of the crisis and the need for policies for the long run. The collaboration between the ILO and the Bretton Woods institutions is important in order to implement this cooperation effectively. The seminar has been an important event in promoting this cooperation.

6. The sharing of the experiences in each country and the international experience should enhance policy dialogue throughout the region.

Ultimately, each country must examine its options to address labor issues. Further tripartite dialogue will be important. The ILO, the World Bank, and the Japanese Ministry of Labor look forward to following up the seminar with technical assistance and further dialogue.

2 The Economic Crisis: Labor Market Challenges and Policies in Indonesia

Rizwanul Islam, Gopal Bhattacharya,
Shafiq Dhanani, Max Iacono,
Farhad Mehran, Swapna Mukhopadhyay,
and Phan Thuy

UNTIL THE EAST ASIAN crisis Indonesia had enjoyed remarkable success with its economic development strategies. Annual GDP growth throughout the 1980s stood at 6.1 percent, rising to 7.6 percent in the first half of the 1990s and to 7.8 percent in 1996. The economy diversified as it grew. The manufacturing sector in particular turned in an impressive performance, growing at a rate of 10 percent yearly between 1985 and 1995 and ultimately accounting for a quarter of the nation's GDP. Indonesia exported a wide range of manufactures, including textiles and apparel, wood products, and petrochemicals. Merchandise exports grew at an average of nearly 15 percent a year in 1986–93 but then began to decline; in 1996 the growth rate was 8.8 percent (World Bank 1997a; ADB 1997; ILO 1996).

Indonesia's gross investment rate went from 24 percent of GDP in 1980 to 32 percent in 1996. Domestic savings also grew, and the economy continued to finance about 90 percent of its investment domestically. In 1996 the domestic savings rate was 31 percent of GDP (World Bank 1997a).

Indonesia's performance on the employment front was less impressive in the years leading up to the crisis. Employment increased more slowly than the size of the labor force (Islam 1998). Between 1988 and 1995 em-

43

ployment grew at 2.3 percent annually, while the labor force grew at 3.1 percent. Annual employment growth actually declined from 2.8 percent in 1985–90 to 1.8 percent in 1990–95. The rate of open unemployment jumped from 3.2 percent in 1990 to 7.0 percent in 1995.[1] In 1996 (immediately before the crisis) approximately 4.4 million people, or nearly 5 percent of the labor force, were already looking for jobs. The problem of unemployment was most serious in urban areas, where the rate rose from 6.1 percent in 1990 to 10.9 percent in 1995. Unemployment also seriously affected those with a university education: for this group, the rate jumped from 6.7 percent in 1990 to 11.5 percent in 1995. The 1996 Labor Force Survey showed that nearly a third of all workers were underemployed (that is, working fewer than 35 hours per week) in 1996. The informal sector accounted for nearly two-thirds of total employment. The labor force continued to expand annually by around 2.2–2.3 million, depending on the source of the data.[2]

Despite the increase in unemployment, Indonesia made progress in reducing poverty. In the two decades between 1976 and 1996, the incidence of absolute poverty (the percentage of the population living below the poverty line) declined from 40.08 percent to 11.34 percent.[3] The benefits of growth appear to have been distributed fairly widely. All provinces experienced increased income, consumption, and employment levels, although at different rates (and beginning at different stages of development). Indicators for life expectancy, infant mortality, literacy, and education also improved (World Bank 1997b).

Indonesia's economy began to show signs of strain in 1996, when export growth slowed to less than 9 percent from its average of nearly 15 percent for 1986–93. GDP growth began slowing in 1997, falling from nearly 8 percent in 1996 to less than 7 percent in the first quarter of 1997 and to less than 6 percent in the second.[4] The growth rate for 1997 as a whole was 4.9 percent. A severe drought during the year adversely affected agriculture, and the production of rice (the staple food in Indonesia) was an estimated 4 percent below 1996 levels. As a result the country had to import food grains for the first time in many years. The worst forest fires in more than a decade exacerbated the agricultural problems and devastated the tourist trade.

In effect the financial crisis hit at a time when the Indonesian economy was already facing dwindling exports, a slowdown in overall growth, sharply reduced rice production, and a sharp increase in food prices. This chapter examines the effects of the crisis on the already strained labor market. In particular it explores the government's policy response to the crisis in three areas: employment creation, labor market services, and vocational education and training.

Recent Macroeconomic Trends

In 1998 Indonesia's GDP contracted by 13.7 percent. Electricity, gas and water, oil and natural gas, and agriculture were the only sectors to record positive growth in that year. A drought induced by El Niño affected agriculture, and the growth rate declined from 3.1 percent in 1996 to 0.7 percent in 1997 and 0.2 percent in 1998. The construction sector was hit hardest by the crisis, experiencing a contraction of nearly 40 percent in 1998. Nonoil manufacturing and services also experienced very sharp declines (14.5 and 16.6 percent, respectively). Inflation, as measured by the consumer price index (CPI) stood at about 78 percent in 1998, contrasting sharply with the price stability of the precrisis period. All components of the CPI increased dramatically, especially food and clothing prices.

Despite the massive depreciation of the rupiah, export revenues stagnated in dollar terms in 1998–99. But the flat export revenues masked robust growth in the export volumes of agricultural commodities such as coca, coffee, palm oil, spices, and tea. But low international prices for many of these commodities in 1998 meant that overall export revenues remained unchanged or declined. Imports declined by 11 percent in 1998–99 over the previous fiscal year. This compression, which was caused by the massive depreciation of the rupiah and the collapse of aggregate demand, included declines in all categories of imports—consumer goods, raw materials, and capital goods. The sharp decline in imports combined with flat export growth to generate a sizeable current account surplus for 1998–99 of $1.4 billion, or 1.1 percent of GDP, in contrast to the 1997–98 deficit of $1.7 billion. This development cannot be regarded as wholly favorable, however, because lower imports of capital goods and raw materials reflect declines in investment and manufacturing output.

The overall macroeconomic picture began improving in 1999. GDP rose by 1.4 percent in the first quarter from the last quarter of 1998. And in the second quarter of 1999, GDP registered positive growth compared with the corresponding period in 1998. The economy appeared to be bottoming out sooner than predicted. For 1999 as a whole, GDP rose by 0.31 percent, and during the first quarter of 2000, the growth rate rose to 5.01 percent. The risk of hyperinflation was contained, and forecasts for inflation were adjusted downward to just 10 percent for 1999. Declining inflation and the relative stability of the currency in late 1999 allowed the central bank to lower interest rates to just over 20 percent—down from the very high rates (30 to 50 percent) that prevailed in 1998 and the first half of 1999.

Labor Force Participation Rates

Indonesia's working-age population grew by 3.5 million persons (2.6 percent) between 1997 and 1998, continuing earlier trends. A stable employment rate of just over 63 percent of this group translates into more than 2 million additional labor market entrants. These new entrants consisted of teenagers just turning 15 and nearly 0.7 million persons from outside the labor force (homemakers and others), who were absorbed primarily into agriculture.

Labor force participation among Indonesians of working age (15 years and older) remained essentially unchanged (at about 67 percent) in 1998. The slight upward trend of the female rate was largely offset by the slight downward trend of the male rate (table 2.1). Participation among adults (25 years and older) increased slightly in the aftermath of the financial crisis, rising from 72.5 percent in 1997 to 73.5 percent in 1998. The decrease in the rate of participation among youth (those ages 15–24) was smaller than anticipated. The rate fell a statistically significant 2.7 percent in 1994–98 (from 53.0 percent to 50.3 percent). Similar standard error calculations for urban and rural trends also show no significant trends. Regional differences in labor force participation rates in Indonesia are relatively small (the spread between the highest and lowest regional participation rate is 18 percentage points).[5] In 1997 children ages 10–14 accounted for 1.6 million workers, or less than 2 percent of total employment. The vast majority of them were engaged part-time in unpaid agricultural work for their families. Around 1.0 million of these children, or just under two-thirds of the total, attended school. Employment among these children did not increase significantly in the first year of the crisis, nor did the number actively looking for work. The number of child workers rose by just 80,000, or 5 percent (mostly boys), and they were relatively evenly divided between urban and rural areas. Most of the children in this age group (over 85 percent) continued to attend school full time in both 1997 and 1998, although the rate for male rural boys dropped slightly. The proportion of teenagers ages 15–19 who were attending school increased slightly.

Unemployment and Underemployment

The economic crisis did not lead to massive open unemployment, as had been feared. In 1997–98 overall employment increased by nearly 3 percent (2.5 million) compared with 1.5 percent in 1996–97.[6] The labor force ex-

TABLE 2.1
Aggregate Changes in the Labor Force[a]

	1994	1996	1997	1998	Annual increase 94–96	96–97	97–98
			(millions)				
Population (10+)	125.3	131.9	135.1	138.6	2.59	2.42	2.58
Labor force	83.7	88.2	89.6	92.7	2.65	1.61	3.50
Unemployed	3.7	4.3	4.2	5.1	8.31	−2.08	20.61
Employed	80.0	83.9	85.4	87.7	2.38	1.79	2.65
Nonparticipating	41.6	43.7	45.5	45.8	2.48	4.07	0.78
Students	9.8	10.8	10.8	11.3	4.87	0.18	4.25
Homemakers	22.1	24.0	25.9	25.2	4.08	7.95	−2.43
Other	9.7	8.9	8.8	9.3	−3.88	−1.70	5.98
			(percent)				
Unemployment[b]	4.36	4.89	4.68	5.44	0.26	−0.21	0.76
Labor force[c]	66.80	66.87	66.34	66.93	0.04	−0.53	0.59
Unemployment	2.92	3.25	3.11	3.65	0.17	−0.14	0.55
Employment	63.88	63.62	63.23	63.28	−0.13	−0.39	0.05
Nonparticipating	33.20	33.13	33.66	33.07	−0.04	0.53	−0.59
Students	7.83	8.19	8.01	8.14	0.18	−0.18	0.13
Homemakers	17.67	18.19	19.17	18.24	0.26	0.98	−0.94
Other	7.70	6.76	6.48	6.70	−0.47	−0.27	0.21

Note: 1994–97 figures exclude 10–14 age group.
a. Defined as those aged 15 and above.
b. Percent of labor force.
c. These and following figures are percent of population.
Source: National Labor Force Surveys; Central Bureau of Statistics.

panded by 3.5 percent between 1997 and 1998, compared with just 1.6 percent in the previous year—a rate of increase 1 percent higher than the growth rate of the working-age population. Though employment increased in almost all age categories, adults over 30 accounted for most additional employment (90 percent).

The open unemployment rate increased by less than 1 percent between August 1997 and August 1998, the first year of the crisis. The increase remained small because displaced workers from sectors such as manufacturing and construction were simply too poor not to work. Thus they were forced to find income-generating occupations in the agricultural and informal sector. For this same reason the open unemployment rate remained low in 1999.[7]

In the first year of the crisis, the number of Indonesians not working and actively looking for work increased by nearly 1 million, or 20 percent, climbing from 4.2 to 5.1 million. This increase followed a decline of 2 percent in 1996, so that the open unemployment rate actually increased from 4.7 percent to 5.4 percent of the labor force (table 2.1). But the crisis also drew nearly 2.5 million new participants into the labor force, about 1.0 million of them from urban households.[8] This number is smaller than the corresponding number for rural areas because the number of urbanites who left or remained outside the labor force actually increased by about 1.2 million persons, half of them students or homemakers. The situation was reversed in rural areas, where over 1.0 million women who had been homemakers and 0.5 million former students of both genders entered the workforce.

A closer look at the statistics for the working-age population outside the labor force shows that the number of people under "nonparticipating" who are neither homemakers nor students increased by 0.5 million (table 2.1). Since this category includes unemployed people who are not actively looking for work (especially in urban areas), the overall increase in both open and disguised unemployment was probably on the order of 1.4 million persons, or a third more than before the crisis.

Unemployment affected men more than women because two of the hardest-hit sectors—construction and manufacturing—employed mostly men. In the first year of the crisis the number of unemployed men rose by 0.6 million, or 26 percent, over the previous year. The number of unemployed women grew at just half this rate. Urban and rural areas were affected equally, although the overall unemployment rate remained much lower in rural areas (around 3.3 percent) compared with urban areas (9.3 percent) (table 2.2).

Job seekers in 1998 differed markedly from those seeking work in 1997. Before the crisis most job seekers were young high school and college graduates looking for their first job.[9] Once the crisis hit, however, many job seekers were older and had prior work experience. The number of those who had worked nearly tripled, rising from just under 0.8 million to nearly 2.0 million. The share of those ages 30 and above, many of them with just a junior secondary school certificate, also tripled, climbing from 11 to 30 percent of the total. Unemployment also increased significantly among those with secondary and some university education. But it *de-*

TABLE 2.2
Characteristics of the Unemployed, 1994–98

	Number				Distribution			
	1994	1996	1997	1998	1994	1996	1997	1998
	(millions)				(percent)			
Total unemployed	3.65	4.29	4.20	5.06	100.0	100.0	100.0	100.0
Male	1.98	2.29	2.26	2.86	54.2	53.3	53.8	56.5
Female	1.67	2.00	1.94	2.20	45.8	46.7	46.2	43.5
Urban	2.14	2.49	2.57	3.10	57.9	57.9	61.2	61.3
Rural	1.51	1.80	1.63	1.96	42.1	42.1	38.8	38.7
Worked before	1.05	0.78	0.77	1.96	28.7	18.1	18.3	38.7
Never worked	2.60	3.51	3.43	3.10	71.3	81.9	81.7	61.3
15–19	1.07	1.39	1.39	1.44	29.2	32.4	33.1	28.5
20–24	1.55	1.65	1.60	1.19	42.4	38.4	38.1	23.6
25–29	0.65	0.77	0.75	0.93	17.7	17.9	17.9	18.3
30+	0.39	0.48	0.46	1.50	10.7	11.3	11.0	29.6
Primary education or less	0.91	1.05	0.98	1.17	24.8	24.4	23.3	23.1
Junior secondary	0.63	0.79	0.74	0.98	17.1	18.1	17.5	19.4
Senior secondary	1.81	2.06	2.11	2.48	49.6	48.2	50.2	49.0
Diploma/ university	0.31	0.40	0.38	0.43	8.5	9.3	9.0	8.5

Source: National Labor Force Surveys.

creased for those at the top of the educational ladder (including university graduates).

Since open unemployment increased only marginally in the first year of the crisis, the real impact was felt in less work and lower real incomes. Underemployment (working fewer than 35 hours per week) increased in the first year of the crisis, while opportunities to work overtime and earn extra income declined. The number of people working fewer than 35 hours a week rose by 3 percent of the workforce, mainly because of the substantial increase in the number of agricultural workers, who often work shorter hours (especially unpaid family workers). Both urban and rural areas were affected, and men were more affected than women. In addition the proportion of those working more than 45 hours per week declined by 4 percent (from 39 to 36 percent) in both urban and rural areas. Again men were more likely than women to bear the burden of reduced hours; in fact women saw their share of overtime increase by 2 percent. Fewer hours and reduced opportunities to work overtime meant a reduction in take-home pay for most workers and contributed to the decline in living standards and increasing poverty (tables 2.3 and 2.4).

Before the crisis underemployment had been falling steadily, in line with the declining importance of agriculture and nonwage employment. In 1997–98, however, the number of people working fewer than 35 hours per week rose from 37 to 40 percent. Underemployment rose more rapidly in urban areas (4 percent) than in rural areas (3 percent). It also rose more rapidly for men (3 percent) than for women (2 percent). Most of this increase reflected growth in the number of agricultural workers (nearly 5.0 million), particularly in the number of unpaid family workers. Underemployment rose even in this sector, however, rising by around 2 percent, just as it did in nonagricultural sectors as a whole. In fact, underemployment rose by nearly 3 percent in manufacturing, compared with 1.0–1.5 percent in trade and services.

Job Losses

Around 2.5 million workers, or 3 percent of the total work force, were displaced by the crisis in 1997–98. Job losses came from all sectors of the economy except agriculture and the small transportation and communication sectors. Most displaced workers were wage employees, and men accounted for three-quarters of all job losses. The manufacturing sector was easily the largest loser, accounting for nearly half of all job losses, followed by construction and mining and trade and services. About three-quarters of the job losses in these sectors were in rural areas. In urban areas many workers displaced from the manufacturing and construction sectors entered the trade and other service sectors, keeping net job losses in the cities minimal. Displaced workers in rural areas did not have this option. Rural workers thus formed the bulk of all displaced nonagricultural workers, and many were forced into agricultural labor.

Job losses in the manufacturing sector exceeded 1.0 million persons, or nearly half the total job losses, with men accounting for around 60 percent (table 2.5). Around three-quarters of all retrenchments in this sector occurred in rural areas. The decline in manufacturing employment was

TABLE 2.3
Trends in Underemployment, 1994–98

	1994	1996	1997	1998
	(millions)			
All employees	80.04	83.90	85.40	87.67
<35 hours/week	30.60	31.86	30.56	34.30
35–45 hours/week	20.12	21.36	21.25	21.87
>45 hours/week	29.32	30.68	33.59	31.50
	(percent)			
All employees	100.0	100.0	100.0	100.0
<35 hours/week	39.3	38.9	36.6	40.0
35–45 hours/week	24.7	25.1	24.6	24.6
>45 hours/week	36.0	36.0	38.8	35.4
Male	100.0	100.0	100.0	100.0
<35 hours/week	29.6	28.4	26.5	29.6
35–45 hours/week	26.7	27.7	26.6	27.6
>45 hours/week	43.6	43.8	47.0	42.8
Female	100.0	100.0	100.0	100.0
<35 hours/week	55.5	56.6	53.8	54.4
35–45 hours/week	24.1	23.0	23.3	20.7
>45 hours/week	20.4	20.3	22.9	24.9
Urban	100.0	100.0	100.0	100.0
<35 hours/week	21.9	20.9	20.9	24.1
35–45 hours/week	26.4	28.0	26.5	27.1
>45 hours/week	51.7	51.1	52.7	48.7
Rural	100.0	100.0	100.0	100.0
<35 hours/week	46.9	47.8	44.9	47.0
35–45 hours/week	25.5	25.0	24.8	23.8
>45 hours/week	27.6	27.2	30.3	29.2

Note: Data are for the general population 15 years and older.
Source: National Labor Force Survey.

not limited to the most industrialized provinces, since 60 percent of workers in the manufacturing sector were self-employed or family workers. Many of these small-scale and household enterprises relied on sales to the general population, whose purchasing power was eroded by inflation.

TABLE 2.4
Underemployment in Selected Sectors, 1994–98

	1994	1996	1997	1998
Agricultural	100.0	100.0	100.0	100.0
<35 hours/week	56.7	58.6	56.7	58.5
35–45 hours/week	23.7	23.8	23.5	23.3
>45 hours/week	19.5	17.6	19.8	18.3
Nonagricultural	100.0	100.0	100.0	100.0
<35 hours/week	24.3	23.4	22.6	24.6
35–45 hours/week	25.6	26.1	25.3	25.7
>45 hours/week	50.1	50.5	52.1	49.6
Manufacturing	100.0	100.0	100.0	100.0
<35 hours/week	24.3	24.9	23.4	26.0
35–45 hours/week	26.6	26.1	25.2	25.2
>45 hours/week	49.1	49.0	51.3	48.8
Trade	100.0	100.0	100.0	100.0
<35 hours/week	27.2	26.5	26.4	27.9
35–45 hours/week	21.7	21.6	20.9	20.8
>45 hours/week	51.2	51.8	52.7	51.3
Services	100.0	100.0	100.0	100.0
<35 hours/week	28.8	26.1	25.5	26.8
35–45 hours/week	33.6	35.5	35.2	35.4
>45 hours/week	37.6	38.3	39.2	37.9

Note: Data are for the general population ages 10 and older. Data for the 10–14 age group are included for 1994–97.
Source: National Labor Force Surveys.

The construction sector suffered job losses of nearly 0.7 million primarily male workers, or nearly a third of all job losses. As with manufacturing, three-quarters of these job losses occurred in rural areas. The other most seriously affected sectors—mining and trade and services—experienced nearly 0.2 million job losses each. Women accounted for two-thirds of all job losses in trade, while men accounted for virtually all job losses in the service sector. In urban areas some displaced workers from the manufacturing and construction sectors found refuge in the informal trade and service sectors, thus increasing urban employment in these sectors by about 0.2 million. However, this increase was insufficient to compensate for the 0.4 million jobs shed by the rural trade sector.

TABLE 2.5
Job Losses and Absorption in Agriculture, 1997–98

	Changes in employment		By location		By gender		By status	
	millions	%	Urban	Rural	Male	Female	Wage	Other
All employment	+2.267	...	0.951	1.316	0.894	1.373	−1.684	3.951
Distribution (%)	100.0	...	42	58	39	61	−74	174
				(percentage)				
Agricultural	+4.625	100	23	77	57	43	9	91
Nonagricultural	−2.358	100	4	96	73	27	88	12
Mining	−0.201	9	(7)	107	61	39	36	64
Manufacturing	−1.075	46	29	71	58	42	66	34
Utilities	−0.085	4	91	9	97	3	100	0
Construction	−0.663	28	27	73	98	2	109	(9)
Trade and hotels	−0.139	6	(166)	266	37	63	201	(101)
Transportation	0.028	−1	207	(107)	40	60	(284)	384
Finance	−0.039	2	38	62	90	10	95	5
Other services	−0.184	8	(104)	204	97	3	51	49

. . . not applicable

Note: Figures in parentheses denote job gains in nonagricultural sectors.
Source: National Labor Force Surveys

Agricultural employment increased by nearly 5 million (3 million men and 2 million women), or 6 percent of the total workforce, and was mostly supply driven. Workers from other sectors who had been displaced by the crisis accounted for nearly half this growth. The other half consisted of new entrants to the labor force, primarily young workers and women seeking work to cope with the crisis. Rural households accounted for most (nearly 80 percent) of the new employment in agriculture. Men accounted for nearly 60 percent of the new agricultural employment, which was predominantly nonwage (self-employment and unpaid family work).

The increase in agricultural employment was not evenly distributed across the country. The large province of Java and the provinces dominated by smallholder agriculture (Maluku, Southern Sumatra, and South Sulawesi) expanded their work force by 1.0–1.6 percent. But the provinces of Aceh, Central Kalimantan, North Sumatra, Riau, and West Kalimantan experienced a contraction in employment. So did the commercial and tourist centers of Bali, Jakarta, North Sulawesi, and Yogyakarta, where the agricultural sectors were (and remain) too small to absorb many workers.

Changes in the Employment Structure

The crisis produced shifts in the country's employment structure. The share of agriculture in overall employment declined between 1996 and 1997, falling from 44 to 41 percent. With the onset of the crisis, however, agricultural employment began climbing again, reaching 45 percent in 1998 (table 2.6). The share of all nonagricultural sectors, which had been increasing, began declining correspondingly. Manufacturing employment, which had reached 13 percent of total employment in 1997, dropped back 2 percent, and employment in trade and services fell by 1 percent each (to 19 and 14 percent, respectively). The gender ratios did not change, how-

TABLE 2.6
Structural Changes in Employment, 1994–98

	Workers				*Distribution*			
	1994	*1996*	*1997*	*1998*	*1994*	*1996*	*1997*	*1998*
	(millions)				*(percent)*			
Total employment	80.04	83.90	85.40	87.67	100.0	100.0	100.0	100.0
Agriculture	36.51	36.50	34.79	39.42	45.6	43.5	40.7	45.0
Nonagricultural	43.53	47.40	50.62	48.26	54.4	56.5	59.3	55.0
Mining	0.72	0.75	0.87	0.67	0.9	0.9	1.0	0.8
Manufacturing	10.59	10.57	11.01	9.93	13.2	12.6	12.9	11.3
Utilities	0.18	0.16	0.23	0.15	0.2	0.2	0.3	0.2
Construction	3.54	3.78	4.18	3.52	4.4	4.5	4.9	4.0
Trade and hotels	13.72	15.84	16.95	16.81	17.1	18.9	19.9	19.2
Transportation	3.36	3.94	4.12	4.15	4.2	4.7	4.8	4.7
Finance	0.62	0.69	0.66	0.62	0.8	0.8	0.8	0.7
Other services	10.79	11.67	12.58	12.39	13.5	13.9	14.7	14.1
Male	49.14	51.91	53.00	53.90	61.4	61.9	62.1	61.5
Female	30.90	31.99	32.40	33.77	38.6	38.1	37.9	38.5
Urban	24.04	27.43	29.35	30.30	30.0	32.7	34.4	34.6
Rural	56.02	56.47	56.05	57.37	70.0	67.3	65.6	65.4
Wage	26.79	28.70	30.28	28.80	33.5	34.2	35.5	32.9
Nonwage	53.25	55.20	55.13	58.87	66.5	65.8	64.5	67.1

Source: National Labor Force Survey.

ever, because while men accounted for most job losses in nonagricultural sectors, many of them moved to employment in agriculture. Similarly, the urban-rural shares of employment did not change, because most of the additional employment was located in rural areas, compensating for the job losses there.

Increases in agricultural employment accounted for much of the rise in total employment in provinces that saw employment expand in 1997–98. These provinces saw the share of agriculture rise by about 10 percent, except for the larger Java provinces, where the increase was 4–6 percent. The average increase in agricultural employment for the country as a whole was 4 percent, in part because it remained flat or declined in East Timor, North Sumatra, South and Southeast Sulawesi, Yogyakarta, and West and Central Kalimantan.

WAGE EMPLOYMENT. The crisis also affected wage employment. Before the crisis the share of wage employment had risen steadily, climbing from 33 to 35 percent in 1994–97, in line with the growth of manufacturing, construction, and other sectors with large numbers of employees. In 1998, however, wage employment declined by nearly 1.5 million, mainly in manufacturing and construction, but also in all other sectors. In contrast non-wage employment increased by nearly 4.0 million, primarily in agriculture but also in the urban informal sector, particularly trade and services. As a result, the overall share of wage employment fell back sharply to 32 percent in 1998 (table 2.7).

Both wage and nonwage employment increased in agriculture. Wage employment rose by around 0.5 million, most of them relocated urban workers who became agricultural laborers, and was divided equally between male and female workers. But nonwage employment increased even faster, mostly in the self-employment category (including hired and family laborers), so that the share of wage employment in total employment actually fell slightly, dropping from 13.4 to 13.0 percent. Wage employment outside the agricultural sector fell by nearly 2.0 million. A third of these losses came from manufacturing and construction, while another tenth originated in the trade sector. Nearly two-thirds of all losses in wage employment originated in rural areas, primarily in manufacturing, construction, and the service sector. The service sector alone accounted for a quarter of the losses in wage employment.

Even nonwage employment outside of agriculture fell (by around 0.5 million) in the first year of the crisis. In fact nonwage employment increased significantly only in agriculture (by nearly 4.5 million). In the ag-

TABLE 2.7
Changes in Employment Status, 1994–98

	Workers				Distribution			
	1994	1996	1997	1998	1994	1996	1997	1998
	(millions)				(percent)			
All employment	82.04	85.70	87.05	89.40	100.0	100.0	100.0	100.0
Self-employment	16.60	18.35	19.98	20.63	20.2	21.4	23.0	23.1
Self-empl.[a]	18.92	21.29	18.05	19.79	23.1	24.8	20.7	22.1
Employer	0.78	1.20	1.48	1.53	1.0	1.4	1.7	1.7
Employee	27.06	28.95	30.49	29.00	33.0	33.8	35.0	32.4
Family workers	18.67	15.91	17.06	18.45	22.8	18.6	19.6	20.6
Nonwage	54.98	56.75	56.56	60.39	67.0	66.2	65.0	67.6
Agriculture	37.86	37.72	35.85	40.61	100.0	100.0	100.0	100.0
Self-employment	5.78	6.23	6.77	7.25	15.3	16.5	18.9	17.8
Self-empl.[a]	12.80	14.48	11.64	13.86	33.8	38.4	32.5	34.1
Employer	0.20	0.31	0.44	0.46	0.5	0.8	1.2	1.1
Employee	4.85	4.94	4.81	5.27	12.8	13.1	13.4	13.0
Family workers	14.23	11.75	12.18	13.77	37.6	31.2	34.0	33.9
Nonwage	33.01	32.78	31.04	35.34	87.2	86.9	86.6	87.0
Nonagricultural	44.18	47.98	51.20	48.79	100.0	100.0	100.0	100.0
Self-employment	10.82	12.12	13.21	13.38	24.5	25.3	25.8	27.4
Self-empl.[a]	6.12	6.81	6.40	5.93	13.9	14.2	12.5	12.2
Employer	0.59	0.88	1.04	1.06	1.3	1.8	2.0	2.2
Employee	22.21	24.01	25.68	23.74	50.3	50.0	50.1	48.7
Family workers	4.44	4.16	4.87	4.67	10.0	8.7	9.5	9.6
Nonwage	21.97	23.97	25.52	25.05	49.7	50.0	49.9	51.3

a. Self-employment assisted by family members and temporary employees.
Source: National Labor Force Surveys.

gregate, therefore, nonwage employment (both self-employment and un-paid family work) increased by nearly 4.0 million. It absorbed not only many of those losing wage employment but also most new entrants into the labor force. Nearly half the additions were self-employed workers assisted by hired labor or family members, while a fifth were unassisted self-employed workers. The remaining third consisted of unpaid family workers. This last category was most important for women, accounting for nearly 60 percent of all new female employment, compared with only a quarter of all new male employment.

In manufacturing the majority (60 percent) of workers who lost their jobs were employees; the rest were self-employed and unpaid family workers. This fact suggests important linkages between the formal and informal manufacturing sectors in Indonesia, particularly for female workers. Non-wage employment losses for women in manufacturing reached more than half (54 percent) of total losses. Likewise job losses in trade and services did not affect only those in the employee category but also self-employed workers assisted by hired labor and family members. Only the number of self-employed persons working on their own expanded in these two sectors. The exception was the service sector, which added female employees but not unassisted self-employed workers.

Wage employment declined in almost all provinces, in line with employment losses in the manufacturing, construction, and trade and service sectors across the country. The only significant exception was North Sumatra, where wage employment expanded a little for women in manufacturing and for both men and women in the service sectors.

Definitive information on how women workers have been affected by the crisis is limited. Labor Force Survey data on open unemployment suggest that women have been less severely affected than men. The unemployment rate for male workers increased 22 percent in 1997–98, reaching 5.04 percent. The rate for females, however, rose less than 9 percent, although the 1998 rate was higher (6.12 percent). The degree of underemployment also increased more for men than for women. These and other such figures can be interpreted in different ways, however. One interpretation suggests that women worked longer hours in order to compensate for lost household income as men were retrenched. In urban areas female workers' real income declined sharply (by 29 percent) compared with the decline for males. In rural areas, however, the reverse was true.

THE INFORMAL SECTOR. Before the crisis the informal sector played an important role in Indonesia's employment structure. But the share of informal employment in total employment began increasing once the crisis hit. Only indirect indicators of this trend are available, as no time-series data exist for the sector. The share of wage employment in total employment is one such indicator. It increased in 1994–97, indicating a concomitant rise in the share of formal sector employment (table 2.6). In 1998 nonwage employment increased sharply, not only in agriculture but also in sectors such as trade and services, while the share of wage employment fell from its 1997 level of 35 percent to 32 percent.

Self-employment statistics provide a second indirect measure of the size of the informal sector. Presumably self-employed workers (with and without temporary hired labor or family help) form the urban informal sector in some industries. Calculations based on this assumption for the wholesale and retail trade sector show an increase of at least 300,000 informal sector units in 1997–98. This finding should be taken as a lower-bound estimate because of the presence in the 1997 data of self-employed workers ages 10–14 who cannot be harmonized with the 1998 data, which do not cover this age group

Clearly, then, arriving at concrete quantitative estimates about informal sector employment is at best difficult. But the precrisis trend toward a decline in the informal sector's share in total employment appears to have reversed itself afterward. Informal sector employment clearly has grown in urban areas, especially in trade, transportation, and services.

MIGRATION. Migration has been an important strategy for the Indonesian labor force in coping with the economic crisis. Reverse internal migration (from urban to rural areas) is in part responsible for the increase in agricultural workers. In 1998 around 1.0 million urban workers took up agricultural work in rural areas while their families stayed in urban areas. Official and unofficial international migration has accelerated, particularly to Malaysia (for men) and the Middle East (for women). A significant proportion of Indonesians—well in excess of 2 million—now work overseas. Some 70 percent of them are women.

The number of contract workers migrating with official permission increased by 75 percent between 1998 and 1999. Contract workers also migrated without such permission, and this group (particularly males entering Indonesia) is estimated to be several times larger than the group of documented migrants (Hugo 1999). Migrant workers did not return from Malaysia in large numbers, as had been feared, for two reasons. First, Malaysia weathered the crisis much better than had been anticipated. And second, redundant construction workers were easily absorbed into plantations, the informal sector, and the trade and service sectors.

Real Wages and Living Standards

Nominal earnings of employees increased by less than 20 percent in the first year of the crisis. Meanwhile consumer prices for workers rose by 100 percent between August 1997 and August 1998, for a drop in real earnings of 40 percent for the period. Subsequent wage surveys of the manufacturing and hotel sectors indicate that employers may have frozen pay between September 1998 and December 1998 and that this practice may be ongoing, considering the relatively low inflation rate in early to mid-1999. Real earnings of workers were probably still 40 percent lower in mid-1999 than they were in mid-1997. Nominal wages in rural areas rose somewhat more than in urban areas owing to a higher-than-average increase in pay for agricultural laborers. Male and female workers were equally affected in the aggregate. While female workers in rural areas did not benefit from the same pay increases as their male counterparts, they did obtain higher pay raises in urban areas.

According to the National Labor Force Survey, nominal wages increased by 17 percent on average in the first year of the crisis, rising from Rp. 241,000 to Rp. 282,000 (around $35) per month between August 1997 and August 1998. Nominal earnings increased by 14 percent in urban areas and by 22 percent in rural areas. Though on average male and female earnings kept pace with each other, in rural areas male earnings increased 23 percent, while female earnings rose just 19 percent. The reverse happened in urban areas, where female earnings outpaced male (16 percent and 13 percent, respectively) (table 2.8).

The statistical authorities do not publish official time series for real wages. An appropriate deflator reflecting increases in the prices of goods and services consumed by workers could be used to derive such a series, but such a deflator is not available. An average consumer price index is available for over 44 cities but not for rural areas. Even if a composite index were available, a consumer price index would have to be developed that reflects a basket of goods for workers earning the low daily average (around $1 per day). For the present purposes we have estimated an approximate worker's consumer price index by weighing the price indices of food and other expenditure categories of the official urban consumer price index against the proportion of expenditures that urban and rural worker households devote to these categories.

SECTORAL EARNINGS. Wage increases varied considerably across economic sectors. National Labor Force Survey data show that agricultural earnings increased almost twice as rapidly (more than 30 percent per year) than average earnings in other sectors (17 percent). The subsistence-level earnings that traditionally prevailed in agriculture ($0.65 per day in 1998) may in part explain the dramatic increase in earnings in this sector, since these initial earnings were only half the average earnings in sectors such as

TABLE 2.8
Trends in Monthly Nominal and Real Earnings, 1994–99

	Index (1997 = 100)						August 1998	US$/month (August)	
				1998		1999			
	1994	1996	1997	Aug	Dec	Mar	Rp. 000[a]	1997	1998
Nominal Index Labor									
Force Survey	65	86	100	117	—	—	282.3	96	35
Male	66	86	100	118			314.3	107	39
Female	62	84	100	118			215.5	73	27
Urban	68	86	100	114			328.0	115	41
Rural	65	87	100	122			227.2	28	75
Agriculture	70	90	100	131			155.3	48	19
Manufacturing	62	84	100	111			253.3	91	32
Construction	68	87	100	115			279.3	97	35
Trade and hotels	70	89	100	120			279.2	93	35
Services	65	84	100	118			333.6	113	42
Farmers' Survey[b]	70	92	100	133	145	155	146.0	43	18
Quarterly Wage Survey									
Manufacturing	66	86	100	122	120		271.3	89	34
Mining (median)	99	97	100	154	216		700.5	182	88
Hotels	80	89	100	140	134		350.9	100	44
Real Index Labor									
Force Survey	83	92	100	59	—	—	135.0		
Male	84	92	100	59			150.4		
Female	79	90	100	59			103.1		
Urban	85	91	100	58			160.8		
Rural	82	93	100	60			107.0		
Agriculture	89	96	100	65			74.3		
Manufacturing	79	90	100	56			121.2		
Construction	86	92	100	58			133.6		
Trade and hotels	88	95	100	60			133.6		
Services	82	90	100	59			159.6		

TABLE 2.8 *(continued)*

	Index (1997 = 100)						*August 1998*	*US$/month (August)*	
				1998		*1999*			
	1994	*1996*	*1997*	*Aug*	*Dec*	*Mar*	*Rp. 000ᵃ*	*1997*	*1998*
Farmers' Survey	89	98	100	65	66	68	71.9		
Quarterly Wage Survey									
Manufacturing	85	93	100	59	57		123.0		
Mining									
(median)	127	106	100	74	103		316.9		
Hotels	102	96	100	67	64		158.7		
Deflator (U+R)ᶜ	79	94	100	200	213	225			
Urban	77	94	100	195	208	218			
Rural	79	94	100	203	218	229			

— not available.
a. $1 = Rp. 2,500 in Aug 1997 and Rp. 8,000 in mid-1998.
b. Weighed ploughing wage (Java, 40 percent; Sumatra, 20 percent; other, 20 percent).
c. Deflator: consumer price index for workers.
Source: National Labor Force Surveys; Farmers' Terms of Trade Surveys; Quarterly Wage Surveys.

manufacturing and construction. Rapid inflation in food prices meant that agricultural workers had to substantially increase their earnings or go without the food they and their households needed to survive. But the increased earnings are also in part the result of the fact that some laborers receive their wages in kind, monetizing the value of food. While agricultural earnings increased, however, manufacturing and construction saw below-average increases (11 and 15 percent, respectively). Increases in service sector earnings were slightly above average at 20 percent per annum for males but not for females.

Other wage surveys confirm the above changes. The Farmers' Terms of Trade Survey indicates that the earnings of hired agricultural laborers rose by 33 percent during the first year of the crisis. They rose by another 22 percent in the subsequent nine-month period ending in March 1999. Quarterly wage survey data show increases in gross earnings in manufacturing (22 percent), mining (54 percent), and hotel work (40 percent) between September 1997 and September 1998. Preliminary data for December 1998 indicate that earnings remained stable in manufacturing and hotels over the next three months while continuing to rise in mining.

In the manufacturing sector, wage increases were modest at first but began rising in earnest after the first year of the crisis, for two reasons. Many firms began dismissing the lowest-paid workers and casual and contract laborers first, while keeping their better-paid regular staff. At the end of the first year, firms began to implement early retirement plans and other measures to reduce their regular work force. In both cases average reported earnings increased for the relatively well-paid staff that remained. For this reason the average figures in the wage surveys may overstate the actual increase in nominal wages.

REGIONAL DIFFERENCES. The labor force survey data show that increases in nominal earnings were well above average in Maluku, all the Sulawesi provinces, and most of the Sumatra provinces except Aceh and North Sumatra (where they were below average). The increases were slightly above average in Bali, the Kalimantan provinces, and Nusa Tengara but remained average in most Javanese provinces. The exceptions were West Java and Yogyakarta, which saw increases that were well below average between August 1997 and August 1998. The provinces that did relatively well in Sumatra (Kalimantan, Maluku, and Sulawesi) have a strong base of smallholder agriculture. The Sumatran provinces that experienced below-average wage increases are dominated by large-scale plantations. Java also experienced substantial layoffs in manufacturing and construction, putting downward pressure on wages in these and other sectors, including agriculture.

Only limited information is available on the income of self-employed and other nonwage workers, despite the fact that these workers account for over two-thirds of the work force. The monthly Farmers' Terms of Trade Survey provides some idea of the changes in the income of landowning farmers in 10 provinces. But only the annual national socioeconomic survey (*Susenas*) shows overall changes in the living standards of households. This survey is of limited use, since the income data are never fully tabulated or published. Expenditures are tabulated and published, but without any corresponding information on the economic sector(s) generating household income.

THE NUMBER OF PEOPLE IN POVERTY. The number of Indonesians who have been pushed into poverty by the economic crisis is a subject of controversy. Projections made in mid-1998 indicated that by the end of 1998, 48 percent of the population (around 90 million people) would fall below the poverty line. However, this estimate was based on the very high inflation rates prevailing at that time and on an assumption of stagnant wages and incomes in nominal terms. Indonesia's Central Bureau of Statistics projected a similar increase in the incidence of poverty—39 percent in June 1998. But a study by Poppele and Pritchett (1999) presents a very different view, suggesting an incidence of poverty of only 14 percent in 1998 (compared with 11 percent in the precrisis period). An independent evaluation of these and other studies challenges this assertion, arguing that more than one-third of all Indonesians (41 percent in rural areas and 21 percent in urban areas) were propelled into poverty in 1998 (Islam 1999). A recent World Bank Poverty update puts the incidence of poverty in Indonesia at 19.9 percent in 1998—also a very sharp increase over the precrisis period.

Employment Creation and Maintenance

In the wake of the economic crisis, the government of Indonesia instituted a number of measures designed to address unemployment and underemployment. These measures create jobs directly and promote other employment opportunities, including self-employment and small and medium-size enterprises (SMEs).

Direct Job Creation

Padat Karya, or labor-intensive job creation programs designed to alleviate poverty in the short term by generating employment, were in vogue in Indonesia in the 1970s and 1980s. Much of the social capital in rural Indonesia, including village roads, schools, and secondary and tertiary irrigation channels, were built during the 1970s under these programs. Over the years, however, the government gradually replaced Padat Karya with other poverty alleviation strategies and in 1994 discontinued the programs altogether.

In the wake of the drought conditions, economic crisis, and political turmoil, the government revived Padat Karya. Padat Karya 1 (PK1) had the sole objective of providing emergency income for displaced workers through direct job creation. It targeted primarily retrenched construction and manufacturing workers in urban Java, which had taken the initial brunt of the crisis. The government quickly disbursed Rp. 42 billion to support the program, which began in December 1997 and lasted four months.

The next generation of Padat Karya programs, PK2, was initiated in April 1998 during a period of widespread unrest. PK2, which was much larger in scope (its 16 subprograms were implemented by different government agencies) and had multiple objectives and a variety of target groups. The budgets for the various programs ranged from Rp. 95 billion to Rp. 1.6 trillion.[10] The ultimate goal of PK2 was to create a total of 226 million person-days of employment.

PK2 was designed not only to provide emergency income but also to create social capital. The target beneficiaries of PK2 included the newly poor and recently retrenched workers as well as the long-term poor and unemployed. The subprograms covered all provinces and targeted specific regions, sectors, and population groups. Some were designed and implemented as top-down programs, while others sought to involve community groups and nongovernmental organizations (NGOs), at least in principle.

PROBLEMS AND CHALLENGES. PK2 suffered from a number of problems, including inadequate coverage and significant leakage of benefits to the nonpoor. A lack of clear objectives, weak program design, insufficient community involvement, and the absence of a functioning decentralized labor market information system made targeting beneficiaries difficult. The best option would have been to allow for self-selection (especially in the case of unskilled labor) by offering below-market wages. Most successful labor-intensive public works programs, like India's Maharastra Employment Guarantee Scheme, keep wage rates low in order to reach the truly needy and keep out those with high reservation wages.

PK2 suffered from two other problems: low wage bills and low female participation rates. The wage bills of a large number of projects were too small compared with expenditures for materials and other costs. Even in highly capital-intensive infrastructure projects, a large untapped potential may exist for increasing labor intensity without compromising quality. Identifying additional essential (if sometimes peripheral) activities that require large quantities of labor can help projects realize this potential. The second problem—the lack of female participation—stemmed largely from the fact that women in most parts of Indonesia (except perhaps Bali) are generally not involved in construction activities. Project planners need to identify and design a range of activities that will attract women.

POLICY IMPLICATIONS. The numerous problems inherent in the second stage of PK2 resulted in substantial cutbacks in the Padat Karya budget for 1999–2000 (to around 50 percent of the previous year's levels). The cutbacks are unfortunate, for the fault lay not in the programs themselves, but in the manner in which they were designed and implemented. Planners did not pay adequate attention to the need for a disaggregated database and supporting community-level structures to ensure proper targeting and sustainability. A centrally designed program targeting the poor and unemployed with virtually no community participation in needs assessment, selection, implementation, or monitoring is unlikely to succeed.

The current situation had a number of important policy implications:

- *Substantial reverse migration, the influx of urban workers into farm-based activities, and a substantial drop in real incomes have created an urgent need for additional income opportunities in the rural sector.* The 1990s saw very little investment in rural infrastructure, for example. Ample opportunities exist for labor-intensive work programs to construct, renovate, and simply maintain school buildings, health centers, and public irrigation facilities. Activities such as forestry and soil conservation offer additional possibilities. Such programs will contribute to the long-term growth of the economy. Careful targeting and sound design, implementation, and monitoring are essential to their success.

- *Effectively managing such programs requires a high degree of coordination among line ministries at every level of government.* Such coordination has been lacking, and the ministries have been duplicating programs in some areas while providing none of the activities that are needed in others. Activities must be rationalized and policies as well as programs coordinated. Provincial and district-level administrations need technical assistance as well as financial resources.

- *Local governments must make sure that they develop projects appropriate to community needs and targeted to those in need.* A necessary condition for ensuring fair and adequate project selection and targeting is community involvement in assessing and implementing projects and in monitoring them for greater transparency. Decentralization must begin at the top and be accompanied by a bottom-up process of institutional strengthening.

- *The process of institutional strengthening requires that local institutions receive adequate funding and technical expertise.* Introducing special quotas for vulnerable segments of the populations (such as the poor and landless, women, and minorities) can make these institutions more representative. Representatives of civil society can also be included in village-level forums—another change that will facilitate the targeting and monitoring of programs and enhance transparency. Strong village institutions are also well placed to identify surplus labor at local levels, and workers' organizations can serve not only as custodians of worker rights but also as important agents of change. Such organizations help identify areas needing special attention and emerging training needs.

Self-Employment Generation and the Role of Microfinance

In Indonesia self-employment on a very small scale—and at the bottom of the economic ladder—has long been the only alternative for displaced agricultural workers unable to enter the fast-growing industrial sector. Yet the informal sector's role in absorbing surplus labor during the country's economic transition went largely unrecognized. Instead the government systematically implemented a range of policy interventions that worked against the interests of the self-employed who operate at the lowest economic levels, including regulatory monopolies that limited production trade for a large range of agricultural commodities. Faulty pricing and fiscal policies are virtually decimating small producers and traders in some markets, such as sugar cane. Indiscriminate taxes and levies imposed by local governments, ad hoc regulations on local trade and transport, and a range of statutory licensing requirements and restrictions on the production and marketing of products pose serious problems for small producers and businesses. The drought, the economic crisis, and historically high inflation only made matters worse.

Despite the severity of these problems, this group of workers has long faced a much more serious constraint: lack of access to working capital. Most credit instruments are not accessible to the assetless poor, since most require collateral or are geared toward those with regular incomes. Even many successful microfinance programs, such as Badan Kredit Desa (which has operated since 1898), cater to the relatively affluent segments of the rural economy. As a result the self-employed at the lower rungs of the income ladder have always depended heavily on informal credit sources.

In the late 1990s the microfinance sector began expanding, although its share in total credit disbursed remains insignificant. The new programs provide some alternatives to very small entrepreneurs needing credit. One such program is the Bank Kredit Kecamatan, which is owned by the provincial governments and has branches in subdistrict capitals. Field staff from these offices travel to the surrounding villages to transact business. The provincial governments also own the Lumburg Kredit Pedesaan, a system of semi-formal financial institutions. Bank Indonesia and the German Agency for Technical Cooperation (GTZ) sponsor the Program Hubungan Bank dan KSM, which operates in 10 provinces. It is designed to help low-income, self-employed workers develop skills in managing and implementing group lending strategies. Finally, the Pembinaan Peningkatan Pendapatan Petani-Nelayan Kecil operates in 18 provinces as a group-based microenterprise credit and development program for the poor.

All these microcredit programs carry high interest rates—far higher than the rates of some of the more formal programs, such as the highly acclaimed Unit Desa network of Bank Rakyat Indonesia. Yet they have been largely successful, with low default rates. Two of these groups—Lumburg Kredit and the Peningkatan program—make only group loans of the Grameen Bank variety. The loans are small (usually less than $100), require no collateral, and have short maturities (from 3–18 months). Some loans require savings deposits.

POLICY CONSIDERATIONS. Most of these programs received initial subsidies from the government or from donors. But with proper management they began breaking even within a few years and now provide a valuable service to low-income households and especially women, who make up most of the borrowers. Their success is in part attributable to sound design that includes measures such as incentives for staff and clients. With the help of a contingent of field staff, programs such as Bank Kredit can reach clients in remote and relatively inaccessible areas. These lenders provide women with the working capital they need to establish themselves (primarily in petty trading activities). The rates are high but affordable— much lower than the implicit rates charged in informal credit markets.

These programs demonstrate that repayment rates can be kept high even with high interest rates. In fact such programs show that contrary to popular belief, microfinance institutions do not need subsidies to turn in strong financial performance. Subsidized credit, which is often provided for political reasons, may in fact undermine the healthy functioning of these programs. Government ownership can also undermine their financial performance through undue political pressures. Bank Kredit and Lumburg Kredit, for instance, face pressures to underwrite large numbers of loans during election times. Government control may do damage in other ways as well. Government regulations can seriously hamper the growth of microfinance institutions. For instance, in Indonesia all microfinance institutions that are too small to become rural banks and abide by the 1992 Banking Act must either become cooperatives or stop taking deposits. And the Badan Kredit Desa, the country's oldest source of microfinancing, was not allowed to expand because of the presence of another network, the Koperasi Unit Desa village cooperatives. This group has not generally followed sound financial principles, and Badan Kredit provided too much competition. The Indonesian government needs to rationalize the existing programs and develop a comprehensive national microfinance policy.

Employment Funds

Employment funds can be used to complement targeted employment generation—job creation programs of the Padat Karya type and microcredit programs for the self-employed. In Indonesia an employment fund needs to have two components. The first would provide retraining and redeployment assistance for retrenched workers, supplementing locally implemented programs that target hard-hit regions and sectors. Resources for this component would come from proportional contributions from regions (under the planned decentralized financial system) and government allocations. Workers' organizations can be included in the management of these funds to improve targeting and transparency. The fund would focus on four areas:

- *Targeting.* The fund would operate in those geographic areas with the most severe retrenchment and unemployment problems, the highest poverty rates, and the most severely hit sectors and industries.
- *Design.* Program design must reflect the needs of the community and provide for effective links to local industry.
- *Female participation.* The fund needs to incorporate measures specifically targeted at increasing female participation—for instance increasing awareness of women's needs and, where necessary, taking proactive steps such as reserving a proportion of training spots for women. The fund could also promote work opportunities for women in nontraditional fields and new occupations that emerge as the country develops.
- *Management.* Procedures for selecting organizations to manage the programs would have to be carefully designed, and ongoing support would need to be provided to the agencies administering the programs. Competitive bids could be used to choose the best candidate among several suitable agencies.

The second component of the fund would be a microcredit program to foster self-employment among the poor, especially in regions hit hard by the crisis. Policymakers would need to draw up a sensible microcredit policy to help bolster self-employment for the poor, as the existing schemes are scattered and ad hoc and need to be rationalized. Such a policy must be developed in tandem with a clear policy on subsidized rural credit schemes, in part since subsidized credit is not necessarily the best way of making credit available to the poor.

A self-employment program of this type would be able to target poor women effectively. A number of small women's organizations cater to the needs of self-employed poor women. These organizations could be promoted and encouraged to participate in public forums (such as village council meetings) in order to bring forward their priorities and requirements.

Small and Medium-Size Enterprises

In 1994 SMEs, including household enterprises, made up 99.8 percent of all businesses and accounted for 39 percent of the country's GDP. The total number of SMEs grew from 34.2 million in 1994 (33.5 million of them household-based enterprises) to an estimated 39 million in 1999. Outside of agriculture SMEs are concentrated in food, beverages and tobacco, textiles and garments, wood and wood products, and nonmetallic mineral production. An important feature of the Indonesia's SME sector is the existence of cooperatives, or loosely knit groups of SMEs that share some common interest. Around 52,000 of these cooperatives function throughout the country.

Two opposing forces are at work in Indonesia regarding policy for SMEs. Donors such as the World Bank, Asian Development Bank (ADB), and International Monetary Fund (IMF), as well as many government officials, support an approach that offers technical assistance to microentrepreneurs. Proponents of the People's Economy Movement, which emphasizes the need to move away from a conglomerate-driven economy to a more diversified one, see the cooperatives as the main vehicle for redistributing assets and economic control to the people. Proponents are using at least 17 different credit schemes in an attempt to pump $1.5 billion of subsidized credit into cooperatives. Early in March 1999 the government set up a state financing company for SMEs with an initial budget of Rp. 1.5 trillion.

This politically motivated agenda may not result in effective long-term economic or social policy and could worsen short-term economic distortions. Pumping credit into cooperatives has caused bank deposits with these institutions to rise rapidly. The cooperatives have been further urged to borrow at subsidized rates of 16–18 percent but can readily deposit their money at more than 30 percent interest. Under these circumstances cooperatives' bank deposits will continue to rise with little real increase in economic activity.

The People's Economy is a political reality and must be considered in designing any broad policy initiative. Accepting and articulating that two different agendas are driving policy formation can have specific benefits.

First, policymakers can identify any policies that are best phased out when the political climate stabilizes. Second, acknowledging the situation can help restore confidence in the economy. Investors, both domestic and foreign, are more likely to accept visible economic distortions if the government states clearly that these distortions are the result of short-term political or social considerations and not part of a long-term economic strategy.

Policymakers themselves need to be able to distinguish between short-term programs that are inspired largely by political considerations and long-term programs that will produce sustainable economic growth. These latter programs are more likely to produce genuine social equity. And common policy initiatives can be developed in areas where the two types of programs overlap.

The policy debate aside, Indonesia has a plethora of programs designed to support SMEs.[11] The technical programs focus on marketing, inputs, manufacturing and processing, the regulatory environment, and linkages to other firms. They are designed to provide two types of assistance: extension services and partnerships. Extension services have been provided in a variety of forms, including the World Bank's Dapati scheme, the cluster development program supported by the United Nations, the Indonesian Business Advisory Network (supported in part by GTZ), and a number of government programs. Several government ministries and agencies have put forward mandatory partnerships using a range of different laws and regulations. These partnerships are based on the premise that SMEs are a weak economic group and require government support.

Government policies and programs frequently overlap or duplicate each other. Duplication wastes scarce resources and leads to interagency inefficiencies that are particularly onerous when they take the form of fixed costs. SMEs generally pay a large proportion of their income in fixed regulatory costs; in fact the burden of taxation and licensing requirements in all forms falls most heavily on these enterprises. And over the last 30 years a complex legal and regulatory system has developed that increases the burden on SMEs. Indonesia's overlapping laws, rules, regulations, licenses, and fees seriously constrain SME development. Some of these schemes (like the World Bank's) are relatively successful, but many (including most of the government's major programs) are not.

ACCESS TO CREDIT. Since the onset of the economic crisis, lending to SMEs has decreased in both absolute and relative terms. This decline has generated some concern among policymakers and international agencies seeking to assist Indonesia. For example various IMF programs have emphasized the need to ensure that adequate amounts of credit continue to flow to SMEs. The lack of in-depth analyses of existing programs makes assessments of this issue particularly difficult. But the general picture of SMEs that is emerging shows that these businesses are reducing their debt burden in the face of high interest rates and increasing savings in response to high deposit interest rates. Obviously many SMEs have been hurt by the increase in interest rates and the consequent high costs of credit. And many are undoubtedly not in a position to take advantage of interest earnings through deposits. But in the aggregate it appears that many SMEs are making rational economic adjustments to the prevailing commercial climate and will continue doing so as long as they enjoy access to a rational financial system that permits it.

At least 24 microfinance and SME credit programs currently operate in Indonesia. These programs differ widely in orientation, methods of operation, and structure. Some are directed primarily at special groups, such as farmers or transmigrants. The range of major commercial and industrial SME programs includes lending by commercial banks that are required to devote at least a fixed proportion of their lending to small borrowers, including SMEs. It also includes subsidized credit targeted to cooperatives and their members, specialized rural banks, and donor-supported SME programs.

Three types of financing are available for SMEs: formal commercial, semi-formal and informal, and directed (table 2.9). The formal institutions epitomize what might be described as the ruling paradigm in small-scale financing and perhaps in financial intermediation in general in Indonesia. They are depositor based and self-sustaining, and they move considerable volumes of credit. A large share of total private finance, perhaps as much as a quarter of the total loans in the banking sector in 1997, flowed to SMEs (approximately Rp 83.3). Undoubtedly some of this credit (perhaps a substantial share) would have been extended to SMEs without any special programs. However, it seems clear that the regulation requiring that 22.5–25 percent of commercial banks' loans be directed to small borrowers has had an influence on the pattern of credit.

Semi-formal and informal credit sources include private moneylenders, rotating savings accounts, credit associations, suppliers, and pawn shops. While most of these financing sources are difficult to examine, anecdotal evidence from people familiar with the market indicates that these arrangements provide significant services. The existence of this robust informal market raises two important points. The first is that these sources may well be essential to the survival of SMEs lacking access to other sources of credit. The second is that these sources of finance are themselves thriving small commercial enterprises. Their role in meeting the credit needs of SMEs has been largely overlooked and merits further study.

TABLE 2.9
Microcredit Providers

Types of institution	Number of branches	Total amount of loans	Number of borrowers	Average loan size	Savings
BRI Unit Desa	3,701	Rp 511 billion in new lending RP 32.3 trillion cumulative	2.5 million	Rp 500,000 (14.6%) Rp 500,000– 1 million (30.3%) Rp 1–2 million (31.8%)	Rp 16 trillion
BPR	2,056	Rp 2 trillion	2 million	Rp 1 million	
Savings and loan cooperatives	37,595	Rp 4 trillion		Rp 500,000	Rp 1.3 trillion
Commercial banks	221	Rp 45 trillion in small loans		Maximum Rp 350 million	

Source: Bishnu P. Shreshta, Rural and Micro Finance in Indonesia, Jakarta: APRACA Consulting Services, April 1999 p. 73, 75. Kebijaksanaan Pemerintah Dalam Mengembangkan Usaha Simpan Pinjam, Ir. Deswamdhy Agusman Jakarta, 5 May, 1999.

STRATEGIES FOR PROMOTING THE GROWTH OF SMEs. Promoting SMEs requires more than targeted programs. It requires emphasizing macroeconomic and sector-specific policy reforms that affect the trade regime and the fiscal, monetary, and regulatory frameworks. Programs that favor SMEs must not be used to compensate for policy distortions; instead the policies causing the distortions need to be reformed. This approach is in keeping with increased reliance on market mechanisms. But it is also in line with the principal of putting in place complementary sets of public policy initiatives to improve the functioning of these mechanisms while also trying to compensate for any market failures.

A second strategy involves establishing appropriate institutional packages that focus on four areas essential to the growth of SMEs. Designing and implementing such packages requires:

• Developing policy, legal, and regulatory environments in each sector that are conducive to competition and trade;

- Improving access to credit and financial services;
- Providing access to general, sectoral, and locality-specific business services; and
- Establishing innovative links between urban and rural markets, as well as relevant intersectoral linkages and backward and forward production and trade linkages, in order to stimulate demand. The process should include large and small domestic firms as well as international firms.

In implementing these approaches, policymakers need to differentiate among emerging, recovering, transforming, and shrinking sectors and subsectors.

SMEs themselves need to become more proactive and to engage in activities that will help them grow and develop. For instance, they need to prepare for increased competition under a free-trade regime. SMEs need to increase their efficiency by introducing modern management styles, improved technology, and best organizational practices. They need to cooperate with each other to overcome their size constraints and improve collective efficiency. And they must integrate themselves in supplier and technological networks, both domestic and international.

Large companies can play an important role in this process by rationalizing their production systems and investing in more efficient supplier networks. A strong business consulting sector is needed to support adjustment and restructuring processes within and among SMEs and between SMEs and large enterprises, as SMEs do not generally have easy, reasonably priced access to professional business advice. The government needs to offer initiatives to facilitate networking among SMEs, create a new balance between public and private service providers, and move from a supply-oriented to a demand-oriented approach to SME promotion in fields such as management advice, human resources development, technology upgrading, and marketing.

Initiatives such as those included in the Asia Foundation's SME program have been particularly helpful in bringing entrepreneurs together and in strengthening links with government officials and NGOs, both locally and nationally. Regional fora have brought together SMEs at the provincial level, raising awareness of the role these enterprises play in the economy and winning them a hearing at all stages of the policymaking process. This kind of work can benefit from broad-based joint efforts that include donors and government and that are widely replicated.

IMPROVING ACCESS TO CREDIT. A recent study examines changes in the availability and terms of credit for SMEs during the economic crisis and assesses possible short-term policy responses (Musa 1998). The study con-cludes that subsidized credit is not the solution to the problems of SMEs and that these enterprises are more concerned with business opportunities, access to information on markets, and a nondiscriminatory business envi-ronment. More than access to credit, SMEs need lower transaction costs, freedom from unnecessary bureaucratic interventions, simplified licensing procedures, and fewer taxes at the regional level. Based on this and simi-lar studies (see, in particular, Wieland 1998), we have identified a num-ber of policy initiatives that will improve the flow of credit to SMEs. First and most important is an environment conducive to the efficient devel-opment and operation of the commercial financial institutions that serve SMEs. Encouraging commercial lending is clearly the most cost-effective means of ensuring credit with minimal intermediation costs. Reducing the costs of commercial lending will increase the volumes of credit that flow through commercial institutions. To reduce these costs the government needs to encourage efficiency-enhancing practices within lending institu-tions and to improve the regulatory and policy environment for the finan-cial sector.

Second, the government can continue requiring banks to set aside a certain proportion of loans for small borrowers. In general this approach increases the volume of credit flowing to SMEs, though it can also have negative consequences. Regulations mandating such set-asides can act as a tax on the financial system by reducing total loan volumes. Further, the regulations require banks to engage in an area of business with which they may have little or no experience. Some banks do well in these markets, while others do not.

Third, the government needs to consider that private credit is more ap-propriate than subsidized credit when it comes to SME financing and to foster the growth of private credit programs for SMEs. Subsidized credit carries high fiscal costs and can impose significant administrative costs on participating institutions. These additional costs undermine repayment discipline and create unfair competition for commercial lending opera-tions. Several of the subsidized credit programs have demonstrated poor re-payment performance over the years. When the government forgives these bad debts, borrowers are left with a transfer of wealth and the perception that it is not necessary to repay loans. The result could well be a "culture of nonperformance" that further undermines repayment performance, jeop-ardizes commercially sustainable SME operations, and offers rent-seeking opportunities for target clienteles.

Given that successful SME lending programs already operate in Indone-sia, the focus of any efforts to expand access to credit should be replicating the most successful aspects of those programs. Lending institutions wishing to develop an SME portfolio can adopt innovations that reduce transaction costs, improve repayment performance, and increase operational efficiency. Moreover, given the difference of opinion among policymakers on how best to support improved access to financing for SMEs, standards for evaluating SME financing operations must be agreed to quickly. Standards for SME financing programs will need to address levels of outreach, cost-effectiveness, and the distribution of benefits. Technical assistance needs to focus on identifying the expected performance of SME financial operations in line with these three factors.

Labor Market Services and Regulations

Indonesia's Public Employment Service is within the Ministry of Manpower, under the Directorate General of Manpower Development and Placement. The service focuses on four areas, each with its own directorate: labor market information and support services, self-employment and job expansion, domestic employment, and overseas employment. Regional and district offices provide outreach and collect information.

The Employment Service has registered more than 1 million workers in 27 provinces each year since 1989. In 1996 and 1997 the number increased sharply, jumping from 1,198,281 in 1995 to 1,497,159 and 1,542,522 respectively. The number of job vacancies registered in these provinces increased from 227,539 in 1989 to 629,464 in 1996 but fell to 593,153 in 1997. Overall placement rates (the ratio of registered placements to registered job vacancies) were 83.90 percent in 1996 and 83.07 percent in 1997. The highest ratios are found in the electricity, gas, and water sector and the mining sector.

Labor Market Information

The Department of Manpower is not only one of the primary sources of labor market information in Indonesia but also one of the major users of this information. The department is responsible for regularly collecting representative data on manpower and employment throughout the country. Three of the directorates are particularly important suppliers of such data:

- *The Directorate of Overseas Employment Placement* maintains and analyzes records of legal overseas workers.
- *The overseas directorates,* where Indonesian workers register before they are placed by private employment agencies, collect data on the arrival and departure of overseas workers

- The *Directorate of Labor Market Information and Support Services to Placement* maintains and analyses administrative records on job seekers, job vacancies, and placements. Employment service personnel in regional and district offices collect and process the data.
- *The Manpower Planning and Information Section* collects aggregate labor market information. This agency is in charge of annual publications on the manpower and employment situation in Indonesia.

The dissemination of timely, accurate labor market information is hindered by several constraints. First, Employment Service officers do very little job canvassing, perhaps because they lack transportation. Second, labor market information received from the regional and district offices arrives late and is not sufficiently disaggregated by job, gender, skills, or age. The offices also do not supply information on layoffs; rather, it is collected by another agency that does not communicate it to the appropriate offices. In addition, job seekers are not required to register with local Employment Service offices. Those workers who register voluntarily are mainly from the formal sector. Further, decisions on where to locate district offices are based on the cost of land, rental prices, and the location of local authorities rather than on job seekers' needs and the location of enterprises. And finally, most data is still processed by hand because of a lack of technical expertise in modern data collection and retrieval systems.

Job Matching at District Offices

The aggregate placement figures cannot serve as a performance indicator for the employment service in job matching at the district level. According to the 1998 National Labor Force Survey, only 4 percent of the unemployed regarded registering with their district office as a primary job-search strategy. Computerized systems have been installed in 15 district offices (9 in Jakarta and West Java and 6 in East Java) to register job seekers and job vacancies. However these pilot systems are neither comprehensive nor fully operational and cannot be considered reliable labor exchange systems, for several reasons. They are not linked to a local area network (LAN) that would allow district offices to access all jobs within a region. In addition the official data on job seekers and job vacancies is neither comprehensive nor accurate, since most job seekers and employers (especially in the informal sector) do not register with their local offices. Likewise the information on job seekers that is collected does not include details of their employment history or training. And finally only basic information on job vacancies is registered—the name and address of the company, job title, and proposed salary. No job descriptions are available.

For these reasons, district-level job-matching services tend to be inefficient and ineffective. The problem is compounded by the Employment Service officers, for several reasons. First, the officers lack the skills necessary for job canvassing, analyzing job vacancies and workers' skills and requirements, and registering data. In addition they have no reference guides, books, or other material that could help them. They also face major problems in transferring laid-off workers from urban areas and industrial sectors to rural areas and agricultural sectors, as Indonesia lacks a coherent redeployment strategy. And finally, Employment Service officers do not hook up job seekers with labor market adjustment programs for youth or women or with social safety net programs in rural areas.

Efforts to place workers are also hindered by economic factors, including:

- A decrease in job vacancies, both domestically and overseas;
- Difficulties in identifying job vacancies in the informal sector and in companies that recruit workers directly;
- Problems shifting job seekers from the formal to the informal sector or to Social Safety Net programs; and
- Difficulties applying regulations on placing disadvantaged groups, such as the disabled.

In February 1999 the Employers' Association of Indonesia established the National Tripartite Coordinating Body for Empowering Manpower. The group has two objectives: to set up a database on layoffs, new job seekers, and vacancies abroad and to do on-line job matching. This body could be a potential competitor for the Public Employment Service.

Private employment agencies, which place workers both domestically and overseas, are strictly regulated in Indonesia. In 1998 the Department of Manpower issued 204 licenses to private agencies. Of these agencies 178 worked with overseas employment, 16 with domestic employment, and 10 with seafaring jobs.

Around 8 million laid-off workers have registered with the Employment Service as companies and factories in the major contracting sectors close. If the Department of Manpower receives notice of mass layoffs in time, the appropriate agencies provide labor standards advice and mediation (if the unions and firm cannot agree on compensation). If mediation fails, the case goes to the Labor Court. The "early warning" system often did not work well during the crisis. Consequently, no planning took place before mass layoffs, and retrenched and dislocated workers did not receive immediate, proactive assistance from government agencies. It was left to the initiative of individual companies to respond to the crisis. In some big multinational companies (over 3,000 employees), the human resources department issued guidelines for mass layoffs, including programs such as early retirement. No retrenchment management program was available to other firms, and no assistance was available to alleviate the hardship of dislocated workers.

Terminating Employment [12]

Several ways of terminating an employment contract are recognized in Indonesia. Termination may occur at the initiative of either the employer or employee or with the agreement of both parties. Employment may also be terminated by a worker's retirement or the expiration of a fixed-term contract. However Indonesian law generally does not support termination at the employer's initiative. This policy is embodied in the law governing termination of employment, which stipulates that employers must do their best to prevent terminating employees. This general prohibition is given legal force in the procedures set up to regulate dismissals. The legislation requires employers to obtain government authorization before terminating employees. Employers may not simply give notice, as they do in other countries, notably the United States.

Employers must have authorization in all but a very few cases. These include terminations made during probationary periods, which last for a maximum of three months; terminations resulting from the expiration of fixed-term contracts; resignations; and retirements that follow company regulations or collective agreements. Dismissal permits are issued in cases of "grave mistakes" such as theft, fraud, and criminal acts.

Despite the general prohibition against dismissal, the law gives employers some discretion in terminating workers. When an employer believes that termination is unavoidable, the law requires that discussions take place with the workers' organization or even with the worker. Only when the discussions have been held and produced no agreement can the employer ask the Regional Committee for the Settlement of Labor Disputes for permission to terminate. Without an agreement the employer may dismiss the worker only after obtaining this permission. In determining whether to permit the termination, the Regional Committee considers labor market conditions and the interests of both the worker and employer.

Parties to a deliberation concerning a dismissal may also apply to the Ministry of Manpower for mediation. The ministry must deal with the matter within 30 days. When mediation fails the matter is forwarded to the regional or central committee. Employees may not be suspended or their employment affected in any way while a request for permission to terminate employment is pending. Employees may appeal a regional or national committee's decision to permit termination within 14 days by appealing to the Central Committee for Settling Labor Disputes.

COLLECTIVE DISMISSALS AND DISMISSALS FOR ECONOMIC REASONS. Indonesian law regulates collective or mass dismissals, which are defined as 10 or more dismissals at one enterprise in one month or a series of terminations that demonstrate an intention to carry out a mass dismissal. The number 10 is somewhat arbitrary; the important consideration is the employer's intention to carry out mass layoffs. Except where such dismissals are effected with consent, employers wishing to carry out mass layoffs must obtain prior authorization in the form of a permit from the National Committee for the Settlement of Labor Disputes. The committee considers the condition of the labor market and the interests of both employers and workers. The committee also holds consultations with the affected workers. When mass dismissals occur as a result of government measures or activities, the government must try to move the affected workers to other areas or to public works projects.

SEVERANCE PAY. Regional and national committees have the discretion to award severance pay and other compensation to workers after granting an employer's request to terminate employment. Severance pay, which is set by ministerial regulations, is paid at a base rate of one month's pay for each year of service, up to a maximum of five months' wages. So-called service monies are also available for long-term employees (those with more than five years' tenure). Severance is payable at the base rate for company closures and changes of location but must be paid at twice the base rate for redundancies for economic reasons and dismissals for reasons other than grave mistakes.

THE REGULATORY IMPACT. Assessing the actual impact of existing legislation and regulations on the functioning of the labor market in general and on job losses in particular is a difficult task because of the shortage of accurate data. Did the manufacturing firms that laid off some 1 million workers in the first year of the crisis actually follow the prescribed procedures? According to Department of Manpower records, some 1,125 enterprises presented cases in 1998 concerning 182,442 workers. If these figures are any indication, then mass layoffs took place that did not adhere to the procedures required by law.

Whether alternatives to layoffs have been the subject of dialogue or consultations with workers and their representatives is also a matter of debate. What is known is that in early 1998, the Federation of All-Indonesia Trade Unions, which until mid-1998 was the only officially recognized trade union federation, set up a team to consult with and assist companies contemplating mass dismissals. The team's main objective was to promote alternatives to layoffs such as reducing the number of hours worked, eliminating overtime, cutting production costs, and sending workers for "home rest." The Indonesian Employers' Association also provided a range of similar advisory services to its members.

The government is currently considering reforms to important components of the country's labor legislation. A degree of uncertainty will prevail within the regulatory framework until the reform process is complete. The Manpower Act, passed in September 1998, was suspended before it could come into force and is being revised to create a number of separate laws. The provisions on termination of employment, for instance, have been noted for possible inclusion in legislation on dispute settlement laws. But these reforms are unlikely to have any immediate impact on regulations governing termination of employment, as the new legislation specifically retains the terms of the previous legislation in this area. However, the new legislation does envisage a series of future implementing regulations that may affect certain provisions.

Vocational Education and Training

The recent economic and financial crisis in the Southeast Asian economies has brought the issue of the relationship between education and training and employment to center stage. The most difficult issue for Indonesia is identifying the precise nature of the training interventions that will provide the relief the country needs as it follows the path of economic recovery. The process of recovery will require a degree of restructuring among as well as within various sectors. For these reasons educating and retraining retrenched workers for redeployment must be regarded as both long- and short-term issues.

Education and Training in Indonesia

The national education and training systems in Indonesia were under review throughout the 1990s in an effort to enhance their efficiency, effectiveness, and relevance. Although the review should have enabled the government to map out a rapid response to the challenges arising out of the crisis, it did not. In addition the financial stringency resulting from the crisis could have a negative impact on education and training, particularly skills training programs for the formal sector. Budgetary allocations for the education sector as a proportion of GDP have in fact declined steadily since 1986–87 (ILO forthcoming). Further underinvestment in new equipment and raw materials and inadequate funding for upgrading the skills of the teaching staff will lower the quality of training.

Education in Indonesia had been expanding rapidly before the crisis. Net primary enrollment reached 92 percent in 1992. In 1996–97 primary school enrollment reached 29.24 million, increasing to 29.27 million in 1998. Junior secondary school enrollment rose from 9.28 to 9.69 million during the same period. The dropout rate had also been declining, falling to less than 3 percent for primary schools and 3.6 percent for junior secondary schools in 1996–97. In 1998–99, however, enrollments declined and the dropout rate increased. The available data show that in 1998–99, the dropout rate at the primary level rose to 5.7 percent. At the junior secondary school level it increased dramatically, reaching 11.5 percent (ILO 1999).

Vocational Education

The Ministry of Education and Culture provides vocational and technical education at the secondary level through the Directorate of Secondary Vocational Education (formal programs) and the Directorate of Mass Education (nonformal programs). In the 1996–97 school year, some 712 government and more than 3,000 private vocational secondary schools were in operation. The contribution made by the private sector in promoting vocational education can be gauged from the fact that in 1996–97, about 83 percent of students in vocational schools were enrolled in private institutions (table 2.10).

The number of government schools increased to 751 in 1997–98. The two largest groups of government-run vocational senior secondary schools focus on economics (340 schools) and technical trades (154 schools). The technical schools offer formal education at the senior secondary level to students ages 16–19. The three-year courses are designed to develop broad-based technical skills in preparation for employment as skilled industrial workers and low-level technicians. In 1996–97 economics schools accounted for 48 percent of the total enrollment of senior vocational secondary schools (1.77 million students), technical schools for 41 percent, and other vocational institutions for approximately 11 percent.

In 1994 the Ministry of Education and Culture introduced the concept of the dual education system (*Pendidikan Sistim Ganda*) to implement its

TABLE 2.10
Vocational and Technical Secondary School Enrollments (1996–97)

School types	Public		Private	
	Number	Percent of total	Number	Percent of total
Economic	245,923	28.8	606,880	71.2
Home economics	45,373	78.9	12,168	21.1
Other vocational	25,483	39.9	38,339	60.1
Social work	7,447	59.9	4,987	40.1
Handicraft industry	11,125	76.8	3,365	23.2
Traditional music	2,537	75.8	824	24.2
Music	503	87.3	73	12.7
Arts	3,012	84.7	543	15.3
Tourism	859	2.9	28,547	97.1
Technical	157,647	22	560,109	78
Agricultural	24,880	66.4	12,597	33.6
Other technical	14,646	38.8	23,116	6.2
Graphics	1,812	46.1	2,117	53.9
Marine engineering, ship building and maintenance	1,181	31.6	2,559	68.4
Chemistry	1,635	50.1	1,627	49.9
Flying	1,128	21.3	4,169	78.7
Development	8,890	100	0	0
Textile	0	0	1,224	100
Maritime	0	0	1,1420	100
Total	513,952	29.1	1,253,209	70.9

Source: Ministry of Education and Culture 1998.

"link and match" policy, which is intended to connect vocational and technical education and training directly to the labor market. The new dual system is modeled after the German system. So far all public and 20 percent of the private vocational and technical schools have participated in this program, along with some 11,000 SMEs.

Skill Training

Skill training in Indonesia is provided through a number of different mechanisms. These include the formal educational system, special training centers, public and private training providers, and some informal training venues. Some 19 government departments have established and regulate 815 training programs (MOM 1997).

But primary responsibility for occupational training in technical, managerial, and entrepreneurial fields, for skill certification, and for establishing skill standards lies with the Ministry of Manpower.[13] The ministry's target group is primarily job seekers, who receive training at the 156 public institutions throughout the country. Other public agencies offering skill training include the Ministries of Trade, Agriculture, Health, and Tourism.

The World Bank (1997b) has identified a number of weaknesses in the Ministry of Manpower's training programs. Among them are low internal and external efficiency, high unit costs, low capacity utilization, weak linkages with employees, and uncertain labor market outcomes for graduates. Despite these weaknesses enrollment in the training centers grew in almost every field between 1994 and 1998 (table 2.11). Enrollments did decline in 1998–99, mostly because of reductions in budgetary support during the economic crisis.

Reduced budgetary support for skill training is not a new phenomenon. Similar reductions in 1984–87 resulted in serious underutilization of training facilities and equipment. In response the Ministry of Manpower initiated "third-party utilization" of its facilities, opening them to private training providers, employment agencies, businesses, and other government agencies. In 1996–97 nearly 31,000 workers attended third-party courses, but that number fell sharply to less than 12,000 in 1998–99 with the onset of the economic crisis. The ministry needs to revisit third-party utilization.

Information on enterprise-based training is scarce. The World Bank (1997b) estimates that some 2,500 companies operate their own training centers for around 230,000 trainees. Prior to the crisis some enterprises were making significant investments in training, especially foreign firms and joint ventures producing high-value goods.

Although private providers make an important contribution to the national training effort, they have not been effectively integrated into the planning process for the national vocational training system—a situation that needs to be rectified immediately. The government can create an environment that fosters efficiency among private training providers by keeping regulation to a minimum. At the same time, however, regulatory polices must ensure that the excesses evident in the private training sector in many countries do not develop in Indonesia.

The Ministry of Manpower has been providing facilities for upgrading the skills of private trainers. However, participants do not rate these pro-

TABLE 2.11
Trainees in Skill Training Programs
(1994–95 to 1998–99)

Fields	1994–95	1995–96	1996–97	1997–98	1998–99	Total
Regular						
Engineering	8,321	10,176	11,176	12,968	9,008	51,649
Electricity	7,955	10,707	12,959	14,269	9,364	55,524
Automotive	8,929	10,162	10,849	12,383	8,608	50,931
Construction	6,736	7,977	9,139	9,568	6,224	39,644
Marketing	4,393	5,872	6,018	7,486	5,280	29,049
Other vocations	11,494	13,882	16,650	19,189	10,992	72,207
Agriculture	11,477	10,231	14,979	19,846	20,592	77,125
Total	59,305	69,007	81,770	95,709	70,068	375,859
Third-party training						
Engineering	4,812	5,123	6,726	6,037	2,848	25,546
Electricity	2,900	3,940	5,304	5,387	2,340	19,871
Automotive	5,441	8,604	9,232	5,008	4,115	32,400
Construction	1,320	942	1,182	797	505	4,746
Marketing	2,074	4,161	5,532	1,191	1,066	14,024
Other vocations	1,503	4,441	2,449	3,790	326	12,509
Agriculture	980	1,688	402	260	441	3,771
Total	19,030	28,899	30,827	22,470	11,641	112,867

grams highly. Participants want less of the theoretical training these programs provide and more hands-on experience in public training centers. This suggestion merits serious consideration, especially in view of the fact that public training facilities are presently underutilized.

In addition, the government needs to foster private sector participation in the national training system. The (sectoral) industry training boards can play an important role in this respect, and the government needs to facilitate their creation. These boards can serve as catalysts in the process of developing links between skill training and industries. The benefits of such linkages would accrue to both partners.

Retraining Retrenched Workers

The Indonesian government recognizes the importance of providing training for the large number of workers retrenched because of the crisis. But the lack of data on retrenched workers, especially educational and skill profiles, hinders efforts to plan and organize retraining programs. To be effective retraining programs must take into account differences in individual workers, in the goals of retraining, and in the systems that deliver it.

Indonesia has four types of retraining programs for retrenched workers, most of them focused on developing income-generating opportunities. These programs include entrepreneurship development and self-employment, micro- and small enterprise development, community-based training (supported by the International Labour Organization [ILO]), and the development of cooperative enterprises.

One of the most successful retraining programs is the Adjustment Training Program (*Pelatihan Penyesuaian*), which is conducted by the Ministry of Manpower. This program provides retrenched workers with the training necessary to secure employment in the domestic market as well as overseas. The government has also used public works to provide income support for the unemployed, including two public works programs specifically targeting retrenched workers.

In the absence of an adequate database providing information on retrenched workers, identifying the specific training methodologies that would be most suitable for Indonesia is difficult. However experiences from other countries (both industrial and developing) suggest some potentially effective approaches. These entail creating learning conditions tailored to specific needs, problems, and potential. For instance modular materials can be used to create an individualized, task-based, learner-paced environment. The modules can be closely matched with individual skill profiles to make training more effective and to minimize the time and costs involved.

The methodology developed by the ILO to generate employment and income sources in rural areas may be the most useful alternative for retrenched workers. Community-based training recognizes the importance of forging effective links between skill training and employment opportunities in rural areas where the market (or the potential market) for newly acquired skills is generally unknown. The methodology involves identifying income-generating opportunities and corresponding training needs, designing and delivering appropriate training programs, and providing follow-up support with a view to ensuring the sustainability of the activities trainees undertake. One of the key elements in the success of this methodology is access to credit. In Indonesia this issue can be appropriately addressed by linking the program with an employment fund like those described earlier.

Maintaining a Skilled Workforce

The Indonesian government is trying to improve the skill profile of the Indonesian workforce in the medium term in order to meet the challenges of globalization and international competitiveness. Meeting this challenge requires improving the effectiveness and efficiency of the training system. Two factors add to the urgency of making these changes. The first is the country's productivity level, which is one of the lowest in Southeast Asia (table 2.12). The second is the large number of expatriate workers in the country (table 2.13a). Indonesia needed close to 17,000 technicians and operators alone in 1996, many of whom were imported (table 2.13b). The fact that this figure represents a downward trend from 23,000 in the previous year is of little comfort given the scope of the problem.

The government needs to take action on several fronts to improve skill training and increase productivity. First, it must increase its efforts to train workers for those industries with the most growth potential over the next two to three years, including agroprocessing, tourism, and certain types of manufacturing (such as rattan furniture) that produce goods for export and do not rely on imported materials. Second, the government must review the functioning of public vocational training centers. Their focus needs to be reoriented so that they assume different roles as functions are devolved, shed some of the training activities the private sector can provide, and offer advanced training courses. One particularly important step involves offering skill upgrading to increase productivity in the agricultural sector, including in agroprocessing.

Third, the government needs to consider ways to improve the quality of teaching in public training institutes. Until 1996 most of the instructors (60 percent) had only a senior secondary school education; 19.8 percent

TABLE 2.12
Productivity Levels of Asian-Pacific Countries
(thousand US$)[a]

Country	1990	1991	1992	1993	1994
Japan	275,689	280,796	280,972	278,570	280,351
Singapore	177,788	182,757	187,286	204,246	217,051
China	116,044	122,503	127,863	134,184	139,821
Malaysia	64,839	68,319	71,518	74,344	78,848
Republic of Korea	83,881	89,205	91,984	95,462	100,954
Thailand	20,691	22,207	22,998	25,109	—
Philippines	17,190	16,757	16,154	16,145	16,352
Indonesia	15,593	16,310	17,021	18,098	19,256

— not available

a. Output per worker per year.

Source: Asian Productivity Organization, 1996.

TABLE 2.13(a)
Expatriate Workers by Main Industry, 1995–97

Agriculture, forestry, hunting, and fishing	1,963	4,243	1,431
Mining and quarrying	6,358	6,946	2,997
Manufacturing	36,429	22,299	19,574
Electricity, gas, and water	948	930	332
Construction	2,196	311	3,086
Wholesale and retail trades, restaurants, and hotels	5,015	525	4,049
Transportation, storage, and communication	792	971	590
Financing, insurance, real estate, and business services	771	882	1,045
Community, social, and personal services	2,485	4,027	4,088
Total	56,957	41,134	37,192

had the Diploma II, and just 7.5 percent had some tertiary education (table 2.14). To compensate for these relatively low educational levels, instructors were exposed to further training. Between 1989 and 1993 some 1,994 instructors attended training within the country, and 393 were sent overseas (MOM 1997). The government needs to continue monitoring the quality of instruction, taking remedial action when necessary.

Fourth, the government can step up its efforts to provide skill certification for workers going overseas. The overseas market has always been an important source of jobs for Indonesian workers and is even more so now. Indonesia expects to export 2.8 million workers in 1999–2003. Skill certification plays an important role in wage setting because it helps ensure fair working conditions for workers. Testing the skills of migrant workers and

TABLE 2.13(b)
Expatriate Workers by Main Occupation, 1995–97

Occupation	1995	1996	1997
Manager	13,624	12,663	8,762
Professional	11,874	11,163	12,969
Supervisor	8,254	8,281	5,409
Technician or/operator	23,407	16,551	10,052
Total	57,159	48,658	37,192

Source: Ministry of Manpower.

TABLE 2.14
Formal Education of Public Vocational and
Skill Training Instructors, 1996

No.	Vocation	SLTA	DI	DII	DIII	SI	Total
1	Automotive	216	0	206	0	59	461
2	Mechanical/Technology	427	0	288	289	47	1,051
3	Electricity/Electronics	392	40	106	46	40	624
4	Construction	347	0	106	0	23	476
5	Business	222	20	0	0	45	287
6	Various vocations	244	20	0	0	22	286
7	Agriculture	308	20	0	0	32	360
	Total	2,156	100	706	335	268	3,565

Note: SLTA, senior secondary school; DI, diploma I; DII, diploma II; DIII, diploma III; SI, tertiary school.
Source: Ministry of Manpower 1997.

providing certification of their competency before they leave should therefore be a priority.

Finally, the Ministry of Manpower needs to step up its overall skill testing initiatives. It has made considerable efforts to establish skill standards and tests for a range of occupations. It has put in place the infrastructure required to support the system and the expertise needed to develop standards, test design, and certification arrangements. But the program suffers from inadequate staffing and funding. The ministry has initiated steps to review the current system with a view to improving its efficiency and ultimately to devolving skill testing and certification functions to the industries themselves. This important initiative needs to be followed up vigorously.

Looking to the Future

Training policies have an essential role to play in promoting employment, especially during economic and financial crises. In terms of the Asian financial crisis, training and human resources development initiatives will be measured by their success in creating and sustaining the country's comparative advantage and meeting the demands of industry for skilled workers, irrespective of the health of the economy. In the aftermath of the crisis in Indonesia, where low-skilled workers are the most deeply affected, retraining programs will also be important to ensure that retrenched workers become (and remain) employable.

The government of Indonesia has initiated a number of important measures designed to develop human resources. It has made nine years of basic education mandatory for all Indonesians and instituted reforms of the technical and vocational education and training systems. The government must now build on these initiatives. Some short- and medium-term concerns include:

- Establishing a structured coordinating mechanism with a clearly defined mandate and sufficient autonomy and authority;
- Evaluating public training centers in order to reorient their focus and enhance internal and external efficiencies;
- Targeting training programs to the needs of industries with the most growth potential and to the most vulnerable groups;
- Increasing the involvement of private training providers in national training efforts and facilitating the establishment of industry training boards;
- Improving the skill testing and certification system;
- Enhancing women's access to educational opportunities and training;
- Creating a viable system for financing training; and
- Collaborating with employer and worker organizations on improving the national training system.

Many of these points were set out in a 1995 report by the Task Force on Technical and Vocational Education, which was appointed by the Minister of Education and Culture.[14] The task force recommendations are an important attempt to look at the vocational educational system in a holistic manner. Two important issues were inadequately addressed, however. The first is funding—a more important issue now than in 1995. In the aftermath of the crisis, efficient utilization of available resources is one of the government's major concerns. The second issue involves linking the vocational education program (run under the school system) and the vocational training program for those who have left school. If any effort to improve the national vocational training system is to succeed, it must effectively integrate all subsystems.

The task force also recognized the need for coordination at the national level and recommended establishing a new body called the National Vocational Education and Training Council (NVETC). Establishing such a body would lead to a duplication of efforts, since another body with a similar mandate (the National Training Council established by the Ministry of Manpower) already exists. The task force's recommendation is reflective of the ongoing "turf wars" among the various major players in the field of technical and vocational education and training. Any coordinating body will have little effect as long as the ministries fail to work together—especially since they are technically not bound by each other's administrative fiats.

Such a body, then, should be set up under a presidential decree. It should be headed by a representative of the private sector and should include, among others, private employers (from both the formal and informal sectors), ministries involved in training, workers' organizations, and private training providers.[15] An effective labor market information system is essential to the smooth functioning of such a body. This information system must include an inventory of public and private training providers, with attendant details such as the location of training centers; the type and length of the training offered; intake capacities; fees payable (where applicable); and entry requirements. Arrangements must be made to disseminate information, including through the employment services.

The government also faces challenges to the educational system in general. At both the national and provincial levels, the educational system faces a number of issues, including access, gender equity, a shortage of facilities, and quality. Some of these problems are specific to individual provinces. Educational quality and opportunities vary widely, indicating that some provinces are experiencing serious funding problems. The issue of access manifests itself in high dropout rates and low educational levels throughout the population, showing that the educational system (particularly at the upper levels) is out of the reach of many Indonesians. The impact of the crisis may drive more people away from the educational system, particularly from the vocational stream, which is perceived as more expensive.

Given these problems and the fact that the depressed economic situation is likely continue for some time, what is the outlook for vocational and technical education? General education may weather the storm because it is less expensive to implement than vocational and technical education, which require expensive inputs in the form of equipment and facilities. In general, however, while the population and workforce continue to expand, the funding available for education continues to decline. This scenario raises two questions. First, how will those with low levels of education secure productive, well-paying employment? And second, how will those with low levels of education manage to send their children to school and keep them there? These are the challenges policymakers and program managers must meet. Unless the government takes steps to make the best use of all available resources, both general and vocational and technical education are likely to continue to suffer.

The government must pay more attention to the availability of educational opportunities and to the quality of the education offered. Merely expanding the school system will not suffice; enhancing access is equally important. Areas where school-age children are not in school must be identified and the causes of their nonparticipation addressed if educational policies are to succeed. More measures need to be initiated to increase enrollments at all levels, for two reasons. First, a sound educational system means a more skilled, more trainable workforce. And second, increasing the number of educated workers will decrease pressure on the labor market in the short to medium term.

Some Final Remarks

Although Indonesia has not yet recovered from the economic crisis that has gripped its economy since the middle of 1997, growth resumed in 1999. But the economy is unlikely to attain the growth levels of the last two decades within the next few years. Current projections indicate that GDP growth for 2000 will remain at around 3 percent. The dilemma faced by local industries because of the crisis is one reason growth will remain low. The domestic market is limited by the ongoing recession, and the quality of local products is not up to the standards of competitive foreign markets. At the moment industries are surviving from year to year, using up savings rather than productive money while waiting for the results of new elections—and ultimately for economic recovery.

The crisis has been a major setback for the Indonesian economy in other ways. Before the crisis Indonesia had been steadily progressing toward its goal of achieving full employment and eliminating underemployment. The crisis has seriously impeded this progress. Unless the government devotes special attention to the problem, unemployment and underemployment are likely to grow worse. Durable solutions to the problems of unemployment and underemployment can be found only in the context of sustained economic growth. For this reason policymakers must not only restart economic growth—a daunting challenge—but also get the economy back on the road to full employment.[16]

The government must begin thinking in terms of a two-pronged integrated strategy of employment-led recovery and reconstruction. This strategy would include policies and measures designed to make the growth process more employment friendly and activities aimed at creating additional jobs through direct employment programs. An employment-friendly, efficient growth process should make it possible to achieve output growth with a lower rate of investment than would otherwise be required.[17] And such a strategy would be consistent with Indonesia's quest to attain pre-crisis growth rates without the same investment rates. Since estimated output growth in the short and medium term is unlikely to generate sufficient employment for the entire labor force, the government also needs to focus on the second element of the two-pronged strategy—additional job creation through direct employment programs.

While macroeconomic stability is essential in order to return to a sustainable growth path, making that growth employment friendly will require macroeconomic trade, exchange rate, fiscal, monetary, and sectoral policies conducive to such a process. Such policies will have to be carefully designed to have the maximum positive impact on labor-intensive sectors, subsectors, and technologies. Sectoral employment issues will have to be a priority. The government needs to examine its strategies and policies (and design new ones) for employment in the agricultural, manufacturing, and informal sector. SMEs are expected to play a major role in growth and employment generation in the medium term.

The government can also introduce appropriate measures to minimize job losses and facilitate the process of restructuring the economy and redeploying workers. It can begin this process with restructuring at the enterprise level, appropriate reforms in labor market policies and institutions, measures to strengthen employment services, and training programs aimed at redeploying workers.[18] Programs are needed that equip employers and managers with the practical concepts and tools necessary to undertake socially sensitive and economically effective enterprise restructuring. Most enterprises can benefit from specific assistance in:

- Designing and implementing appropriate measures for repositioning financing and debt, production capacity, human resources, research and development, technology, and marketing;
- Refocusing overall business strategies from both a short- and medium-term perspective;
- Developing strategies to meet various types of international standards and norms;
- Increasing competitiveness and productive efficiency;
- Installing modern human resources management, corporate citizenship, and social responsibility policies; and
- Becoming involved in the newly emerging democratic environment by advocating policies that are of particular benefit to specific industries.

Reforms in labor market institutions and legislation need to use tripartite consultation to achieve an appropriate balance between efficiency in the workplace and effective worker protections. Given the economic restructuring that must take place in response to the changed realities following the East Asian crisis, retraining workers in general and retrenched workers in particular is a priority. Retraining programs must be carefully formulated, keeping in view the changing demands for skills and differences in regional requirements. Labor market information will play a crucial role in formulating such programs and identifying target groups of workers. Self-targeting mechanisms offer the best means of selecting workers for retraining. Employment services also need reforming, in part by linking the assistance they provide to retraining programs. Incorporating "rapid response" capabilities will allow employment services to provide more effective assistance to retrenched and dislocated workers, as well as to companies and communities.

Notes

1. The data presented above are from censuses and intercensal surveys. The Labor Force Survey for 1996 shows a much lower rate of unemployment (4.89 percent of the total economically active population in 1996). But even that figure represents a sharp increase in the rate of unemployment from 2.6 percent in 1986 to nearly 5 percent in 1996.

2. The Labor Force Surveys yield higher figures for the total workforce than the census and intercensal data. The reason(s) for this difference are difficult to understand. Godfrey (1993) provides an overview of the difficulties of comparing figures obtained from various sources.

3. Data compiled by the Central Bureau of Statistics, based on the National Socio-Economic Survey of Consumption. The poverty line is calculated based on the daily minimum nutritional requirement of 2,100 calories per capita, plus a minimum amount of nonfood items such as clothing, education, transportation, and other basic household and individual needs.

4. Based on data available in Central Bureau of Statistics, Statistical Indicators, December 1997, GDP growth during the first two quarters of 1997 over corresponding periods in 1996 was 6.94 and 5.95 percent respectively.

5. Dki Jakarta has the lowest rate (58.2 percent) and Bali the highest (76.8 percent). The spread and the highest and lowest rankings did not change between 1997 and 1998.

6. This increase occurred because the job losses in nonagricultural sectors (2.5 million) were offset by the increases in agricultural employment (5 million).

7. The open unemployment rate was highest in the relatively industrialized and commercialized provinces of Bali, Java, North Sumatra, and South Sulawesi. Most other provinces experienced lower increases of 0.3–1.0 percent.

8. Some 56 million persons, or 40 percent of the working-age population of 139 million, lived in urban areas in 1998, compared with 53 million, or 39 percent, in 1997.

9. Even before the economic crisis, the government had expressed concern about the increase in graduate unemployment in Indonesia. To address this concern it implemented the Young Professional Entrepreneurship Development Program to help young unemployed graduates create self-employment opportunities.

10. Some of the PK2 projects were conceived as part of the Social Safety Net program induced by the crisis. But only US$1 billion of the Social Safety Net budget of US$15.7 billion was allocated to these projects, and a large proportion of even this amount apparently suffered leakages.

11. The most prominent government-funded programs are managed by the Ministry of Industry and Trade and the Ministry of Cooperatives and Small-Scale Industry. Donor-funded programs include those supported by the World Bank, U.S. Agency for International Development (USAID), Asia Foundation, German Agency for Technical Cooperation, United Nations International Development Organization (UNIDO), and Swisscontact.

12. The description of legislation in this section is based on ILO forthcoming.

13. The ministry is also responsible for training that enhances productivity and promotes self-employment and for programs targeting overseas workers and apprentices.

14. The task force argued for technical and vocational education that is driven by industry and guided by market signals. Training should meet nationally recognized standards, provide multiple entry and exit points and flexible delivery, and recognize competencies wherever and whenever obtained. Importantly it should cater to the informal as well as the formal sector. And finally, it should be oriented toward (and able to facilitate) the integration of education and training and supported by a decentralized system of management.

15. The functions of such a body are discussed in ILO (forthcoming).

16. The economy's observed employment elasticity stood at 0.2936 from 1985 to 1995. The government's rule of thumb regarding employment elasticity is that a 1 percent increase in GDP will generate 400,000 jobs. Using this measure Indonesia needs a growth rate of over 5 percent annually just to absorb the 2.2 million workers who join the labor force each year—and this statistic does not take into account the backlog of the unemployed and underemployed. The 1.2 million additional jobs that should accompany the projected growth rate of 3 percent for 2000 are clearly insufficient.

17. Such a strategy would not create a trade-off in terms of productivity and incomes. As Indonesia still faces the problems of unemployment and underem-

ployment and wages are still relatively low (and also flexible), it should continue to enjoy a comparative advantage in producing and exporting labor-intensive items. It is of course important to ensure that factor prices do not get distorted because of government policies.

18. For more details, see ILO (forthcoming).

References

ADB (Asian Development Bank). 1997. *Asian Development Outlook 1997*. Manila.
_____. 1998. *Asian Development Outlook 1998*. Manila.
_____. 1999. *Country Economic Review, Indonesia*. Manila.
APO (Asian Productivity Organization). 1996. *Productivity Statistics: Productivity Indexes and Levels in APO Member Countries*. Tokyo.
Godfrey, Martin. 1993. *Labor Market Monitoring and Employment Policy in a Developing Economy: A Study of Indonesia*. New Delhi: International Labour Office and Asian Regional Team for Employment Promotion.
Hugo, G. J. 1999. "The Impact of the Crisis on International Population Movement in Indonesia." Paper prepared for the International Labour Organization Employment Strategy Mission.
ILO (International Labour Office). 1996. *World Employment 1996–97*. Geneva.
_____. 1999 (forthcoming). *International Digest on Termination of Employment Laws*. Geneva.
_____. Forthcoming. *Indonesia: Strategies for Employment-led Recovery and Reconstruction*. Report of an Employment Strategy Mission. Geneva.
Islam, Iyanatul. 1999. "Poverty, Inequality and the Indonesian Crisis: What Do We Know?" Jakarta: United Nations Support Facility for Indonesian Recovery.
Islam, Rizwanul. 1998. *Indonesia: Economic Crisis, Adjustment, Employment and Poverty*. Issues in Development Discussion Paper 23. Geneva: International Labour Office.
MOEC (Ministry of Education and Culture). 1998. *Education Statistics in Brief 1996–97*. Center for Informatics, Board of Research and Development. Jakarta.
MOM (Ministry of Manpower). 1997. *Profil Balai Latihan Kerja Menyongsong Kemandirian*. Directorate General for Training and Productivity Development, Jakarta.
Musa, Agustina. 1998. "Access to Credit for SMEs in Indonesia Before and During the Economic Crisis (1997–98)." Jakarta: Asia Foundation and U.S. Agency for International Development. Working paper.
Poppele, J., and Lance Pritchett. 1999. "Social Impact of the Indonesian Crisis: New Data and Policy Implications." Social Monitoring and Early Response Unit, Semarang.
Widarti, D. 1999. "Skills training in Indonesia." Paper prepared for the International Labour Organization, Jakarta. Unpublished.

Wieland, Robert. 1988. "SME Finance in Indonesia: An Assessment." Washington, D.C.: Institute for International Economics.

World Bank. 1997a. *World Development Report 1997.* Washington, D.C.

_____. 1997b. *Training and the Labor Market in Indonesia: Productivity Gains and Employment Growth.* Washington, D.C.

_____. 1998. *Education in Indonesia—from Crisis to Recovery.* Washington, D.C.

3 Korea: Labor Market Outcomes and Policy Responses after the Crisis

Soon-Hie Kang, Jaeho Keum,
Dong-Heon Kim, and Donggyun Shin

THE THREE DECADES leading up to 1997 were a time of phenomenal economic growth for Korea. But the financial crisis at the end of 1997 and the subsequent structural reforms and macroeconomic stabilization programs constricted economic activities on a large scale. In 1998 real GDP growth was –5.8 percent, and inflation rose to 7.5 percent.

Korea's precrisis growth sharply increased the demand for labor. The unemployment rate hovered around 2 percent from 1989 to 1997, and as 1997 approached the country faced a severe labor shortage. Analysts argued that the unemployment rate had fallen too far below the nonaccelerating wage rate of unemployment.

Wage increases soon began to outstrip productivity increases, discouraging potential investors. Until the mid-1980s Korea had enjoyed cheap labor costs compared with competing countries such as Hong Kong, Singapore, and Taiwan. However, the rapid rise in wages after 1987 increased unit labor costs, and Korea could no longer count on cheap labor to give the country an edge in international competition. After the democratization of 1987, trade unions with relatively advantageous collective bargaining contracts were often successful in wage negotiations with employers. Nominal wages doubled within just four years. Real wages came close to doubling between 1987 and 1997, while the growth rate of nominal wages continued to climb, rising by approximately 13 percent in 1990–97.

One profound effect of the crisis, then, was to accelerate the restructuring of the labor market to achieve labor market flexibility. Jobs—which in Korea had often been perceived as having a lifetime guarantee—are no longer protected. Labor market policies are now deigned to protect overall employment. This change is not without costs. The Korean labor market experienced record levels of unemployment along with very strong labor mobility.

The official unemployment rate for the first quarter of 1999 reached 8.4 percent, with the number of unemployed exceeding 1.7 million. Most of the unemployed had been employed in the construction, trade, and manufacturing sectors. They were primarily nonprofessionals, including technical personnel and laborers (53.6 percent) and workers in services and sales positions (22.1 percent). The proportion of regular workers in the work force continued to decrease, while the proportion of temporary and daily workers rose.

The crisis also increased procyclical nominal and real wage movements. The growth rate of nominal wages decreased from 12 percent in 1996 to 5 percent in 1997. The results of wage bargaining through July 1998 show that wage increases declined an average of 2.4 percent. Of 3,337 workplaces 2,259 agreed to a wage freeze, and another 559 agreed to wage cuts. In 1998, as the inflation rate rose to 7.5 percent, real wages dropped by almost 10 percent.

As growth in wages fell, so did the rate of unionization. Most collective bargaining in Korea takes place at the enterprise level, as it does in Japan and the United States. Union membership had been decreasing since the late 1980s and with the crisis declined to a little over 12 percent of the total work force—a smaller percentage than in the United States, where the rate of unionization is only 14 percent.

As a result of the painful economic restructuring, the Korean economy began recovering from its deep recession. Growth resumed as private consumption increased, and private investment continued its slow (but sizable) recovery. Real GDP grew by 4.6 percent in the first quarter of 1999, and inflation stood at only 0.7 percent. Although the unemployment rate stood at 8.4 percent in the first quarter, this high rate was the result mainly of lags in the effect of business cycles on the labor market. The unemployment rate started to decrease significantly in April, and as of September 1999 stood at 4.8 percent, with 1.07 million people unemployed.

Employment and Unemployment

The East Asian financial crisis resulted in massive job destruction in Korea. Total employment, which had stood at 21.1 million in the fourth quarter of 1997, was reduced to 19.8 million by the fourth quarter of 1998 and to

19.0 million in the first quarter of 1999. The average quarter-to-quarter employment reduction for January 1998–March 1999 amounted to 0.4 million. The reduction in total employment was close to 20 percent.

This fall in total employment is attributable primarily to job losses in the manufacturing and construction industries. From the fourth quarter of 1997 until the fourth quarter of 1998, employment fell by 583,000 in manufacturing and 533,000 in construction, for a total decline of 1.1 million—more than 90 percent of total job losses. Employment in wholesale and retail also fell significantly. The community, social, and personal services industry grew by 17,000, even during the economic downturn, reflecting the massive public works program implemented as part of the government's unemployment policy. In keeping with expectations of countercyclical behavior, employment in agriculture increased sharply for the first three quarters of 1998 but fell dramatically in the first quarter of 1999, reflecting the recent economic recovery.

Across industries the hardest-hit jobs were those in manual production and clerical work. The number of managers and professional workers actually increased by 2.5 percent, rising from 3,722,000 in the fourth quarter of 1997 to 3,815,00 in the fourth quarter of 1998. This increase suggests that job losses during the economic crisis in Korea were not evenly distributed across different occupations, with workers at the lower echelons bearing most of the burden.

The downturn negatively affected the structure of the Korean labor market. The number of regular workers decreased by 733,000 between the fourth quarter of 1997 and the same quarter of 1998, accounting for approximately 60 percent of the total reduction in employment during this period. Temporary workers accounted for the next largest proportion. However, the number of daily workers, which had dropped sharply in the first quarter of 1998, began increasing steadily over the year, rising from 1,933,000 in the fourth quarter of 1997 to 1,961,000 in the same quarter of 1998.[1] The number of unpaid family workers also increased by a small amount for the same period.

According to a recent World Bank survey (Hallward-Driemeier and others 1999), 60 percent of Korean manufacturing firms employed fewer workers after the crisis than they had before. This difference is the highest among the five countries under discussion (Indonesia, Korea, Malaysia, the Philippines, and Thailand). Korea and Thailand had the largest proportions of redundancies, with over a quarter of the firms reporting a decline in employment of more than 25 percent.

Perhaps the single most important indicator of labor market performance is the unemployment rate. As we have seen the recent economic downturn destroyed a large number of jobs, and the unemployment rate is high by historical standards. The annual average unemployment rate for 1989–97 was 2.2 percent, with little yearly variation. The recent financial crisis and resulting cyclical and structural adjustments sharply raised the unemployment rate, which climbed to 6.8 percent in 1998 and then to 8.4 percent noted for the first quarter of 1999 (figure 3.1).

Who Is Unemployed?

Breaking the unemployment rate down by gender helps us to understand the recent increase in overall unemployment. There is little difference between genders in terms of the number of unemployed. But in Korea men tend to remain in the labor force when they lose their jobs, while women tend to leave the labor market. As a result the difference in male and female unemployment rates increased from 0.5 percentage points in 1997 to 2 percentage points in 1998, rising to 2.3 percentage points in the first quarter of 1999. Since the unemployment rate measures the percentage of the labor force that is actively looking for work, it may underestimate the actual number of job losses if some jobless workers become discouraged and stop seeking work.

FIGURE 3.1
Unemployment Rates

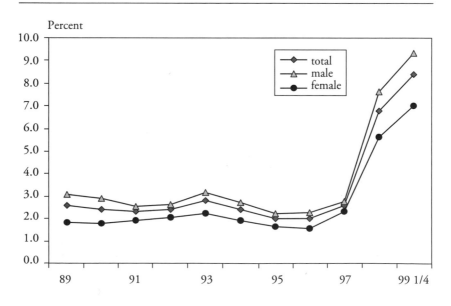

Source: National Statistical Office.

FIGURE 3.2
Labor Force Participation Rate

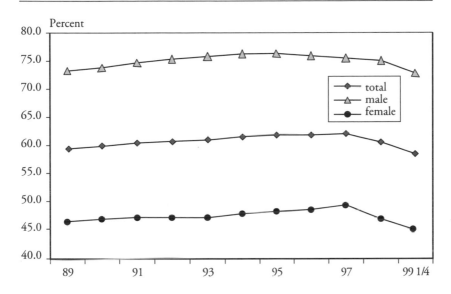

Source: National Statistical Office.

Korea's overall labor force participation rate had been increasing until 1997, reaching 62.2 percent in that year. It decreased sharply to 60.7 percent in 1998 and to 58.6 percent in the first quarter of 1999, largely because of the huge exodus of women from the labor force (figure 3.2). In 1997–98, the number of women in the labor force decreased by 330,000, while the number of men increased by 120,000, for a reduction of 210,000 in absolute terms. If these women had not left the labor force, the unemployment rate would have been 7.8 percent instead of 6.8 percent in 1998.[2]

Traditionally the unemployment rate in Korea is higher for workers with a college-level education than for those with a high school education or less. However, the unemployment gap between the two groups narrowed over time, and the crisis reversed the situation of these two groups of workers (figure 3.3).

What lies behind this shift in unemployment trends? Empirical evidence shows that the recent structural adjustment process is associated with significant downward mobility for less educated workers as their jobs are filled by those with more education (NSO various issues). Often these less skilled workers remain unemployed. Another explanation for the nar-

FIGURE 3.3
Unemployment Rate by Educational Attainment

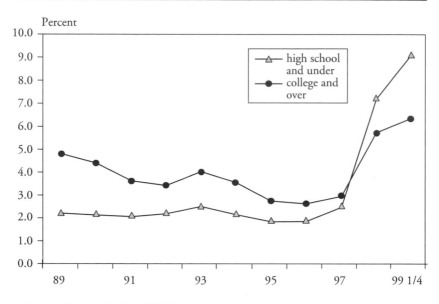

Source: National Statistical Office.

rowing of the unemployment gap between highly educated workers and those with less education lies in the growing demand for college graduates relative to the demand for high school graduates. The unemployment rate in the first quarter of 1999 was 9.1 percent for workers with a high school education or less and 6.4 percent for those with a college-level education.

According to a recent study (Shin 1999), the monthly averages for January 1998–February 1999 show that 567,000 people joined the ranks of the unemployed, while 496,000 left the unemployment pool. Net growth in unemployment therefore amounted to 71,000 people. Among the 567,000 newly unemployed workers, 58 percent had had jobs in the previous month and 42 percent had not. Among the 496,000 people who left the unemployment pool, 64 percent found jobs, and the other 36 percent left the labor force. The monthly hazard rate from the unemployment pool was 31.8 percent. To put it another way, for every 10 unemployed people in a month, roughly 1 person left the labor market, 2 found employment, and the other 7 remained in the unemployment pool for the following month. This 1:2:7 relationship remained stable after the crisis, supporting the notion that labor mobility was very strong.

If we apply the 31.8 percent average monthly exodus rate from the unemployment pool to the 934,000 unemployed in January 1998, we find that fewer than 10,000 should remain in the unemployment pool after 12 months. However, the actual number of unemployed persons who remained in the unemployment pool continuously between January 1998 and January 1999 was around 40,000—almost 4 times the expected figure. These calculations show that people who experienced long-term unemployment had a smaller probability of escaping from unemployment than people who were unemployed for only a short period. This fact in turn suggests that the overall duration of individual periods of unemployment in Korea was relatively long.

One of the most important and least visible consequences of a deep recession or structural change is in fact a large and expanding pool of people who have been unemployed for a long period of time. The term long-term unemployment rate (LTUR) is traditionally used to represent the proportion of people who are continuously unemployed for 12 or more months. Figure 3.4 illustrates how the LTUR changed after 1998. A systematic pattern tends to emerge when the LTUR series is contrasted with

FIGURE 3.4
Long-Term Unemployment Rate

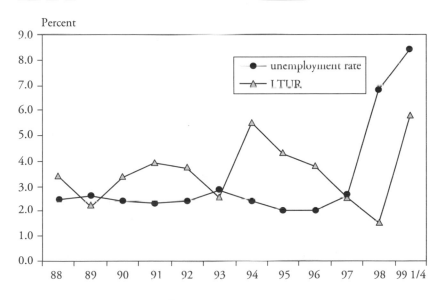

Source: National Statistical Office.

the usual unemployment rate series. The LTUR tends to fall with sharp increases in unemployment, when large numbers of newly unemployed workers join the pool of jobless workers. As the newly unemployed workers find jobs and the overall unemployment rate decreases, the LTUR tends to rise. Korea experienced this pattern in 1993–94, after a mild recession. In 1993, the year when the unemployment rate reached its local peak, the LTUR fell slightly. In 1994, however, it went up by 3 percentage points, rising from the 1993 levels of 2.5 percent to 5.5 percent.

The recent—and much more severe—downturn produced a similar pattern in the LTUR. As the unemployment rate jumped by 4.4 percentage points in 1998, the LTUR dropped by 1 percentage point. The LTUR in the first quarter of 1999 was 5.8 percent. Although the LTUR fell in 1998, the absolute number of long-term unemployed almost doubled. Traditionally, the LTUR is higher for men than for women and is positively correlated with education level. These patterns still prevail in Korea.

The rising unemployment rate only partly reflects the consequences of the crisis in terms of employment. The number of hours worked also decreased significantly during the downturn. The average number of hours worked per week fell from 47.3 in 1996 to 46.7 in 1997, dropping to 45.9 in 1998. The increase in the proportion of part-time workers (those working fewer than 36 hours a week) in the total labor force partly explains this decline. The proportion of part-time workers rose from 7.2 percent in 1997 to 9.3 percent in 1998.

Industrial Relations

When it comes to the development of Korea's industrial relations, the 1987 Declaration of Democratization is considered a turning point. The declaration amended the constitution to endorse the principle of freedom of association and autonomy for labor and management. The pre-Declaration period is classified as the period of employer-dominated industrial relations, and the post-1987 period, which was marked by massive industrial disputes, as the period of confrontation and conflict. During this period employers and employees strenuously sought to establish a "power equilibrium." Before 1987 the number of labor disputes averaged 200 a year. In 1987, however, the number totaled 3,749. As they went through massive labor disputes, trade unions strengthened their organizing capacities. The number of unionized workers increased from 948,000 in June 1987 to 1,270,000 at the end of the year and to 1,930,000 in 1989.

The number of labor disputes peaked in 1987 at 3,749 cases. But in 1989 the government began to take strong action against illegal strikes, and the number of disputes dropped remarkably, falling to 1,616. It fell again in 1992 to just 234. In 1995 there were only 88 labor disputes, and in 1996 only 85. The number of unionized workers also continued to fall, decreasing from 1,930,000 in 1989 to 1,610,000 in 1995. However, these developments did not mean that industrial relations in general stabilized. They indicated only that the time of turbulence that followed 1987 began to stabilize somewhat after 1990. But labor and management still had not quite shed their age-old tendency toward confrontation and conflicts. Evidence shows that the total number of work days lost due to labor disputes increased from 392,581 in 1995 to 892,987 in 1996 (KLI 1998).

In 1997, recognizing that an economy with inefficient labor-management relations cannot survive in an age of borderless competition, the government, labor, and management reached an agreement. Korea needed a new system of harmonious industrial relations in order to achieve sustainable development. Korea's labor laws, which had not been significantly changed since they were enacted in 1953, were thoroughly revised. In particular, the Act Concerning the Promotion of Worker Participation and Cooperation, promulgated in March 1997, required all enterprises with 30 or more workers to organize a *labor-management council*. Each council would be composed of an equal number of labor and management representatives and would hold quarterly meetings.

The labor-management councils discuss, among other things, ways of improving productivity and workers' welfare, preventing labor disputes, and addressing environmental issues. They have the authority to introduce and manage education and training plans and welfare facilities in the workplace. The Central Labor-Management-Government Council is the highest national tripartite body and is composed of labor, management, and public interest groups. It deliberates on labor policies and their relationship to industrial, economic, and social policies. And it considers any other matters that may have a bearing on industrial peace.

As the mood of industrial relations changes from one of confrontation and conflict to one of participation and cooperation, labor and management are seeking solutions through dialogue and negotiation. Nevertheless, Korea needs a dispute resolution system. In principle the Trade Union and Labor Relations Adjustment Act prescribed that whenever disputes occur that involve working conditions, labor and management must work to resolve the dispute autonomously. The new law also narrowed the scope of and imposed stricter conditions on compulsory arbitration. Only essential public services such as water, electricity, gas, oil, telecommunications, railroads, hospitals, inner-city bus services, and banking services would be subject to compulsory arbitration. The Labor Relations Commission could conduct compulsory arbitration if the Special Mediation Committee, which is composed of three public interest representatives, recommended it.

Problems in the Labor Market

The question of whether the rise in the unemployment rate was cyclical or structural is difficult to answer, as dramatic cyclical changes induce structural adjustments. Nor is it simple to compare the degree of labor market flexibility among economies. However, the above statistics show that most labor market variables responded very quickly and procyclically during the recession, suggesting that the Korean labor market was not excessively rigid. Moreover, Korea made efforts to improve labor market flexibility during the adjustment process. Newly introduced measures allowed for a system of flexible work hours, dismissals for economic reasons, and a worker dispatch system.[3]

The primary problems facing the Korean labor market after the Asian financial crisis were wage rigidity, a worsening employment structure, long-term unemployment, youth unemployment, and family unemployment (unemployment among heads of households with no other wage earners).

WAGE RIGIDITY. Although labor market variables show very procyclical movements, some are functionally very rigid. In particular individual wages do not appear to reflect productivity differentials, creating functional wage rigidity. According to the 1996 Survey on Collective Bargaining on Wages conducted for employers and workers at 262 unionized workplaces in the manufacturing sector, the most common wage determination system is based on seniority. As of 1996 the cost of the labor needed to produce one unit of output was approximately 30 percent higher in Korea than in France and Japan, 15 percent higher than in the United States, and 10 percent higher than in Taiwan (KLI 1997). This fact explains why the international competitiveness of the Korean labor market gradually declined, even when the economy was growing rapidly. The wage system can be rationalized, however, through the promotion of an annual salary system based on ability and performance rather than on seniority. Functional wage flexibility should be the primary policy goal if the labor market is to be healthy and competitive.

THE EMPLOYMENT STRUCTURE. As previously discussed the proportion of well-paying jobs and "regular" employment decreased dramatically during and after the crisis. But the trend toward increasing numbers of non-regular workers also appeared in many industrial countries. The most sensible way to address such a phenomenon is by asking how these workers can best be protected and to what extent they should be. These questions concern not only basic labor standards but publicly administered social insurance programs.

LONG-TERM UNEMPLOYMENT. The LTUR reached 3.8 percent in 1999— still low relative to the rate in industrial countries. But with Korea's social safety net in the early stages of development, concern about the long-term unemployed in Korea could be justified. By 1999 this class of unemployed workers numbered around 51,400, and these workers seemed destined to form a new underclass.

YOUTH UNEMPLOYMENT. As of 1998 the highest proportion of the unemployed (approximately 36 percent) belonged to the 20–29 age group. The next-highest proportion came from the 30–39 age group. Workers ages 15–19 accounted for a smaller proportion of the total unemployed but faced an unemployment rate of 20.8 percent in 1998. (The unemployment rate stood at 11.4 percent for the 20–29 age group.) When the crisis began, the practice of hiring new graduates from high schools and colleges virtually halted, generating a large pool of unemployed new graduates who would have trouble finding employment even when the economy started its recovery. The government initiated a sizable number of ready-made public jobs and internship programs for this group, but these publicly funded programs were not expected to last indefinitely.

FAMILY UNEMPLOYMENT. The problem of family unemployment in Korea is becoming increasingly serious. As of 1998 some 668,000 of the 1,463,000 unemployed, or 45.7 percent, were family heads, compared with 34.5 percent in 1997. Moreover, about 19.1 percent of this group were heads of families with no other income earners. The majority were low-paid workers even before becoming unemployed. Statistics show that 60,000 were temporary workers, 90,000 daily workers, and 39,000 unpaid family workers, new entrants to the labor force, or those with work experience who had been jobless for more than one year (NSO various issues).

Employment Creation and Maintenance

In response to rapidly rising unemployment, in March 1998 the Korean government began implementing comprehensive measures to address a number of labor market issues. These issues included job protection and creation, vocational training, job placement, and social protection (Lee and Choi 1998; Uh 1999).

The job-protection program was intended to minimize unemployment in two ways. First, it would help keep viable profit-making firms from collapsing. Second, it would provide firms experiencing short-term financial difficulties with subsidies to help them retain employees. The Employment Insurance System (EIS) would provide workers with financial support and assistance. The job-creation program aimed to provide new jobs through public investment projects, public works projects, and support for business startups. The vocational training and job placement programs were designed to enhance the employability of the jobless and to expand the networking system for job matching. The social protection program would provide income support to unemployed workers and their families. Included among the social protection programs were unemployment benefits (through the EIS), public works, temporary livelihood protection, and loan projects for the unemployed.

To implement these unemployment policy measures, the government spent almost 10 trillion won in 1998 (table 3.1). Public expenditures on labor market programs were almost negligible in Korea before the crisis

TABLE 3.1
Public Expenditures on Unemployment Measures, 1998

Unemployment measures	Budget (billion won)	No. of persons covered
Job creation	**3,817**	—
Expansion of SOC investment	3,295	—
Support for venture enterprises	522	—
Job protection	**2,117**	**781,000**
Support for efforts to retain employees	122	781,000
Support for managerial stabilization of SMEs	1,995	—
Vocational training and job placement	**901**	**363,000**
Social protection	**3,235**	**1,843,000**
Public works projects	1,044	438,000
Unemployment benefits	850	441,000
Loan projects for the unemployed	750	109,000
Temporary livelihood protection, etc.	591	855,000
Total	**10,070**	**5,611**

— not available.
Source: Ministry of Labor, White Book on Labor, 1999.

(Park and Lee 1999). For example, Korea spent 0.1 percent of GDP on active labor market policies in 1996 (Martin 1998). However, the picture changed significantly after the crisis, and total labor market–related expenditures expanded to 2.2 percent of GDP in 1998.[4] In 1999 a total budget of 16 trillion won was allocated for unemployment policies (including a supplementary budget): 6.5 trillion won to create jobs in the private sector, 2.5 trillion won to create public works jobs for 300,000 people, 0.5 trillion won to support firms that retain employees, 1.1 trillion won to support vocational training and job placement, and 5.4 trillion won to support the social safety net (OECD 1999).

Although the basic framework of measures to address unemployment had not changed since the programs were enacted, the government's priority shifted from assisting the unemployed to creating jobs. Job creation was the top priority among unemployment policies in 1999. The government's efforts centered on creating a favorable environment for the private sector to create jobs (KOILAF 1999; MOL 1999). These efforts included:

- Providing necessary infrastructure (such as business management consulting resources and start-up information);
- Increasing the number of small business support centers and business "incubators" to help support the start-up of small and medium-size enterprises (SMEs) and venture enterprises with high potential for employment;
- Supporting service industries such as tourism that have high job-creation potential; and
- Increasing investment in social overhead capital and extending housing construction projects.

Income Support for the Poor and Unemployed

As we have seen the government made a number of provisions to help support the vulnerable and unemployed. These social safety nets include the EIS, public works projects, and temporary livelihood protection. In addition, the government offers special loans for the unemployed and a wage claims guarantee system for workers from bankrupt firms.

The Employment Insurance System[5]

In the early 1990s the government began discussing an unemployment insurance scheme that would be an institutional device offering comprehensive employment-related services (KOILAF 1998). There was some concern that such a system would reduce workers' motivation to seek employment and thus prolong the period of unemployment. Finally, however, a social consensus was reached to adopt the EIS as part of an active and comprehensive manpower policy. The Employment Insurance Act mandating the EIS was enacted in December 1993 and took effect on July 1, 1995.

The EIS was intended to serve two purposes. First, it would provide unemployed workers with unemployment benefits, and second, it would offer workers the chance to upgrade their job skills and thus enhance their chances of finding and retaining stable employment. The program combined traditional unemployment benefits and active labor market programs such as skills training and job matching. For this reason the system was called the *employment* insurance system rather than the unemployment insurance system.

The EIS has three major components: unemployment benefits, an employment stabilization scheme, and a vocational competency development scheme. Unemployment benefits aim not only to stabilize unemployed workers' living conditions but also to promote reemployment through job-seeking and employment promotion allowances. The employment stabilization scheme aims to prevent unemployment from massive layoffs and to stimulate reemployment at those times when changes in the industrial structure or technology result in extensive corporate restructuring. The vocational competency development scheme seeks to develop the vocational skills of workers through life-long vocational training.

Each of the three schemes has its own premium. The premium for unemployment benefits is 1.0 percent (0.5 percent each from employers and employees) of total payroll.[6] The premium for the employment stabilization scheme, which is financed entirely by employers, is 0.3 percent of total payroll. The vocational competency development scheme is also financed by employers and carries a premium ranging from 0.1 percent to 0.7 percent of total payroll, depending on the size of the firm.

Compared with other contingencies covered by social insurance programs, unemployment is subject to a much greater degree of uncertainty (Yoo 1999a). Economic fluctuations affect the level of unemployment and thus the financial situation of the employment insurance fund. The Korean government maintains a reserve for the employment insurance fund to cover any unexpected demand. When the economic crisis began at the end of 1997, Korea had a sufficient amount of reserves in the fund—2 trillion won, the equivalent of almost 18 months' expenditure in an environment of high unemployment. These reserves allowed Korea to cope with high unemployment after the crisis.

UNEMPLOYMENT BENEFITS. Unemployment benefits include job-seeking and employment promotion allowances. To receive unemployment benefits, claimants must have been insured for 6 months or more during the 12-month working period prior to the date of termination. Workers who are voluntarily unemployed without good cause or who are terminated for cause are ineligible for unemployment benefits. Claimants must register at their local labor office as job seekers. They must be ready and able to work and actively searching for a job. The duration of unemployment benefits is set at between 60 and 210 days, depending on age and length of enrollment in the EIS.

Unemployment benefits are paid to eligible claimants every two weeks following a two-week waiting period. Thus even workers who register immediately following a layoff must wait four weeks for the first payment. The amount of the benefits workers receive equals 50 percent of their average wage rate during the three months immediately preceding layoff. Because unemployment benefits are nontaxable, the level of income replacement is often higher than it is in other countries.

Unemployment benefits were initially limited to workers in firms with more than 30 employees, but coverage was extended rapidly after the financial crisis (table 3.1). Coverage was extended to workplaces with more than 10 employees in January 1998 and to workplaces with more than 5 employees in March 1998. It was further extended in October 1998 to employees in firms with fewer than 5 workers, temporary workers employed at least one month, and part-time employees working more than 18 hours a week. In addition a special 60-day extension was granted to unemployed workers whose benefits expired between July 1998 and June 1999. The extension was renewed in the second half of 1999.

As of July 1999 the government had granted a combined 1.5 trillion won to 718,000 people in the three years since July 1, 1996, when unemployment benefits first began (table 3.2).[7] Claims for unemployment benefits had increased sharply by the end of 1997 but showed a downward trend as the economy gradually picked up. The average duration of unemployment benefits was 85 days in 1997, 91 days in 1998, and 126 days in July 1999. Over the three-year period, men accounted for 70 percent of recipients.

As of August 1999 the ratio of unemployment benefit recipients to the total number of unemployed stood at 12.3 percent—considerably lower

TABLE 3.2
Workers Receiving Unemployment Benefits, 1996–99

	1996	1997	1998	As of June 1999
Males	8,017	37,960	305,280	128,192
	(79.1)	(74.4)	(69.6)	(67.6)
		13,057	133,185	61,390
		(25.6)	(30.4)	(32.4)
Females	2,116	5,563	119,550	56,739
	(20.9)	(10.9)	(27.3)	(29.9)
		12,463	133,808	52,920
		(24.4)	(30.5)	(27.9)
		13,942	95,664	38,354
		(27.3)	(21.8)	(20.2)
Under 30	854	16,163	79,820	35,988
	(8.4)	(31.7)	(18.2)	(19.0)
30–39	2,264	2,886	9,623	5,581
	(22.3)	(5.7)	(2.2)	(3.0)
40–49	3,335			
	(32.9)			
50–59	3,087			
	(30.5)			
Over 60	593			
	(5.9)			
Total	10,133	51,017	438,465	189,582
	(100)	(100)	(100)	(100)

Note: Numbers in parentheses are percent of total participants.
Source: Ministry of Labor.

than in industrial countries (table 3.3). The government aims to increase the figure to 20 percent by 2002. In addition the government expects 7.6 million workers, or 80 percent of the workers eligible for employment insurance (about 9.5 million), to have insurance coverage by that year (MOL 1999).

EMPLOYMENT STABILIZATION. The employment stabilization scheme has two parts: aid for employment adjustment and aid for employment promotion. Aid for employment adjustment consists of employment maintenance and hiring subsidy programs. Hiring subsidy programs assist employers who contribute to the stabilization of the labor market by hiring

TABLE 3.3
Unemployment Benefit Coverage
(millions of employees)

	July 1996	January 1998	March 1998	October 1998	June 1999
Scope of coverage	30 employees or more	10 employees or more	5 employees or more	All workplaces	All workplaces
No. of employees to be covered (A)	4.31	5.67	6.11	8.50	8.60
No. of insured employees (B)	4.3	4.30	4.69	4.90	6.00
B/A (%)	99.8	75.8	76.8	57.6	69.8

Source: Korea Labor Institute.

laid-off workers from restructuring enterprises. Employment maintenance subsidy programs offer wage subsidies to firms that retain redundant workers during periods of short-term financial difficulty (OECD 1999; Yoo 1999b). The programs provide subsidies of one-half to two thirds of employees' wages (depending on the size of the firm) for six months to firms that provide their employees with at least one month's paid leave, transfer workers to affiliates, or switch to a new line of business while retaining at least 60 percent of their employees.[8] Other subsidies cover:

- *Temporary shutdown.* Firms that close for at least two days a month can receive one-half to two-thirds of the temporary shutdown allowance they must pay employees.
- *Reduced working hours.* Firms that reduce regular working hours by more than 10 percent can receive up to one-tenth of the wage bill from before the reduction.
- *Training to retain employees.* Firms that provide training for their workers receive one-half to two-thirds of wages for trainees and are reimbursed for training expenses.

In 1998 a total of 1,805 firms received employment maintenance subsidies that covered nearly 660,000 workers. Some 91 firms received hiring subsidies for employing 5,210 displaced workers (table 3.4). Contrary to initial expectations, these employment subsidy programs were used by less

TABLE 3.4
Participation in Employment Subsidy Programs, 1998[a]

	Number of employees						
	Total	5–49	50–99	100–299	300–499	500–999	1000+
All firms	199,272	179,902	11,100	6,477	911	580	302
Firms participated	1,896	755	366	445	118	103	109
Participation rate (%)	0.95	0.41	3.29	6.87	12.95	17.75	36.09

a. Employment maintenance and hiring subsidies only.
Source: Korea Labor Institute.

than 1 percent of private employers. A strong association exists between the size of the firm and the likelihood of utilizing the subsidy programs, suggesting that small firms did not utilize the subsidy programs because they simply did not know the programs existed or could not cope with the complex rules.

The employment maintenance subsidy program was expanded in 1999, allowing firms to receive more than one type of subsidy instead of just one at a time. In addition, the duration of the subsidies was temporarily increased from 6 to 8 months for the first half of 1999. A recent study investigated the effects of these subsidy programs on employment maintenance, using employer surveys as well as case studies (Kim and Park 1999). Samples were drawn from 533 firms that received the subsidies between January 1, 1998, and March 20, 1999.

Fay (1996) posits that, theoretically, the net employment effect of a subsidy can be computed as follows:

net effect = gross effect – deadweight loss – substitution effect – displacement effect.[9]

By definition the substitution effect does not occur in wage subsidy programs designed to maintain employment. Therefore we can compute the net employment effect by estimating precisely the magnitude of the deadweight loss and displacement effect—an often difficult task. Thus the study estimated the net employment effect of the employment maintenance subsidy using the percentage of layoffs that might have occurred among subsidized employees in the absence of the subsidy. The result was 22 percent on average, suggesting a deadweight loss in the 70 percent range. Although judging the robustness of the result is also difficult because the study was based solely on interviews with employers, this result roughly coincides with the experiences of OECD countries (Fay 1996). Studies of the wage subsidies in Europe in the late 1980s have found that most such programs yielded small net employment effects. According to an OECD report, the estimated net employment effect of wage subsidy programs in Australia, Belgium, Ireland, and the Netherlands was a mere 10 percent (Martin 1998).

The results by type of subsidy program are as follows: paid leave subsidy, 29 percent; unpaid leave subsidy, 26 percent; and temporary shutdown, reduction of working hours, and training, around 20 percent each. Analyzing these results by industry, we find that in nonmanufacturing industries, 28 percent of the subsidized employees would have been laid off in the absence of the subsidy program—higher than the 21 percent in the manufacturing industries. Looking at the results by firm size (number of employees), we find that firms employing fewer than 10 workers would have eliminated a third of their subsidized employees in the absence of the subsidy program. Firms employing 100 workers or more would have reduced 16–19 percent of their subsidized employees. These results suggest that the smaller the size of the firm, the higher the employment maintenance effect of the subsidy program.

THE VOCATIONAL COMPETENCY DEVELOPMENT SCHEME. The vocational competency development scheme under the EIS is an incentive system that promotes voluntary in-house training by providing financial support to employers and employees from the EIS fund. The scheme offers two types of financial support. Employers that implement training programs receive support for in-plant and other types of education and training and paid leave for employees enrolling in training. Employers can also apply for a loan or subsidy from the EIS to establish training facilities, purchase training equipment, or both. To promote training in SMEs, the EIS helps arrange and provide financial support for group vocational training.

Support for employees covers education and training and includes training incentives for the elderly and tuition loans. Unemployed workers can engage in any training activity regardless of their eligibility for unemployment benefits. This scheme is based on the notion that receiving training with the goal of becoming reemployed in a secure job is preferable to the passive protection of unemployment benefits.

In 1997 approximately 13,888 firms and 3,422,444 individual workers were entitled to use the vocational competency development programs. Of the workers 48 percent were in the manufacturing industry and 51 percent in the service sector (19 percent in finance, insurance, and real estate and 13 percent in transportation, warehousing, communication, and related industries). These figures indicate that the focus of vocational training is shifting from the manufacturing to the service sector. Only 1 percent of workers were in the agricultural sector.

In 1999 EIS funds supported a total of 199,880 people. Of these 81,324 (41 percent) received support for in-plant training, 102,683 (51 percent) received support for alternative types of education and training, 5,559 (3 percent) took paid leave for education and training, 1,949 (1 percent) undertook training during a period of unemployment, and 8,365 (4 percent) received tuition loans. Total financial support for the programs was about 59 billion won.

Public Works Projects

Public works programs have two policy objectives: to create temporary job opportunities and to reinforce social safety nets for the unemployed (Yoo 1999a). By providing temporary job opportunities for the unemployed in the public sector, these programs guarantee the basic livelihood of unemployed families. In principle those who are eligible for public works projects must be between 18 and 60 years old at the time of application. They must be unemployed or daily workers without regular income. Homeless individuals whose status can be verified by administrative agencies or approved organizations are also eligible. Those receiving unemployment benefits are not eligible, regardless of the amount of benefits they receive. However, spouses of those who receive less than 300,000 won in unemployment benefits are eligible for jobs with public works projects.

Public works are divided into central and local government projects. Selection criteria for workers may differ for central government projects. Screening decisions for local government projects are made based on scores in nine categories: age, status in household (head or otherwise), number of dependents, property status, gender (for household heads), handicap, duration of unemployment, public works experience (including in previous stages of the same project), and household income.

The budget for public works projects amounted to 1 trillion won in 1998 and 2.5 trillion won in 1999. Public works projects are carried out in stages. The first two stages take place over three months, with a 10-day break so workers can look for jobs. Those who participate in three stages consecutively are excluded from participating in the next stage. Although designed primarily for male heads of household, the projects also attract

TABLE 3.5
Public Works Project Participants, 1998–99
(percent)

	1998	
	Stage 1	Stage 2
Male	67.7	57.0
Female	32.3	43.0
Under 20	1.2	0.7
20–29	12.0	8.8
30–39	20.7	19.6
40–49	26.1	26.9
50–59	27.6	30.6
60–65	12.4	13.4

	1999		
	Stage 1	Stage 2	Stage 3
Male	58.7	50.5	45.6
Female	41.3	49.5	54.4
Primary school or less	37.4	36.0	34.7
Middle school or dropouts	22.3	23.3	21.3
High school or dropouts	27.2	27.3	27.1
Two-year college or dropouts	5.0	4.9	6.1
University dropouts or higher	8.0	8.5	10.7
Under 20	1.0	0.9	1.3
20–29	11.6	13.5	16.0
30–39	22.7	21.4	18.8
40–49	32.4	30.4	27.2
50–59	27.4	22.5	29.0
60–65	5.0	11.2	7.8

Source: Ministry of Labor.

many female workers who have been excluded from other job opportunities (Park and Lee 1999) (table 3.5). In 1998 some 41 percent of the participants were female. By 1999 the female participation rate had risen to an average of 49 percent during the first three project stages.

The daily wage rate for participants depends on the type and difficulty of the work. In 1998 the wage rate for stage 2 projects ranged from

22,000–35,000 won. However, the wage rate was cut by 3,000 won in October 1998 and by a further 3,000 won in 1999. Currently the daily wage rate ranges from 19,000–29,000 won, higher than the minimum wage.[10]

Short-term job creation projects target special groups. For example in 1998 the government began sponsoring an internship program in response to the problem of unemployment among young people. The program was originally introduced to provide new college graduates with short-term jobs and was extended to unemployed high school graduates in 1999. The internship program is a kind of wage subsidy program. Participating firms are offered 500,000 won per month for 6 months if they hire new college (high school) graduates who cannot find a job. The internship program, which in 1999 had a budget of 209 billion won, benefited 58,000 unemployed college graduates and 10,000 unemployed high school graduates.

The public works program was often criticized. Some public works projects are considered to be unproductive or even wasteful (Yoo 1999a). Early in the program some well-off people were able to participate and many poor unemployed people were excluded, largely because local governments often selected participants on a first-come-first-served basis regardless of the selection criteria. The high wage rate for public works was also criticized as having the potential to distort the labor market. In response the government cut the wage rate by 6,000 won.

Temporary Livelihood Protection

The Livelihood Protection Program, created by the Livelihood Protection Act in 1961, provides support to those who are unable to work, including the handicapped, the elderly, and children. It is a means-tested program designed not for the unemployed but for the poor in general (Yoo 1999a). In 1998 the program protected 1.16 million people—approximately 2.5 percent of the total population. If no one in a poor household is able to work, the government subsidizes living, educational, medical, maternity, and funeral expenses. If anyone in the household is able to work, the government subsidizes educational, medical, maternity, and funeral expenses and supplies free vocational training and education but not living expenses. Instead, the government offers a long-term loan with a low interest rate to help set up and operate a business. If an unemployed person is unable to work, the program supplies direct income support.

The government expanded the program and introduced the Temporary Livelihood Protection Program for the unemployed in March 1998 in order to protect poor unemployed people who do not qualify for unemployment benefits. The original program had stiff eligibility criteria: incomes of less than 230,000 won monthly and property valued at less than 29 million won. Some of the strict eligibility criteria were later eased to allow participants to own property worth up to 44 million won.

This program offers long-term, low-interest loans for livelihood expenses, housing costs, and business operations and supplies medical care and education. If an unemployed person is unable to work, the program offers direct income support. The program protected 310,000 unemployed low-income people in 1998 and 760,000 in 1999. However, it is still too limited in its coverage and generosity. For example, a household of four members can receive 250,000 won per month under the program. But in 1999 the minimum living expenses for such a household were estimated at 880,000 won.

The government plans to reform the social safety infrastructure with the Act on Ensuring People's Basic Living Standards (MOL 1999). With this reform the government aims to ensure that people in the lowest income brackets have the basic necessities, including clothing, food, medical services, and education. The act will take effect in October 2000, and the Temporary Livelihood Protection Program, together with the Livelihood Protection Program, will be integrated into the Program for Ensuring People's Basic Living Standards.

Other Social Safety Nets

An unemployed person needing direct income support or money for urgent medical, wedding, or funeral expenses, children's school fees, housing costs, or business-related expenses may apply for a long-term loan. This special loan project was introduced by the tripartite agreement of February 1998. In order to get the loan, the applicant must register at the local labor office as an unemployed person prior to applying for the loan and must be actively seeking work. The applicant must also satisfy certain criteria in terms of income, housing, and number of dependents. The amount of a loan ranges from 3 million won for livelihood maintenance, urgent medical, wedding, or funeral expenses, or school tuition to 30 million won for operating a business.

As of June 1999, 596 billion won remained of the original 1.85 trillion won in the loan fund. The original amount was funded with the sale of employment security bonds. The loan project was expected to continue until the fund was completely paid out (MOL 1999).

The government operates other loan funds. Some of these programs have highly beneficial effects, especially the loans to jobless female household heads and funding for the long-term unemployed to start businesses. These programs will be considered for permanent implementation.

A large number of firms went bankrupt after the crisis (Park 1999).[11] Many of the bankrupt firms could not make severance payments or even pay wages to their employees. The government established the Wage Claims Guarantee System for such employees in July 1998. Under this system these workers receive wage arrears for up to three months and severance payment equal to their wages for the last three years at the bankrupt business. In 1998 the system was financed by a levy on firms of 0.2 percent of the total payroll and a budget outlay of 190 billion won (OECD 1999). The levy was raised to 0.3 percent in 1999. As of June 1999, 39.5 billion won had been paid to 12,210 workers at 278 workplaces. About 72 percent of the recipients were male.

The Financial Crisis and Labor Market Services

The impact of the crisis on workers was particularly severe because Korea had only minimal social safety nets. Families broke apart; violent and petty crime alike increased sharply; and many small children were left at orphanages and other institutions. As a result the government undertook a number of programs designed to mitigate soaring unemployment.

In order to minimize job losses, the Korean government encouraged the private sector to adopt more flexible management practices, allowing part-time employment, work-sharing, and flexible work hours.[12] Wage flexibility was also an important part of the government's response to the crisis. Employers and workers are encouraged to agree to a performance-based wage system and to consider pay cuts instead of retrenchment.

Dismissals

Responding to criticism that labor hoarding within firms was one of the causes of the financial crisis, the Central Labor-Management-Government Council initiated an amendment to the Labor Standards Act. The amendment gives firms the legal right to dismiss workers in what are termed "managerially urgent" cases in order to lower labor costs and build competitiveness. Previously firms had been unable to fire workers without running the risk of lawsuits, and it was generally understood that job security was guaranteed unless a worker committed a serious crime. Before the new legislation, firms (especially large ones) forced workers to quit "voluntarily" by removing their desks or transferring employees to a distant area or a lower-level position.

The Tripartite Committee was established in January 1998 as a forum for organized labor, business, and government to discuss appropriate labor market policy responses to the crisis. The committee considered the recommendations of the Central Labor-Management-Government Council to amend the Labor Standards Act and allow dismissals for economic reasons. The agreement reached by the committee amended the act to allow dismissals, providing that every effort to avoid retrenchment had been explored, that rational and fair standards had been used to select employees for dismissals, that employees had been given advance notice, and that sincere consultations had been held with trade unions or worker representatives. Large firms were also obliged to notify the Ministry of Labor in advance of any layoffs.

Conditions for dismissals are still relatively strict. Moreover, a firm is required to make efforts to rehire the dismissed workers if it intends to recruit workers at all within two years of the day of dismissal. In 1998 only 115 firms notified the Ministry of Labor of their intention to lay off 12,000 workers. The EIS reported that dismissals made according to the legislation totaled just 7.1 percent of all job separations, or roughly 140,840 workers (table 3.6). However 14.2 percent of the unemployed who had job experience had been dismissed from their previous jobs (KLI and KIHASA 1998). This figure is far higher than the figures reported by the EIS and Ministry of Labor, suggesting that most dismissals did not meet the required conditions and violated the necessary procedures. Many firms, especially SMEs, where labor unions have little influence and management has the upper hand, laid off their employees arbitrarily, without due process. Moreover, the legalization of dismissals "for managerial needs" encouraged this phenomenon, since many firms regard this legislation as permission to dismiss workers unconditionally.

Act for Dispatched Workers

The Tripartite Committee also tried to enhance employment flexibility by legalizing the use of dispatched workers. Even though many temporary work agencies lease workers such as secretaries, maintenance personnel, and drivers, the law had prohibited dispatching workers. The Act Protecting Dispatched Workers, passed in February 1998, changed the legal climate in this regard.

TABLE 3.6
Reasons for Job Separation
(percentage of sample)

Reason	EIS data	Survey on Unemployment and Welfare Needs
Voluntary resignation (to change jobs)	50.3	41.5
Voluntary resignation (to marry, care for children, or related reason)	2.3	2.6
Resignation (health reasons, age)	1.2	4.2
Dismissal (for managerial needs)	**7.1**	**14.2**
Bankruptcy or shutdown of firm	6.6	24.0
Termination of contract	2.6	1.2
Early or honorable retirement (usually with allowances)	15.9	2.0
Regular retirement	0.8	0.8
Others	10.0	9.5
Total	100.0	100.0

Source: EIS data: Phang (1999); Survey: KLI and KIHASA (1998).

Under the act dispatched workers can be used for up to one year in 26 occupations deemed to require specialized knowledge, skills, and experience. The act permits one-year extensions if both parties agree. Employers must make potential workers aware of the working conditions. And to protect dispatched workers, the act stipulates that employers must not discriminate between them and regular workers. Their contracts cannot be terminated because of religion, gender, or social status. By the end of 1998, some 789 agencies had been established that employed a total of 42,000 dispatched workers.

Employment Services and Labor Market Information

The Korean government expanded and reinforced public employment service agencies and created a nationwide network for job information.[13] The number of public employment service agencies managed by the central government increased from 52 in February 1997 to 134 in March 1999 (table 3.7). The number of public workers specializing in job placement services also increased, climbing from 141 to 2,684 during the same period.[14]

TABLE 3.7
Employment Service Agencies

	February 1997	March 1999
Central government		
Local labor office	46	—
Manpower bank	3	20
Employment security center	3	99
Employment center for daily workers	—	15
Subtotal	52	134
No. of counselors	141	2,684
Local government		
Employment center	251	253
Information center	34	28
Subtotal	285	281
Private agencies	1,432	1,756
Total	1,769	2,156

— not available.
Source: Ministry of Labor.

In addition to dramatically increasing the number of public employment service agencies and counselors, the government launched several projects designed to provide easy access to labor market information. The government formally launched an electronic labor exchange system, Work-Net, in May 1999, using Canada's WorkInfoNet as a standard. Work-Net, which workers can access via the Internet, provides information on job vacancies, vocational training, career guidance, employment policies, employment insurance, labor market statistics, and labor laws. In July 1999 the government published the *Occupational Outlook Handbook*, along with various career guidance books and a CD-ROM version of the Dictionary of Occupational Titles.[15] It is currently developing an occupational preference test and in 1998 piloted two other tests, the General Aptitude Test Battery and the Occupational Interest Test Battery, which were administered nationwide to 300,000 people and 150,000 people, respectively.

To improve the quality of employment services and make them more user friendly, the government combined the employment insurance and employment security sections of local labor offices into employment security centers. These centers, which are based on the concept of one-stop service, are designed to provide job seekers with all the information and services they need for their job search, from job vacancy information to vocational training. The primary advantage of these centers is that unemployed workers can receive unemployment benefits and job search assistance in the same place. The central and provincial governments run a joint manpower bank that specializes in job-matching services and an employment center for daily workers.

The government also eased regulations on and increased its support for private employment agencies. In 1998 some 1,902 private agencies helped 1,537,857 workers find jobs.[16] The government also supports trade unions and employers' organizations that provide job placement services. In June 1998 the requirement that employers report all vacancies to the government was eased, and unnecessary requirements (such as regulations governing office space) were eliminated. For-profit enterprises that provide labor market information such as job vacancies through newspapers, periodicals, and the Internet must register with the Ministry of Labor. By the end of 1998, 47 such enterprises had registered with the government.

Finally, the government initiated the development of a set of databases of unemployed workers and introduced the Worker Profiling System, a statistical model based on the reemployment experiences of previously unemployed workers with similar characteristics.[17] The purpose of profiling is to identify hard-to-employ workers early on and refer them to services that can help them find jobs quickly.

The Effectiveness of Employment Services

As a result of the government's efforts to expand public employment services, the number of job seekers using the public employment system jumped from 243,467 in 1997 to 2,130,687 in 1998 (table 3.8). The number of job vacancies posted with public services also increased dramatically. A survey conducted in September 1998 reported that the ratio

TABLE 3.8
Outcomes for Public Employment Service Agencies

Year	Vacancies (A)	Job seekers (B)	Placements	Employed (C)	(A/B) × 100	(C/B) × 100
1994	225,652	148,597	180,248	28,141	152	18.9
1995	196,319	116,147	175,416	20,938	169	18.0
1996	215,925	150,668	306,501	20,939	143	13.9
1997	245,223	243,467	644,295	36,425	101	15.0
1998	410,005	2,130,687	2,356,881	157,442	19	7.4

Source: Ministry of Labor.

of unemployed registered with public employment service agencies rose from 4.8 percent in 1996 to 22.5 percent in 1998 (KLI and KIHASA 1998).[18] Only 9.1 percent of the unemployed used private employment services, suggesting that public employment services played an increasingly important role in job matching in 1998.

However, the effectiveness of these services is still in question. Even though the absolute number of job seekers finding jobs through the public system more than quadrupled, the employment rate ([*employed/job seekers*] $\times$ 100) decreased only by half from 1997 (15.0 percent) to 1998 (7.4 percent). In part this disparity reflected a tight labor market still feeling the effects of the economic downturn. But other statistics show that only 5.8 percent of the unemployed found jobs through the public employment services. According to the September 1998 survey, unemployed workers used an average of 2.36 job search methods. These findings suggest that public employment services are relatively inefficient compared with other job search methods such as friends and relatives and direct contacts.[19]

Many of the unemployed visited public employment service agencies such as local labor offices and manpower banks. But the general feeling was that the current system did not provide customers with timely and reliable information on the supply of and demand for labor (table 3.9).

TABLE 3.9
Evaluation of Public Employment Services
(percentage of respondents)

	Agree completely	Agree somewhat	Disagree somewhat	Disagree completely
Staff is kind and friendly	18.8	54.0	19.0	4.5
Staff know their duties very well	14.7	53.8	19.4	3.4
I can find plenty of job openings	2.5	10.8	47.7	32.1
Services are provided quickly	2.1	18.9	41.2	30.2
Job openings suggested are adequate for me	0.9	8.7	28.3	54.2
I received in-depth counseling on career development	3.1	10.9	32.8	42.0

Source: KLI and KIHASA (1998).

Most job seekers believed that public employment services failed to provide adequate job opportunities and counseling on career development.

Most of the employees working in public employment service agencies had less than one year of experience in this field. Furthermore, both the quality and quantity of the information the system supplies were seriously limited. Before the financial crisis, information on job openings was usually sufficient for job seekers. However, in an environment of high unemployment and economic contraction, job seekers want information not only on available job opportunities, but also on vocational training, career development, the labor market situation, and occupational prospects.

The government's failure to provide much-needed information becomes clearer when we compare Work-Net with labor market information systems in other countries, including Canada's WorkInfoNet and the America Labor Market Information System (ALMIS) in the United States. Work-Net did not supply occupation-specific information, local labor information, or occupational prospects. These services are essential to helping workers plan their careers and fully utilize Korea's limited human resources.

Additionally, the number of public employment agencies and counselors was insufficient. Even after the initial drastic increase in the number of public employment service agencies and counselors, the number of workers per counselor stood at 3,901 in 1997, compared with 364 in Germany, 325 in Sweden, and 745 in the United Kingdom (table 3.10). Japan's figure was closer to Korea's, but Japan's unemployment rate was still relatively low. In any case the number of unemployed (as opposed to workers) per counselor was 150 in Japan but 664 in Korea.

Vocational Education and Training

In 1967 the government established a national training system with the enactment of the Vocational Training Law. In 1973 the National Techni-

TABLE 3.10
Public Employment Service Agencies and Counselors, 1997

Country	Agencies	Counselors	Workers per counselor
Japan	619	15,320	3,401
Germany	842	93,000	364
Sweden	570	11,000	325
United Kingdom	1,159	34,000	745
Korea[a]	119	2,684	3,901

a. Data are for March 1999.
Source: Ministry of Labor.

cal Qualification Law put in place a system of skill certification. Laws enacted in 1976 introduced and formalized mandatory in-plant vocational training and established a Vocational Training Promotion Fund financed by a training fee levied on firms that did not meet the stipulated training requirements. In 1982 the Ministry of Labor founded the Korea Manpower Agency (KOMA) as its training arm. In 1989 the Korea Institute for Technology and Education was established to provide teacher training programs for the vocational training centers.

By 1998 approximately 500 vocational training institutes were providing various levels of training for a broad range of occupations (table 3.11). KOMA is in charge of 40 public vocational training institutes aimed at providing the skills industries need most but cannot teach in in-plant training. The remaining institutions are in-plant training centers (237) and authorized training centers (178) run by nonprofit organizations and private sector firms. Between 1967 and 1998 approximately 3.3 million people attended training courses at these institutions.

Government support for vocational and technical education and training in Korea was important in developing the skills that have helped fuel Korea's rapid growth. Having concentrated on expanding primary education during the 1950s, Korea focused on vocational secondary schools during the 1960s and 1970s. In the late 1960s and 1970s, the government stepped up efforts to develop skilled and technical workers outside the formal education system and established many vocational training centers. In the mid-1970s the government began encouraging firms to offer in-service training. During the 1980s enrollment in vocational secondary schools and in-plant training began to decline, although enrollment in junior vocational colleges rose. In 1991, in response to perceived shortages of skilled workers, the government once again began emphasizing vocational education in secondary schools. In 1994 the government initiated a review of vocational education and training policies as part of a comprehensive ex-

TABLE 3.11
Vocational Training Institutes

		Public			
	Total	KOMA	Central government	Local government	In-plant	Authorized
1990	316	37	38	7	122	112
1998	509	40	46	8	237	178

Source: Ministry of Labor.

amination of human resource development policies by the Presidential Commission on Educational Reform.

The most important development in technical education at the upper secondary level and in public vocational training programs occurred in the 1970s, however. Government policy specifically addressed these areas, and appropriate financial support was made available to provide a first-class teaching environment in these programs. Also important in developing these programs was foreign assistance—both financing and technical services—especially in establishing public training centers.

Ongoing efforts were made to adapt the vocational education and training system to changes in the economic environment. When the construction boom in the Middle East in the late 1970s offered opportunities for skilled construction workers, special attention was paid to training workers in those trades. In the early 1970s, when the rural electrification project was implemented, rural training centers were established in each province. These centers provided short-term training in electrical trades so that locally trained workers would be available to help implement projects.

Vocational training programs are classified as initial training, upgrade training, retraining, and job transfer training. But there are no clear distinctions among the last three categories, and in general further training or in-plant training covers all three.[20] Initial training, as recognized by law, is for trainees who are recruited specifically for vocational training and new employees who have been on the job less than one month. Initial training programs include three things:

- General education, which is coordinated with practical training;
- Basic training in the knowledge and skills necessary to the occupation, provided by a training institution or in a plant, either on or off the job; and
- Specialized training to improve employability.

In 1997 the number of people completing initial training programs accounted for 27 percent of all trainees completing craftsmanship training. Of the people who completed in-plant training, which focuses primarily on more advanced training, 84 percent were enrolled in further training and only 16 percent in initial training (table 3.12).

Recent Reforms in Vocational Training

The Korean government attempted to correct market failures in the area of training by imposing levies on firms that do not provide training, imple-

TABLE 3.12

Vocational Training by Program in 1997

(number of trainees)

Institution	Total	Initial training	Further training		
			Upgrade	Retraining	Job transfer
Total	245,044	66,015	156,067	22,199	763
Public	49,257	15,644	33,107	506	—
In-plant	173,686	28,312	122,918	21,693	763
Authorized	22,101	22,059	42	—	—

— not available.

Source: Ministry of Labor, Yearbook of Vocational Training, 1997.

menting a national technical qualification system, and providing public vocational training. Until the 1980s these systems served the needs of economic development well. During the 1990s, however, the levy system failed
in its goal of encouraging firms to undertake and upgrade training programs voluntarily. The most visible evidence of this failure was the lack of
upgrade programs in enterprises. Training programs for blue-collar workers
(including new entrants to the workforce) concentrated on basic skills to
enhance employability and did not improve the technical knowledge and
skills of existing employees.

This emphasis on basic skills training can be traced to a policy designed
to channel youths who were not in school into the industrial sector during the economic expansion of the 1970s. This compulsory training system, like the levy system, contributed to an initial expansion of in-plant
training. But it did not meet the training demands of private firms because
it did not respond to changes in the Korean economic environment. It
also did not provide employers with the incentives and assistance they
needed to invest in the further education and training of their workers,
largely owing to the regulations governing the use of training funds, the
qualifications of trainers, and training materials and equipment.

Early in the 1990s training provided by companies on a voluntary basis
increased sharply. At the same time the number of youths undertaking vocational training decreased markedly owing to the declining proportion of
young people in the overall population and the growing number of youths
entering universities. Some of the hottest issues in designing the EIS were
determining how to encourage the private sector to provide more training
voluntarily, boost upgrade training and retraining for in-service workers,
and offer job transfer training to the unemployed.

The government decided that it was premature to abolish the compulsory system, which had existed for almost two decades. For the time being, it was decided to apply the system to companies of 1,000 or more that still needed a large number of trained workers. As a result, enterprises with fewer than 1,000 employees were exempted from the compulsory vocational training system after July 1995. These companies then came under the jurisdiction of the EIS, which leaves the decision to provide training up to the employers and provides financial support based on actual costs.

Promoting Vocational Training for Workers

As discussed previously, the Basic Vocational Training Act, including the compulsory training system, helped workers acquire certain skills but did not meet the changing demand for industrial manpower. In addition, the law limited the ability of enterprises to provide upgrade training to their employees. In response to this situation, in 1997 the government passed the Act Promoting Workers' Vocational Training. The act establishes a system of vocational competency development and encourages enterprises to provide further training for their employees on a voluntary basis. The act went into effect in January 1999, replacing the Basic Vocational Training Act (table 3.13).

Under the new legislation, the Ministry of Labor can offer financial support to employers implementing vocational competency development programs. The Ministry can also offer support to employees seeking to develop their vocational competency by enrolling in vocational competency development training programs, programs designated in the Education Law, or certification programs.

The enactment of the law provided momentum for another transformation in vocational training. The act removes restrictions on in-plant training, encouraging voluntary training, demand-oriented training, and job competency training for the employed. The government will play a supportive assisting role.

Vocational Training for the Unemployed

The severe economic downturn, recent bankruptcies, and the downsizing of many companies resulted in rapid unemployment growth in Korea. The government responded by providing training programs for the jobless in order to increase employability. In 1998 vocational training programs for the unemployed were provided to 362,941 persons, approximately 8 times as many as in the preceding year. Almost a quarter of all the unem-

TABLE 3.13
Legislation on Vocational Training in Korea

	Basic Vocational Training Act (1976–98)	Act Promoting Workers' Vocational Training (1999)
Premise	Compulsory system of training.	Companies encouraged to provide voluntary training.
Target group	Most training is initial training for graduates.	Training includes vocational competency development for the employed, the unemployed, and graduates.
Training area	Training concentrates on production work in the manufacturing industry.	Training is expanded to include clerical, managerial, and service workers.
Classification of training	Training may be public, in plant, or authorized. Programs include initial, upgrade, and job transfer training as well as retraining.	Standard training is based on standards set up by the Ministry of Labor. Vocational competency development includes initial, upgrade, and job transfer training.
Training materials	Training materials compiled or approved by the government.	Any training materials can be used.
In-plant training	Enterprises with 1,000 or more employees in certain industries are required to provide training or pay a training levy.	The government provides financial support to all companies for vocational competency development programs.

Source: Ministry of Labor.

ployed received government-sponsored training. The total budget for vocational training in 1998 amounted to 738 billion won, approximately 13 percent of which was spent on programs for the unemployed (table 3.14).

About half of those who received training once worked at enterprises covered by the EIS. These workers are therefore eligible for reemployment training lasting from one month to one year. They may take training up to three times until they find a new job. However, training allowances are cut in half for the second period of training and are reduced to zero the third

TABLE 3.14
Training for the Unemployed, 1998

Type of training	Budget (billion won)	Number in training plan (A)	Number of participants (B)	B/A	Number of participants (1997)
Total	737.7	320,000	362,941	113.2	42,182
Reemployment training for the unemployed	327.5	289,000	333,541	115.4	27,738
Reemployment training for the unemployed from enterprises covered by the EIS (trainees receive a training allowance of up to 90 percent of the minimum wage, except those receiving unemployment benefits)	178.5	141,000	170,096	120.6	1,949
Training for employment promotion (for the unemployed from enterprises not covered by the EIS, especially economically disadvantaged groups and women)	96.9	110,000	101,709	92.5	25,789
Training to return to agriculture	1.2	2,000	5,126	256.3	—
Training for the newly unemployed who are not entitled to unemployment benefits, such as new graduates (especially from polytechnic colleges and universities)	46.1	26,000	43,012	165.4	—
Training to start a business, especially for the white-collar unemployed	4.8	10,000	13,598	136.0	—
Manpower development training	69.6	31,000	29,400	94.8	14,444
Initial training to be a craftsman (to promote employment for workers with no skills who do not go on to a higher education)	9.6	11,000	14,515	132.0	5,900
Training for the 3-D (difficult, dirty, dangerous) fields	35.0	10,000	11,000	110.0	2,985
Paid leave training (for workers from enterprises covered by the EIS)	25.0	10,000	3,885	38.9	5,559
Other	340.6	—	—	—	—

— not available

Source: Ministry of Labor.

time. Trainees who do not qualify for unemployment insurance receive a monthly benefit of 200,000 to 300,000 won (60–90 percent of the minimum wage) during the training period, including allowances for transportation, family support, and child care. Trainees learning skills used in the "3-D" (dirty, difficult, and dangerous) industries, which still face a labor shortage, receive an additional bonus. Similar training opportunities and benefits are offered to the unemployed who are not covered by the EIS.

A pilot program of training vouchers was launched in 1998. The objectives of the voucher system are to provide the unemployed with more choices for receiving training and to promote competition among institutions providing it. Colleges, universities, and other educational institutions became involved in training activities. In addition the program makes monitoring registration and course attendance easier. Despite some confusion in the program early on, in late 1999 the voucher initiative expanded from just three cities to all of Chungchong province (in central South Korea). An evaluation at the end of the year will help determine whether the initiative should be expanded nationwide.

Vocational training for the unemployed in 1998 had a number of positive effects, increasing employability, stabilizing livelihoods, and providing a degree of mental security for the unemployed. Despite their success, however, these programs were not without their problems. Some training institutions participated in the programs simply to receive government money and did not provide appropriate training. And some trainees were interested in receiving the training allowances but not in attending the programs.

Two other difficulties associated with the programs were the underdeveloped labor market information system and the lack of expert managers. Training programs were selected based on what existing training institutions had to offer (for instance, in equipment and facilities) with little thought for either labor market demands or the needs of the unemployed. Thus training institutions often provided the same training programs they were offering before the financial crisis. The placement figures for those completing the training reflect these problems. As of 1998 the employment rate for individuals completing training programs for the unemployed was 19.8 percent.

New Measures in 1999

In 1999 the Korean Ministry of Labor began implementing plans to provide training for 341,000 jobless workers (200,000 of them under the

EIS), and the training budget rose almost 19 percent to 880 billion won. Government policy for vocational training in 1999 placed top priority on enhancing employability and increasing the efficiency of the training itself. To improve the relevancy and efficiency of vocational training for the unemployed, the government implemented the following initiatives:

- *Transforming the vocational training system to meet trainees' needs.* Training courses would be evaluated and redesigned to respond to demand. Regulations governing such things as instructors and curricula would be adjusted to meet training needs, and training providers would have more autonomy.
- *Expanding the kinds of training offered to include more topics and to cover promising job fields.* Training programs would give priority to such high value-added fields as information technology. Training programs for currently employed workers would be upgraded. The examination criteria of the National Technical Qualification Test would be revised to meet the needs of knowledge-based industries.
- *Making training more efficient.* As a means of controlling the quality of training programs, the government began developing an effective evaluation system. To increase the placement rate for trainees, a "tailor-made" training system was introduced in March 1999. The system assists trainees by securing employment contracts with companies and then providing any necessary training. The companies receive 10 percent of the monthly training costs as an incentive to provide courses that result in placement rates of 50 percent or more within the 3 months following the course. Comprehensive evaluations are to be performed of the job placement rate of training institutions, the number of trainees obtaining qualifications, trainees' satisfaction, and the management of trainees after training. The individual evaluation system was designed to increase the probability of job placement.
- *Enhancing information systems.* The government sought to improve the labor market information system in order to supply industries with workers that have relevant skills, thereby fulfilling demand and at the same time ensuring employment. To this end the government began constructing a vocational training information system, enhancing counseling for trainees using individual profiles, and improving the available information on training, especially on employer demand.
- *Increasing private participation in training.* The Act Promoting Workers' Vocational Training, as we have seen, was designed to encourage

the private sector to become more involved in vocational training. The act helps adjust training and subsidies to the needs of customers and reduces regulations on training. The government committed itself to conducting a comprehensive review of the current training subsidies with an eye to further adjustment.

The government targeted specific groups and firms in its effort to boost private involvement in training, including trade unions and small to medium-size enterprises. In general trade unions in Korea had not been involved in vocational training. The government encouraged trade unions and employers to consult about matters related to training under the auspices of the labor-management councils at the firm level. Furthermore, the government encouraged SMEs to install training facilities and equipment with a view to boosting the firms' participation in training. It also began examining the possibility of granting subsidies to large enterprises (and their associate companies) that develop training programs. Finally, the government sought to identify companies and training institutes with outstanding performances in order to disseminate their experiences as "best practices" to others involved in vocational training.

Looking to the Future

The financial crisis that began at the end of 1997 had severe consequences for the Korean labor market. In the wake of the crisis, the government responded by providing an arsenal of both active and passive labor market programs. The EIS is the most important social safety net for the unemployed in Korea (Yoo 1999b). However the EIS covers only about 12 percent of all the unemployed. To expand the number of unemployment benefit recipients, every effort must be made to include in the EIS all workers in small workplaces and temporary workers. In addition, the government needs to carefully review the possibility of applying the EIS to daily workers.

Since unemployment benefits cover only a limited group, the government created a large number of public works jobs to assist the unemployed. But these programs have their problems. Some ineligible parties received benefits, and others drew double benefits; meanwhile those most in need of assistance were left out of the projects. Alleviating this situation will require establishing a database of participants in public works projects in order to ensure an unbiased selection process and reduce the possibility that participants draw double benefits. Efforts to monitor the projects will help make implementation more efficient. In the long run public works projects need to target unemployed groups and establish links with vocational training providers and job search agencies (Park and Lee 1999).

Because high unemployment is expected to persist in Korea some years into the 21st century, vocational training to enhance workers' employability and job search assistance through the public employment service are increasingly important. Job search assistance is usually the most inexpensive active labor market program, and evaluations from other countries show consistently positive outcomes for this type of activity. To speed up the reemployment process of unemployed workers and enhance labor market efficiency, the public employment service system requires ongoing improvement. The government plans to increase the ratio of job seekers utilizing the public service to 30 percent within a few years. Meeting this goal will require establishing a comprehensive labor market information system and opening more public employment agencies staffed with skilled counselors.[21] Finally, even though many of the key components of the infrastructure needed to build a comprehensive program of public employment services are in place, more can (and should) be done, including:

- Revising the current occupational classification system, which is inadequate, to meet labor market needs;
- Improving Work-Net, the integrated labor market information system;
- Developing career guidance information;
- Improving research on occupational prospects;
- Enhancing the connection between private and public employment services;
- Improving internal coordination within the Ministry of Labor and with local governmental employment service centers;
- Emphasizing data development, improving the quality of data, and expanding dissemination of labor market information;
- Developing standard job manuals for counselors; and
- Enhancing the expertise and morale of staff working in employment service agencies.

Owing to a faster-than-expected economic recovery, the unemployment rate began declining after reaching a record high of 8.6 percent (1.78 million) in February 1999, dropping to 4.8 percent (1.07 million) in September 1999. At the same time, however, the employment structure worsened, and the proportion of long-term unemployed increased rapidly. Further, the share of nonregular work in the labor market is expected to persist. To address these issues effectively, the government needs to carefully evaluate its policy responses.[22]

Although Korea developed various social safety nets for the unemployed after the crisis, their absolute level of social protection is still much lower than in industrial countries. The government should make every effort to reinforce the role of the EIS as the primary social safety net and initiate other income support activities to prevent unemployed workers and their families from slipping into poverty. In addition to the income support activities, more active labor market measures are needed. What is equally crucial, however, is the evaluation of these measures to ensure that they are being implemented effectively.

Notes

1. For statistical purposes regular employees are defined as workers with an implicit or explicit employment contract of more than one year. Temporary workers have an employment contract of one month to one year, and daily workers have a contract of less than one month.

2. Recent empirical findings suggest that the overall labor force participation rate is procyclical (NSO, various issues.)

3. A worker dispatch system allows an employer to lease its employees to another firm. The dispatching firm retains an employment relationship with its leased employees.

4. Korea's GDP was 449.5 trillion won in 1998. Park and Lee (1999) exclude expenditures on job creation and support for the managerial stabilization of small and medium-size enterprises, perceiving these as expenditures on *indirect* unemployment measures. Thus their calculations reflect only *direct* public expenditures on unemployment measures (table 3.1).

5. The following description of the EIS draws heavily on Yoo (1999a, 1999b).

6. The premium had been 0.6 percent until 1998. It was lowered in January 1999, when Korea found itself facing high unemployment.

7. *Korea Herald*, August 31, 1999.

8. Subsidies for manpower reassignment are paid for one year following the completion of the reassignment.

9. Most evaluation studies show that subsidies to private sector employers have both large deadweight losses and substitution effects (Fay 1996; Martin 1998). Deadweight losses occur when the outcome of a wage subsidy program is no different from the outcome in the absence of the subsidy (that is, employers use the subsidy to hire workers they would have hired anyway). The substitution effect occurs when a worker hired by a firm in a subsidized job is substituted for an unsubsidized worker who would have been hired. Typically, the displacement effect refers to displacement in the product market.

10. Specifically 19,000 won or less for positions such as simple office and outdoor work; 24,000 won or less for work that requires certain skills or qualifications or has a high labor intensity; and 29,000 won or less for professional and

skilled work. The minimum wage rate applicable from September 1, 1999, to August 31, 2000, is 1,600 won per hour (361,600 won per month).

11. More than 15,000 firms went bankrupt between December 1997 and April 1998.

12. For an in-depth discussion on the issue, see KOILAF (1998).

13. The government neglected employment services until the financial crisis. Until the onset of the crisis, the government's share of job matching was roughly 2 percent.

14. Most of the newly hired counselors have civilian status. And these counselors are involved not only in job-matching services but also in other areas, such as employment insurance. Thus only a portion of the new counselors are involved full time in job-matching services, a factor that tends to lower their morale.

15. Unlike similar handbooks in other countries, Korea's handbook is not based on a rigorous econometric model. Such a model still needs to be developed.

16. However, there is no reliable data on the proportion of private agencies involved in job matching.

17. The worker profiling system is similar to the one developed by the Australian government, which is used mainly as an advisory tool in the field. For detail, see Eberts and O'Leary (1996) and Deety (1998).

18. However, a large number of unemployed workers register in order to participate in programs such as vocational training and public works rather than to seek jobs.

19. Since 22.5 percent of unemployed workers registered with the public employment service agencies and unemployed workers used an average of 2.36 job search methods, 9.5 percent of the unemployed had to succeed in finding jobs through the public employment services if the services are as efficient as other methods. But the data show otherwise.

20. Further training is generally regulated under the EIS as part of the vocational competency development training component.

21. In particular, the government must concern itself with counselors' morale and expertise.

22. As previously discussed, although the EIS has been extended to all employers, the system does not protect a large number of workers classified as daily workers. Daily workers make up an estimated 70 percent of construction workers, and the unemployment rate of the daily construction workers is the highest of all occupational groups. A comprehensive employment stability plan for daily construction workers is urgently needed.

References

Deety, A. 1998. *Job Seeker Classification Instrument.* Canberra, Australia.

Eberts, R. W., and C. J. O'Leary. 1996. *Profiling Unemployment Insurance Beneficiaries.* Kalamazoo, MI: W.E. Upjohn Institute.

Fay, Robert G. 1996. "Enhancing the Effectiveness of Active Labour Market Policies: Evidence from Programme Evaluations in OECD Countries." OECD Labour Market and Social Policy Occasional Papers 18. Paris: OECD.

Hallward-Driemeier, M., and others. 1999. "Asian Corporate Recovery: A Firm-level Analysis." Paper presented at the conference organized by the World Bank and the Korea Economic Research Institute, May 27.

Kim, Dong-Heon and Eui-Kyoung Park. 1999. "Evaluating the Efficiency of Employment Maintenance Subsidies." Seoul: Korea Labor Institute.

KOILAF (Korea International Labor Foundation). 1998. *Labor Reform in Korea Toward the 21st Century.* Seoul.

_____. 1999. *Unemployment Measures: From Desperation to Reconstruction.* Seoul.

KLI (Korea Labor Institute). 1997. *1996 Overseas Labor Statistics.* Seoul.

_____. 1998. *Overseas Labor Statistics.* Seoul.

KLI and Korea Institute for Health and Social Affairs. 1998. Survey on Unemployment and Welfare Needs. Seoul: Ministry of Labor.

Lee, Won-Duck, and Kang-Shik Choi. 1998. *Labor Market and Industrial Relations in Korea.* Seoul: Korea Labor Institute.

Martin, John P. 1998. *What Works among Active Labour Market Policies: Evidence from OECD Countries' Experiences.* OECD Labour Market and Social Policy Occasional Paper 35. Paris: OECD.

MOL (Ministry of Labor). 1999. *Midterm Unemployment Policy.* Seoul.

NSO (National Statistical Office). Various issues. *Annual Report on the Economically Active Population Survey.* Seoul.

OECD. 1999. *OECD Economic Surveys: Korea, 1998–99.* Paris: OECD.

Park, Funkoo, and Joohee Lee. 1999. "The Social Impact of the Financial Crisis: Labor Market Outcomes and Policy Responses in Korea." Seoul: Korea Labor Institute. Unpublished Paper.

Park, Young-bum. 1999. "Social Safety Nets for the Unemployed: The Korean Case." Paper presented at the Institute for Social Sciences International Conference on Unemployment, Job Creation, and Employment Relations, October 29–30.

Phang, Hanam. 1999. *Characteristics of the Unemployed Who Received Unemployment Benefits in 1998.* Seoul: Korea Labor Institute.

Shin, D. 1999. *Unemployment Structure in Korea.* Seoul: Korea Labor Institute.

Uh, Soo-Bong. 1999. Employment: Structure, Trends and New Issues. In *Labor Relations in Korea,* edited by KOILAF. Seoul.

Yoo, Kil-Sang. 1999a. Employment Insurance and Social Safety Nets for the Unemployed. In *Labor Relations in Korea,* edited by KOILAF. Seoul.

_____. 1999b. *The Employment Insurance System in Korea.* Seoul.

4 Malaysia: Protecting Workers and Fostering Growth

Norma Mansor, Tan Eu Chye,
Ali Boehanoeddin, Fatimah Said,
Saad Mohd Said

From 1987 until the onset of the East Asian financial crisis in July 1997, the Malaysian economy had been one of the fastest-growing economies in Southeast Asia, with an average annual growth rate of 8.5 percent (table 4.1). The crisis trimmed Malaysia's growth rate to 7.7 percent in 1997 and in 1998 plunged the country into a severe recession, reducing the growth rate to –7.5 percent. Prior to the crisis, Malaysia's growth had been driven largely by private investment in productive capacities with increasingly sophisticated technology.[1] The country had also generally been enjoying a merchandise trade surplus.[2] The surplus has become even more significant in light of the growth in exports and the dramatic slowdown in imports amid the recessionary circumstances.

For almost 10 years the manufacturing sector rather than the agriculture sector was the mainstay of the economy (table 4.2). In 1987 the two sectors contributed around the same amount (22 percent) to Malaysia's GDP. But the manufacturing sector recorded average annual growth of 13.8 percent in 1987–97, while the agriculture sector averaged just 2.9 percent. In 1997 the agriculture sector accounted for only 11.9 percent of Malaysia's real GDP, but the manufacturing sector weighed in at 35.7 percent. The construction sector's real GDP contribution rose only marginally in 1987–97 (from 3.4 percent to 4.8 percent in 1997). The mining and quarrying sector appears to be playing an increasingly small role in the Malaysian economy, given the contraction in the sector's share in real

141

TABLE 4.1
Selected Macroeconomic Indicators

Year	Real GDP growth (%)	Inflation (%)	Unemployment rate (%)	Population (millions)	GNP per capita at current market prices (US$)
1985	−1.1	0.4	6.9	15.68	1,896
1986	1.2	0.6	8.3	16.11	1,595
1987	5.4	0.8	8.2	16.52	1,814
1988	8.9	2.5	7.2	16.94	1,869
1989	9.2	2.8	6.3	17.4	2,064
1990	9.7	3.1	5.1	17.8	2,311
1991	8.7	4.4	4.3	18.2	2,474
1992	7.8	4.7	3.7	18.6	2,882
1993	8.3	3.6	3.0	19.6	2,970
1994	9.3	3.7	2.9	20.1	3,515
1995	9.48	3.4	2.8	20.7	3,960
1996	8.6	3.5	2.6	21.2	4,463
1997	7.7	2.7	2.6	21.7	4,284
1998	−7.5	5.2	4.0	22.2	3,013

Source: Treasury, Economic Report, various issues.

GDP from 10.5 percent in 1987 to 6.7 percent in 1997. The share of the services sector has remained relatively stable at around 41 percent in 1987–97.

During the high-growth era of 1987–96, Malaysia experienced relative price stability. Inflation never exceeded 5 percent, largely because of prudent monetary policy and government intervention. The government imposed direct price controls (especially on consumer essentials), improved distribution and marketing channels, and curbed profiteering and other unethical business practices. Despite the threat of stagflation following the abrupt depreciation of the ringgit and the danger of imported inflation (owing to the economy's heavy dependence on imported intermediate and capital goods), the government succeeded in containing inflation at 5.2 percent in 1998.

Malaysia has been experiencing a population growth rate of 2 percent a year. The population rose from 16.52 million in 1987 to 22.2 million in 1998 (table 4.1). The government's relatively prudent macroeconomic management has resulted in a remarkable 66.1 percent rise in per capita GNP, which climbed steadily from US$1,814 in 1987 to US$4,284 in

TABLE 4.2
Industry Shares in GDP, 1986–98[a]
(RM million)

	1985	1986	1987	1988	1989	1990	1991	1992	1993	1994	1995	1996	1997	1998
Agriculture, livestock, forestry and fishing	11,854 (2.5)	12,348 (4.2)	13,216 (7.0)	13,933 (5.4)	14,768 (6.0)	14,827 (0.4)	14,828 (0.0)	15,531 (4.7)	16,205 (4.3)	16,047 (-1.0)	16,231 (1.1)	16,584 (2.2)	16,804 (1.3)	15,813 (-5.9)
Mining and quarrying	5,985 (-1.4)	6,368 (6.4)	6,409 (0.6)	6,803 (6.2)	7,383 (8.5)	7,757 (5.1)	7,944 (2.4)	8,075 (1.6)	8,039 (-0.4)	8,241 (2.5)	8,979 (9.0)	9,381 (4.5)	9,475 (1.0)	9,399 (-0.8)
Manufacturing	11,263 (-3.8)	12,111 (7.5)	13,734 (13.4)	16,151 (17.6)	18,444 (14.2)	21,340 (15.7)	24,307 (13.9)	26,859 (10.5)	30,324 (12.9)	34,842 (14.9)	39,790 (14.2)	44,684 (12.2)	50,270 (12.5)	47,354 (-5.8)
Construction	2,738 (-8.4)	2,354 (-14.0)	2,077 (-11.8)	2,133 (2.7)	2,380 (11.6)	2,832 (19.0)	3,240 (14.4)	3,619 (11.7)	4,023 (11.2)	4,589 (14.1)	5,385 (17.3)	6,150 (14.2)	6,732 (9.5)	5,439 (-19.2)
Electricity, gas, and water	948 (6.5)	1,027 (8.3)	1,109 (8.0)	1,211 (9.2)	1,344 (11.0)	1,526 (13.5)	1,697 (11.2)	1,931 (13.8)	2,176 (12.7)	2,474 (13.7)	2,797 (13.0)	3,134 (12.1)	3,543 (13.0)	3,791 (7.0)
Transport, storage, and communication	3,630 (4.8)	3,851 (6.1)	4,055 (5.3)	4,412 (8.8)	4,839 (9.7)	5,487 (13.4)	6,079 (10.8)	6,481 (6.6)	6,921 (6.8)	7,776 (12.4)	8,852 (13.8)	9,711 (9.7)	10,530 (8.4)	10,835 (2.9)
Wholesale and retail trade, hotels and restaurants	6,911 (-2.8)	6,147 (-11.1)	6,423 (4.5)	5,988 (8.8)	7,687 (10.0)	8,807 (14.6)	10,068 (14.3)	11,190 (11.1)	12,428 (11.1)	13,427 (8.0)	14,781 (10.1)	16,163 (9.4)	17,290 (7.0)	17,047 (-1.4)
Finance, insurance, real estate and business services	5,094 (4.1)	5,071 (-0.5)	5,482 (8.1)	6,088 (11.0)	6,771 (11.2)	7,759 (14.6)	8,733 (12.6)	9,644 (10.4)	10,650 (10.4)	11,713 (10.0)	12,938 (10.5)	14,825 (14.6)	16,240 (9.5)	16,911 (4.1)
Government services	6,957 (2.1)	7,253 (4.3)	7,543 (4.0)	7,819 (3.7)	8,185 (4.7)	8,579 (4.8)	8,964 (4.5)	9,201 (4.9)	10,073 (9.5)	11,022 (9.4)	11,454 (3.9)	11,931 (4.2)	12,654 (6.1)	12,958 (2.4)
Other services	1,301 (4.1)	1,353 (4.0)	1,400 (3.5)	1,454 (3.9)	1,522 (4.7)	1,678 (10.2)	1,831 (9.1)	1,983 (8.3)	2,146 (8.2)	2,298 (7.1)	2,478 (7.8)	2,687 (8.4)	2,880 (7.2)	2,923 (1.5)
Less: Imputed bank service charges	1,834 (15.0)	1,891 (3.1)	2,235 (18.2)	2,820 (26.2)	3,356 (19.0)	4,076 (21.5)	4,804 (17.9)	5,376 (11.9)	6,411 (19.3)	7,381 (15.1)	8,503 (15.2)	10,032 (18.0)	11,498 (14.6)	12,280 (6.8)
Add: Import duties	2,245 (-11.0)	1,759 (-21.6)	1,650 (-6.2)	2,131 (29.2)	2,442 (14.6)	2,947 (20.7)	3,458 (17.3)	3,728 (7.8)	4,043 (8.4)	4,927 (21.9)	5,090 (3.3)	5,402 (6.1)	5,765 (6.7)	3,747 (-35.0)
GDP at market prices	57,093	57,751 (1.2)	60,863 (5.4)	66,303 (8.9)	72,409 (9.2)	79,463 (9.7)	86,345 (8.7)	92,866 (7.8)	100,617 (8.3)	109,976 (9.13)	120,272 (9.4)	130,621 (8.6)	140,684 (7.7)	133,939 (-4.8)

a. In 1978 prices.

Note: Figures in parentheses are annual percentage changes.

Source: Treasury, *Economic Report*, various issues.

1997. But the steep depreciation of the ringgit following the de facto devaluation of the Thai baht has severely eroded Malaysians' living standards, scaling down per capita GNP to USUS$3,013 in 1998—a hefty 29.7 percent decline. In fact, the per capita income target of RM 14,788 set for the year 2000 has become impossible to meet. Instead, the per capita income (both in nominal and real terms) for 2000 is projected to be lower than in 1997.

Labor Market Trends

The manufacturing sector has become not only an increasingly important source of national income but also a prime generator of national employment. Manufacturing employment accounted for 27.1 percent of total national employment in 1998, up from 15.7 percent in 1987. The share of the agriculture sector in national employment fell considerably, dropping from 31.9 percent in 1987 to 16.5 percent in 1998. This decrease can be traced in part to the adoption of mechanized production processes and intensive farm management practices, and in part to the growing emphasis placed on developing other sectors. The share of the mining and quarrying sector has been relatively stable at around 0.005 percent. Both the construction sector and the services sector registered a moderate expansion in their shares. Construction saw its share of employment expand from 6 percent in 1987 to 8.8 percent in 1998, and employment in the services sector grew from 45.8 percent to 47.1 percent.

The national unemployment rate declined steadily, falling from 8.2 percent in 1987 to 2.6 percent in 1997, primarily because of the government's progrowth policies (table 4.1). In fact, Malaysia had already achieved full employment in 1993 with an unemployment rate of 3 percent, and the labor market tightened further in the years that followed.

Employment

The deflationary effect of the financial market turmoil led to a surge in the unemployment rate, which rose to 4.0 percent in 1998. Despite this increase, the crisis has had a limited effect on job opportunities in Malaysia. Workers have been retrenched as firms restructure their operations, but many of those retrenched have been the foreign workers Malaysian industries had come to depend on in the overheated precrisis economy. Despite the retrenchments, then, Malaysia continues to face labor shortages in certain sectors of the economy owing to a lack of intersectoral mobility and the strong preference among locals for jobs that are not perceived as menial. Since February 1998 the government has required employers to inform the Department of Labor at least one month in advance of any retrenchments, wage cuts, or temporary layoffs in order to monitor workers' welfare.

THE INFORMAL SECTOR. Malaysia has no unemployment insurance. Some of those who have lost their employment in the formal sector have ventured into the informal sector, becoming petty traders and street vendors or operating from their residences, performing odd jobs and engaging in other income-generating activities. Hawker stalls have proliferated in cities. While no studies have been made of the informal sector per se, it is safe to assume that in Malaysia, as in many developing countries, the sector serves as an important source of employment for the poor and unemployed, especially during shocks.

The absence of a social safety net makes informal ventures more compelling. In order to promote self-employment and self-reliance, in 1996 the government implemented a revolving fund of RM 300 million (the *Amanah Ikhtiar Malaysia*). This program to aid the poorest in setting up small businesses has disbursed a total of RM 289.8 million in interest-free loans to 54,856 participants, and its success is reflected in the 100 percent repayment rate. The number of participants has increased because of the economic downturn and is projected to reach 4,260 participants in 2000.

Another program designed to assist petty traders and informal sector workers is the *Yayasan Tekun Nasional*, which has disbursed loans totaling RM 8.7 million to 2,890 entrepreneurs. While these programs help some retrenched workers maintain an income, the informal sector cannot be expected to provide full insulation from shocks such as the Asian crisis. Businesses in the informal sector are also likely to suffer as the formal sector falters.

UNEMPLOYMENT. During the high-growth period before the crisis, Malaysia recorded an absolute decline in the number of job seekers, especially among workers in the 15–19 and 25–29 age groups. In what may be a reflection of Malaysia's success in providing greater access to tertiary education, those in the 20–24 age group constituted the bulk (44 percent) of total job seekers in 1997.

Women appear to be having more trouble finding jobs than men. While males constituted 63.2 percent of the total number of registered job seekers in 1987, they accounted for about 52.1 percent in 1997 (table 4.3). The number of female job seekers, however, rose from 36.8 percent in

TABLE 4.3
Registered Job Seekers by Sex
(end of period)

End of	Total job seekers	Males	Females
1985	80,681	49,279	31,402
1986	86,896	55,857	31,039
1987	78,553	49,642	28,911
		(63.2)	(36.8)
1988	78,200	49,478	28,722
1989	72,127	46,130	25,997
1990	54,387	33,915	20,472
1991	50,159	30,050	20,109
1992	42,344	25,287	17,057
1993	31,617	18,594	13,023
1994	26,445	15,095	11,350
1995	25,546	13,935	11,611
1996	21,747	11,863	9,884
		(54.5)	(45.4)
1997	23,762	12,386	11,376
		(52.1)	(47.8)
July	34,514	18,423	16,091
1998		(53.4)	(46.6)

Note: Figures in parentheses refer to percentage shares in the total number of job seekers.
Source: Treasury, *Economic Report,* various issues.

1987 to 47.8 percent in 1997. In part, this phenomenon is attributable to the increasing entry of females into the labor force as Malaysia modernizes (table 4.4). The overall labor force participation and male labor force participation rates are relatively stable, but the female participation rate increased from 44.9 percent in 1987 to 47.3 percent in 1997. This increase in women seeking work may also mean that women are feeling the consequences of the East Asian crisis slightly more than their male counterparts.

Full employment has also contributed to the rising incidence of job switching—workers who are already employed seeking alternate employment. The share of the employed registering as job seekers expanded from 9 percent in 1987 to 33.8 percent in 1997. The economic recession brought forth by the financial market turbulence has helped reduce the percentage of employed job seekers, however, and their number fell to 20.7 percent of total job seekers in 1998. Prior to the crisis, the labor market seemed to favor those with less education. The percentage of those

TABLE 4.4
Labor Force Participation Rates by Gender

Year	Labor force (millions)	Labor force participation rates		
		Total[a]	Male[b]	Female[c]
1985	6,039.1	65.8	87.4	44.3
1986	6,222.2	65.8	87.5	44.2
1987	6,408.9	65.9	86.9	44.9
1988	6,658.0	66.1	85.8	46.5
1989	6,850.0	66.3	85.8	46.9
1990	7,042.0	66.5	85.6	47.3
1991	7,204.0	66.6	85.7	47.5
1992	7,370.0	66.7	85.7	47.6
1993	7,627.0	66.8	87.0	46.1
1994	7,834.0	66.8	87.1	46.5
1995	8,256.8	66.9	86.8	47.1
1996	8,641.4	66.7	86.6	47.2
1997	9,038.2	66.6	86.9	47.3
1998	9,006.5	64.3	86.7	46.8

a. Total number of people economically active as a percentage of total working age population (15–64 years).

b. Total number of males economically active as a percentage of total number of males in the working age population.

c. Total number of females economically active as a percentage of total number of females in the working age population.

Source: Treasury, Economic Report, various issues.

with little education registered as job seekers contracted from 27.2 percent in 1987 to 14.1 percent in 1997. The percentage of job seekers with some higher education increased, while their share in the labor force fell.

Labor Productivity and Wages

The economic slowdown of 1985–86 had already forced establishments to make productivity improvements as part of the adjustment process. Rising unemployment and retrenchments exerted pressure on employees to boost productivity in order to retain their jobs. For the economy as a whole, labor productivity, or value added per worker, increased from RM 10,160 in 1985 to RM 10,867 in 1988, an increase of 2.2 percent annually. The manufacturing sector, which underwent severe adjustments (including retrenchments), recorded an increase of 6.5 percent per year in value added per worker. In the agriculture sector labor productivity increased by 2.5 percent annually during 1985–88. The economic conditions that prevailed during 1986–88 did not warrant the rapid wage increases of the first half of the 1980s, and wages were moderated because of the need for economic adjustment. In the manufacturing sector, average nominal earnings of workers increased by 2.2 percent per year, while the increase in real earnings was close to 1 percent. Overall, average wage increases in collective agreements negotiated in 1986 was 4 percent for 3 years. For the manufacturing sector, the rate was 4.3 percent. In 1987 the average rate dropped to 3.2 percent and 2.5 percent, respectively.

Labor productivity continued to increase in the years before the financial crisis. Despite the strong demand for labor in 1991–95, labor productivity rose across all sectors. For the economy as a whole, labor productivity measured as GDP per worker in constant 1978 prices increased by 5.1 percent a year, rising from RM 11,870 in 1990 to an estimated RM 15,200 in 1995. (This rate of growth exceeded the overall labor productivity growth of 3.3 percent during 1986–90.) Output per worker in the manufacturing sector, which stood at RM 19,410 in 1995, was higher than for the economy as a whole. Overall economic growth averaged 3.9 percent annually between 1990 and 1995. Labor productivity growth in the agriculture and services sectors was 6.1 percent and 5.9 percent, respectively, during this period. At 5.9 percent a year, growth in GDP per worker in the services sector was particularly impressive. A growth rate of 1.8 percent in 1986–90 indicates increased efficiency in the use of labor resources and the widespread use of information technology.

In 1991–95, however, the tight labor market resulted in upward pressure on wages. Average nominal manufacturing wages rose by about 27 percent between 1990 and 1994, or 6.2 percent annually. With productivity growth lagging behind wage growth in the sector, pressure on unit labor costs increased. This phenomenon was particularly marked in 1990–92, when high wage growth unaccompanied by productivity growth resulted in rising unit labor costs. Productivity growth in the manufacturing sector began rising at the end of 1992, however, climbing 4.6 percent and 6.8 percent in 1993 and 1994, respectively. Consequently, unit labor costs in the manufacturing sector began declining in the mid-1990s.

The tight labor market situation since 1995 has exerted pressure on wages, with wage increases outstripping productivity growth. Nominal wage rates grew by 5.7 percent in 1996 and 6.1 percent in 1997 but increased at just 4 percent in 1998. However, labor productivity grew at a slower rate during those years, rising to only 3.5 percent in 1996 before dipping slightly to 3 percent in 1997. Moreover, productivity growth reg-istered a negative 3.8 percent owing to the underutilization of existing capacity—the result of the 1998 economic slowdown. In the manufactur-ing sector, average nominal wages increased by 10 percent a year during 1996–97, but productivity rose by a mere 1 percent. The result has been pressure on unit labor costs, particularly in 1996 and 1997, when they rose by 4.8 percent and 2 percent before declining by 4.5 percent during the 1998 economic slowdown.

Although the economy appears to have recovered, many firms are still paying wages that are lower than they were before the crisis. However, this situation can be viewed as a technical correction, as the country had sus-tained a loss of competitiveness in the precrisis years, with wage growth outstripping productivity growth. Bank restructuring and mergers, which are gathering momentum in the country, and the gloomy outlook for the electronics industry argue for at least a cap on further wage increases.

Industrial Relations

The number of trade unions increased from 479 in 1992 to 516 in 1996 (table 4.5). The government favors in-house rather than national unions. Many of the unions (316 out of 516 in 1996) are for workers in the man-ufacturing and services sectors. The number of trade unions increased in four sectors—agriculture, forestry, and fishing; manufacturing; electricity, gas, and water; and commerce—but consolidation and rationalization in other sectors prevented the unions from expanding. Inclusive of employ-ers' trade unions, the number of trade union memberships increased steadily from 680,647 in 1992 to 728,246 in 1996 (table 4.5). Private-sector employees accounted for slightly more than half the memberships (table 4.6). These developments suggest that the government allows work-ers to organize.

Although recently the Malaysian Trade Union Congress has pushed for a minimum wage law, no such law has been enacted. Collective agree-ments appear to be an significant means of determining wages. The num-ber of collective agreements concluded increased from 334 in 1992 to 398 in 1996 (table 4.7). In 1996 over half of the agreements (210 out of 398) were in the manufacturing sector. The tendency to link wages to workers' productivity is growing and may help to contain inflation and enhance the country's international competitiveness. In 1994 about 60 percent of the collective agreements in force contained productivity- or performance-related incentives.

TABLE 4.5
Trade Unions and Membership, by Sector, 1992–96[a]

Sector	1992		1993		1994		1995		1996	
	Number	Membership	Number	Membership	Number	Membership	Number	Membership	Number	Membership
Agriculture, forestry and fishing	35	84,415 (12.4)	37	82,742 (11.9)	36	83,943 (12.0)	39	86,421 (12.2)	43	91,983 (12.6)
Mining	5	3,110 (0.5)	5	2,921 (0.4)	5	2,186 (0.3)	4	1,531 (0.2)	3	1,491 (0.2)
Manufacturing	102	149,569 (22.0)	106	147,487 (21.3)	117	147,359 (21.1)	119	141,021 (20.0)	119	144,814 (16.9)
Construction	7	3,402 (0.5)	7	4,588 (0.7)	6	4,661 (0.7)	6	2,849 (0.4)	6	4,032 (0.6)
Electricity	26	33,585 (4.9)	26	36,625 (4.7)	24	32,725 (4.7)	27	51,436 (7.3)	30	54,843 (7.5)
Commerce	30	465,01 (6.8)	32	53,035 (7.7)	31	54,574 (7.8)	45	102,803 (14.6)	45	100,480 (13.8)
Transport and communication	73	60,123 (8.8)	78	55,413 (8.0)	78	55,908 (8.0)	75	46,018 (6.5)	73	42,963 (5.9)
Services	201	299,302 (44.0)	205	314,770 (45.4)	204	318,017 (45.5)	189	274,174 (38.8)	197	287,640 (39.5)
Total	479	680,007 (100.0)	496	693,581 (100.0)	501	699,373 (100.0)	504	706,253 (100.0)	516	728,246 (100.0)

a. Does not include Employers' Trade Union and Federation of Trade Unions.
Note: Figures in parentheses are percentages of total numbers.
Source: Department of Trade Union Affairs, Ministry of Human Resources.

TABLE 4.6
Trade Unions by Membership, 1992–96

Category	1992		1993		1994		1995		1996	
	Number	Membership	Number	Membership	Number	Membership	Number	Membership	Number	Membership
Employees' trade unions										
Private-sector employees	258	373,288 (54.8)	276	384,867 (55.4)	281	384,867 (55.0)	281	396,663 (56.1)	292	407,303 (55.9)
Government employees	131	215,304 (31.5)	132	219,579 (31.6)	133	225,897 (32.3)	135	226,823 (32.1)	136	241,411 (33.1)
Statutory body and local authority employees	90	91,415 (13.4)	88	89,402 (12.9)	87	88,609 (12.7)	88	82,767 (11.7)	88	79,532 (10.9)
Employers' trade unions	18	640 (0.1)	16	616 (0.1)	16	616 (0.1)	13	572 (0.1)	13	528 (0.1)
Total	497	680,647 (100.0)	512	694,197 (100.0)	517	699,989 (100.0)	517	706,253 (100.0)	529	728,246 (100.0)

Note: Figures in parentheses are percentages of total numbers.
Source: Department of Trade Union Affairs, Ministry of Human Resources.

TABLE 4.7
Collective Agreements, 1992–96

Sector	1992			1993		
	No of C/A	Workers involved	Wage increase (%)	No of C/A	Workers involved	Wage increase (%)
Agriculture and estates	12	6,515	8	15	27,916	5
Mining and quarrying	4	1,784	7	3	2,439	5
Manufacturing	191	51,042	11	199	54,940	11
Construction	—	—	—	—	—	—
Electricity, gas, and water	—	—	—	—	—	—
Commerce	46	3,404	8	44	6,727	10
Transportation, storage and communication	40	14,277	8	31	3,633	8
Service	34	32,177	10	39	10,001	9
Others	7	614	6	1	2	5
Total	334	109,813		332	105,658	

— data not available.
Note: C/A: Collective agreement.
Source: Industrial Relations Department, Ministry of Human Resources.

Job Creation and Maintenance and Income-support Activities

Rapid economic growth during the 1990s led to an expansion of employment opportunities in Malaysia. Most of the new jobs were in the manufacturing, construction, and services sectors, highlighting the importance of these areas (table 4.8). Private investment continues to be the primary source of new jobs, but the government has supported job creation directly (through public work and privatization programs) and indirectly (through loan and grant programs). While it is still too early to assess the full effects of these initiatives, they have contributed to the net gain in job opportunities and have aided unemployed workers seeking to support themselves in the informal sector.

Private Direct Investment

Private direct investment (including foreign direct investment), particularly in manufacturing, was the primary source of employment creation in

	1994			1995			1996	
No of C/A	Workers involved	Wage increase (%)	No of C/A	Workers involved	Wage increase (%)	No of C/A	Workers involved	Wage increase (%)
15	1,481	10	14	91,863	15	32	12,990	15
—	—	—	—	—	—	6	1,342	9
196	53,468	9	216	58,656	28	210	47,674	11
—	162	—	1	1,237	10	—	—	—
—	20,452	—	—	—	—	9	29,713	5
53	10,080	11	95	15,116	12	42	4,866	13
31	3,093	15	35	32,399	12	55	9,918	10
46	214,77	9	38	8,458	11	38	6,364	9
6	25,51	9	5	232	7	6	466	9
348	112,764		404	207,961		398	113,333	

1996–98. It is expected to be the primary source of jobs in 1999–2000 as well, creating a total of 129,900 jobs, or 39 percent, of all new jobs.

The financial crisis has not seriously affected private investment in Malaysia. The latest figures on direct investment projects prove that Malaysia continues to attract both local and foreign capital. In the first quarter of 1999 (January–March), Malaysia received 160 applications to set up manufacturing projects worth RM 2.67 billion. Of these, 78 were for new projects and 82 for expanding and diversifying existing investments. A total of 145 manufacturing projects were approved, with total capital investments totaling RM 1.81 billion. Of this amount, RM 1.32 billion was foreign direct investment. Of the 145 approved projects, 75 were new and 70 expansion and diversification. Clearly investors recognize that Malaysia is an attractive and viable manufacturing and export base.

Direct Job Creation

Since 1996, the government has sought to increase employment opportunities through direct job creation. To this end it has funded public works projects and undertaken privatization projects with the private sector.[3] The major public work programs include infrastructure projects, agricul-

TABLE 4.8

Net Job Creation by Sector, 1996–00

Sector	Average annual growth rate (percent)		Net job creation (thousands)	
	1996–98	1999–00	1996–98	1999–00
Agriculture, forestry, livestock and fishing	–2.0	–0.3	–90.6	–7.9
Mining and quarrying	1.1	0.5	1.2	0.4
Manufacturing	3.8	2.8	243.9	129.9
Construction	0.7	2.1	15.6	30.3
Electricity, gas, and water	5.7	3.1	11.8	4.9
Transport, storage, and transportation	3.2	2.2	39.2	19.8
Wholesale and retail trade, hotels, and restaurants	3.1	1.8	124.2	53.4
Finance, insurance, real estate, and business services	3.6	3.9	41.9	32.7
Government services	0.2	0.2	5.5	4.0
Other services	5.7	4.1	121.1	65.4
Total	2.1	1.9	513.8	332.9

Source: Government of Malaysia, Midterm Review of Seventh Malaysia Plan, 1996–2000.

tural development projects, and rural development projects. Public works projects had a generally positive impact on job creation in 1996–98 (table 4.8).[4] The exceptions were in the agriculture, forestry, livestock and fishing sector, which lost jobs during the period. Privatization occurred under the government's privatization program from 1996–98. Both the public sector and privatization programs were directed toward expanding capacity to support the private sector and meet the needs of Malaysia's modernizing economy.

The government's allocation of development resources shows the extent of the public sector projects. In the Seventh Malaysia Plan for 1996–00, economic and social programs accounted for the major part of development expenditure. Of RM 89.5 billion in total expenditure, almost 80 percent is allocated to economic and social programs. Some RM 43 billion, or 48.2 percent, is allocated to economic sectors and RM 27.6 billion, or 30.9 percent, to social sectors. In the economic sector, the largest portion (22.1 percent) is reserved for transportation and communication, with another 9.6 percent going to commerce and industry, 9.3 percent to agriculture and rural development, and 4.3 percent to water resources. The breakdown of social sector spending is 17.8 percent for education and training, 3.9 percent for housing, 3.8 percent for health and population, and 2.0 percent for local authorities and welfare services.

INFRASTRUCTURE PROJECTS. In its quest to become an industrial economy by the year 2020, between 1996 and 1998 Malaysia devoted a large share of its development expenditure to the transportation and communication subsectors (around RM 13.5 billion, or 28 percent). Most of the funds were used to develop railroads, ports, highways, and the new government administrative center at Putrajaya, as well as to support sewerage, waste disposal management, and water supply projects. Among the large infrastructure projects completed in 1996–98 were the North-South Highway, the West Port in Selangor, the Light Rail Transit (LRT) in Klang Valley, and the telecommunication and television satellite.

During the period of economic slowdown, the government reviewed the expenditures of both economic and social programs. As a result, it redirected policy to give more weight to helping those most severely affected by the crisis, particularly low-income groups and the poor. Specific steps to redirect policy to meet this goal include:

- *Continuing to develop infrastructure projects.* For the remainder of the Seventh Malaysia Plan, the government will continue to develop infrastructure projects essential to an industrial economy. The government has provided RM 5.243 billion for developing infrastructure and public utilities and will give priority to projects that are regarded as catalysts for economic growth, including ongoing projects and those nearing completion.
- *Reducing operating and maintenance cost through the privatization.* Since 1993, a total of 434 projects have been completed under the Privatization Program. From 1996 to 1998 alone, the total costs of 68 projects amounted to RM 667 trillion. The program is said to be relieving the government's financial and administrative burden and improving the efficiency and productivity of the economy. The program is believed to be facilitating economic growth while helping to meet planned targets in pursuing growth and equity, including enhancing the participation of Malaysia's indigenous people (*Bumiputra*) in the corporate sector.

During the crisis, the privatization program has continued to play an important role in facilitating economic recovery and growth. To ensure the effectiveness of the programs, the government is taking steps to streamline procedures, provide effective coordination and monitoring, and strengthen the regulatory aspects. Priority is given to those projects with the greatest multiplier effect.

• *Providing funding for infrastructure projects.* To help finance infrastructure projects and projects involving large public facilities, the government has established the Infrastructure Development Fund with an initial allocation of RM 5 billion. The fund aids companies undertaking infrastructure projects that require large capital outlays, particularly the strategically important privatized road projects. The government provides financing in the form of soft loans through the newly restructured Development and Infrastructure Bank Malaysia Berhad. The fund not only helps the companies undertaking such projects but also indirectly creates and maintains employment.

AGRICULTURAL DEVELOPMENT. The government's agriculture development projects are designed to improve productivity through commercialization and private-sector participation. The government has two approaches to furthering its goals: the In-Situ Development Program and the New Land Development Program.

The *In-situ Development Program* focuses on integrated agricultural development, drainage, irrigation, replanting, and land consolidation for smallholders. In 1996–98 it developed a total of 156,000 hectares. The program helps smallholders group themselves into larger production units, creating economies of scale by increasing productivity and alleviating labor shortages. The program is projected to develop another 120,000 hectares of land in 1999–2000 and will include rehabilitation programs.

The *New Land Development Program* developed a total of 65,000 hectares of new land for agricultural purposes in 1996–98. In line with the policy of limiting the government's role in this area, the private sector developed another 50,000 hectares. The program will develop a projected 72,000 additional hectares in 1999–2000. The private sector will be responsible for 55.5 percent of this figure.

RURAL DEVELOPMENT. The government's rural development policy emphasizes improvements in the living standards of the rural sector. The new rural development philosophy places equal emphasis on human and physical development. The government has introduced several programs, including the Rural Vision Movement, One Village One Product, Home Rehabilitation, Uplifting the Village Economy, and Entrepreneurial Development, among others.

In 1996–98, the government undertook a total of 3,000 rural water supply projects, 270 road projects, 10,000 projects under the Home Rehabilitation Program, and 6,000 projects under the Uplifting the Village Economy Program. In 1999–2000, 1,800 villages will be developed under the Rural Vision Movement and 1,400 under the Community Enhancement Program. In addition, the government will increase its actions to promote entrepreneurship, develop infrastructure, promote organized farming activities, implement the One Village One Product program, establish rural industries, and foster agro- and ecotourism ventures. These measures are expected to generate employment as well as to expand development in rural areas.

Indirect Job Creation

During the economic slowdown that has followed the financial crisis, the government has actively supported workers seeking to become entrepreneurs. It offers a variety of schemes providing loans and grants for both individuals and small to medium-scale industries (SMIs). Funds for SMIs are intended to promote new productive capacity in targeted sectors.

MEASURES FOR THE SELF-EMPLOYED. In an effort both to ensure that the self-employed are able to continue their activities during the crisis and to create new self-employment opportunities, the government has allocated RM 200 million for petty traders and another RM 214 million for vendor development programs. It has also introduced a venture capital financing scheme and a "graduate entrepreneurs" scheme aimed at developing entrepreneurs. In particular, the programs provide support for self-employment in the distributive trades, including petty trading (vegetable cultivation and livestock rearing, for instance), hawking, farming, and running small businesses. Allocations from the development fund allocation for such activities during the Seventh Malaysia Plan increased from RM 249.4 million to RM 638.7 million (table 4.9).

Other financial schemes available to entrepreneurs are the Islamic Financing Scheme, the Incubator Financing Scheme, and the General Financing Scheme (run by the Bank Pembangunan Malaysia). Funds are also available through Tabung Amanah Ikhtiar Malaysia, the Small-Scale Entrepreneur Fund, and the Economic Business Group Fund (which includes assistance for women entrepreneurs). The funds are expected to help around 12,000 petty traders and small businessmen set up or expand their businesses. Institutions such as the Board of People's Trustees (MARA), the State Economic Development Corporation, Perbadanan Usahawan Na-

TABLE 4.9
Funds Allocated to Distributive Trade and Supporting Services,
1996–2000
(millions of RM)

Program	Seventh Malaysia Plan allocation		Estimated expenditure 1996–98	Balance 1999–2000
	Original	Revised		
Fund for petty trades	—	200.0	—	200.0
Upgrading and modernization of trade services	28.8	30.8	10.1	20.7
Business premises	212.7	400.0	130.1	269.9
Trading and constancy services	7.9	7.9	7.9	5.8
Total	7.9	638.7	142.3	496.4

— not available.
Source: Government of Malaysia, Midterm Review of Seventh Malaysia Plan, 1996–2000.

sional Berhad and Perbadanan Nasional Berhad (PNS), and the Urban Development Authority have similar programs.

During the economic slowdown, the government further assists franchisers and franchisees with the Franchise Financing Scheme and the Small-Scale Entrepreneur Financing Fund.[5] The Franchise Development Assistance Scheme assists entrepreneurs in starting a business and developing a product.

Measures for Small and Medium-Scale Industries

In Malaysia firms with paid-up capital amounting to RM 500,000–1.5 million are considered SMIs. SMIs make up a significant portion of the manufacturing sector. At present, however, their output of intermediate goods is limited, and they operate at a low level of technology. Further, the industrial linkages between SMIs and the manufacturing sector are inadequate.

To address these problems, the government implemented eight development programs in 1996–98 through the Small and Medium-scale Industries Development Corporation. These programs include initiatives aimed at creating industrial linkages, developing and acquiring technology, developing enterprises and markets, and providing financial support and skills training. More than 400 SMIs received grants totaling RM 25.1 million for industrial linkage and technology-related programs. Another 527 enterprises received a total of RM 5.0 million for marketing development programs.

SMIs suffered a setback during the crisis because of insufficient demand, increases in production costs, and a credit squeeze. On January 2, 1998, the government established the RM 1.5 billion SMI Fund to promote new productive capacity and improve the utilization of existing capacity in manufacturing, agriculture-based, and supporting services industries. In 1998 participating financial institutions approved disbursements of RM 882.23 million for 873 applicants. The fund will run until December 2005 and will provide between RM 50,000 and RM 5 million per customer. All Malaysian-owned SMIs in the target sectors are eligible to apply to the fund.

In response to the crisis, on November 23, 1998, the government established the Rehabilitation Fund for Small and Medium-scale Industries. The fund provides financial assistance during the period of crisis to viable SMIs with nonperforming loans and temporary cash flow problems. The fund has a budget of RM 750 million and is available to all SMIs in the manufacturing, agriculture-based, and services industries. While the SMI Fund and the Rehabilitation Fund are meant to be used by existing businesses, prospective entrepreneurs can use the New Entrepreneur Fund to start a new business. This fund has been in existence since 1989 and has been used by over 2,000 entrepreneurs.

Employment Maintenance

Neither work sharing nor wage support is practiced in Malaysia, since the layoff rate for skilled workers is not alarming. Despite the absence of a wage support system (either before or after the crisis), workers in certain essential professions in both the public and private sectors enjoy some kind of wage support. Generally these workers receive additional allowances on top of their monthly pay as an incentive to stay in their professions. For example, public-sector employees in certain professions, such as medicine, receive a Critical Service Allowance as well as their regular monthly salary.

The Malaysian government has changed its policy on retrenchment because of the economic crisis. In August 1998 the government introduced measures that encourage companies to maintain their workers. These measures include support for retraining workers; recommendations for pay cuts, temporary layoffs, and voluntary separation schemes; and flexible working hours and part-time employment.

To encourage companies to send their workers for training during the crisis, the government has agreed to reimburse registered employers for the full costs of training (up from the previous reimbursement rate of 75–80 percent). At the end of July 1999, the government had approved 181,032 training centers at a total cost of RM 74.4 million. During the same period, a total of 806 participants received approval to follow courses at certificate and diploma levels to upgrade their existing skills and knowledge.

The government also encourages employers to maintain their workers by reducing salaries. Since August 1998 the Ministry of Entrepreneurship Development has been collecting the data on companies that have followed this recommendation. Employers appear to prefer voluntary separation to temporary layoffs. Between August and December 1998 only 4.4 percent of employers opted for temporary layoffs. Another 28.4 percent opted for voluntary separation, with the remaining 67.2 percent choosing pay cuts. Most of the firms opting for voluntary separation were in the manufacturing sector, particularly in areas with an oversupply of women workers.

On August 1, 1998, the government introduced flexible working hours and formalized part-time work by amending the Employment Act of 1955. The amendment is aimed at reducing the country's dependence on foreign workers by encouraging more women to participate in the labor force. The government is also contemplating the introduction of "career breaks" that would allow women to leave and reenter the workforce without losing their statutory benefits.

Table 4.10 shows the actions employers took in 1998–99 when faced with the need to cut labor costs. The most popular course of action among

TABLE 4.10

Employer Actions during Recession, Peninsular Malaysia, 1998–99

(January–June)

Type of action taken	Number of employers		Number of employees	
	1998	1999	1998	1999
Retrenchment	4,485	1,342	75,432	20,292
Salary reduction	795	369	22,516	13,246
Layoffs	52	26	6,342	5,277
Voluntary separation scheme	336	255	5,982	8,152
Total	5,668	1,992	110,272	46,967

Source: Labor Department, Ministry of Human Resources.

the 4,485 employers was retrenchment, followed by salary reductions and layoffs. Retrenchments seemed to slow down somewhat in the first half of 1999, with 1,342 employers retrenching a total of 20,292 workers.

In 1998 some 41,877, or 55.5 percent, of the retrenched workers were male. Of this group 9,415, or 22.6 percent, were professionals and technical workers. But almost half of the female workers retrenched in 1998 were skilled and semi-skilled production workers. The same pattern appeared in 1999.

The only data available on retrenchment and related activities are compiled from the mandatory reports filed by employers. These reports cover only manual workers (regardless of wage level) and other workers with monthly wages of not more than RM 1,500 (the definition of employee given in the First Schedule of the Employment Act of 1955). Employers retrenching other categories of workers are not compelled to report to the Labor Department.

Income-support Activities

As has been noted, unemployed Malaysian workers do not receive any form of income or in-kind support. However, employed workers are protected against old age and incapacitation and their survivors cared for in case of death (from any cause) through a compulsory saving scheme, the Employees Provident Fund (EPF). The EPF is financed directly by monthly contributions from both employers and employees (12 and 11 percent, respectively, of the worker's monthly wage).

Employees can withdraw their outstanding deposits with the fund either in full or in part, depending on the circumstances. Employees who are incapacitated, intend to emigrate, or have reached the age of 55 can withdraw the full amount, as can relatives of an employee who dies. Employees may also withdraw part of their deposit when they reach 50 and when they need money to build or purchase a house, repay a housing loan, invest in funds managed by approved fund management institutions, or pay for medical treatment for specified illnesses.

Employees are also protected against the contingencies of industrial accidents, occupational diseases, disability, and death from any cause through two social security schemes, the Invalidity Pension Scheme and the Employment Injury Insurance Scheme. These schemes apply to all private-sector employees earning less than RM 2,000 per month. The Workmen's Compensation Act of 1952 requires private-sector employers to insure legally employed foreign employees against the same contingencies.

In-kind Support

Through collective agreements, some employees enjoy benefits such as private health insurance, car and housing loans, crèches, prayer rooms, and all kinds of leave, including leave for pilgrimages, prolonged illnesses, and drug rehabilitation and leave in consideration of long service. With the exception of private health insurance, public-sector employees enjoy the same benefits.

Severance Pay

Severance pay in Malaysia is known as *termination benefits* and is regulated under the Employment Act of 1955. Employers are required to pay this benefit to any employee who has been employed under a continuous contract for a period of not less than twelve months. The amount of the termination benefit the departing employee receives varies from 10 to 20 days of wages for each year of service. During the crisis termination benefits have been extended to cover employees who leave their jobs under a voluntary separation scheme.

Labor Market Services

For more than two decades Malaysia has had employment services that match workers' qualifications with employers' specific requirements. The job-matching process is intended to reduce the length of time it takes workers to find jobs, contributing to the efficient functioning of the labor market while making the best use of available human capital. The Department of Manpower of the Ministry of Human Resources is responsible for employment services, including registration and placement, counseling, occupational guidance, and technical training for workers. The department also registers and regulates private employment agencies and collects and disseminates employment information. It maintains regional and state Manpower Offices throughout the country and has its own website where vacancies are posted.

Public Employment Services

The Department of Manpower's Public Employment Services Section provides free employment assistance to domestic job seekers and employers. It is assisted by four units: the Operational Unit, the Private Employment Agencies Licensing Unit, the Enforcement Unit, and the Occupational Guidance Unit. The section not only registers and places job seekers but also provides employers with lists of qualified candidates (usually within two working days of a request).

Private Employment Agencies

Private employment agencies cater to both domestic and foreign job seekers. These agencies complement the registration and placement activities of the Public Employment Service. Based on the services they provide, private employment agencies in Malaysia can be grouped into three categories:

- *Regular private employment agencies*, which cater to white-collar and blue-collar workers. They provide placement services for local and overseas job seekers and charge a registration fee;
- *Consultant management agencies*, which cater to top managerial and professional job seekers; and
- *Labor contracting agencies*, which cater to certain industries, usually domestic and construction work.

As of the end of 1998, a total of 898 licenses had been issued under the Private Employment Agencies Act. Some 324 of the registered agencies were active, and 574 were considered inactive. Table 4.11 shows the registration and placement activities of the private employment agencies based on the monthly reports received by the Manpower Department.

Prior to 1998 the government required private employment agencies to submit reports on registration on a quarterly basis and reports on placement on a monthly basis. But since the crisis these agencies have been required to submit monthly reports for both activities. Demand for the services of private agencies has increased markedly and was particularly high in 1998, when 29,135 job seekers registered—an increase of more than 100 percent over the previous year. But in the first half of 1999, the number of job seekers using the agencies declined to 6,773 (compared with 19,398 in the first half of 1998). This decrease in demand could reflect either of two scenarios. First, some job seekers may have become discouraged and withdrawn from the labor force as the probability of finding a job fell and the expected value of wages declined to less than the reservation wage. Married women and teenagers, in particular, may have given up the job search altogether in favor of nonmarket activities such as looking after children, pursuing further studies, or just consuming leisure. Second, the decline reflects Malaysia's nascent economic recovery, which was evident in a positive economic growth rate of 4.1 percent for the second quarter of 1999.

TABLE 4.11

Malaysia: Registration and Placement by Private Employment Agencies, 1997–99

(January–June)

	Registration			Placement		
	1997	*1998*	*1999*	*1997*	*1998*	*1999*
January		911	1,319	71	790	493
February		0	816	61	847	206
March	1,047	9,595	2,382	131	880	372
April		412	1,552	84	730	268
May		345	196	90	809	53
June	1,016	8,135	508	87	769	578
July		142		148	911	
August		1,589		201	627	
September	2,356	6,493		295	596	
October		1513		565	610	
November		—		834	—	
December	9,587	—		915	—	
Total	14,006	29,135	6,773	3,482	7,569	1,970

— not available.

Source: Ministry of Human Resources, Manpower Department.

The placement rate of private employment agencies does not appear to be high. Of 29,135 job seekers in 1998, a total of only 7,569 job seekers, or 26 percent, were reported as successfully placed. The actual performance of private employment agencies could be evaluated by calculating the overall penetration rate. But the lack of both data on vacancies and a detailed breakdown of registrants, vacancies, and placement makes such an assessment impossible.

Services for Retrenched Workers

The government provides a number of services for retrenched workers, including registration and placement through the Public Employment Service. It also provides a job link program, occupational guidance, and job counseling.

REGISTRATION AND PLACEMENT. Since the government introduced registration and placement programs for retrenched workers in January 1998, a total of 17,622 workers, or 29 percent of all those retrenched, have registered with the Public Employment Service. Of these, 12,062, or 68.4 percent, were successfully placed in 1998 (table 4.12). The other 53,333 retrenched workers—71 percent—cannot be traced. Presumably they have been absorbed by other firms or have obtained jobs through other channels, such as advertising or personal contacts. About 16 percent of the retrenched workers were high-level professional workers, and 15,042, or 19.9 percent, were skilled production workers. These groups are more likely than others to find new positions without having to turn to the Public Employment Service for help.

The performance of the Public Employment Service in registering and placing retrenched workers improved significantly in the first half of 1999. The percentage of untraceable workers has fallen from 83 percent in the first half of 1998 to 58 percent. In the same period, the service successfully placed 83 percent of the registered retrenched workers, up from 71 percent in 1998. Publicity campaigns may be partly responsible for this improvement.

JOB LINK PROGRAM. When the Public Employment Service receives notification of an impending retrenchment, it informs registered employers searching for workers about the potential supply of labor. This program has had some success. For example, in July 1998 some 713 of the 4,128 workers retrenched by a company in Penang were rehired immediately. A total of 2,203 of those workers have been reemployed by other companies, while the rest have turned to self-employment or withdrawn from the labor market.

OCCUPATIONAL GUIDANCE AND JOB COUNSELING. Since the crisis the Public Employment Service has continued to play its traditional role in providing occupational guidance and job counseling services for job seekers and retrenched workers. However, its emphasis has shifted. As well as providing job seekers with information about wages, it offers information about the current labor market situation. Job seekers are briefed on employers' requirements for new hires, industries producing the most new jobs, and available training.

To improve the capabilities of those providing guidance and counseling, the Manpower Department organized a number of training seminars and courses for them. In 1998 a total of 830 officials and staff from the Manpower Department were trained overseas and locally.

As of December 1998, the Manpower Department had conducted a total of 103 occupational guidance talks throughout the country with 55,318 participants and had held 9 job fairs. The activities took place at headquarters and at sites throughout Malaysia.

TABLE 4.12
Registration and Placement of Local Retrenched Workers, 1998–99
(January–June)

Month	1998					1999				
	Total	Alternative employment	Untraced	Registrants	Placement	Total	Alternative employment	Untraced	Registrants	Placement
January	1,654		1,653	1		2,613	104	1,820	689	376
February	6,590	40	6,498	52	29	4,565	277	2,387	1,901	1,679
March	9,945	2	9,665	278	247	2,496	355	889	1,252	1,174
April	6,028	2	5,959	67	17	1,092	136	639	317	207
May	5,591	20	5,504	67	18	2,135	91	1,396	648	500
June	5,391	355	4,071	965	720	1,022	28	777	217	213
July	10,488	2,307	4,504	3,677	2,608	1,047	21	797	229	207
August	6,427	112	5,006	1,309	830					
September	6,099	246	1,040	4,813	3,749					
October	6,434	541	2,397	3,496	2,064					
November	5,083	120	3,372	1,591	678					
December	5,169	199	3,664	1,306	1,102					
Total	74,899	3,944	53,333	17,622	12,062	14,970	1,012	8,705	5,253	4,356

Source: Manpower Department, Annual Report, 1998.

Labor Market Information

In Malaysia a number of agencies are responsible for collecting and disseminating labor market information and formulating labor market policies. These agencies include the Ministry of Human Resources, the Department of Statistics, the Ministry of Education, the Public Service Department, the Economic Planning Unit, and the Malaysian Administrative Modernization Manpower Planning Unit.

The economic recession following the financial crisis has created additional demand for new sources of data that are essential to implementing successful remedial policies. The labor market information system during the recession must be related to the policy framework for employment creation for target groups such as the unemployed, the poor, and retrenched workers. Successful planning, implementation, and monitoring depend on having detailed information on the characteristics of labor and the structure of labor markets. To meet this requirement, the Labor Department of the Ministry of Human Resources is producing a statistical report on retrenchment to facilitate policy formulation during periods of economic recession.

The National Recovery Plan provides the most comprehensive labor market information and has been one of the main public policy responses to the economic downturn. It is the result of collaboration and coordination between those who produce labor market information and those who use it. The government put together the plan with organizations representing universities, employers, workers, and consumers. Among other things, the plan contains information on the causes and effects of the economic crisis, the policy response and its objectives, and actions that will be taken.

Labor Market Regulation

Employers in Malaysia are restricted in the actions they can take against employees. Since the financial crisis, laws have been amended to cover increasing numbers of retrenchments. First, however, it is important to make a distinction between *dismissal* and *retrenchment*, two common modes of terminating a contract of service between employers and employees. Employers cannot terminate a contract of service without proper cause, as provided by Section 5(2)(a) of the Industrial Relations Act of 1967.

- *Dismissal* refers to a disciplinary action taken against an employee who is found guilty of industrial misconduct. Section 14(1)(a) of the

Employment Act, 1955 states that "an employer may, on the grounds of misconduct . . . [and], after due inquiry, dismiss the employee without notice."

- *Industrial misconduct* refers to actions related to duty, discipline, and morality. In cases of industrial misconduct an employee's contract of service can be terminated immediately, without a prior notice from the employer.

TERMINATION BY RETRENCHMENT. Under the Industrial Law, retrenchments, redundancies, and reorganizations all fall into the same category. Companies retrench workers for various reasons, including a decline in aggregate demand during a recession, closures, mergers and takeovers, and technological changes that introduce labor-saving techniques of production. Employers wishing to retrench employees are required to serve them with a notice of termination. The termination takes effect on the expiration date of the notice.

The Employment Termination and Layoff Benefit Regulations of 1980 (under the Employment Act of 1955) govern benefits for terminated employees. The amount of a termination benefit is determined by the terms of the contract of service. However, it should not be less than the amount provided for in the regulations. The Employment Act of 1955 was amended on August 1, 1998, to prevent inappropriate retrenchments and unlawful dismissals and to promote fair labor practices.

REGULATIONS GOVERNING LABOR MOBILITY. Malaysia has no regulations on occupational and internal geographical mobility. The government promotes the migration of workers from west Malaysia to the state of Sabah. Both the Public Employment Service and the Malaysia Migration Fund Board (the statutory body within the Ministry of Human Resources responsible for promoting geographical mobility) foster worker mobility. The Migration Fund Board oversees transfer schemes that give grants and allowances to workers migrating to Sabah. This program has gained in importance because the migrant workers from Peninsular Malaysia who once worked in Sabah are no longer willing to make the move. Working conditions on the plantations of Peninsular Malaysia are favorable, and the cost of living in Sabah is high. As the number of Malaysians emigrating to Sabah decreases, the number of workers from Indonesia and the Philippines willing to travel there increases. The government's program is designed to make the area more attractive to Malaysians.

Malaysian law classifies international labor mobility into two categories: Malaysian workers seeking foreign employment, and foreign workers seeking employment in Malaysia. Private employment agencies play an active role in recruiting Malaysians for foreign employment, and their activities in this regard are regulated by the Private Employment Agencies Act of 1981. Foreigners seeking employment in Malaysia are placed in one of two categories: semi-skilled and unskilled foreign workers, and expatriates. They are governed by Malaysia's Immigration Guidelines for Foreign Workers (1995).

Assessing the Public Employment Service

The Public Employment Service in Malaysia has been viewed as one of the instruments for achieving and maintaining the goal of full employment set out in the National Labor Policy. The service mobilizes the country's manpower and improves human resource utilization through its traditional function as intermediary between employers and employees in job search and placement activities. Since the crisis, demand for the programs the service offers has risen dramatically (table 4.13). The number of new registrants increased by 32.7 percent between 1997 and 1998, although it fell

TABLE 4.13
Malaysia: New Registrants, Vacancies, and Placement
in the Labor Market, 1992–99
(January–July)

Year	New registrants	Vacancies	Placement	Penetration rate[a] (percent)
1992	102,644	83,300	27,060	32.5
1993	102,624	77,031	25,901	33.6
1994	94,045	57,410	23,425	40.8
1995	85,768	58,412	22,552	38.6
1996	84,736	57,539	25,134	43.7
1997	91,491	64,463	26,233	40.7
1998	121,396	74,610	21,170	28.4
1999	76,074	57,214	12,513	21.9

a. The penetration rate is the total number of placements expressed as a percentage of total hires.

Source: Manpower Department, Ministry of Human Resources, Malaysia: Labor and Human Resources Statistics, 1992–96.

TABLE 4.14
Malaysia: Vacancies by Sector, 1996–99
(January–June)

Sector	1996	1997	1998	1999
Agriculture, forestry, hunting, and fishing	1,993	1,855	5,231	10,991
Mining and quarrying	122	109	188	64
Manufacturing	36,107	40,645	52,159	25,645
Electricity, gas, and water	178	200	122	13
Construction	2,755	3,785	2,156	1,450
Wholesale and retail trade, restaurants, and hotels	6,159	6,420	5,281	2,354
Transport, storage, and communication	2,245	2,555	1,066	800
Finance, insurance, real estate, and business services	3,264	3,868	3,070	1,628
Other services	4,716	5,026	5,337	2,549
Total	57,539	64,463	74,610	45,494

Source: Manpower Department, Ministry of Human Resources.

again in the face of the nascent recovery in 1999. This large increase in the number of job seekers signals a manpower surplus and a loose labor market. It also reflects the "added-worker effect" that occurred as the recession encouraged secondary workers to join the labor market to maintain household income.

Despite the increase in unemployment, the number of vacancies also rose (from 64,463 in 1997 to 74,610 in 1998, or 16 percent) because certain sectors, such as agriculture, are experiencing labor shortages. Most of the new vacancies have been in the agricultural sector, which has seen its need for workers double each year since 1997 (table 4.14). The increase in vacancies in the sector is the result of the opening up of oil palm estates in the districts of Miri, Bintulu, and Sibu in Sarawak. The manufacturing sector also recorded an increase in new job vacancies of 28.3 percent in 1998. This increase may originate with export-oriented companies that are responding to Malaysia's improved export performance.

Despite the increases in the number of registrants and vacancies reported in 1998, the number of placements has decreased. The percentage of total vacancies filled by the Public Employment Service, or the overall penetration rate that measures the effectiveness of placement services, is low. It stood at just 28.4 percent in 1998 and fell to 21.9 percent in the first half of 1999, compared with 40.7 percent in 1997. The penetration rate by occupational categories also varies from a high of 70.7 percent for clerical and related workers to a low of 3.3 percent in agriculture. The limited number of vacancies available relative to the number of job seekers makes the Public Employment Service's job more difficult, contributing to the low overall penetration rate.

The extremely low penetration rate in the agricultural sector can be traced to the unwillingness of workers to take agricultural jobs, particularly on the plantations. Relatively low wages in the sector result in a high incidence of rural-urban migration, leading to labor supply constraints in the plantation sector. The low percentage of vacancies filled in other job categories is the result largely of the mismatch between job seekers' aspirations and characteristics and employers' requirements. When unemployment is relatively high, employers tend to look for workers with more experience and skills than would usually be required, and employment services can face difficulties in meeting demand. Perhaps for this reason, retrenched workers have a high placement rate. In 1998 the Public Employment Service successfully placed 68 percent of all retrenched workers.

Most active registrants seeking employment with the Public Employment Service are already unemployed. In 1998, 80.2 percent of the active registrants were unemployed, compared with 69.9 percent in 1997. In 1999 that figure increased by 10.3 percent. Further, in 1998 only 6.7 percent of the active unemployed in the country registered with the Public Employment Service, so that calculating the unemployment rate in terms of all Malaysians is virtually impossible.

TABLE 4.15

Malaysia: Active Registrants, by Employment Status, 1997–99

(January–June)

Employment status	1997	1998	1999
Unemployed	194,071	298,250	197,187
Employed	70,287	55,441	35,847
Self-employed and family workers	13,251	18,203	14,966
Total unemployed in the economy	233,100	443,200	—
Unemployed active registrants (% of total unemployed)	8.3	6.7	—

— not available.

Source: Manpower Department Bulletin, various issues; Treasury Report 1998/99.

Assessing the Impact of Regulations on Retrenchment

The Malaysian government has passed new regulations or revised existing statutes to protect workers in the aftermath of the Asian financial crisis. While it is difficult to assess the exact effects of these changes, statistics show that termination benefits are being paid. Some employers, however, are taking advantage of the economic slowdown to replace local workers with cheaper foreign labor.

TERMINATION BENEFITS. According to the regulations, in 1998 a total of RM 301.5 million should have been paid to 56,292 retrenched workers (table 4.16). Of this amount, 3,061 employers disbursed RM 249 million, or 83 percent of the required sum. Even though the law states that the benefit must be paid in full within 7 days of the contract termination date, in some cases the benefits have not been paid 10 months after workers have been retrenched. However, the figures show a high degree of compliance among employers undertaking retrenchments.

UNFAIR DISMISSAL. Workers may be dismissed unfairly during the recession for one of two reasons. First, employers may wish to replace local workers with cheaper foreign labor. And second, employers may simply neglect to comply with the law, dismissing workers without prior notice or without complying with the principle of "last in, first out." The first reason is more commonly given for dismissing workers. Some employers in the manufacturing sector have seen the recent economic downturn as an opportunity to substitute foreign for local workers. Since foreign workers are willing to accept lower wages than local workers, these firms are able to reduce their labor costs.

COLLECTIVE BARGAINING. In 1998, 442 trade disputes involving 93,530 workers were reported, a decrease of 3 percent from 1997 (table 4.17). Of these disputes 175 (40 percent) concerned mainly the terms and conditions of collective agreements. Although deadlocks in collective bargaining accounted for only 112 (29 percent) of the total disputes reported, they affected almost 55 percent of total workers. Disputes involving unfair labor practices represented only 5 percent of the total disputes in 1998, but this figure represents a 600 percent increase over 1997 levels. Many of the 1998 disputes (216, or 49 percent) occurred in the manufacturing sector—the only sector to experience an increased number of disputes during the recession.

TABLE 4.16

Statutory Benefits Paid to Retrenched Workers, 1998

(Peninsular Malaysia, by state)

State	Number of employers	Number of employees	Amount required (RM)		Amount settled (RM)	
Federal Territory of Kuala Lumpur	532	4,740	34,223,114.69	(100)	25,797,200.19	(75)
Johore	391	5,327	17,101,673.84	(100)	14,135,585.51	(83)
Kelantan	48	982	1,416,289.51	(100)	1,358,518.67	(96)
Malacca	84	1,035	3,783,855.09	(100)	3,345,709.68	(88)
Negeri Sembilan	144	1,709	6,520,227.52	(100)	5,839,149.32	(90)
Pahang	83	2,830	5,593,475.95	(100)	4,629,672.56	(83)
Perlis/Kedah	167	4,474	24,671,691.82	(100)	23,684,456.04	(96)
Penang	275	15,284	78,967,250.17	(100)	76,021,118.22	(96)
Perak	386	4,714	15,516,975.23	(100)	15,045,190.73	(97)
Selangor	904	12,449	109,583,602.40	(100)	75,749,915.34	(69)
Terengganu	47	2,748	4,154,177.74	(100)	3,298,858.77	(79)
Total	3,061	56,292	301,537,333.50	(100)	248,905,374.50	(83)

Note: Figures in parentheses denote percentage of total.
Source: Labor Department, Ministry of Human Resources.

TABLE 4.17

Malaysia: Trade Disputes, 1994–98

Reasons for disputes	Number of disputes					Number of workers involved				
	1994	1995	1996	1997	1998	1994	1995	1996	1997	1998
Refusal to enter into collective bargaining	25	25	0	12	19	3,924	2,106	6,356	4,003	2,644
Deadlock in collective bargaining	119	131	137	112	126	53,716	25,437	21,367	39,370	51,209
Terms and conditions in collective agreement and other service contracts	236	254	211	223	175	22,638	12,660	18,181	70,861	30,393
Retrenchment and layoff	7	10	17	4	9	833	634	1,368	151	971
Promotion, reallocation of duties, transfer, and other management prerogatives	28	8	1	17	24	259	55	18	13,426	1,282
Demotion, suspension, warning letter, and other disciplinary actions	23	16	3	17	37	93	60	22	2,242	1,103
Noncompliance with labor standards	15	10	8	7	2	929	2,418	180	565	97
Infringements of workers' rights and unfair labor practices	14	9	22	3	21	1,751	1,225	1,784	9	4160
Other	36	48	57	63	29	3,332	4,062	3,062	8,090	1,671
Total	503	511	476	458	442	87,575	48,657	52,338	138,717	93,530

Source: Industrial Relations Department, Ministry of Human Resources.

Limitations of Current Labor Market Information

As we have seen, Malaysia has several sources of labor market information. However, the collection and dissemination of the data need to be improved. Some of the problems with obtaining the labor market information are:

- *Delays in the dissemination of information.* Delays hinder the effectiveness of using data to monitor changes in the labor market. For example, the latest published issue of the Manpower Department's *Labor and Human Resource Statistics* is for 1992–96. The Labor Force Survey is conducted only once a year, and publishing the data takes at least a year.
- *Inadequate statistical coverage.* Major gaps in statistical coverage of the labor market exist in Malaysia. First, little information is available on the labor market at the local level and on the informal sector. Currently, only information on Peninsular Malaysia is available through the Labor Force Survey and the population census. Second, there is a dearth of information on unemployment and underemployment by season, age, sex, level of education, skills, and family obligations. Another gap is lack of published information on the characteristics of those involved in the informal sector (sex, economic activity, level of education, skills, and income, for instance). And finally, nothing has been published on the number of workers holding more than one job.
- *Shortage of wage rate and earnings data.* Surveys and reports on wages are not conducted and published at regular intervals. The Occupational Wage Survey, which provides information on salary and earnings in selected industries, was initially a biannual survey but has been conducted annually since 1991 (the latest data are from 1993). The Annual Survey of Manufacturing Industries also provides wage data by employment category but at a highly aggregative level. The recent publication of the Fringe Benefit Survey for Executives and Nonexecutives by the Malaysian Employers Federation has helped fill the gap in information on wages and earnings.

Vocational Education and Training

Education and training have always been an important component of Malaysian economic development. However, vocational training started to receive greater government attention only in the mid-1980s under the Fifth Malaysia Plan (1985–90). The focus on vocational education and training (VET) supports Malaysia's efforts to become a more industrial and technology-based economy.

Since 1985 VET has focused on high-tech jobs that involve labor-saving technology and robotics work production and on skills related to information technology. This focus supports the government's efforts to create a knowledge-based economy, as outlined in the Seventh Malaysia Plan. Private-sector participation in training has increased, with companies not only providing input but also forming partnerships with public-sector organizations to offer training. More private training institutions have also emerged since 1985, although VET continues to be an activity led by the public sector.

The Ministry of Human Resources is responsible for overall human resource development issues. Its objectives are to contribute efficiently and effectively to the government's efforts to produce a skilled, competent, disciplined, innovative, and efficient workforce with positive values, consistent with the nation's industrial needs, technological changes, and economic growth.

To meet these objectives, the ministry has developed several strategies. It aims to:

- Establish strategic alliances through consultations and cooperation with employers, workers' organizations, and enterprises to produce a highly skilled and productive workforce to meet the government's planning goals;
- Hold dialogues with industrial organizations and employers' associations to encourage greater private-sector participation in skills development and upgrading;
- Expand the capacity and improve the quality of training programs at industrial training institutes; and
- Adopt innovative and progressive strategies to market customized courses at the industrial training institutes.

The Policy Research and Planning Division of the Ministry of Human Resources monitors policies and strategies within the ministry. The division has several important functions:

- Assessing and identifying training needs for industry and analyzing both public and private training institutes;
- Implementing government initiatives related to human resource development, such as the Cabinet Committee on Training and the Industrial Technology Development Action Plan, among others; and

- Representing the ministry at international and national forums related to human resource planning and development.

Along with the Ministry of Human Resources, the Ministry of Education makes important contributions to VET. A key part of its mandate is to ensure that school curricula are in line with the qualifications workers need in a high-tech labor force.

Institutional Framework

A number of key players are involved in manpower planning in Malaysia (figure 4.1):

- Central planning agencies like the Economic Planning Unit, the Ministry of Human Resources, and the Public Service Department;
- Supporting principal agencies like the Ministry of Education, the Ministry of International Trade and Industry, and the Statistics Department; and
- Agencies directly involved in producing skilled labor, such as the Ministry of Education, MARA, and the Ministry of Youth and Sports.

Other agencies that play a role in human resource development include the National Vocational Training Council (NVTC), which is tasked with establishing a coordinated and comprehensive system of vocational and industrial training in line with Malaysia's economic development goals and technological development needs. At the end of 1998, some 158 institutions had registered with the NVTC. The Manpower Planning Subcommittee of the National Development Planning Committee is responsible for the overall manpower policy and determines national education and training policies. These policies are then translated into specific programs by the supporting and implementing agencies. The Human Resource Development Council (HRDC) has a special role. It encourages retraining and skills upgrading for employees of firms registered with the council. In 1997 a total of 1,181 employers from the manufacturing sector and 405 employers from the service sector registered with the HRDC.

Public Vocational Training

In 1995–98, the intake of public training institutions increased from 15,428 to 22,630 trainees (table 4.18). Over the same time period, their output (the number of trainees successfully completing courses) increased

FIGURE 4.1
Manpower Planning Machinery

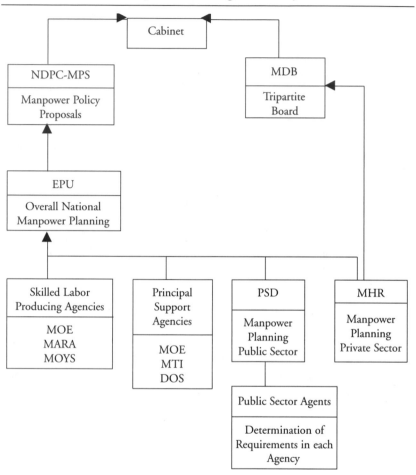

PC-MPS : Manpower Planning Subcommittee of the National Development
         Planning Committee
MDB   : Manpower Development Board
EPU   : Economic Planning Unit
PSD   : Public Service Department
MHR   : Ministry of Human Resources
MOE   : Ministry of Education
MOYS   : Ministry of Youth and Sports
MTI   : Ministry of Trade and Industry
DOS   : Department of Statistics

Source: General Circular No. 2, 1986, Government of Malaysia.

TABLE 4.18
Intake of Public Training Institutions 1995–2000, by course

Course	1995 Intake	1995 Percent	1998 Intake	1998 Percent	2000 Intake	2000 Percent	Average annual growth rate (%) 1996–98	1999–2000
Engineering trades	10,574	68.5	14,333	63.8	16,605	58.5	10.8	7.5
Mechanical[a]	5,991	38.8	8,508	37.6	9,769	34.4	12.1	7.5
Electrical[b]	4,323	28.0	5,406	23.9	6,306	22.2	7.7	8.0
Civil[c]	260	1.7	519	2.3	530	1.9	25.9	1.1
Building trades[d]	1,660	10.8	2,312	10.2	3,063	10.8	11.7	15.1
Printing trades[e]	154	1.0	244	1.1	210	0.7	16.6	7.2
Others[f]	2,457	15.9	3,541	15.6	6,338	22.3	13.0	33.8
Skill upgrading	583	3.8	2,100	9.3	2,166	7.6	53.3	1.6
Total	15,428	100.0	22,630	100.0	28,382	100.0	13.5	12.1

Notes: [a] Includes general mechanics, general machining, tool and die making, motor vehicle mechanics, welding, and sheet metal works and fabrication.
[b] Includes electrical installation and maintenance, radio and television servicing, refrigeration and air conditioning, electrical fitting, and armature winding and engineering.
[c] Includes construction.
[d] Includes carpentry and joinery, woodwork machining, bricklaying, and plumbing.
[e] Includes hand composing, machine composing, offset printing, and bookbinding and letterpress.
[f] Includes surveying, architectural draftsmanship, photography, laboratory science, dispensing optics, computer programming, information processing, heavy plant operation, architecture, quantity surveying, hotel and catering and home economics.

Source: Government of Malaysia, *Midterm Review of the Seventh Malaysia Plan, 1996–2000.*

from 15,844 to 20,898 (table 4.19). Malaysia has four basic training schemes.[6]

THE SBL SCHEME (TRAINING SUPPORT SCHEME). This scheme allows employers to develop their own training programs relevant to their business goals. It also permits various modes of training, namely:

- In-house training, either on or off the job or both, using internal, external, and even foreign resources;
- Institution-based training, with public and private training institutions offering evening and weekend programs;
- Training by employers' or industry associations such as the Federation of Manufacturers Malaysia;
- Training by industry-managed training centers such as the Penang Skills Development Center;
- Cooperative training, with large companies offering their programs to smaller employers; and
- Overseas training when domestic offerings do not meet employers' needs.

The PROLUS SCHEME (APPROVED TRAINING PROGRAM SCHEME). This scheme aims to facilitate the retraining of workers through preapproved programs, sparing employers the burden of applying for approval themselves. Training providers, including government agencies, private organizations, and consultants, are encouraged to register with the HRDC. All training providers must satisfy certain conditions in order to win Approved Training Program status. A committee with majority employer representation assesses the trainers.

PLT SCHEME (ANNUAL TRAINING PLAN SCHEME). Under this scheme employers are encouraged to submit annual training plans covering the next year. Smaller employers may engage training consultants for this purpose and have the HRDC reimburse their costs.

The PERLA SCHEME (TRAINING PROVIDER AGREEMENT SCHEME). Unlike the above three schemes, which provide reimbursement only after the training has been completed (and fees incurred), PERLA provides the employers with the opportunity to participate in training programs while paying an approved minimum in fees. The HRDC provides the trainer with the balance of the fees, using a fund supported by employer contributions.

TABLE 4.19
Output of Public and Private Training Institutions, 1995–2000, by course

Course	1995			1998			2000			Average annual growth rate (%)			
										1996–1998		1999–2000	
	Public	Private	Total	Public	Private	Total	Public	Private	Total	Public	Private	Public	Private
Engineering trades	10,758	7,496	18,254	12,857	9,823	22,680	15,014	11,615	26,629	6.1	9.4	5.3	8.7
Mechanical	6,804	1,679	8,483	7,958	2,100	10,058	8,932	2,416	11,348	5.4	7.7	3.9	7.3
Electrical	3,734	5,743	9,477	4,471	7,628	12,099	5,616	9,087	14,703	6.2	9.9	7.9	9.1
Civil	220	74	294	428	95	523	466	112	578	24.8	8.7	2.9	8.6
Building trades	1,792	205	1,997	2,122	255	2,377	2,780	290	3,070	5.8	7.5	9.4	6.6
Printing trades	108	25	133	213	31	244	210	37	247	25.4	7.4	-0.5	9.2
Others	2,623	576	3,199	3,676	718	4,394	3,780	828	4,608	11.9	7.6	0.9	7.4
Skills upgrading	563	—	563	2,030	—	2,030	2,116	—	2,116	53.3	—	1.4	—
Total	15,844	8,302	24,146	20,898	10,827	31,725	23,900	12,770	36,670	9.7	9.3	—	8.6

— not available.

Note: Does not include output from courses such as commerce, agriculture, home science, and other "soft" skills.

Source: Midterm Review of the Seventh Malaysia Plan, 1996–2000.

TABLE 4.20
Major Public Vocational Institutions

Ministry	Institution
Human Resources	Industrial Training Institute (CIAST)
	The Center For Instructor and Advanced Skills Training (CAST)
Education	Polytechnics, Technical Secondary School, Vocational School
Entrepreneur Development	Institut Kemahiran MARA (IKM)
Youth and Sports	Institut Kemahiran Belia Negara (IKBN)

The Ministry of Human Resources and HRDC introduced the Retrenched Workers Retraining Scheme as a specialized occupational mobility program in May 1998. It is designed to make workers more employable by upgrading their skills and to provide employers with highly skilled workers (especially when the economy has recovered).

The government has also established a number of vocational institutions, some of them under various ministries (table 4.20). Two advanced skill-training institutes have also been set up. The British-Malaysian Institute offers courses in electrical and electronic engineering, medical electronic engineering, communication engineering, computer system engineering, and information technology. The Japan-Malaysia Technical Institute specializes in computer engineering technology and industrial electronic technology. In addition, France and Germany have signed bilateral agreements with Malaysia to provide VET in highly advanced technical programs.

The HRDC has also introduced an 18-month special apprenticeship program designed particularly for graduates and retrenched workers. The Hotel Industry Apprenticeship Scheme prepares workers for the service industry, and the Mechatronics Apprenticeship Scheme provides training in electronics, electrical, mechanical, and other technical fields. The Entrepreneur Development Ministry has set up another apprenticeship program, the Graduate Entrepreneur Scheme, which trains graduates to become entrepreneurs.

Private Vocational Training

In 1994 around 40 private vocational institutions trained 6,278 workers in 39 different areas. Most of the trainees were in five areas: electrical engineering (2,193 trainees, or 34.9 percent); microcomputers (785 trainees, or 12.5 percent); mechanical engineering (573 trainees, or 9.1 percent); radio and television (393 trainees, or 6.3 percent); and computer graphics design (287 trainees, or 4.6 percent). Of the trainees, 50.6 percent completed their courses with a diploma. The other 49.4 percent received certificates.

The government has developed a scheme that could benefit private vocational institutes. The Human Resource Development Fund (HRDF), established under the Human Resource Development Act of 1992, offers employers incentives (in the form of grants) to establish and accelerate systematic training programs. The fund is supported by contributions from employers equal to 1 percent of the monthly payroll. Companies can either hire trainers or send employees for training at private vocational institutes. The HRDF focuses on three types of training:

- Skill areas such as computers, crafts, technology, and professional education, as well as specialized training for trainers, research and development, and basic education;
- Management and supervisory training; and
- Companywide productivity and quality improvement.

To make it easier for employers to train their workers, the HRDF offers distance learning, joint training schemes, and cluster training schemes. The HRDF has pumped RM 15 million into an apprenticeship scheme in machining, mechatronics, tool and die manufacturing, and hotel work, using both on- and off-the-job training. By the end of 1998, a total of 694 trainees had been trained under the apprenticeship program. A Special Skilled Apprenticeship Program has also been developed.

Long-term Perspectives

Public and private vocational institutions are producing a growing number of skilled and semi-skilled workers to meet the country's needs (table 4.21). But Malaysia still suffers from imbalances in the labor market, with surpluses in some areas and shortages in others, for two reasons. First, *the number of semi-skilled workers is increasing faster than the number of skilled workers*. The overall number of skilled and semi-skilled workers increased in 1993–97 in a number of major industries (automotive, electronics, electrical, carpentry, and printing, for example). However, the increase in semi-skilled workers has been larger than the increase in skilled workers, leaving a shortage of highly skilled labor in these industries.

TABLE 4.21

Expected Demand for Skilled and Semi-skilled Workers, 1990–98

(by industry)

Industry	Basic skills	Computer-aided design	Semi-skilled	Total	Percentage
Food	1,271	436	6,160	7,867	1.84
Drinks and tobacco	53	—	520	573	0.13
Textile	1,660	3,831	31,391	36,882	8.62
Wood products and furniture	5,829	3,291	48,884	58,004	13.56
Paper and printing	1,716	180	6,536	8,432	1.97
Chemicals	1,389	1,207	10,880	13,467	3.15
Coal and petroleum	1,173	124	734	2,031	0.47
Rubber products and plastic	2,897	2,056	25,913	30,866	7.22
Nonmineral material	1,558	980	10,531	13,069	3.05
Basic minerals	7,421	207	8,996	16,624	3.88
Manmade minerals	4,153	360	4,956	9,469	2.21
Electrical and electronic	7,811	5,973	174,300	188,084	43.96
Engineering and vehicle tools	8,238	531	18,242	27,011	6.32
Measurement tools	151	42	1,840	2,033	0.47
Other	1,518	773	11,184	13,475	3.15
Total	46,838	19,991	361,067	427,896	100.0

— not available.

Source: Ministry of Human Resources, Research and Planning Division, *Prospective Employment in the Manufacturing Sector 1990–98.*

Second, demand for labor and labor absorption of both skilled and semi-skilled workers) are highest in a handful of industries (table 4.21). These include the automotive, electrical, electronics, metal-based, rubber- and plastic-based, textile, and wood-based industries.

These industries are the country's primary source of growth. Demand for both skilled and semi-skilled workers in these areas is expected to continue as the industries expand.

Based on its projections of future demands for labor, the Ministry of Human Resources has identified the training areas that need to be emphasized:

- *Electrical and electronics industry group.* Computers, mechatronics, and advanced manufacturing technology such as micromechanics, robotics, digital imaging, micro- and nanofabrication.

- *Automotive and transportation industry group.* Industrial and engineering design, automobile engineering, automotive ergonomics, automotive testing analysis, tools, mold and die, general machining, and machine operation.
- *Textile and apparel industries.* Textile science and technology, fashion design and marketing, engineering design, and manufacturing processes.
- *Rubber-based industries.* Computerized manufacturing, robotics for SMIs, advanced processing techniques, measurement and sensor technology, computer modeling (in compounding), computer simulation in rapid prototyping for design work on rubber engineering applications, precision machining, and precision tool-and-die fabrication.
- *Wood-based industries.* Specialized industrial training in advanced wood-based methods and sciences.
- *Metal-based industries.* Metallurgy and metallurgical engineering.

Evaluating Public Training

Despite the relative success of public institutions in training and retraining workers, the public VET delivery system suffers from several serious shortcomings. Predominant among these is a lack of coordination and haphazard planning that leads to duplications in curricula. This situation is the result of each institution's tendency to promote its own strategic interests and the lack of effective overall coordination at the national level.

To address this problem, the NVTC acts as a focal point for vocational and skills training. Unfortunately, it does not have the necessary jurisdiction to implement a coordinated VET delivery program in public and private training institutions, although the government envisages giving the council the necessary mandate. The government has also set up a standing committee, the Coordinating Committee for Public Training Agencies, to deliberate on common issues faced by the public skills training provider. But this committee has also proved inadequate to the task of providing an effective delivery system.

As a result most training centers have their own separate curricula and types of certification, all of which differ from one another. Most of the public institutions offer similar courses in a few areas (such as heavy transportation mechanics, electrical wiring, air conditioning and refrigeration, industrial electronics, and welding) and cover a limited range of skills. This duplication suggests that public training institutions are unable to identify market trends and offer courses relevant to them. Contributing to this situation is a problem discussed earlier: a lack of timely and relevant information. The public agencies involved in planning VET are poorly informed about the human resource requirements of industries and the state of the labor market.

Another serious problem is the quality of the students who attend vocational institutions. Most have not succeeded in other educational programs and opt for vocational training as a last resort. Of those opting for VET, those taken in by public vocational institutions are generally less academically qualified than those who attend private vocational institutions. In addition, the students themselves tend to perceive vocational training as the least-best option. VET lacks the status of more traditional educational programs in the Malaysian schools. And public servants tend to earn less than their private-sector counterparts and often have little opportunity for promotion. Experienced trainers often move to the manufacturing sector, which offers higher remuneration and benefits, leaving public training institutions without enough qualified trainers.

For all these reasons, industries have questioned the quality of the training the public institutions provide. The trainees are not up to industry standards, so that much of the effort that has gone into training them is wasted. Many firms are unwilling to hire graduates of these public vocational institutes as skilled workers, taking them on as semi-skilled workers. Manufacturers complain that graduates of public training institutions are unable to fit into a high-tech occupational environment. In other words, public training providers are not market driven.

Collaboration between public-sector training institutions and industry is imperative in order to correct this problem. Public training institutions need to enhance their ability to respond to rapid technological changes. The tasks of identifying the competencies that are actually required in the manufacturing sector, assessing the competency of trainers and institutions, and overseeing certification lie with the NVTC. It has instituted a new five-level skill qualification framework for vocational training and certification to help provide workers with the skills they need and create a systematic career path for skilled craftsmen. The new qualification framework will encourage trainees to seek advanced training after completing lower-level courses.

The Government Response

The government has embarked on a few encouraging initiatives to improve both public and private VET. Among these are the RM 5 million retraining program for retrenched workers and an exemption from HRDC contributions for employers in sectors facing severe difficulties. This last measure is intended to ease employers' financial burden and thus moderate the level of retrenchment.

The NVTC has developed the National Occupational Skills Standards in an effort to standardize training curricula and requirements in certain areas. The accreditation system is based on a continuous assessment of the trainees and has been fully implemented in all public training institutions offering courses covered by the standards. Implementing the accreditation system is essential not only to producing highly skilled manpower but also to developing a career path for skilled workers that runs parallel and is seen as equal to academic-based career development.

As part of its efforts to encourage greater private-sector participation in industrial and skill training, the government has raised the industrial building allowance from 2 to 10 percent a year. This allowance helps offset the cost of constructing buildings that will be used for VET by allowing businesses to write off the costs within 10 rather than 45 years. Further, the government has provided financial support to skill development centers managed by the private sector in the amount of RM 35.7 million.

Policy Implications and Recommendations

The Malaysian government has responded to the effects of the financial crisis with a number of labor market reforms and initiatives that address unemployment problems. The reforms speak to both the short-term consequences of the economic slowdown and the long-term need for an adequate supply of labor in all sectors. They also seek to ensure the insensitivity of unemployment in the event of future declines in economic activity. Despite these efforts, more can be done in the areas of employment creation and maintenance and income-support activities, labor market services, and vocational education and training.

Employment Creation and Maintenance and Income-support Activities

Both the government and private sector must assume responsibility for creating and maintaining employment. The government has two important roles to play.

- First, it needs to continue to actively *create employment through public works projects*, especially when faced with economic slowdowns and market failures (when the private sector is unlikely to take on certain responsibilities).

- Second, the government must *ensure that the private sector observes all rules and regulations regarding employment*, particularly during the period of crisis.

The private sector meanwhile should play a positive role in employment creation during periods of economic boom. During economic slowdowns, private firms *should actively seek alternatives to retrenchment in order to maintain employment levels.* One way the private sector can fulfill this responsibility is by adhering to government regulations concerning retrenchment, which offer alternatives to eliminating jobs.

The government of Malaysia has repeatedly stressed that it does not need an income-support policy for the unemployed. Besides not wanting to incur the financial burden, the government feels that such a policy would discourage the unemployed from seeking jobs, prolonging the period of unemployment. As an alternative to unemployment schemes, the government has elected to provide training in skills required by industries and to work to ensure that enough job opportunities are available in the country.

However, the government should seriously *consider implementing an unemployment insurance scheme* to provide financial support for retrenched workers. Such a scheme would minimize the financial burden involuntarily retrenched workers face, particularly in the period of crisis. The government can design the scheme so that it is financed by worker and employer contributions, particularly from those sectors that tend to be most affected by economic slowdowns or that have high turnover rates among workers. The scheme would also provide employers with another reason to seek alternatives to retrenchment, since firms would be partly responsible for financing the cost of their unemployed workers.

The increase in the unemployment rate in Malaysia during the crisis can be considered a temporary phenomenon. Employment should increase as the economy improves. In the short run, then, the best policy is to let the market make the necessary adjustments. However, the government can introduce a series of measures to speed up the adjustment process. Among these are:

- *Creating labor market information centers with rigorous employment search services and improving coordination between the government and private sector.*
- *Promoting part-time work and temporary employment in the medium and long term.* The objective of such measures is to enhance flexibility in the job market, thus reducing dependency on foreign workers in

sectors facing labor shortages, such as manufacturing, agriculture, and services. Legislation expanding opportunities for part-time employment has already been introduced. Expanded part-time opportunities will increase women's participation in the labor market and help ensure an adequate supply of workers, particularly in service-related sectors.

- *Offering part-time workers some of the benefits available to full-time workers* will further encourage women to join the labor force. Providing day-care centers for children of employees at the workplace should encourage mothers to reenter the work force and discourage women who become pregnant from quitting their jobs.
- *Introducing temporary employment* can help eliminate the high turnover rate in some sectors.[7] Temporary employment needs to be properly monitored to ensure that employers do not abuse this form of hiring. Government guidelines on the hiring of part-time and temporary workers need to be particularly clear, for instance. Experience suggests that temporary workers who are employed for a specified period are reemployed to do the same job. Establishing more temporary employment agencies throughout the country can also help promote both part-time and temporary employment.
- *Instituting tax and subsidy incentives designed to create and preserve employment in the long term.* Income subsidies can be an incentive to encourage employment in sectors that are facing labor shortages. Subsidies can also encourage employers to hire individuals they would not normally take on, such as young people and the elderly.

Labor Market Services

The labor market services currently available in Malaysia need to be more effective. As discussed earlier, a number of shortcomings prevent the Public Employment Service from providing the best services to those seeking employment, including a lack of coordination and a shortage of timely information. The government and private sector can take several steps to improve the available services. Increasing the effectiveness of labor market intermediaries would ensure better matches between job seekers and vacancies, reducing the time and cost of the job search for both employers and workers. For instance:

- *Establishing regulations governing the Public Employment Service and private agencies.* In Malaysia, the Public Employment Service is the main instrument for organizing the labor market. It issues licenses and implements rules regulating the placement activities of private employment agencies. It can promulgate regulations that safeguard the interests of both job seekers and employers and ensure that information is compiled, analyzed, and disseminated.

- *Improving coordination between public and private employment agencies.* To expedite the placement of unemployed job seekers in times of recession, public and private employment agencies need to cooperate closely and exchange information. The Public Employment Service is within the Ministry of Human Resources, which has direct access to information on labor market conditions and policies. Private agencies need to have close contact with the service in order to obtain timely labor market information that will help improve their placement activities.

- *Enhancing the quality of the Public Employment Service.* The effectiveness of the placement service must be judged in qualitative as well as quantitative terms. Quality placement from the employers' side involves satisfying their demands for qualified workers. On the employees' side it involves providing well-paying, stable job opportunities.

- *Requiring businesses to register vacancies with the Public Employment Service.* Especially when the number of job seekers considerably exceeds the number of vacancies, compulsory listings can facilitate the job search. These listings also make it easier for the Public Employment Service to assess employment opportunities and match workers with jobs. Such data also provide essential information in terms of available jobs and retrenchment activities.

- *Placing more emphasis on vocational and employment counseling, especially in periods of recession.* When unemployment rates are high, the Public Employment Service needs to encourage unemployed workers to undertake entrepreneurial activities or to become self-employed. Counselors can identify those job seekers with the initiative to venture into business and provide them with financial and management assistance. An employment guidance program can help change job seekers' perception of the job market and shorten the time unemployed workers spend seeking work. Such a program helps reduce frictional and structural unemployment.

- *Reassessing and increasing retrenchment benefits.* Retrenchment creates major financial problems for workers, especially those who are sole breadwinners. For this reason retrenchment benefits set out in the Employment Act of 1955 (which was revised in 1983) can be reexamined and increased. Such a revision will take into account the de-

terioration in the real value of benefits from inflation. Employees'
unions are one of the best ways to ensure that workers get the optimum amount of retrenchment benefits (over what is provided in the
Employment Act of 1955).

Employers are unlikely to agree to such a recommendation. Although the government requires them to inform the Labor Department of intended retrenchments, many apparently do not. Estimating
the actual percentage of employers that do report their retrenchment
exercises is difficult. One of the reasons employers are reluctant to provide such information is that companies often operate at a loss during
the recession and are unable to afford the retrenchment benefits and
other payments the law requires.

- *Increasing the efforts of the Manpower Department and the HRDC to
  disseminate information on registration, placement, and retraining services.* Only 24 percent of retrenched workers register at employment
  offices. HRDC figures indicate that less than 1 percent of retrenched
  workers seek retraining under the Retrenched Workers Retraining
  Scheme. These low percentages may reflect the fact that many workers are not aware that such services exist. Publishing vacancies regularly and establishing regular contact with employers, employees, and
  government agencies to coordinate and disseminate labor market information will also improve labor mobility.
- *Providing adequate training for staff entrusted with generating labor
  market information.* Successful training efforts require carefully designed training programs with appropriate course offerings and effective trainers and course material. Courses such as data analysis are
  relevant in this regard.

Vocational Education and Training

The list of recommendations for improving vocational training is long.
The government, private sector, and training institutions themselves need
to take steps to improve the VET delivery system. These steps include:

- *Having an independent central agency with the tools and mandate it
  needs to oversee and guide all public and private-sector VET.* The
  NVTC, for instance, cannot function effectively unless it includes
  not only government and private-sector representatives but also representatives of trade and workers' unions and manufacturers' groups.
  This group can draft appropriate programs and requirements for

VET, coordinate and monitor programs as they develop, and make recommendations to the government. The recent economic crisis has shown that those involved in VET have not studied the impact of the crisis on human resource development in Malaysia. The only organization known to have evaluated its VET is MARA, but only in its branches.

- *Fully implementing national standards for curricula and certification at both public and private training institutions.* A national policy must be in place that requires all vocational institutions to offer courses in line with national objectives. The government has already begun taking such steps with the new skill standards. More should be done, including developing a national assessment system and a national certification system. A National Reference Structure for Vocational Qualifications can provide a basis for comparing the various types of diplomas and certificates offered, helping students choose appropriate courses and employers find the types of workers they need.

- *Encouraging employers to provide training.* The government needs a firm directive and guidelines on training for employers in the manufacturing sectors. These employers need to provide opportunities for trainees to undergo practical training with their companies.

- *Improving the collection and dissemination of information on labor market trends and future demand for workers.* Institutions must be able to base their course offerings on demand—that is, they must design their curricula to meet the needs of the labor market.

- *Upgrading the quality of the students who enter public (and private) vocational institutions.* Since Malaysia is moving into high-tech, capital-intensive industries, the quality of students selected to undergo skills training must be upgraded accordingly. The task is to set a higher standard of admission requirements and to give VET the same status as other forms of education. The Ministry of Education should try to change the curriculum at the secondary level by giving equal status and significance to vocational subjects.

- *Encouraging the participation of foreign expatriates and vocational institutions from industrial countries in VET.* The government should be more flexible in allowing foreign expatriates to work with both public and private vocational institutions, especially in areas where local expertise is scarce. At the same time, the government must encourage vocational institutions from other countries to operate in Malaysia by providing attractive incentives and infrastructure support.

- *Offsetting costs for both trainees and employers.* Costs for training in the most-needed specialties must not be too high, and scholarships, infrastructure facilities, equipment, and trained instructors must be made available. Constraints on space, staff, budgets, and equipment have often been responsible for the overabundance of courses that promise few prospects in the job market.
- *Setting up centers of excellence for specific industries.* Such centers provide state-of-the-art, industry-specific training that will help develop a work force suited to the demands of the high-tech workplace. These centers will also make the delivery system for VET more professional and acceptable to employers.
- *Improving coordination between training institutions and local organizations.* Each training institution must establish a close rapport with employers in its area in order to gather up-to-date and relevant data on labor market demands. Such data will help in designing courses that meet employers' demands.
- *Amending course offerings to include nontechnical skills that improve job performance.* Areas such as English language competency, creativity, initiative, entrepreneurial know-how, and teamwork are often neglected. However, these skills can improve a candidate's chance of obtaining employment.
- *Ensuring the competency of training providers.* Training providers need to meet certain standards. They need to keep abreast of the latest technological developments in the workplace. They must be effective presenters able to conduct and evaluate the material they are providing. The pace of change in technology and in labor market needs is such that the VET system must itself be capable of rapid change. Modular courses are one way to increase flexibility by allowing students and employers to select only the modules they need. Incorporating a variety of delivery methods, including on-the-job and distance learning, can also keep training flexible, as can ensuring that decisions are made at the local level so that training is responsive to the needs of local industries.

Notes

1. In 1987 and 1997, however, exports fueled the country's growth, and in 1992 public investment played the leading role, recording the fastest growth rate of all the demand components of GDP.
2. The exceptions were 1991 and 1994–97.

3. It is difficult to calculate the exact number of jobs created by public work projects, since the private sector is also directly involved in developing these projects. The government administers and funds the projects, and private companies that have been awarded the tender do the actual construction.

4. Public works projects were clustered primarily in four sectors: construction; electricity, gas and water; transportation and storage; and government services.

5. The fund was launched in June 1998 with an initial capital of RM 90 million. The funds have been disbursed to more than 8,500 applicants. Demand for disbursements has been substantial enough that the government is providing an additional RM 300 million to augment the fund.

6. Total output exceeds input because some courses take longer than one year to complete. Some students may also have been "repeaters."

7. Temporary employment in this context does not include the probation period for employment, although employees are classified as temporary during this time.

OIS J24 195-244
J64 J31 J68 J23
J38

5

The Philippines: Labor Market Trends and Government Interventions Following the East Asian Financial Crisis[1]

Jude Esguerra, Arsenio Balisacan
and Nieves Confessor

In the last half of the 1990s, the Philippines has experienced both high unemployment rates and low productivity growth. In the wake of the East Asian financial crisis, unemployment and underemployment have increased, and the impact on households has been profound. This chapter examines the effects of the crisis on low-income groups and the success of the government programs designed to support unemployed and underemployed workers. These programs include income support, job creation, loans for small enterprises, and labor market services. The evidence suggests that the majority of these programs need to be strengthened and that targeting needs to be improved. The training and vocational education system, which is also examined here, is likewise in need of reform, and some measures have already been drafted. These improvements and reforms will provide workers in the Philippines with improved security during future crises and shocks.

The Situation before the Crisis

Unemployment was already high before the crisis, particularly among youth. Productivity was low, in part because of the high reservation wages of the unemployed. The crisis only made matters worse: more unskilled workers became unemployed or underemployed, and the country's output became less and less competitive. Firms and workers adjusted by shortening hours, but the impact remained severe.

High Unemployment Rates

Unemployment rates in the Philippines were already high before the financial crisis struck in 1997. During most of the 1990s they hovered between a little below 8 percent and 9.5 percent. The El Niño phenomenon and the financial crisis brought these rates up even more.

In Europe high unemployment rates are blamed in part on overgenerous unemployment and social insurance schemes that workers can resort to as an alternative to work. A similar phenomenon may be at work in the Philippines, even though the rudimentary programs that are found in the country cannot be compared to the mature social security systems in Europe.

On the face of it, high unemployment rates in the country are largely a youth-related phenomenon. Theoretically, reducing unemployment among young people in the 15–24 age group—especially those with some high school or college education—will largely solve the country's unemployment problem (Canlas 1997). But that observation does not yet constitute a diagnosis. In January 1997, before the crisis, only those with a high school education and those who had some undergraduate college credits registered rates of unemployment significantly higher than the overall unemployment rate of 7.75 percent (table 5.1). Unemployment among college graduates was also above the overall rate, but only by less than a per-

TABLE 5.1
Educational Attainment and Unemployment

	Unemployment rates (percent)		
	Jan–97	*Jan–98*	*Jan–99*
Overall unemployment	7.75	8.42	8.98
No grade completed	5.94	7.34	7.45
Elementary	5.63	6.13	6.04
High school	10.42	11.14	12.12
College undergraduate	12.78	13.47	14.80
College graduate	8.63	10.22	12.07

Source: Bureau of Labor and Employment Statistics, *Current Labor Force Statistics 1999.*

centage point. As the crisis progressed, the unemployment rate rose among all workers regardless of their educational attainment but especially among those with college degrees. It would be wrong, however, to conclude that crisis-related job losses were highest among well-educated workers.

One hypothesis that deserves closer study posits that the reservation wage of educated young people in search of employment is high because of overseas income from family members and relatives.[2] The amount of this type of income compares favorably with the local value added of Philippine manufactured exports and allows young people, especially those from relatively well-off families, to endure long periods of unemployment as they look for work. An overly generous social security system would have similar effects. This hypothesis is further supported by the fact that the prevalence of households that rely on foreign remittances as their main source of income rises noticeably between the lowest and highest income deciles. In 1991, for example, for household heads in the first and second deciles, only 0.7 and 1 percent relied on foreign remittances as their main source of income. The percentages for the 9th and 10th deciles, however, were as high as 13.2 percent and 19.8 percent, respectively. The proportion of unemployed heads of households who are dependent on remittances increases as income increases. Only 16.8 percent of unemployed households heads in the 1st decile receive remittances,[3] but more than half (53 percent) in the 10th decile do.[4]

In contrast to Europe, however, there is no easy response to the situation such remittances create. Social security benefits can (at least in theory) be reduced or redesigned to ameliorate the perverse effect on unemployment in industrial countries. But the same cannot be said of the Philippines. These remittances from abroad are, after all, private transfers. Given this situation we are able to say that the observed unemployment in the country before the crisis was not really entirely the result of distress—that is, it was not entirely involuntary. A significant portion of it was likely the effect of unemployment among young educated people who had high reservation wages because their families could afford to support them for long periods during the job search.

In the long term, when overall productivity and wages have caught up with the reservation wages of this segment of educated youth, unemployment will go down. Productivity growth is the crucial factor that will allow the economy to catch up to the high expectations and reservation wages of these young people and their families. Indirectly we are therefore also saying that productivity growth can be linked to unemployment. The question then becomes one of how to raise productivity.[5]

TABLE 5.2

Employment in Agriculture and Services, 1990–98

(percent)

Industry shares (percent)	1990	1991	1992	1993	1994	1995	1996	1997	1998
Agriculture	44.97	44.93	45.30	45.71	45.10	43.43	42.84	40.83	39.2
Industry	15.42	15.85	16.15	15.61	15.78	16.13	16.30	16.71	16.4
Services	39.62	39.22	38.55	38.68	39.12	40.44	40.86	42.46	44.4

Source: Current Labor Statistics (DOLE).

Productivity and the Reservation Wages of the Unemployed

The Philippine labor force was around 30.3 million in 1997 and 31.1 million in 1998. Among those older than 15, labor force participation averaged 65.8 percent from 1987 to 1997. In 1998 it was 66.1 percent, or slightly lower relative to 1996 and 1997. Where did these people work? Table 5.2 tells the story of an agricultural sector that is contracting, an industrial sector that has been stagnant, and a services sector that has become the last resort for people who cannot find work elsewhere.

In the past productivity growth has stalled because of stagnation in agriculture and the failure of manufacturing to create job openings. The contribution of the manufacturing sector to the country's GDP inched down from more than 27 percent in 1980 to 24.9 percent in 1998. As a result, industry's contribution to employment remained at around 16 percent throughout the 1990s.

Industry has failed to employ labor that cannot be employed in agriculture. This fact has many causes, including an inhospitable macroeconomic environment that in the past has led to the intensive use of capital rather than labor. Failures in the exchange rate policy of recent years are central to this development. The loss of competitiveness in the tradables sector, in addition to factors such as deficient infrastructure, is the result of the real (at times nominal) appreciation of the peso during the first half of the 1990s (box 5.1). While there was some economic growth before the crisis, much of it occurred in construction, public utilities, real estate, and banking—sectors that are not subject to competition from imported substitutes made cheap by an overvalued currency and the progressive reduction of import tariffs and restrictions. Investments moved toward these sectors because of the loss of profitability in tradables (manufacturing and agriculture).

BOX 5.1
Loss of Competitiveness and Declining Labor Costs

Unit labor costs fell in the years before the crisis, but the decline was generated by falling wages rather than by rising productivity. Productivity had in fact been down in a number of key sectors. Rising productivity in the tradables sector was the result of labor shedding (World Bank 1997). It is possible to classify the different sectors according to whether they are open to competition or not, and analysis has shown that those most open to competition have lost share in total employment even while experiencing increased productivity (Lim 1997).

The wage-setting system the government introduced in the 1990s did not cause rigidities in the labor market serious enough to threaten competitiveness (Reyes 1996a). Compensation indexes had been declining in the years before the crisis, and ironically, in the run-up to the crisis, Philippine wages in foreign currency terms were high and rising. They were in fact on a par with those of Thailand, which had a per capita income almost twice that of the Philippines, and much higher than wages in Indonesia, which has a similar per capita income (World Bank 1997).

Since overall compensation in real peso terms has been relatively stagnant in the 1990s, the nearly 40 percent real exchange rate appreciation between 1990 and mid-1997 must bear much of the responsibility for the increased remuneration, measured in foreign currency terms.[6] Higher wages may in turn have contributed to the relative stagnation of traditional manufacturing industries (such as garments and footwear) in recent years. This trend is probably premature, since the Philippines has a large pool of surplus labor and a rapidly growing labor force relative to its major competitors.

Productivity also slowed because periodic cycles of boom and bust prevented firms and workers from accumulating the know-how and mastering the technologies that would have allowed them to sell in bigger and more demanding markets and that would have spurred job creation. The economy's tenuous foothold in the demanding export market—the result in no small part of an overvalued currency prior to the crisis—also diminished the demand for product innovation and efficiency enhancement among firms. During the recovery, which is already under way, this initial condition also means that increasing demand in major Asian commodity and component importers such as Japan and the Republic of Korea will have a limited impact on prospects for the Philippines.

Agriculture, which continues to employ the biggest chunk of workers in the Philippines, has also been suffering from the effects of very low investment rates owing to the prolonged uncertainty over land ownership and the land reform program that was started in 1988. The land reform program was supposed to have been completed in 1998 but at that point had been implemented on only 40 percent of target lands. The country's fiscal problems and the fact that the lands to be distributed in the coming years are relatively expensive make it difficult to be optimistic about the resolution of this problem.

When the crisis brought down the overvalued peso, it also inadvertently addressed one of the most important reasons for the economy's weak capacity to absorb labor into high-productivity sectors while maintaining its competitiveness. The financial crisis may therefore have marked an important turning point for the Philippines, even if (on the surface at least) economic policy has exhibited more continuity than change.

Labor Market Flexibility

Labor regulations can cause high unemployment rates. Philippine labor regulations, however, including wage setting and retrenchment, are not in general related to the high precrisis unemployment rates. The possible exceptions are regulations on nonregular work—specifically certain prohibitions pertaining to labor-only contracting that existed before 1997. Further, during the crisis both workers and employers found flexible means of keeping firms from shutting down altogether. In the formal sector these methods resulted in underemployment among workers who had not been retrenched.

WAGE SETTING. Wage fixing in the Philippines has been decentralized since 1990 to allow for more sensitivity to regional economic circumstances. Regional Tripartite Wage and Productivity Boards are responsible for setting wage levels. The law itself allows for many exceptions, although this fact does not mean that setting a minimum wage will not influence the levels at which other wages are set. One study reveals that a significant proportion of entry-level employees in the years after the regionalization of wage setting received the minimum wage (Reyes 1996a). The same study showed that in the period after wage setting was regionalized (1989–95), wage adjustments did not contribute to inflationary pressures. The minimum wage increases granted by the regional wage boards since the crisis have been below inflation rates.

SEPARATION PAY. The authorities have recently strengthened the enforcement of separation pay provisions in the Labor Code.[7] There is no ceiling on the amount of separation pay an employee may receive, but the Labor Code mandates that permanent workers who are laid off must be given the equivalent of one month's salary for every year of service. Little is known about the consequences of this provision on the behavior of managers, but it did not prevent the Philippines from having the highest level of layoffs among older workers of any country hit by the crisis (Lamberte, Guerrero, and Orbeta 1999). In the absence of unemployment insurance in the country, tightening the legal mandate on separation pay was a logical step for the government to take during the crisis.

NONREGULAR WORK. In the years before the crisis, prohibitions on "labor-only contracting" created an institutional disincentive to the emergence of a flexible labor market and negatively affected small and medium-size enterprises (SMEs) and their potential to create jobs. To protect workers' rights, the Labor Code expressly prohibited the contracting out of labor. The regulations also prohibited subcontracting, preventing employment creation through that channel.

In 1997, however, the Labor Department revised these regulations.[8] The new rules declare that labor contracting and subcontracting arrangements are legal as long as the contractor or subcontractor has sufficient capitalization and contractual employees are assured of their rights. The principal employer is jointly liable for any violations of labor standards by the subcontractor. The new rules specify which services can be contracted out or subcontracted:

- Work or services that are needed to meet unusual production volumes and that the regular work force cannot handle;
- Occasional work or services requiring experts or highly technical individuals;
- Services for the promotion of new products, but only for the duration of the promotional period;
- Services not directly related to the main business or operation of the principal, including janitorial and security work, landscaping, messenger work, and tasks not related to manufacturing;
- Merchandising or publicly displaying a manufacturer's products, but not selling them or performing any work that involves issuing a receipt or invoice;

- Specialized work involving unusual or specific skills, tools, or equipment; and
- Temporary services that substitute for those of a regular employee during a period of absence, including during suspensions but not during legal strikes.

The practices of hiring temporary in-house workers through agencies and subcontracting parts of production to outsiders are prevalent in the Philippines despite the legal prohibitions.[9] The use of nonregular workers differs considerably across industry groups, however. They are a significant presence in construction, in some segments of manufacturing, and to some extent in the financing, community services, sales, and utility industries. They are used the least in the mining and quarrying sector.

The Effect of the Crisis on Labor Market Flexibility

Many firms and their workers were able to be flexible in adjusting to the weakness in demand caused by the crisis, although low demand is the main reason for retrenchments and factory closures. The adjustments—in particular reduced hours—ameliorated the impact of the crisis on unemployment, but at the cost of greater underemployment, even in the formal sector. In January 1998 the rate of visible underemployment began to increase over previous years (figure 5.1). The rate had not gone down as of October 1998 as it normally does when agricultural underemployment falls.

By October 1998 the full impact of the crisis was being felt (independent of the effects of the drought on agriculture). Both wage and salary workers adjusted by working shorter hours based on various forms of job rationing (de Dios 1999). Daily work hours were reduced, work weeks cut, and workers put on job rotation or forced vacation leave. Because visible underemployment in the formal sector translated into lower pay, firms were able to achieve a flexible downward adjustment in their wage bill corresponding to the business cycle. Industrial relations did not seem to worsen, however. In fact, indicators of strike activity declined throughout the crisis period.

Involuntary Unemployment and Underemployment during the Crisis

For the poor underemployment is normally a more viable option than outright unemployment. For the whole of 1997, employment continued to rise in all three major industrial sectors—agriculture, manufacturing,

FIGURE 5.1
Visible and Invisible Underemployment Rates, 1996–99
(percent of total employed)

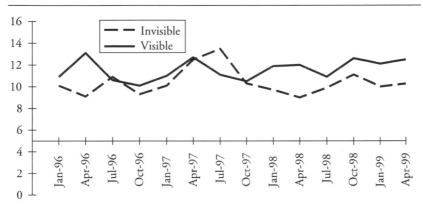

Source: National Statistics Office, Labor Force Surveys.

and services—although at a declining rate. This slowing down in employment was one of the first effects of the crisis that began in July of that year.

Even in 1998, with GDP declining after the second quarter, the economy still managed to generate slightly more employment than in the previous year. But the number of new entrants to the labor force was greater than the number of new jobs created. Labor Force Surveys for 1998 show that aggregate employment began to decline only in April 1998, at the height of the El Niño phenomenon. Employment growth picked up after that point, even though GDP for the rest of 1998 declined at an increasingly rapid pace before posting a modest recovery during the first quarter of 1999 (figure 5.2).

Unemployment and underemployment affected workers most severely in October 1998, more than one year after the crisis struck. The rise in unemployment in April 1998 (to more than 13 percent) was primarily the result of the effects of the El Niño phenomenon and not of the financial crisis. Throughout 1998 the various subsectors of the economy were still creating net positive employment, though not at a pace sufficient to employ all new entrants to the labor force (figure 5.3).

By October 1998 there were 6.7 million underemployed workers in the Philippines, an increase of 894,000 (or 15.4 percent) over the number in the previous year. The October unemployment rate rose to 9.6 percent in 1998, compared with 7.9 percent in 1997, and underemployment was 2.2

FIGURE 5.2
Employment Creation in 1998

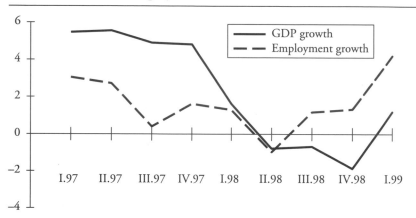

Source: National Statistics Office, Labor Force Surveys.

percent higher than it had been the previous October. Generally unemployment takes a seasonal downturn during this month, reaching its lowest point for the year. In 1998, however, this downturn did not occur—another reason for our contention that October 1998 was the worst month for workers in terms of unemployment. This finding contrasts with the analysis of the Department of Labor and Employment (DOLE), which dates the most severe impact of the crisis to the first quarter of 1998. DOLE relies heavily on administrative reports on closures and retrenchments in formal sector establishments.

UNDEREMPLOYMENT: AN INDICATOR OF DISTRESS AMONG THE POOR. The social impact of the crisis did not necessarily begin to abate once the unemployment rates began to go down, as they did in January and April 1999 (compared with the same periods in 1998). In the Philippines underemployment remains a serious consequence of the crisis. The country's most deprived sectors are found among the ranks of the underemployed. We define underemployment as employment that does not pay enough to meet basic needs, so that workers (often unskilled) must search for additional sources of income. Balisacan (1994) shows that self-employed subsistence farmers and fishers, seasonal workers, and informal sector workers—regarded as among the poorest groups—are also among those who are most frequently underemployed. Results obtained by Alba and Esguerra (1999) also suggest that the average worker "*would prefer to be fully employed* until his unemploy-

FIGURE 5.3

Unemployment and Underemployment Rates, January 1996–April 1999

(in percent)

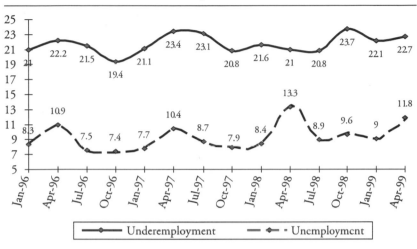

Source: National Statistics Office, Labor Force Surveys.

ment income exceeds 9,000 pesos. Only then does unemployment begin to dominate all the other forms of labor force participation as the worker's preferred mode" (de Dios 1999, p. 21; italics added). Outright unemployment is something that the poor would avoid completely if the choice were up to them. For this group the period of unemployment is thus bound to be short, even if keeping it short means settling for a job that pays poorly. The income deficit that may result is manifested in the search for additional work, even for those who are already employed full time. The phenomenon of full-time workers seeking additional income sources in order to make ends meet is known as *invisible underemployment.*

Underemployed workers are not always poor, although a rise in underemployment often signals difficulty among the very lowest echelons. However, the invisibly underemployed—those working at least 40 hours a week and still in search of more employment—tend to be worse off than the visibly underemployed. The visibly underemployed seek work because they are working part time and would prefer to work more.

Unlike the poor, workers who have had some college education are more likely to be unemployed than underemployed. Alba and Esguerra (1999) conclude that additional education possibly raises a worker's reservation wage and that the job search tends to be longer for individuals with

TABLE 5.3
Unemployment and Underemployment, April 1999

	Number (millions)	Percent of labor force	Increase from previous year's levels
Unemployed	3.95	11.8	−324,000
Underemployed	6.69	22.7	857,000
TOTAL	11.54	34.5	535,000

Source: Labor Force Surveys.

higher reservation wages. Using panel data from the four quarterly Labor Force Surveys for 1998 (5,890 households), Balisacan and Edillion (1999) show that the period of unemployment increases with precrisis income, regardless of the sector in which the individual is employed. This result squares with the findings of Alba and Esguerra (1999) and supports the notion that unemployment of a household head is not a good predictor of distress.

In this regard, although unemployment had already gone down by April 1999, the number of the underemployed still rose by 857,000 during that month over April 1998. This scenario indicates that the effects of the crisis on poorer households were persisting and may have worsened (table 5.3). Half the underemployed were in the agricultural sector, although output and growth and employment creation in the sector had already resumed (figures 5.4 and 5.5).

The Impact of the Crisis on Households

The Ministry of Labor's 1998 Annual Poverty Indicator Survey includes two questions pertaining to the crisis. The first asks whether the household has been affected by price increases, job loss, reduced wages, or El Niño. Table 5.4 shows the percentage of households affected by each event, distributed by income deciles that are based on the 1997 Family Income and Expenditure Survey, which is conducted by the National Statistics Office.

The number of households affected by price increases and El Niño varies across income deciles. Price increases affected poor households more than relatively wealthy ones. Job loss within the country and reduced wages affected middle-income deciles the most, while overseas job loss affected more upper-income households than households from other deciles.

FIGURE 5.4
Employment Creation (January 1997–April 1999)

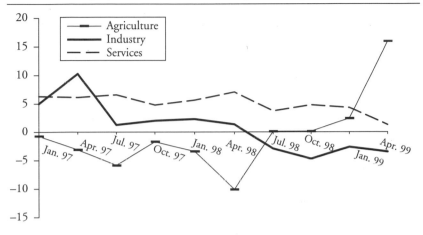

Source: National Statistics Office, Labor Force Surveys.

FIGURE 5.5
Output Growth in the Major Sectors

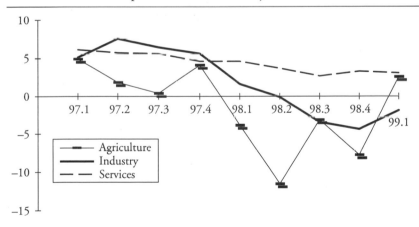

Source: National Statistics Office and Coordination Board.

How Households Responded to the Crisis

Around half of all households (especially among the poorest deciles) responded to the crisis by changing their eating patterns (table 5.5). Households (mostly those in the lower-income deciles) also increased their work-

TABLE 5.4
Impact of the Crisis on Households
(percent)

Income decile[a] (poorest)	Price increases	Job loss in country	Job loss of migrant worker	Reduced wages	El Niño
1	93.5	17.0	3.8	15.4	78.6
2	91.5	16.6	3.2	13.9	72.7
3	90.9	18.3	2.9	15.5	68.3
4	91.7	18.5	4.1	17.1	64.5
5	90.0	21.5	4.5	17.1	61.7
6	90.2	20.5	3.8	16.8	55.0
7	89.7	20.7	4.7	17.1	51.4
8	89.6	19.4	4.8	15.2	45.2
9	88.3	18.3	5.1	14.2	43.5
10	84.7	14.7	4.8	11.2	37.8
Overall	90.0	18.5	4.2	15.3	57.9

a. The sample consisted of 2,315 households per decile, or 23,150 households. These households represent the overlap between the sampling frame of the 1998 Annual Poverty Indicator Survey and the 1997 Family Income and Expenditure Survey.

Source: 1997 Family Income and Expenditure Survey, National Statistics Office.

ing hours and took their children out of school. Administrative reports and labor force surveys show that high school students were the most likely to be removed from school. The proportion of households receiving assistance from friends and relatives was consistently higher than the proportion of households receiving assistance from government agencies. More poor households than middle- and upper-income households depended on government assistance, but households in all the income deciles (including the wealthiest) received assistance from relatives and friends.

Income Support, Job Maintenance and Creation, and Employment Services

The Philippine government responded to the crisis with a number of policies aimed at maintaining workers' income and jobs, creating new jobs, and easing the job search. Specifically, it provided emergency loans, subsidized rice, and established public works programs for displaced workers.

TABLE 5.5
Households' Response to the Crisis
(percent)

Income decile (1997 FIES) (poorest)	Response					
	Changed eating patterns	Took children out of school	Migrated to city or other countries	Received assistance from friends/ relatives	Received assistance from government	Increased working hours
1	56.7	12.4	7.8	16.5	10.7	37.5
2	52.3	9.3	5.4	17.1	8.8	36.8
3	50.7	7.3	5.4	16.3	8.4	33.6
4	51.0	8.7	5.2	17.0	6.8	33.1
5	47.8	7.1	4.5	17.2	5.9	29.4
6	48.3	5.6	3.8	16.4	5.7	27.0
7	47.0	5.0	3.7	15.0	4.5	26.1
8	44.1	3.5	3.4	12.5	2.9	22.3
9	41.4	3.2	3.1	13.8	3.9	23.1
10	33.3	1.2	3.5	12.0	2.6	18.2
Total	47.5	6.4	4.6	15.4	6.1	28.9

Source: Panel data constructed from the overlap between the 1997 Family Income and Expenditures Survey and the 1998 Annual Poverty Indicator Survey (21,602 households). See Balisacan and Edillion (1999).

The Emergency Loan Facility for Displaced Workers

The Philippines has no unemployment insurance system. However, during the crisis, the Employees Compensation Commission initiated the Emergency Loans Program. The program supported the Emergency Loan Facility for Displaced Workers in the amount of 500 million pesos and the Emergency Loan Facility for Displaced Sugar Workers in the amount of 100 million pesos. Ordinary workers who did not usually have access to loans from the banking sector were able to use emergency loans for consumption smoothing.

The program started on March 25, 1998, under the Social Security System. From March 1998 up to May 1999, a total of 433.4 million pesos in loans was released from the displaced workers' fund to 40,491 persons, and 36.6 million pesos in loans was released to 3,481 displaced sugar workers. Displaced workers were able to apply for loans of twice their monthly salaries (up to the 12,500 pesos maximum) at the subsidized interest rate of 6 percent per year. The loans were payable within two years, with a one-year grace period. Workers wishing to borrow from the emergency loan program must have been up to date in their payments on any other loans before their separation from their job.

Similar funds had been set up for workers enrolled in the Social Security System who were affected by the eruption of Mount Pinatubo in Central Luzon and the electricity shortages of 1991–92. Thus the loan funds were a fairly routine institutional response to a crisis situation. Such schemes are not, however, a replacement for a full-fledged unemployment insurance system for the private sector that responds to the needs of workers displaced as a result of the normal dynamics of a highly open market economy.

As of January 2000 the Social Security System does not even have the flexibility to allow unemployed workers to benefit from past contributions. Such a mechanism would allow workers to borrow from their own future retirement benefits, which they would replenish after finding employment. Under the system's rules, workers who lose their jobs also temporarily lose their access to loans from their future retirement benefits. Because employers must approve loans that use salaries as guarantees, workers who lost their jobs as a result of the financial crisis had no other recourse but the emergency loan facility.

Because the DOLE and Emergency Loans Program databases are not linked, identifying the characteristics of displaced workers who took out loans is difficult. What is immediately apparent, however, is that at least 60 percent of those who did are from Manila and nearby provinces. This percentage roughly corresponds to the regional distribution of workers in formal establishments who were affected by temporary and permanent layoffs, job rotation, and other adjustment measures. The loan facilities were not designed to respond to the record unemployment and underemployment in the agricultural sector. Thus the profile of beneficiaries corresponds to those retrenched from formal sector establishments because these workers are monitored by the agencies of the Labor Department. Also, for a worker to gain access to a loan, the DOLE must certify that the potential borrower is an employee of a firm listed in the department's roster of formal establishments that are encountering difficulties. The pattern of formal establishment difficulties does not correspond to the general pattern of distress, however. The regional and sectoral distribution of unemployment and underemployment as reflected in the Labor Force Surveys, rather than the administrative reports, is the more reliable basis for assessing social distress.

We do not know if contractual workers have been able to access these benefits. Even if some of these workers are enrolled in the Social Security

System, the frequency with which informal workers experience unemployment makes it unlikely that their contributions to the system would be current. In 1998 some 19.25 million of the 32 million workers in the labor force were registered with either the regular Social Security System or the system for government employees. Workers' contributions to the system are automatically deducted from their pay, and employers are supposed to remit these payments together with the employer contribution. Many employers fail to do so, however. The compliance rate among employers in 1993 was estimated to be anywhere from 35 to 55 percent (World Bank 1995a). Self-employed workers and workers in family-based enterprises are not usually enrolled.

Subsidized Rice

The National Food Authority (NFA) administers a subsidy scheme that allows it to purchase unmilled rice (*palay*) at a high price and sell milled rice at a low price. For the last six years, the NFA has been able not only to procure at least 3 percent of the country's total palay production but also to store, process, and even distribute the rice. The government provides the NFA with a direct subsidy of roughly 1 billion pesos annually. But the major portion of the NFA's budget actually comes from domestic bank credits guaranteed by the government.

The NFA's subsidy scheme is basically a general food subsidy program. Around 90 percent of its price support funds go to rice rather than palay, so the scheme fails as a subsidy program for producers. There are three reasons for this failure:

- *The NFA is unable to influence farm-gate prices.* The agency's paddy procurement support prices for 1995–98 were below actual palay prices. The support price was fixed at 8 pesos per kilo in 1996, while farm-gate prices averaged 8.20 pesos per kilo until 1997.
- *Buying levels have been low and declining.* From 1975 to 1996 the NFA procured a yearly average of just 5 percent of total palay production. It was able to exceed its target procurement level only in 1990.
- *There have been persistent delays in procurement.* The NFA usually buys one or two months after the peak season, so only relatively wealthy farmers and traders—those with storage capabilities or access to postharvest facilities—benefit from the agency's program.[10]

As a food subsidy program, the NFA's untargeted scheme is also deficient. Balisacan (1994) shows that a general food price subsidy such as the one commonly employed by the NFA in its poverty alleviation efforts is not cost-effective. The price subsidy for rice exhibits substantial leakage of benefits to the nonpoor, who account for about one-half of total rice consumption. Arguably the NFA's operations need to be rationalized, and the agency itself has recently moved in the direction of improving the targeting of the rice subsidy program.

Joseph Estrada's government has implemented a food safety net program specifically for the poor. This new program represents a shift from general subsidies that allow anyone to buy discounted NFA rice to subsidies targeting families living below the poverty line. In collaboration with the Department of Social Welfare and Development (DSWD) and the Department of the Interior and Local Government, the NFA in 1999 piloted targeted rice subsidy programs in 12 municipalities in the provinces of Antique, Iloilo, Sorsogon, and Surigao. If the program moves beyond the pilot stage, it will require a subsidy larger than the 1.19 billion pesos the NFA received in 1999. Assuming no leakages and no additional administrative costs, the program would require a budget of around 5 billion pesos (calculated using a 5 pesos subsidy, multiplying it by a per capita consumption of 100 kilos, and multiplying the result by around 10 million people living below the poverty line).[11]

The NFA maintains a number of programs tailored specifically to the poor, including the Enhanced Retail Access for the Poor (ERAP) program. This program sells cheap basic commodities such as canned goods, cooking oil, milk, noodles, rice, sardines, and sugar. By the middle of 1999, 2,784 privately owned stores and 434 market stalls had been set up under the program. ERAP also fielded 384 rolling stores for those in remote and depressed areas.

The Philippine government is in no position to implement a general rice subsidy, and in fact one is not needed. The key to increasing the impact of the NFA's operations is effective targeting of its interventions. Administrative costs for targeting, however, can be anywhere from 10 to 30 percent of delivery costs. The most reasonable starting point would be to increase the volume of the NFA's operations in the poorest provinces. Administratively undemanding schemes such as the provision of low-quality rice may also be needed to reduce leakages to the nonpoor. Finely tuned targeting mechanisms may be considered after these adjustments have been introduced.

While rural households are net buyers of rice, this fact should not prevent the government from realizing that government interventions in the rice price market will negatively affect farming households or from identifying areas that will suffer. For this reason the government may want to consider shifting to food stamp programs that deliver the subsidy to households as a direct income support. Food stamp programs can also reduce the significant leakages that tend to occur when subsidies are implemented in urban areas with high numbers of displaced workers.

Direct Job Creation

When the crisis unfolded, the Philippines had no sizable public employment programs that could respond appropriately to large-scale economic shocks. Past government infrastructure programs—notably the Community Employment Development Program (CEDP) during the administration of Corazon Aquino and *Kabuhayan 2000* under the administration of Fidel Ramos—had focused on rural poverty. Kabuhayan 2000 was, however, incoherent under the Ramos administration. Subbarao, Ahmed, and Teklu (1996) observe that the program never managed to ensure employment among the poorest groups. In fact, the bulk of the infrastructure program benefited nonpoor areas. Evidence shows that of the two programs, the CEDP was the more successful in terms of reaching poor households in poor regions (Quibria 1996).

The CEDP program was intended to hasten the economy's recovery from the deep recession of the mid-1980s. The program aimed to create employment opportunities for an estimated 1.2 million workers by the end of 1988. The emphasis was on small-scale infrastructure projects such as small, often dirt roads, communal irrigation systems, and school buildings. These projects accounted for nearly 70 percent of the total allocation of 9.1 billion pesos, roughly 90 percent of the approximately 53,000 of the projects supported by the program, and close to 80 percent of the total employment target. Nongovernmental organizations (NGOs) were active in the delivery of these programs. The CEDP, however, often had to delay project implementation—primarily because of slow funding and disbursement procedures—and political pressures tended to distort priorities in project selection. Cases of graft and corruption during project implementation were also reported (Quibria 1996).

The CEDP, however, achieved results that were favorable compared with the outcomes of previous programs. A 1988 National Economic Development Authority survey covering 11,086 workers showed that a large portion (54 percent) of the workers hired under the program were unemployed before the CEDP. In addition 54 percent also had monthly incomes below the minimum food consumption threshold, 82 percent had monthly incomes below the poverty threshold, and 86 percent had incomes below the minimum wage. The program also aimed to utilize workers from the project areas. In this respect the CEDP was again successful, because 78 percent of the workers did come from the project areas. The CEDP was also exceptional among public infrastructure programs in its efforts to evaluate outcomes, and its evaluations showed similar results in almost all the regions.

PROBLEMS WITH PUBLIC WORKS PROJECTS. A major problem in employment-creating infrastructure programs in the country (including past food-for-work programs) is the government's policy of compensating beneficiaries with at least the minimum wage. The experience of other countries has shown that a compensation level lower than the prevailing market wage is an important feature of public works schemes, because low wages discourage the nonpoor from participating and preempting slots intended for distressed workers. The CEDP was successful under the Aquino administration despite this constraint.

The Estrada administration has yet to formulate its own public works strategy. The present pattern of infrastructure provision remains largely an inheritance from the Ramos administration, so that the jobs created in the course of infrastructure provision are largely incidental. Even programs that trickle down to poor agricultural areas, such as the construction of farm-to-market roads, are delayed by complications in budgetary release processes. The delays significantly reduce the ability of the already limited rural infrastructure programs to provide temporary employment from March to April, the period of highest unemployment and underemployment in the agricultural sector. The "thinness" of rural industrialization in the Philippines means that off-farm employment opportunities are highly covariant with peak farming and harvesting seasons. In other words, the seasonal scarcity of income opportunities on farms is not offset by off-farm income opportunities.

Under the new Estrada administration, the only public works initiative as of this writing has been the formulation of a task force. An executive order signed in March 1999 stipulates that the Department of Public Works and Highways (DPWH) and the DOLE will head an interagency task force designed to formulate and recommend steps to increase the labor content of the government's infrastructure programs.[12]

Despite official intentions to enhance the ability of infrastructure programs to employ labor, no significant public works programs are available to workers on demand. The initiative that comes closest to an employment-creation program designed to reduce the risk of falling into poverty because of seasonal joblessness is the DOLE's 14 million pesos pilot Rural Works Program (originally the Emergency Employment Program). This program offers jobs in school repair and maintenance projects; drainage and waterworks systems; health and day care centers; roads, bridges, and irrigation networks; and reforestation, cleanliness, and beautification programs. Workers are paid the minimum wage. The DOLE pays 60 percent of the workers' wages, and local government units and NGOs shoulder the rest of the burden. The government also sponsors a food-for-work program that is spread over 13 cities and has an annual budget of 15 million pesos. The program was started in 1995 but is already in the process of winding down its operations.

LABOR-BASED TECHNIQUES. The promotion of labor-based techniques is in many ways an appropriate response to the problem of unemployment and underemployment in rural areas that have suffered from the lingering effects of the Asian financial crisis and the El Niño and La Niña weather disturbances. Importantly, the labor-based public works approach would not require new expenditures.

This approach is of course not entirely new. The DPWH itself has a "labor-based advisory and training team." In 1994 the DPWH stated that 14 percent of infrastructure programs for that year under Kabuhayan 2000 would use labor-based equipment-supported methods and began providing training in using this approach. These projects, amounting to 1.9 billion pesos, included the construction and maintenance of secondary roads, water supply projects, and flood control structures. Between 1987 and 1993, the Second Rural Roads Improvement Project of the DPWH (funded in part by the World Bank) had a labor-based component that received technical assistance from the International Labour Organization (ILO). This component produced 250 kilometers of small roads between 1987 and 1993 and generated around 1 million person-days of employment in 1988–93. The wage rate adopted for the project was 25–30 percent above the minimum wage. The project was not seasonally targeted, so it may have competed with agricultural activities.

Such projects face a number of roadblocks. The first is the perennial delay and uncertainty of fund releases from the Department of Budget and Management. These delays prevent agencies oriented toward rural areas, like the Department of Agrarian Reform (DAR), from initiating all of their infrastructure projects on time during the hot first half of the year. If and when the DAR learns the funds are available, it is usually too close to the planting season (which is ushered in by the rains) to initiate projects. Labor becomes scarce, and the race against the oncoming rains makes the choice of mechanized methods that require the least amount of labor a very practical one. The second issue is the problem of specifying and introducing incentives and regulations that will induce private contractors (for example, in low-cost housing programs) to employ more labor. Significant trade-offs may exist between efficiency and job creation that need to be studied, especially for categories of public works like housing. Existing guidelines to encourage labor-based production have not been effective because they have not addressed these difficulties.

Reforms that succeed in reducing the uncertainty concerning the availability of funds and the timing of budget releases will go a long way toward putting rural infrastructure programs in a better position to respond to the seasonal employment needs of the rural poor (see, for instance, World Bank 1995b). Such reforms may also provide the agencies with greater scope for employing labor-based technologies, even if these are not always as efficient or as fast as technologies that require more equipment support.

There are other pressing issues—for instance, the skewed distributions of infrastructure projects toward areas that do not necessarily have an urgent need for them. The Kabuhayan 2000 experience indicates that assessments of the depth of poverty in different parts of the country do not seem to play a defining role in legislative and executive decisions to allocate infrastructure across and within regions. This deficiency in the public investment program persists. For instance, the proposed national budget for the year 2000 allocates one-half of the 2.5 billion pesos School Building Program of the Department of Education, Culture, and Sports (DECS) and the DPWH on the basis of student populations in congressional districts rather than on the basis of assessed shortages of facilities. A public works act that allots 30 million pesos in infrastructure funds to every congressional district, even those that are highly urbanized, has been receiving wide support in the Congress. The solution to the problems of public works schemes, however, may have to go beyond training more engineers in LB-ES methods. It may need to include a change in the political incentives that underpin the system of intergovernmental transfers and lead to the irrational allocation of infrastructure funds.

Livelihood Programs

The government has been able to generate employment indirectly through various livelihood and income-generating programs and projects under the DAR, DSWD, Department of Trade and Industry (DTI), and the Labor Department. Incomplete reports submitted by these agencies show that in 1997 a total of 89,780 individuals benefited from the government's various livelihood and income-generating programs.

These livelihood programs, however, have reflected a supply-led credit policy. Consequently they have high default rates and excessive administrative costs. They have also failed to identify and serve the poor and are not sustainable, in part because of the way the loans are structured. The loans are from government agencies and not financial institutions, so borrowers have tended to see them as one-time grant opportunities, and repayment has been low. One inventory showed that only 13 out of 111 programs in existence in 1995 were directed to the ultra-poor (table 5.6).

The DSWD is the government agency that has had the most success providing credit for the poor through its Self-Employment Assistance (SEA) program, a livelihood scheme aimed at developing the capacity of the poorest segments of society for self-reliance and improving their socioeconomic status. The program provides no-interest, collateral-free loans payable in two years, social development assistance, capital skills development assistance, and legal administrative support. Its various livelihood projects benefited some 31,043 persons in 1997. The SEA organizes and supports *kaunlaran* associations, small local groups designed to provide community-based, self-

TABLE 5.6
Government Livelihood Programs

| | Borrowers targeted | | | | |
	Agricultural credit	*Ultrapoor*	*Salaried and self-employed*	*Small and medium-scale enterprises*	*Total*
Number of programs	39	13	21	38	111
Number of implementing agencies	19	4	12	9	—
Estimated funds available (billions of pesos)	>P11.06	—	>P3.2	>P16.7	>P30.9
Annual interest rate (percent)	6–14	0–6 to market rate	3–18	7–24	—

— not available.
Source: Ledgerwood (1995).

managed credit facilities and access to community social services. The associations have around 25 members each and receive technical assistance and seed capital for microenterprises that averages 150,000 pesos (at 4,000–5,000 pesos per member). Starting with a revolving fund of 65 million pesos in 1993, the SEA Project has provided technical and capital assistance to 3,492 successful associations all over the country and 86,890 member families that are engaged in various microenterprises, for a total of 337 million pesos. In 1997 alone, the DSWD extended seed capital of 73.7 million pesos to 633 associations with 16,542 member families.

DOLE runs a small self-employment scheme, PRESEED, in rural areas. PRESEED, which delivers a package of interlinked services for new entrepreneurs, has been subjected to better-than-average monitoring. The program is directed at landless rural workers who want to learn new entrepreneurial skills and are capable of providing equity of at least 10 percent of the total project cost. Participants qualify only if their incomes fall below the poverty threshold. PRESEED released a total of 117 billion pesos from 1989 to June 1996, funding a total of 11,869 projects and benefiting 27,738 workers. In 1993–94, however, only 7.7 percent of the beneficiaries had been unemployed prior to the program. Some 60 percent had existing livelihood projects or businesses even before they applied for the loans, 19 percent were employed in various firms and agencies, and others were working on personal or family endeavors—an indication that PRESEED could have tapped the wrong target beneficiaries.

Support for Small and Medium-Size Enterprises

Assessments of the situation before the crisis estimate that deregulating the financial sector made it much easier for SMEs to gain access to formal credit markets (see, for instance, Llanto and Sanches 1997). According to Llanto and Sanches, the 10 new foreign banks granted licenses to operate since 1995 cultivated a client base among SMEs. The study says that this development was aided by the abolition of the antiusury law, which prescribed limits on the interest rate lenders can charge. The law had the perverse effect of making it difficult for lenders to recoup the higher transactions costs that accompanied lending to small borrowers. With deregulation, even the progressively rising mandatory lending requirements on commercial banks for SMEs (under the country's Magna Carta for SMEs) were exceeded.[13]

These changes did not mean that any eligible SME that wanted to take out a loan could do so, and SMEs continued to be rationed out of the credit market. Increased access to credit markets was just the start of a process that was bound to take a long time, even if there were no reversals (World Bank 1998). In spite of the progress that had been made, SMEs lost access to credit during the crisis, once again highlighting the problem they have obtaining adequate, affordable credit. The Philippine experience suggests some positive lessons.

Using a firm-level survey of 300 firms as well as a control group, the World Bank (1998) showed that between 1985 and 1995, firms receiving on-lent credit from a project in support of SMEs generated more jobs more quickly than similar firms without such credit. Beneficiary firms in the sample created 4,821 new jobs over a decade, or 27 new jobs per firm, while nonbeneficiaries lost 1,400 jobs, resulting in an average of 10 fewer jobs per firm. Moreover the employment generated by beneficiary firms grew more than twice as fast as the Philippine labor force over this period (5 percent annually, compared with the economywide rate of 2.4 percent). The on-lending activities to SMEs were so successful that they can be seen as adding, within limits, to the social safety net for workers. Such activities can, for instance, help address high urban unemployment rates (World Bank 1998).

The Small Business Guarantee Fund

The lesson from the World Bank evaluation cited above did not include the claim that guarantees were effective in preserving and creating jobs. Guarantees were rarely used in the World Bank on-lending programs in the Philippines, because in cases of default, commercial banks that lacked sufficient collateral for their loans were required to go through a long and uncertain bureaucratic process before they could utilize the World Bank guarantee. Actual payments on claims were made only after two to seven years.

The Small Business Guarantee Fund is an offshoot of the Magna Carta for SMEs. It aims to increase the flow of funds from formal lending institutions to SMEs, especially those without collateral. The fund was originally expected to provide large-scale guarantees for SMEs by encouraging financial institutions to lend to these enterprises. It offers a guarantee of up to a maximum of 90 percent on loans to qualified entrepreneurs. The guarantee works primarily as a collateral substitute or supplement. But since its inception in 1993, the fund has had an average volume of guaranteed loans of only around 400 million pesos. Because the Philippines has many credit and guarantee facilities for SMEs, and efforts to rationalize these programs are ongoing, guarantee programs such as the fund may not be the most appropriate source of support for these enterprises.

Wage Subsidies

In some countries wage subsidies have been used to induce firms to train and employ workers who would not otherwise be employed. In Canada for instance, wage subsidies coupled with reimbursements on training costs have been used to encourage firms to create slots for the long-term unemployed. In the Philippines, the government provides wage subsidies through the Special Program for the Employment of Students and the Work Appreciation Program.

The program for students helps children of the long-term unemployed pursue their education by providing employment during summers and Christmas vacations. The program places students in public and private establishments, with the employer paying 60 percent of the prevailing minimum wage and the DOLE footing the other 40 percent in the form of vouchers. The DOLE spent 174 million pesos on this project in 1997, benefiting a total of 86,018 of the 113,939 students registered with the DOLE regional offices and the Public Employment Service. In 1998 the program received 110.4 million pesos and placed a total of 96,557 beneficiaries out of the 118,265 registered. Since the onset of the Asian crisis, children have been receiving priority over displaced workers. This program therefore becomes something of a direct transfer scheme for displaced workers. It does not just displace costs that the private sector might have been willing to incur on its own. Rather, it results in the employment of young people who may not be the most qualified workers that firms could have recruited.

The Work Appreciation Program aims to develop a respect for work and ethics in young people by exposing them to actual work situations. The program teaches them work procedures, the use of machines and tools, and other practical knowledge relevant to specific occupations. This program facilitated the placement of 14,126 youths in different private establishments nationwide in 1998.

Passive Public Labor Market Services[14]

The Philippines has a number of passive labor market programs in place. They include the Public Employment Service and an automated system that provides applicants with information on jobs. These services are aimed at shortening the job search for the unemployed by providing timely labor market information.

PUBLIC EMPLOYMENT SERVICE. In establishing a Public Employment Service Office in every province, key city, and highly urbanized municipality, the government has several goals. It aims to facilitate the exchange of labor market information between job seekers and employers, establish a national manpower skill registry, and serve as a referral and information center for employment placement. The offices also serve as clearinghouses for the various employment promotion programs and services offered by both government and private agencies.

To date, there are 1,825 offices situated in local government agencies, NGOs, and schools nationwide. From 1993 to the first quarter of 1999, a total of 1,685,282 job applicants—or about 62 percent of the 2,722,858 who registered—were placed or otherwise assisted. In 1998 the nationwide network of offices registered a total of 418,617 job applicants; referred 347,606 applicants for wage employment, self-employment, and training; provided employment counseling to 209,641; and tested 23,143. Further linking these offices is a priority on the DOLE's legislative agenda. House Bill 7127, otherwise known as the Public Employment Service Office Act of 1999, is intended to be the enabling law that will ensure a national facilitation service network in every province and key city in the Philippines.[15]

PHILIPPINE JOB EXCHANGE NETWORK (PHIL-JOBNET). The Phil-Jobnet, launched in November 1998, is an automated job and applicant matching system that aims to facilitate job seekers' search for work and employers' search for human resources. The Phil-Jobnet maintains information on existing vacancies and the corresponding qualifications required by employers and can be accessed via the Internet. Applicants can open a file containing information such as their age, educational attainment, skills, and other qualifications. Workstations accessible to the public have been installed in 43 DOLE regional offices and local government units nationwide.

JOB AND LIVELIHOOD FAIRS. Job and livelihood fairs allow job seekers, employers, and overseas recruitment agencies to meet in one venue on a specific date in order to reduce cost, time, and effort, particularly for applicants. Applicants can ask about positions and receive an on-the-spot interview and are sometimes hired immediately. Government agencies are also invited to provide information on self-employment and training assistance. In 1998 some 246 job and livelihood fairs drew 47,828 registered job applicants, and 6,442 were hired. In the first quarter of 1999, 67 job fairs were conducted, drawing 13,666 registered applicants and generating 2,694 placements.

ASSISTANCE FOR DISPLACED OVERSEAS WORKERS. The Placement Assistance Program provides employment referral services to returning workers. The program matches workers' skills and qualifications with the requirements of local employers to facilitate access to employment for this group.

Private Labor Market Service Initiatives

The private sector offers services for job seekers and employers. Traditional private employment agencies recruit for both domestic and overseas positions. In some cases the private sector is trying out innovative approaches. One such approach is a job-matching radio program that provides information on openings at local firms.

MATCHING JOBS ON THE AIR. An excellent example of a private sector initiative in employment facilitation is a public service program offered by 702 DZAS, a Far East Broadcasting Company AM radio station. Since 1986 the program, *Action Line*, has aired job openings, profiled job seekers, and referred workers to positions that suit their qualifications. The radio sponsor tied up with DOLE to provide a format for airing important public announcements and discussions on labor issues on a regular basis. The program, considered a first in the history of Philippine radio broadcasting, is featured twice each weekday and receives an average of 30 calls daily from job seekers and companies in need of personnel.

RECRUITMENT AGENCIES. Recruitment agencies provide employment facilitation services for local and overseas workers for a fee (the fee is charged to the job seeker or employer or is shared by both). The network of agencies and services is an important link between companies and job seekers and reports a significant number of placements. In 1998 alone local agencies recruited about 60,345 job seekers, of which 39,895 were placed. In the first quarter of 1999, these agencies placed 11,397 of 13,927 job seekers. The government monitors and regulates the operations of these agencies. In 1998 it issued 77 licenses to newly established local recruitment agencies and renewed 101 licenses for existing agencies. In the first quarter of 1999, 33 new licenses were issued and 11 were renewed.

Recruitment agencies for overseas employment numbered about 1,053 as of May 1999. Of these 705 specialize in land-based employment and 348 in sea-based jobs. While no system for monitoring placements made by these agencies is in place, their contribution is clearly significant. The scope of their services can be deduced from the large number of workers who leave for overseas employment via formal or authorized channels.

Labor Department Services during the Crisis[16]

The labor market services available in the Philippines during the Asian financial crisis may be likened to a half-finished house that suddenly had to be used for shelter from a storm. In general terms, the available government labor market services (provided by the DOLE) sought to prevent job losses wherever possible and to make an effective and efficient match between workers and companies seeking them—that is, to help job seekers find employment in the shortest possible time and at the least possible cost. One reason for the temporary nature of the DOLE's safety net programs is that the department has no direct mandate to provide social protection services. Within its limits, however, the DOLE has provided a number of useful labor market services that formed an important, if not entirely effective, safety net for some displaced workers.

The most significant set of policies is directed at workers displaced either as a result of the economic crisis or because of adjustments to the opening up of the economy via trade liberalization. These measures make up a package of assistance that reaches mainly workers in formal sector establishments.[17] Local labor offices try to identify firms in distress early on, before labor underutilization, permanent or temporary layoffs, or a permanent closure of the whole establishment. In certain instances the field offices are able to help prevent firm closures and layoffs by assisting in negotiations (social accords) that can be crucial in transforming potential solvency problems into more manageable temporary liquidity problems. In most instances these negotiations reduce labor costs through techniques such as job rotation and shortened work weeks, relieving firms of the burden of having to provide full payment for partially employed or underutilized labor. Since the early 1990s the DOLE has had specific guidelines that make these flexible responses to depressed market demand not only possible but also in compliance with the country's labor laws.

The DOLE is the third party in conflicts that could result in mutually disadvantageous outcomes for both the other parties. The department provides information about possible modes of adjustment that the two parties acting by themselves may not have considered and, by assuring labor that proposals are fair, increases the likelihood that the agreement will be mutually beneficial. And the DOLE acts as a witness to agreements that might not be self-enforcing in the absence of a third party.

In the event that layoffs become inevitable, the DOLE provides workers with four essential services:

- It ensures that workers get the benefits due them by law.
- It sees that workers receive counseling and information about job prospects.

- It provides information on ways to help smooth consumption, helping workers gain access to emergency loans and income-augmenting possibilities for children who need to continue schooling.
- It helps workers gain access to livelihood possibilities such as temporary employment through public works programs, self-employment through livelihood programs, and retraining.

PROBLEMS WITH THE DELIVERY OF LABOR MARKET SERVICES. In implementing its social protection and active labor market policies, the DOLE inadvertently concentrates mainly on workers in large formal sector establishments. Many of these workers are among the most highly skilled segment of the labor force and are not usually the poorest workers. Further, they are usually among the most capable of finding new employment. The DOLE is not intentionally biased, but because the department's original mandate centers on industrial relations and not on employment or social protection, the focus on formal sector establishments was inevitable. Agriculture, for instance, is not within its purview. It also works mostly with large firms that have the capacity to comply with labor standards and voluntary reporting requirements. Smaller firms have little incentive to seek the DOLE's assistance, not only because they lack the capability to comply with labor standards (such as minimum wages), but also because they are unlikely to be able to offer laid-off workers the requisite separation pay.

For these reasons displaced workers from smaller firms are not usually in the DOLE's roster of establishments and thus have limited access to DOLE's programs. The same is true for agricultural workers. Aside from assistance for sugar workers, the DOLE has only small livelihood programs and rural works programs to offer. These programs are too limited to make a significant impact in times of large shocks, and no other agency has programs for agricultural workers. The country's existing agricultural programs concentrate mainly on perennial poverty and low productivity, but not transient poverty. Covariant shocks—such as those caused by the El Niño weather phenomenon and the recent financial crisis—require responses that differ systematically from the present programs for rural areas.

The DOLE's programs for displaced workers exclude virtually no one, however, because the eligibility criteria are so general. The department can say that its services are available to everyone, not just to workers affected by economic crises. Job seekers in general may avail themselves of job fairs, job-matching services, and some degree of job counseling; skills acquisition and upgrading (for formal sector workers); employment and livelihood assistance (for informal sector workers, including assistance to help them enter formal sector employment); services for returning or displaced overseas contract workers; and assistance to improve employability (for new entrants to the labor force), including some assistance in making the transition from school to work. Yet because the most significant services are delivered on site to workers in formal sector establishments, an informal screening mechanism is in fact operative.

LABOR MARKET INFORMATION AND ITS EFFECT ON SERVICES. The DOLE's programs do not make sufficient use of the labor market information that already exists. The Family Income and Expenditures Survey, the Quarterly Labor Force Surveys, and the Annual Poverty Indicator Survey can be very useful instruments in rationalizing the allocation of funds within the DOLE and other agencies with active labor market policies. The DOLE's most significant programs rely mainly on administrative reports prepared by the Regional Layoffs Monitoring System, which tend to overrepresent large formal sector establishments. At present DOLE officials believe that these field reports provide the best statistics of the impact of the crisis on employment. The department disputes this study's claim, for instance, that the impact of the crisis on unemployment was most marked in October 1998. This judgment is based on administrative reports from the monitoring system showing that the lowest number of firm closures for 1998 occurred during the fourth quarter. The administrative reports suggest that the worst effects of the crisis were evident sometime in the first quarter of 1998. After October 1998 no major assessments of the impact took place because of the DOLE's confidence in the regional monitoring system. It felt that the quarterly Labor Force Surveys were not timely enough and did not have the right focus for the DOLE's information needs.[18]

If the DOLE begins paying attention to the most complete sources of labor market information, the department will begin to see that its programs are inadequate relative to the magnitude of the problem and that they usually fail to address the needs of the most distressed workers. This realization should call attention to the need to redesign and scale up programs such as the public works schemes. According to the Institute for Labor Studies, "if given more funds," the DOLE "would want to expand the Phil-Job Net and the rural public works component of the adjustment program."[19]

Training and Vocational Education Programs

Until the establishment of the Technical Education and Skills Development Authority (TESDA) in 1994, responsibility for vocational and technical training was divided among several agencies. This subsector overlaps with basic and higher education, as technical and vocational education programs are conducted at both the secondary and postsecondary levels. In 1994 the education department was split into three departments—the DECS, which is in charge of primary and secondary education; the Commission on Higher Education (CHED), which is in charge of tertiary and higher education; and TESDA. At that time 207 high schools were transferred to TESDA, of which 163 were subsequently transferred back to the formal high school authority because they did not meet the criteria for vocational and technical high schools.

The problem of the overlap of technical and tertiary education has existed for many years. CHED-supervised institutions and state universities and colleges account for an estimated half of the spending on the technical and vocational subsector (TESDA 1999). But TESDA does not oversee and regulate these institutions; rather, they are supervised by the CHED, which is not particularly qualified to do so (figure 5.6).

TESDA, which is primarily a regulatory agency, does not have a mandate to run training centers, much less schools, on a day-to-day basis (box 5.2). The Director General believes that it is possible to improve the situation of the CHED-supervised institutions without necessarily ceding them to TESDA by placing only those programs that offer technical,

FIGURE 5.6
Technical and Vocational Education in the Philippines

	PRIVATE		PUBLIC
Enrollment	♦ ♦ ♦ ♦ ♦ ♦ ♦ ♦ 80 percent		♦ ♦ 20 percent
Type	Nonformal[a]	Formal[b]	Formal
Funding sources	🏛 🏛 Almost exclusive private (commercial establishments, NGOs, nonprofit organizations, and religious groups), mainly through tuition fees and endowment income. 👤 Minor exceptions, such as Private Education Student Financial Assistance, which provides public scholarships that benefit 3 percent of students enrolled in private schools.		🏛 Government subsidies to public schools (high schools and regional and provincial training centers) from TESDA's regular annual budget, with contributions (often in kind) from some local governments. 🏛 Enrollment charges and subsidies for programs under the purview of state colleges and universities, which have their own charters and annual budgets.

[a] Organized programs that are part of the school system.
[b] Organized classes outside the school system.

BOX 5.2
TESDA's Responsibilities

Mandated by law (largely regulatory and facilitative)	Inherited tasks (provided directly by TESDA)
1. Overall regulation and direction of the technical and vocational education system • School-based training • Center-based training • Enterprise-based training 2. Regulatory functions • Development of industry-based standards and certification • Registration and accreditation of training establishments • Training of trainers • Research on the subsector • Promulgation of information about supply and demand for midlevel skills and advocacy for clientele, including enterprises	1. Direct operation of over 50 high schools with postsecondary technical enrollment 2. Direct operation of network of 59 regional and provincial training centers 3. In the future: regulation and operation of technical programs in state colleges and universities that are at present formally under the Commission on Higher Education

vocational, and middle-level skills under the agency's supervision. Given the fact that state universities and colleges have their own charters and are therefore autonomous, the agency is unlikely to be able to extend its authority further. Gaining responsibility for these programs is one of the most urgent reforms on TESDA's advocacy agenda. Another key initiative already listed in the National Technical Education and Skills Development Plan would set up a system for gathering data so that schools and TESDA itself could assess the effectiveness of training.

In 1999 TESDA administered only 2 percent of the education sector's spending. Even when state universities and colleges are included, the technical and vocational subsector in the Philippines is much smaller and less mature than it is in other developing countries in Asia (Maglen and Manasan 1996). TESDA's main task is not the direct administration of training institutions. TESDA's mandate enjoins it to take on a facilitative, regulatory, and standards-setting role (figure 5.6). However, at present, TESDA operates most of the public training institutions outside of the universities and colleges in 14 regional and 45 provincial centers. The vocational schools and centers use up two-thirds of TESDA's budget. Aside from asking for a larger allocation from the national government, TESDA is cautiously testing schemes to shed itself of the financial burden of running these institutions.

Private versus Public Funding

Funding for vocational and technical education is inadequate. TESDA received only a modest budget of 22 billion pesos in 1997–99. The proposed budget for 1999 of 2.2 billion pesos did not include any adjustments for inflation; nominally, it was the same as the 1998 budget. The budget for tertiary training is around eight times the budget for vocational education. However, it is unclear how much money universities spend on vocational courses and similar training.

Aside from this lack of funds, there are other very good reasons for enticing the private sector to take on more responsibility for running the country's technical and vocational schools. Highly subsidized public institutions tend to squeeze out private institutions, which are known to be more cost-effective in delivering services. They have higher utilization rates for both facilities and teachers and employ more teaching than nonteaching staff. The higher utilization rates for facilities and faculty may well reflect the efficiency that derives from the strong link between private providers and the labor market that they serve—in other words, their courses sell better. The emerging consensus appears to be that the scope for government financing of training remains, but that the government's comparative advantage does not appear to be in setting up or maintaining training institutions (see table 5.7).

The government's role in financing technical and vocational education is in part the result of the failure of financial markets to operate properly. If banks lend at all, they demand a high premium from borrowers. The private supply of training outside enterprises is constrained by the unwillingness of financial institutions to fund training organizations that do not possess adequate collateral. One way to circumvent this problem is to consider subsidizing private training facilities directly. The draft National Plan provides for the adoption of a rational scheme of resource allocation with "institutional capability" as the first criteria. The plan involves establishing a system of competitive tendering (bidding) for training provision. Al-

TABLE 5.7
Public and Private Training and
Vocational Education Institutions (December 1997)

	Technical-vocational schools	Tertiary institutions, nondegree programs	Industry-based training centers	NGO-based training centers	Others	Total
Private	825	374	64	92	28	1,383
Public	240	182	57	137	107	723

Source: National Technical Education and Skills Development Plan.

though the details are not yet in operational form, presumably both private and public training institutions may bid through this system.

Private training and vocational education are financed almost exclusively by tuition fees and endowments. The government does not channel financial resources directly through private institutions, with one exception. It operates the Government Assistance to Students and Teachers in Private Education through the voucher system of the Private Education Student Financial Assistance program. The Private Education Student Financial Assistance scheme is one mode of financing that continues to address the government's equity concerns, and there is certainly room to expand it. It provides performance-based scholarships for a maximum of three years. Qualifying exams help screen the applicants. These scholarships function like vouchers, so that students may choose to enroll in either private or public institutions. More than 7,600 scholarships were awarded in 1997 and 1998, and a budget for 10,300 scholarships was allotted for 1999.

The scheme serves two purposes. First, it is a scholarship fund that targets poor students. To qualify, the student's family must have an income below the official poverty line. Vouchers for each region are allocated according to a quota system, so that regions with a greater share of people living below the poverty line receive more vouchers.[20] Regions that have a higher share of people in the labor force who reached high school but not college also receive more vouchers. The vouchers are an important resource that help keep private training institutions liquid by supplying them with students whose fees are paid for by the government. The vouchers are therefore an indirect means of supporting the private sector. A "containment" strategy requires students to use vouchers within the local region, assuring that the program benefits private providers in all regions. Despite this restriction, however, the system creates incentives for schools to compete with other private providers and to offer courses the students demand.[21]

Outcomes of the Training and Vocational Education System

The collection of data concerning the performance of technical and vocational education graduates is spotty, to say the least. The Congressional Commission on Education (1992) reported that these graduates find obtaining employment difficult. Employment rates were 31 percent for graduates of postsecondary nondegree courses. Graduates of short-term, generally nonformal courses had slightly more success, with an employment rate of 54 percent.

Godfrey and Hunting (1996) show that graduating from vocational or technical training does not reduce unemployment and that the unemployment rate for graduates of these programs is in fact higher than the prevailing unemployment rate for nongraduates in similar age brackets.[22] However, the same study argues that training increases labor force participation rates. This finding may reflect the fact that people who have undergone training are less likely to give up on the search for work. Training also appears to open up opportunities in paid employment (rather than in entrepreneurial or family-based modes), and private training (as opposed to government programs) affects how much workers earn. The private training institutions surveyed had slightly higher unit costs per graduate for nonformal training than their government counterparts, but nonformal welding, business studies, automotive, and electrical technology courses boosted trainees' employment prospects.

Training and Vocational Education as a Response to the Crisis

TESDA was able to train only about 1,500 displaced workers in 1998. The displaced workers in the formal sector that were monitored by the DOLE for 1998 numbered 155,000. Several factors might explain the weakness of TESDA's response thus far.

First, the effects of the crisis were not apparent until well into 1998. Consequently, there was little sense of alarm. The national budget for 1999 was prepared by line agencies and made ready for passage in Congress by July 1998, when the full impact of the crisis was not yet apparent. Second, a degree of complacency may have been bred by the constant public pronouncements that the Philippines was the least affected of all the countries affected by the crisis. The fact that national output growth was far healthier than it was in other East Asian economies (which experienced free fall earlier on) doubtless contributed to this complacency.

Third, there was a substantial fiscal constraint. A precautionary program with the International Monetary Fund (IMF) entered into by the Ramos government in early 1998 involved reducing the appropriated budgets of all agencies by 25 percent (the level of mandatory reserves). The Ramos government, however, was also involved in a window-dressing operation of its fiscal situation. While it reported a slight fiscal surplus at the end of 1997, the accounts subsequently showed that the administration owed government contractors more than 100 billion pesos. The Estrada administration inherited the need for drastic fiscal adjustment just as the impact of the crisis was worsening.

Finally, the national elections and the new administration—which was formed around a new party—may have prevented a rapid transition from taking place. Because of the winner-take-all character of Philippine presidential elections, a new president always has a chilling effect on government activity, as middle- to upper-level public officials are customarily obliged to hand in their resignations as a courtesy to the new government. Against this backdrop, TESDA was in its first full year of operation as an integrated structure.

Private and Public Resource Use[23]

By 1997 there were 723 publicly funded vocational-technical institutions and centers in the Philippines and 1,383 private vocational and technical institutions and centers. Private institutions account for 80 percent of enrollment in technical and vocational programs. Both public and private training providers have dropout rates of 10–15 percent. However, the two systems differ sharply in the effectiveness with which they use resources. The costs per graduate of private formal training centers are only 45 to 70 percent of those for graduates of public training institutions (Godfrey and Hunting 1996; Johanson 1998) (table 5.8).

The low staff-to-student ratios in public training institutes is consistent with findings that show widespread underenrollment in some courses. However, this generalization requires a caveat, because public training institutions are heterogeneous. The regional training centers generally have very high utilization ratios, in part because they have the best facilities.

The expansion of private vocational training is hindered by one important factor: the credit constraint faced by small private providers. These small enterprises generally have no collateral, a factor that prevents them

TABLE 5.8
How Public and Private Institutions Use Their Facilities
(percent)

	Public	Private
Utilization rate for laboratories	74	44
Utilization rate for workshops	80	55
Providers with staff-to-student ratios of more than 1:12	90	66

Source: TESDA (1999).

from accessing credit markets. If they do gain access to credit, the lender charges very high interest rates to compensate for the risk. Public credit windows are available, but transaction costs are high and processing an application can take up to two years. Some observers theorize that a second constraint to the expansion of private training provision exists in the form of unfair competition from highly subsidized public training institutions, which often do not charge fees (Johanson 1998). Given the large market share of private institutions, however, any unfair competition is likely to occur in areas that have a disproportionate share of public institutions.

If the phenomenon of unfair competition is widespread, a voucher scheme that allows students to choose their institution is one solution. Subsidies to public training institutions can also be reduced using a scholarship scheme similar to the Private Education Student Financial Assistance program, which allows students to choose either public or private providers.[24] A complementary approach would involve allowing public institutions to charge fees and use some of the funds generated to compensate for reduced government subsidies. Still another solution would involve giving private institutions access to government subsidies—but this notion is somewhat unrealistic, given TESDA's miniscule budget.

Vocational Training within Firms

A recent survey of firms in the Philippines found that more than 40 percent had made significant expenditures on training for their employees (Johanson 1998). More than one-half (55 percent) of firms with more than 500 employees and around one-third of firms with 50 to 499 employees had developed training units and human resource development plans. Nearly half of these medium-size and large firms also had staff members specifically for training, and slightly more than 10 percent had their own training centers. All the firms were keenly aware of the incentives the government provides for private training,

Small firms are less able to institute their own training programs. There is a clear market failure here, because small firms invest less in training and are particularly vulnerable to the free-rider problem (the poaching of staff trained by other firms). Other countries have used various methods to overcome this market failure, including direct subsidies for employers that provide training. Subsidizing employers' expenses is one promising approach, as Singapore's experience shows. In Singapore such subsidies have encouraged small employers to provide training. The Philippines, however, has no single strategy to encourage small firms to provide training.

The Philippines has two apprenticeship programs. First, the apprenticeship law governs training provided by the enterprises themselves. In 1997 some 20,000 apprentices were enrolled in such training, a figure that represents less than 0.1 percent of all wage and salary employees in the country. Several standing proposals (including one from TESDA) argue for revising the law. The draft National Technical Education and Skills Development Plan (TESDA 1999) states that employers are using the apprenticeship law to exploit workers by treating apprentices as a source of cheap labor. In any case the law is ineffective, because it does not require firms to draw up training schemes for approval. The law also restricts training to a maximum of six months—too short a time for trainees to acquire many skills. And TESDA is unable to monitor the apprentices, as they are not considered workers.

The dual training system, which is modeled on the German apprenticeship system, is the second kind of enterprise-based training. Trainees spend 70 percent of their time working in a firm and the rest of the time in designated learning centers. Trainees receive three-fourths of the minimum wage but retain only 30 percent, with the rest going to the training provider. The system brings together on-the-job experience and theoretical instruction. Firms are not obliged to hire trainees after the 30–36 month training period, and they do not spend as much as German firms, which shoulder most of the cost. However, this type of training can be expensive. While the annual cost per trainee of the dual system in Germany is about the same as the country's per capita GNP, simulations show that this ratio is much greater in other countries that have adopted the system. It is more than 2:1 in Korea, more than 3:1 in Indonesia, and more than 4:1 in Egypt.[25]

The program is in its very early stages of implementation and outside of Manila is constrained by the lack of trained personnel. Monitoring mechanisms remain weak, and despite recent gains the adoption rate has been slow. In 1997 the number of graduates was only 235, down from the 273 of the previous year. The weakest link in the dual training system appears to be the rate at which training institutions are accredited. Twenty-seven training institutions had been accredited as of 1998, but the target was 48.[26]

Making Training and Vocational Education Responsive to Market Signals

A major step in TESDA's medium-term planning involved an exercise to elicit from its institutional constituency a roster of skills and industries that should be given priority in 1999–2004. Included in this exercise were staff in the regional offices, schools and training centers, chambers of commerce, and labor unions. What emerged from this exercise was a long list of "sectoral priorities" and "critical skills" for each industry and region. Unfortunately, the exercise included no quantification, so the results cannot be used as a tool to decide exactly how TESDA should use its limited resources. A crude first approximation might, for instance, have involved identifying professions for which compensation indices have been rising faster than average in the past few years. The country's exports of skilled labor could have provided another measure. It makes sense to think twice about investing skills in sectors with a surplus, as indicated by the disproportionately large human resource exports in recent years.

The human resource planning exercise also failed to identify the professions and skills that enterprises and private training institutes are most likely to underprovide or the reasons for not emphasizing them. The government's role in training provision will vary depending on the cause of these market failures. TESDA can begin providing the needed training in these areas. Subsidies (in the form of directed credit and teacher training assistance for private sector providers) can help correct policy distortions (such as excessively high wages for trainees) that cause enterprises to underprovide training. Career counseling can address the lack of information.

The requirements of human resource planning can be daunting, and attempts at such planning elsewhere have not proved successful. Others have arrived at the conclusion that manpower planning does not work (Schweitzer 1994). In this case it becomes very important to make sure that both private and public training providers have the capacity and incentives to respond to market signals rather than being guided by manpower plans. Several means of ensuring this response are available.

TRAINING VOUCHERS. Vouchers such as those available under the Private Education Student Financial Assistance program allow trainees to choose a training provider. The National Technical Education and Skills Development Program includes a plan to expand the number of vouchers under the current program, which is a more efficient mode of providing vocational education than direct government provision. A 200 million peso fund for vouchers benefits 10,000 trainees, while a similar 200 million peso fund benefits only 5,000 student under TESDA.[27]

A VOUCHER SYSTEM FOR THE PUBLIC SECTOR. Voucher systems can also be applied to public schools and training centers. At present TESDA provides block grants for its schools and training centers, and some local government units participate by making school buildings and agricultural lands available. Enrollment is highly subsidized, and there is no means testing in the allocation of the slots. Because grants routinely increase by a certain percentage each year, public schools and centers have no incentive to improve their productivity, resource use, or the quality of their course offerings. A voucher system can create a link between the amount of public resources a school can attract and the number of students it draws. As of the middle of 1999, however, there were no plans to set up such a system.

DEVOLUTION AND THE RATIONAL ALLOCATION OF RESOURCES. A voucher system for the public sector is only one possibility for using resource allocation to create incentives for schools and training centers to perform better. However, in some settings the existing capabilities of a provincial or a regional training center depend on either past investment or past neglect. In these situations the number of voucher holders a school is able to attract may not give an accurate picture of the efforts the institution has made. An incentive system based mainly on vouchers could reward those training outfits that perform well primarily because they have been favored with capital investments in the past or because they are located in highly urbanized centers.

The absence of a voucher system for public providers therefore does not mean that reforms are not being planned. One specific strategy being considered is the establishment of a competitive bidding system for training providers (TESDA 1999). While the formulation may seem general at this point, the language of the provision allows for a wide range of possibilities. People at the policy planing staff do not believe that this reform would force public providers to compete with private providers for contracts. However, if TESDA's training facilities are devolved to local government units, they will undoubtedly have to compete. In deciding which regions or provinces will receive the larger share of training resources, other criteria over and above institutional capability, program equity, and program relevance may be considered, such as a system of matching grants.

This system would allocate more resources to provinces (regions do not have funds) that show a willingness to invest some of their own resources in training.

The proposal to devolve training functions to local government units will encounter many difficulties. Having seen the experience of the devolution of hospitals, TESDA regional staff members are naturally wary. The devolved hospital functions were matched with compensating increases in the Internal Revenue Allotment of the receiving local government units.[28] But it proved difficult to compel local governments to use the additional funds to maintain facilities and pay personnel. The concern of trainers is an especially valid one because the local government unit has the legal authority to declare their positions redundant. The concerns arising from proposals to devolve functions raise almost the same concerns as the proposal to shed the central administrative functions of public training facilities through management contracts with NGOs or the private sector.

RESOLVING THE PROBLEM OF SUPERVISION. Improving responsiveness is particularly difficult in schools run by the CHED and by chartered universities, because it is often difficult to make rapid changes in the curriculum. School-based training has been known to succeed only when the link between the schools and enterprises is strong. Labor market responsiveness also improves when employers are linked directly to the school—for example, by direct employer financing or involvement in school governance. Because more than half of the budget for training and vocational education is being spent by state universities and colleges and institutions supervised by the CHED, creating a channel for TESDA to introduce broad supervision will potentially have a tremendous impact.

Some Recommendations for Future Policy

The government of the Philippines has taken a number of steps to address the problems arising from the East Asian financial crisis. However, much remains to be done. The government can take a number of steps in the near to medium term that will build on the efforts already made.

UNDERTAKE FURTHER RESEARCH. Such research will help policymakers determine the depth of needed labor market interventions. The initial condition of high unemployment in the Philippines—a situation that sets the country apart from its neighbors—deserves further consideration. If unemployment is once more between 7 and 9 percent after the crisis, research can resolve the issue of whether or not the country needs extensive safety nets, active and passive labor market policies, and training. If labor regulations or structural mismatches between the supply and demand for skills are causing market rigidities, safety nets and labor market policies can improve social welfare. We did not find any obvious instances of labor market inflexibility in wage setting or the decision to hire and fire. Even the political power that unions are normally able to wield appears to have been overwhelmed by the overriding need to preserve jobs in the face of a precipitous decline in aggregate economic demand.

STRENGTHEN LABOR MARKET POLICIES. Labor market policies can be strengthened to assist displaced workers. Falling aggregate demand did indeed result in significant job losses and involuntary unemployment. In addition, and possibly to an even greater extent, job losses since the middle of 1997 had another cause. They were also the result of the belief that the drastic shift in relative prices would mean a recovery of aggregate demand insufficient to restore the profitability of many of the enterprises that thrived when the overvalued peso was at its highest. A period of adjustment and economic restructuring, not just of growth recovery, is most likely already under way. Labor market policies, especially training for displaced workers, will be useful as labor is shed and shifted into temporary unemployment or long-term redundancy.

IMPROVE PRODUCTIVITY. Productivity needs to be improved to reduce unemployment. One novel hypothesis proposed here is that a significant portion of the unemployment in the Philippines, even during the crisis, is voluntary and requires a long-term process of sustained productivity growth rather than a high dose of labor market policies. Economywide productivity improvement may be a necessary condition for reducing the high level of unemployment. Many of those who are unemployed simply have unusually high reservation wages because they receive support from their families (which receive significant income from foreign remittances) for extended periods during the job search.

USE INFORMATION TO IMPROVE TARGETING. Labor market information can improve targeting. The phenomenon of underemployment, especially during periods of economic shocks, provides a good first approximation of the location of distress. Quarterly labor force surveys, in conjunction with other economywide surveys like the Annual Poverty Indicator Surveys and Family Income and Expenditure Surveys, can provide insight into the kinds of policies needed. The failure of agencies like the DOLE and the Social Security System to launch adequate poverty-targeted responses can be traced to their reliance on monitoring schemes that are able to capture only the most obvious manifestations of the crisis.

STRENGTHEN SOCIAL SAFETY NETS. Stronger safety nets will help support income during crises. As in the past the Social Security System and the Employees Compensation Commission were able to provide a welcome safety net in the form of emergency loans. But the number of people affected by the East Asian crisis was far greater than in previous calamities. The Social Security System's response had clearly been inadequate, in several senses. First, 13 million people working in the informal sector do not fall within the ambit of the system. A systematic inventory of the government's possible role in encouraging formal and informal safety net mechanisms for these workers is essential. Policymakers must also understand the adequacy and limits of safety net mechanisms such as transfers from relatives in order to establish effective policies. Second, emergency loans are a cumbersome replacement for drawdowns that members of the Social Security System should be able to get routinely from their accumulated savings. The system needs to explore ways to allow members to access funds they have accumulated in the pension fund through the years. Finally, in the medium term the Social Security System should further increase its capacity to monitor and punish employers who do not remit contributions for their employees.

REFORM PUBLIC WORKS PROJECTS. Public works programs need to be made more effective. Previous programs such as the CEDP offer some positive lessons. Any serious effort to use rural works programs to confront covariant risks in the farm and nonfarm sectors of the rural Philippines must begin by reforming the system of intergovernmental transfers that undermines poverty-focused infrastructure allocations for the provinces. The national government's system of budget planning and releases also needs to be reformed to provide the predictability that agencies implementing labor-intensive infrastructure programs require.

INCREASE PROVISION OF LABOR MARKET SERVICES. The DOLE is an agency in transition. Its original mandate was to oversee industrial relations, but in recent years that mandate has changed in two ways. The agency has been involved in disaster relief through job fairs and employment creation in areas affected by volcanic eruptions and earthquakes. It has also been called on to concern itself with problems of employment even in sectors where there are no strict employer-employee relationships. For example, it has stepped up efforts to monitor the enforcement of key labor standards among subcontracting firms. In these situations it strives to provide job-matching services, counseling, retraining, rural works, and livelihood programs and to facilitate access to other government programs such as emergency loans and basic labor standards enforcement, especially in distressed firms.

The DOLE can usefully explore these directions further. In particular it can help to fulfill the need for a lead agency in the creation of social protection institutions, since it is strategically placed to take on this role. The DOLE can move in this direction by:

- *Strengthening and scaling up the delivery of its establishment-based services while looking beyond them.* At present these services are simply inadequate. The DOLE can go beyond formal sector establishments by using economywide databases more intensively. These databases include the Annual Poverty Indicator Survey, the quarterly Labor Force Surveys, and the Family Income and Expenditure Surveys. These databases can be enhanced further and may be used to gauge the adequacy of existing programs and target beneficiaries and to calibrate the timing and extent of needed labor market interventions.

  The depth of agricultural unemployment and underemployment even in early 1999, for instance, was not reflected in the DOLE's administrative reporting system. If it had been, the agency might have seen the potential contribution scaled-up versions of its own public works programs could have made in rural areas. In addition, it could have implemented an interagency initiative on labor-based infrastructure programs. Again, economywide surveys in the fall of 1998 would have allowed the DOLE to see that unemployment and underemployment were rising in many industries, particularly manufacturing and construction. Using only establishment reports on closures and layoffs led the DOLE to believe that the worst effects of the crisis had been felt during the first quarter of 1998.

- *Influencing other agencies with a key role in social protection.* With a more comprehensive grasp of the crisis (beyond what the administrative reports indicate), the DOLE could undertake important advocacy. For instance, during the East Asian crisis it could have argued for relaxing the eligibility requirements for emergency loan programs for distressed workers and increasing the scope for on-lending to SMEs.

- *Designing its own programs and influencing those of other agencies to prevent leakage to the nonpoor.* Because of the fiscal crisis, services should increasingly be targeted to poor areas (the rice subsidy) and means-tested where necessary (retraining). Workers in formal sector establishments are not normally the most vulnerable segments of the work force, even though they are also affected by unemployment and job rationing. Because resources are always in scarce supply, the DOLE needs to identify early on a set of selection mechanisms for beneficiaries that will allocate limited resources (the limited slots for retraining, for instance) to those who need these services but cannot afford them. These may include older workers, people with disabilities, people with low educational levels, minorities, and others. Moving away from an almost exclusive reliance on establishment-centered administrative reports will go a long way toward improving the impact and equity of the government's programs. It will also allow the DOLE to assume a larger role in the provision of services and to develop an economywide constituency for its programs.
- *Reforming training and vocational education programs to improve delivery and efficiency.* Reforms are being contemplated in a number of areas. Possible reforms include:
  - Reducing the number of public training centers in areas where they offer the private sector too much competition;
  - Privatizing maintenance for training facilities by transferring responsibility for it from the central agency to local governments;
  - Implementing user charges; and
  - Auctioning training funds to the private sector or enhancing scholarships for use in the private sector.

Notes

1. The authors would like to thank Marites Cruz, Mina Pangandaman, Aleli Rosario, and Mariflor Liwanag for their able assistance. We also gratefully acknowledge the assistance of the senior staff of the Philippine Department of Labor's Institute of Labor Studies, the Bureau of Labor and Employment Statistics, and the National Wages and Productivity Board.

2. Balisacan and Edillion (1999) reveal that 12–16 percent of the more prosperous half of Philippine households receive transfers from friends and relatives, although the proportion of families in the poorer half that receive transfers from relatives is higher still.

3. The term *unemployed* as it is used here is not comparable to the official definition of unemployment. Household heads who are not seeking work—and are therefore not in the labor force—are included here.

4. Based on an examination of the 1991 Family Income and Expenditure Survey (Reyes 1996b)

5. Note that high firm-level productivity will not translate into higher real wages throughout the economy so long as there are many involuntarily unemployed workers at the factory gates who are qualified replacements for the employed workers who want to bid up wages. Sustained job creation is a necessary condition for bridging the gap between reservation wages and prevailing real wages.

6. Capital inflows outpaced the increases in the current account deficit and resulted in the real appreciation and stabilization of the currency as international reserves grew. The real (and sometimes nominal) appreciation of the peso in a period of heavy and expanding trade and growing current account deficits led to the overvaluation of the currency. For a discussion of the relationship between the appreciation of the peso and the onset of the crisis see de Dios and others (1997)

7. Personal communication with staff of the Labor Department's Institute for Labor Studies (1999).

8. Order Number 10, Series of 1997, which amended the rules implementing Books 3 and 4 of the Philippine Labor Code.

9. For a statistical overview see BLES (1998).

10. See *Bleeding Agency*, Margarita Debuque's three-part article in the *Philippine Daily Inquirer*, August 23–25, 1999.

11. *Bleeding Agency*, Margarita Debuque's three-part article in the *Philippine Daily Inquirer*, August 23–25, 1999.

12. The order is titled *Establishing the Policy Direction and Institutional Framework to Implement Labor-based Equipment Supported Infrastructure Program.*

13. The Magna Carta for Small Enterprises (Republic Act 6977) aims to promote, develop, and assist small and medium-size enterprises through the creation of a council and the rationalization of government assistance, programs, and agencies concerned with the development of these firms.

14. Information for this section was put together by the DOLE's Institute for Labor Studies

15. President Estrada signed this bill into law in January 2000.

16. These programs are formally enumerated in Department Order No. 6, Series of 1998 of the Department of Labor and Employment.

17. The Special Program for the Employment of Students and training scholarships at the Technical Education and Skills Development Authority give priority to displaced workers. These programs are the most generously funded and the easiest to access. The 500 million peso Emergency Loans Program under the Social Security Administration is also accessible mainly to workers displaced from formal sector establishments. PRESEED and the pilot Rural Works Program of the Bureau of Rural Workers, which are the key programs designed for rural workers, are very small.

18. A more detailed presentation of the DOLE's position can be found in BLES (undated).

19. Personal communication with Teresa Soriano, Executive Director of the Institute for Labor Studies.

20. We should note that no regions have been designated as poor, although some provinces and municipalities have. A formula sensitive to poverty incidence within regions would improve targeting. The Family Income and Expenditure Surveys can be used to derive a ranking of provinces according to poverty criteria, for instance.

21. Caveat: around half of the vouchers are spent on computer-related courses. No assessment of the program has yet probed the possibility that students' decisions do not maximize their chances of becoming employed. There are, however, doubts within TESDA's planning office as to the wisdom of enrolling in computer classes instead of agriculture or fisheries courses.

22. We cannot discount the self-selection and screening problems involved here, however. If employers think or know that those who ordinarily qualify for college slots go to college instead of vocational and technical schools, then they tend to believe that those who have "only" technical or vocational credentials are not bright enough to be accepted to college.

23. The data from this section may also be found in NTDSD 1999 (May draft).

24. Current recipients of Private Education Student Financial Assistance scholarships do not attend public institutions.

25. An evaluation of the costs of the scheme in the Philippines is presently being conducted.

26. Personal communication with Guy Adrias, Office of Apprenticeship, TESDA.

27. Meeting with TESDA Director-General Edicio dela Torre (1999).

28. Intergovernmental transfers from the national government comprised a mandatory 40 percent of the national government's internal revenue of two years ago.

References

Alba, M., and E. Esguerra. 1999. "Estimating the Modes of Labor Force Participation in the Philippines." Discussion Paper 9903, School of Economics, University of the Philippines.

Annual Poverty Indicator Surveys. 1998 and 1999. National Statistics Office, Income and Employment Statistics Division, Manila, Republic of the Philippines.

Balisacan, Arsenio. 1994. "Design of a Poverty-Targeted Food subsidy Program in the Philippines." Policy paper for the Agribusiness Assistance Program, School of Economics, University of the Philippines.

Balisacan, Arsenio, and Rose Edillion. 1999. "Human face of the Asian Crisis: What Do Nationwide Panel Data Philippine Households Show?" Paper presented at the national conference of the political Science Association, University of the Philippines, Diliman, Quezon City.

BLES (Bureau of Labor and Employment Statistics). 1998. "Trends and Patterns in Nonregular Employment in the Philippines." *Labstat Updates* 2(2) Department of Labor and Employment, Manila.

_____. 1999. "Statistics on DOLE Assistance Provided to Displaced Workers Affected by the Economic Crisis" *Labstat Updates* 3(7). Department of Labor and Employment, Manila.

_____. Undated. "An Alternative Approach to Monitoring Labor Market Response." Manila.

Canlas, Dante. 1997. "Unemployment and Monetary Policy in the Philippines." In Esguerra Emmanuel and Kazuhisa Ito, eds., *Employment, Human Capital and Job Security: Recent Perspectives on Philippine Labor.* Tokyo: Institute for Developing Economies.

Congressional Commission on Education. 1992. *Post-Secondary Education.* Vol. 2 of Book 2 of *Making Education Work.* Manila.

de Dios, Emmanuel. 1999. "The Economic Crisis and Its Impact on Labor." Philippine Center for Policy Studies. Unpublished working paper.

de Dios Emmanuel, Benjamin Diokno, Raul Fabella, Felipe Medalla and Solita Monsod. 1997. "Exchange Rate Policy: Recent Failures and Future Tasks." *Public Policy.* October/December.

Family Income and Expenditure Surveys. 1997. National Statistics Office, Income and Employment Statistics Division, Manila, Republic of the Philippines.

Godfrey, Martin, and Gordon Hunting. 1996. "Evaluation of the Technical education and Skills Deveopment System." Washington, D.C.: World Bank. Unpublished discussion paper.

Johanson, Richard. 1998. "Philippines Technical-Vocational Education and Training (TVET)." Background paper for Education Sector Study, Asian Development Bank and World Bank. Manila.

Labor Force Surveys. Bureau of Labor and Employment Statistics. Manila, Republic of the Philippines.

Lamberte, Mario Cesar Cororoton, Marge Guerrero, and Aniceto Orbeta. March 1999. "Results of the Survey of the Philippine Industry and the Financial Crisis." Unpublished discussion paper.

Lim, Joseph. 1997. "Macro Labor Statistics and Sectoral Employment." In Esguerra Emmanuel and Kazuhisa Ito, eds., *Employment, Human Capital and Job Security: Recent Perspectives on Philippine Labor.* Tokyo: Institute for Developing Economies.

_____. 1999. "The East Asian Crisis and Child Labour in the Philippines." Tokyo: Institute for Developing Economies. Draft.

Llanto, Guilbert, and Teresa Sanches. 1997. *Impact of Financial Liberalization on Micro and Small-scale Manufacturing Industries.* Manila: Philippine Institute for Development Studies.

Maglen, A., and Manasan, Rosario. 1996. *Education Sector Study.* Manila: Asian Development Bank and World Bank.

Quibria, M.G. 1996. *Indonesia, Republic of Korea, Philippines and Thailand.* Vol. 2 of *Rural Poverty in Developing Asia.* Manila: Asian Development Bank.

Reyes, Celia. 1996a. "An Assessment of the System of Minimum Wage-Setting." Policy and Development Foundation, Inc. Available at the National Wages and Productivity Commission, Department of Labor and Employment. Manila.

_____. 1996b. "Monitoring Systems for Poverty Tracking." Micro Impacts of Macro Adjustment Policies Project Research Paper Series 30. Legaspi Village Makati: Policy and Development Foundation, Inc.

Schweitzer, Julian. 1994. "Vocational Education and Training: the Role of the Public Sector in a Market Economy." Human Resources Development and Operations Policy Working Paper 16. Washington, D.C.: World Bank

Subbarao, Kalanidhi, Akhter Ahmed, and Tesfaye Teklu. 1996. "Selected Social Safety Net Programs in the Philippines: Targeting, Cost Effectiveness and Options for Reform." Discussion paper 317. Washington D.C.: World Bank.

TESDA (Technical Education and Skills Development Authority). 1999. The National Technical Education and Skills Development Plan, 1999–2004, "A Vision and Strategy for the Development of Middle-Level Manpower." Manila.

World Bank. 1995a. "The Philippines: An Agenda for the Reform of the Social Security Institutions." Sector Report 3400. Washington, D.C.

World Bank. 1995b. "The Philippines: Public Expenditure Management for Sustained and Equitable Growth." Sector Report 14680. Washington, D.C.

World Bank. 1996. "A Strategy to Fight Poverty: Philippines." Working Paper 16118 Country Operations Division, East Asia and the Pacific. Washington, D.C.

_____. 1997. *Philippines: Managing Global Integration.* 2 vols. Poverty Reduction and Economic Management Sector Unit Report 7024-PH. East Asia and the Pacific Regional Office. Washington, D.C.

_____. 1998. *World Bank Support for Small and Medium Industries in the Philippines: An Impact Evaluation.* Operations Evaluation Department Report 18041. Washington, D.C.

6 The Labor Market and Labor Policy in a Macroeconomic Context: Growth, Crisis, and Competitiveness in Thailand

Moazam Mahmood and Gosah Aryah

THIS APPRAISAL OF Thailand's labor market and labor policy comes at a critical juncture for the Thai economy.[1] The crisis in growth and employment the country is experiencing at the beginning of the 21st century is unparalleled in Thailand's recent history. The country's recovery—especially to the high growth and full employment that characterized the 1980s and much of the 1990s—is uncertain, largely because of the variability in labor market policy. Past policies may have delivered high trend growth in output and employment, but they also engendered structural weaknesses in the economy that helped bring about the crisis. These problems aside, such policies are unlikely to be effective in the changed global environment. This chapter attempts to fill the current policy "gap" in Thailand by analyzing the related problems of the labor market and the economy. It argues that new policies are needed to foster growth in both output and employment.

The Current Labor Market Situation

In the fall of 1999, the Thai economy was embroiled in the Asian financial and economic crisis. The economy had contracted by 9.4 percent

TABLE 6.1
Growth Rate of Real GDP (percent per year)

Year	1980–90	1990–96	1995	1996	1997 Q1	1997 Q2	1997 Q3	1997 Q4	1998 Q1
GDP	7.6	8.3	8.8	5.5	3.8	5.1	-3.2	-7.5	-13.4

since 1998 (table 6.1). But the rate of contraction slowed in the last quarter of the year, falling from its earlier high of 13 percent to just 4 percent. Estimates of economic growth for 1999 projected an increase to 3 percent. Trend growth was expected to remain low, ranging between 3 and 5 percent, until 2003.

The situation is made more dramatic by the high growth that preceded it. Trend growth in Thailand in 1980–96 topped 8 percent and in 1990–95 neared 9 percent (table 6.1). It declined in 1996 and the first half of 1997, ranging between 4 and 6 percent. The financial crisis hit Thailand in the third quarter of 1997, causing the economy to contract by 3 percent and then to shrink by 8 percent in the last quarter alone. Growth is expected to remain low—in the area of 3 to 5 percent—in 2000–2003.

The Thai economy had attained a per capita GNP of around $3,000 in 1996. The crisis is broadly estimated to have reduced real per capita income by about 20 percent (Kakwani 1998). In 1996 the unemployment rate stood at 2 percent—virtually full employment (table 6.2). By 1997, however, the rate had doubled and continued to climb to around 7 percent. By one estimate the crisis generated approximately 90,000 redundancies, raising the level of unemployment to 2.2 million as of June 1999.[2] Real wages declined following the precrisis tightening of the labor market. Real wage growth, which stood at over 2 percent per year in 1996, reversed itself. The real wage fell by more than 7 percent in 1998 and by 1.5 percent in 1999.

The large debt overhang underscores the difficulty of generating a strong financial and economic recovery. Almost one-half of all debt now consists of nonperforming loans. Private investment is virtually nonexistent, and capacity utilization has collapsed (table 6.2). The exchange rate has also plummeted. The Thai baht was pegged to the dollar at 25:1 in 1996, but the exchange rate is expected to remain around 40:1, up from 55:1 in July 1997. Despite the depreciated baht, exports have dropped from their 1997 level of $57 billion to $53 billion for 1998. The depreciation of the baht has led to a severe compression of the import market, with imports falling from $64 billion in 1996 to $37 billion in 1998. The

1998 Q2	1998 Q3	1998 Q4	1999 Q1	1999 Q2	1999 Q3	1999 Q4	2000	2001	2002	2003
−12.8	−9.5	−3.7	−9.4	4.0	−9.4	3.3	4.8	4.6	4.8	5.1

high precrisis growth of GDP and exports was in part financed by large capital inflows (5 percent of GDP in 1996). Thailand had a significant current account deficit of 8 percent of GDP in 1996, but the currency crisis (which reversed the inflows) and the fall in imports resulted in a large current account surplus—13 percent in 1998.

The major impact of the reduction in growth, employment, wages, asset prices, and income has been a degradation of human development indicators (table 6.2). Between 1992 and 1996 Thai poverty levels had virtually halved, with only 11 percent of the population falling below the poverty line. The crisis has raised the poverty level from 11 to 13 percent, pushing 1 million more people into poverty.

Macroeconomic policies designed to combat the crisis have been based largely on financial sector reform. At the onset of the crisis, the Thai government committed itself to an economic reform package that was a condition of a $17 billion loan from the International Monetary Fund (IMF). Until the year 2000, fiscal and monetary policy will be shaped largely by the terms of this commitment. The IMF program is based on several key measures. First, the indefensible pegged exchange rate has been floated and the depreciating baht propped up by interest rate increases to attract capital inflows. Second, fiscal contraction and a cap on the budget deficit are being used to curtail the threat of inflation. Third, the ailing financial sector is being revived through bank closures, restructuring, and recapitalization. However, the current state of the economy shows that the economic sectors have not recovered.

Devising policies to revive the economic sectors, generate employment, and improve labor conditions requires understanding both the roots of the high growth that preceded the crisis and the reasons it collapsed. For instance financial sector recovery may be necessary to increase employment levels, but it may not be sufficient. If the factors that caused the financial and economic crisis were purely financial, then financial reform will spur economic recovery. But if the causes are a more complex combination of financial and economic sector weaknesses, then economic sector reform will be required as well.

TABLE 6.2
Macroeconomic and Social Indicators in Thailand

	1996	1997	1998	1999	2000
GDP growth	5.5	−0.4	−9.4	0.9	2.9
Inflation (%)	5.6	5.7	8.1	2.4	4.7
Budget balance (% of GDP)	2.3	−0.9	−2.3	−3.5	−3.4
Current account balance	−8.1	−1.9	11.5	8.7	5.1
(% of GDP)	54.4	56.7	52.9	54.6	58.3
Exports (US$ bn.)	63.9	55.1	36.5	42.0	49.0
Imports (US$ bn.)		27.0	29.5	32.34	
Gross reserves (US$ bn)	33.1	28.1	38.0	31.3	28.8
Savings ratio (% of GDP)	40.8	32.3	26.7	24.4	25.2
Gross fixed investment					
(% of GDP)			−23.5	−16.6	
Private investment index			(Dec.)	(May)	
		65.0	52.1	57.6	
Capacity utilization (%)				(May)	
	13.4	13.7	15.2	12.0	11.0
Interest rate (%)	B25.3	B31.4	B41.4	B38.2	B39.5
Exchange rate against					
US$ (baht)	32.0	32.5	33.0	33.4	33.7
Labor force (million)	2.0	3.7	5.2	7.5	6.8
Unemployment rate				2.2	
(% labor force)				(June)	
Unemployment level					
(millions)	2.3	1.4	−7.4	−1.6	2.4
	728		911		
Real wages	11.4		12.9		
Poverty line (baht/person/					
month)	6.9		7.9		
Population below (%)					
No. (million)					

Source: Finance Ministry, Labor Ministry, and the National Economic and Social Development Board. Economic Intelligence Unit Forecast (3rd and 4th quarters, 1999).

We argue that the economic sectors of the country exhibit fundamental weaknesses that helped cause the crisis. These weaknesses exacerbated the problems caused by financial sector weaknesses, which have been widely acknowledged as key factors in the crisis. Our analysis of Thailand's high precrisis growth levels reveals that production efficiency had declined for both labor and capital, especially in the 1990s. This decline in competitiveness has affected exports, the major engine of the country's growth. Macroeconomic policy to revive growth and employment has concentrated so far on eliminating the financial inefficiencies. But the weak state of the economy argues for additional macroeconomic policies directed specifically at redressing the inefficiencies in production. We look at the policy actions the government has taken to combat the crisis—including employment-creation and income-support measures, measures to improve and intensify public employment services, and training programs—and assess their ability to deal with the current economic situation.

The Economy and the Labor Market before the Crisis

Before the crisis Thailand enjoyed high growth in both output and employment. The growth in output caused a shift in the relative importance of various sectors, with agriculture losing share in GDP and manufacturing gaining. Participation in the labor force was also high, especially for women. Despite these positive factors, the informal sector continued to flourish, and underemployment persisted.

Output Growth

Thailand had very high output growth in the 15 years leading up to the crisis. The rate of growth throughout the 1980s was 8 percent annually (table 6.1)—a rate exceeded in the region only by the Republic of Korea (with 9 percent) and China (with 10 percent). From 1990 until 1996 only China's growth rate (12 percent) was higher. Industry, and especially manufacturing, led this high growth, expanding at 10 percent. The services sector grew at 7 percent, while agriculture expanded at only 4 percent.

The high growth in industry and stagnation in agriculture changed the relative shares of these two sectors. In 1980 agriculture accounted for 23 percent of GDP, while industry had a 29 percent share and services a 48 percent share (table 6.3). By 1996 agriculture's share had shrunk to 11 percent, industry's had expanded to 40 percent (owing primarily to manufacturing), and services had remained relatively constant.

The Structure of the Labor Market

The high output growth and sectoral change that characterized the 1980s and 1990s had a major impact on the labor market in Thailand. Thailand's population grew at a rate of 1.6 percent over this period to an esti-

TABLE 6.3
Structure of Output

Thailand	1980	1996
Value of GDP (US$ billion)	32.4	185.0
GDP share		
Total	100.0	100.0
Agriculture	23.0	11.0
Industry	29.0	40.0
(Manufacturing)	22.0	29.0
Services	48.0	50.0
	1980[a]	1989[b]
All manufacturing	100.0	100.0
Food, beverages, tobacco	55.0	21.3
Textiles, apparel, leather	8.0	15.2
Wood, paper, printing	—	21.0
Chemical, rubber	—	17.0
Minerals	—	6.3
Metals	—	5.5
Machinery, transportation	9.0	14.2
Jewelry, others	21.0	1.4

— Not available
a. World Bank 1998.
b. Report of the 1989 Industrial Survey.

mated 61.6 million in 1999.[3] In 1998 some 53 percent of the population over the age of 13 was economically active (including the employed, the unemployed, and the seasonally inactive), making up a labor force of 32 million (table 6.4). Those older than 13 who were not in the labor force accounted for another 15 million, including students (6 million), women doing housework (4 million), and the very young and elderly (4 million). Thailand's 77 percent mean labor force participation rate (LFPR) was high for the region, and its female LFPR the region's highest (59 percent).

Thailand's LFPR declined in the 1990s, falling from nearly 80 percent to its 1998 level. The male LFPR declined from 85 percent to 77, while the female LFPR declined more, from 74 percent to 59 percent. As a result, while the labor force grew at 3 percent in the second half of the 1980s, its growth rate dropped to 0.4 percent in the 1990s. Falling population growth rates and increased school enrollment ratios (the result of an increase in compulsory education levels) are responsible for these declines.

TABLE 6.4
Structure of the Labor Force, 1998

	Total (million)	%	%	Males (million)	%	Females (million)	%
Total population	61.10	100		30.48		30.62	
> 13 years	47.15	77.2	100.0	23.60	100.0	23.73	100.0
Economically active	32.17	52.7	68.22	18.07	76.6	14.09	59.4
Employed	28.55		60.55	16.57	70.2	11.98	50.5
Unemployed	1.61		3.41	0.86	3.6	0.75	3.2
Seasonally inactive	2.00		4.24	0.64	2.7	1.36	5.7
Not in labor force	14.98		31.77	5.34	22.6	9.64	40.6
Household work	4.27		9.06	0.08	0.3	4.19	17.7
Studies	6.05		12.83	3.06	13.0	2.99	12.6
Too young/old	3.84		8.14	1.68	7.1	2.16	9.1
Others	0.82		1.74	0.53	2.2	0.29	1.2

Source: Labor Force Survey (1998).

Even after the sectoral changes of the 1980s and 1990s, half the Thai labor force was still in agriculture in 1998, but almost all of these workers lived in rural areas (table 6.5). After agriculture the three sectors with the largest shares of employment were manufacturing, sales, and services, all with approximately 13 percent. Construction and transportation had much smaller shares (6 and 3 percent, respectively). In urban areas sales and services occupied nearly a third of the labor force, and manufacturing accounted for less than a fourth. In rural areas agriculture had just under a two-thirds share of the rural labor force, followed by manufacturing and sales with a 10 percent share each and services with a 9 percent share.

The high concentration of women in certain sectors has resulted in high LFPRs for females in these areas. By 1998 there was virtually no gender gap in manufacturing, commerce, or services, while agriculture had a small gender gap of 6 percent. The major gender gaps remained in construction, utilities, and transportation. According to an Asian Institute of Technology study (AIT and ILO 1999), this reduction in the gender gap is the result of the feminization of particular export industries. High growth in exports propelled growth in manufacturing, drawing women into assembly lines as production workers. Before the crisis women constituted an estimated 65 percent of the labor force in the six leading export industries. Women had a 65 percent share in the food sector, a 61 percent share in textiles, a 74 percent share in garments and leather, a

TABLE 6.5
Sectoral Employment across Urban and Rural Areas, 1998 (percent)

Sector	Total	Urban	Rural	Female (percent of total)
	100.0	100.0	100.0	0
Agriculture	50.3	1.9	62.6	0
Nonagriculture	49.7	98.1	37.4	1
	12.9	22.9	10.4	0
	6.1	5.2	6.3	4
Manufacturing	13.9	30.7	9.6	5
	3.0	7.5	1.8	4
Construction	13.1	30.3	8.8	0
Sales	7.0	1.5	0.5	5
Transport				
Services				
Other				

Source: Labor Force Survey, 1998.

75 percent share in electronic products, a 64 percent share in jewelry, and a 45 percent share in plastic products.

In 1996, just before the crisis, employees made up the largest occupational category, accounting for 14 million workers, or just under half the labor force of 30 million (table 6.6). Self-employed workers were the next largest category, with just under 10 million (one-third of the labor force), followed by unpaid family workers with 6 million (one-fifth of the labor force).

Women are still underrepresented in the wage employee category (25 percent, compared with 30 percent for men) and the self-employed category (18 percent, compared with 41 percent for men) (ILO 1999). And in fact women are strongly concentrated in the family worker category. At 54 percent their share is twice that of men's. While leading export industries may have been strongly feminized, women constituted a high proportion of unskilled labor in these industries, with correspondingly low proportions in engineering and management (AIT and ILO 1999).

High output growth resulted in a tight labor market before the crisis, and the unemployment rate stood at just 2 percent of the labor force in 1998, or a little more than half a million unemployed (table 6.2). Given the high proportion of seasonal unemployment in total unemployment, a 2 percent unemployment rate verged on full employment. (Seasonal fluc-

TABLE 6.6
Employment by Status, February 1996–99 (in millions)

	1996	1997	1998	1999
Employers	0.84	0.77	0.78	0.94
Government employees	2.31	2.42	2.67	2.64
Private employees	11.68	11.64	10.68	10.22
Self-employed	9.37	9.30	9.48	10.09
Unpaid family workers	5.90	6.14	5.80	6.13
Total labor force	30.10	30.27	29.41	30.02

Source: Labor Force Survey, ILO, CEPR.

tuations, which render a portion of the agricultural workforce inactive each year, may have accounted for up to 2 million unemployed in the wake of the crisis, or more than half the total unemployment then.)

The tight labor market resulted in real wage growth of approximately 3.5 percent per year between 1987 and 1997, or approximately the same as real wage growth in Malaysia (but only around half that in Korea) (table 6.7). Women's wages as a proportion of men's wages are estimated to have increased from 64 percent in 1991 to 71 percent in 1994. This proportion dropped down to 68 percent in 1995, however (ILO 1999). It is possible that the increased supply of women workers became a source of cheap labor, raising the wage differentials.

Despite the precrisis tightening of the labor market, two of its characteristics endured: the dualism inherent in the existence of a burgeoning informal sector alongside the formal sector, and underemployment (ILO 1999). Data from the Labor Force Surveys show that the informal labor market has not changed significantly over the last decade (ILO 1999). In fact in absolute terms informal employment increased from 1.8 million to 2.4 million in 1988–96. Underemployment, defined here as working fewer than 35 hours per week, stood at an estimated 2.43 million in 1997, or a significant 7.6 percent of the labor force (NSO 1999).

Sources of Output Growth and Employment

Two primary sources of growth and job creation are important to Thailand's future growth. The first is the export sector, which has increased in importance throughout the 1990s. The second (and related) source is gross domestic investment, aided by capital inflows.

TABLE 6.7
Manufacturing Wage Rates

Year	Thailand (baht/month)			Korea (won/month)			Philippines (pesos/month)			Malaysia (ringgit/month)		
	Nominal wage rate	CPI	Real wage rate	Nominal wage rate	CPI	Real wage rate	Nominal wage rate	CPI	Real wage rate	Nominal wage rate	CPI	Real wage rate
1988	—	—	—	393.1	100.0	393.1	2995	100.0	2995	620	100.0	620
1989	2996	100.0	2996	491.6	105.8	464.7	3441	112.1	3070	640	102.8	623
1990	3357	105.9	3170	590.8	114.7	515.1	4263	128.0	3330	660	106.0	623
1991	3688	111.9	3296	690.3	125.4	550.5	4831	151.9	3180	719	110.6	650
1992	3986	116.5	3421	798.5	133.3	599.1	5386	165.5	3250	794	115.9	685
1993	4138	120.4	3437	885.4	139.7	633.8	5584	178.0	3133	848	119.9	707
1994	4229	126.6	3340	1002.5	148.3	689.5	6272	194.2	3230	928	124.4	746
1995	4994	133.9	3730	1123.9	155.0	725.1	6654	209.8	3172	1002	128.7	779
1996	5502	141.7	3883	1261.2	162.6	775.2						
1997	5935	149.5	3970	1326.2	169.9	780.6						
Annual growth, 1989–97 (percent)	...	...	3.5	...	...	7.6	...	...	0.8	...	...	3.3

— not available.
... not applicable

Source: ILO (1999a).

THE EXPORT SECTOR. Sources of growth are indicated by the competing demand for resources within an economy. In Thailand the largest increase in demand for resources has come from the export sector, which expanded by 15 percent between 1980 and 1996, raising its share of GDP from 24 to 39 percent (table 6.8). Between 1986 and 1996, indicators of Thailand's integration into the world economy more than doubled (table 6.9). External trade rose from 15 percent of GDP (in terms of purchasing power parity) to 31 percent. Of the other countries in the region, only Malaysia and the Philippines matched this achievement.

Increased demand in the export sector resulted in a very high growth rate for exports. Thailand's export growth rate in 1980–90 was 14 percent, and it increased further in 1990–95 to 21 percent, for an average growth rate for 1980–96 of 17 percent. In each period Thailand's export growth rate was the highest in the region. In value terms Thai exports rose from $6 billion in 1980 to $56 billion in 1996. Manufactured exports showed the strongest growth. The share of food and raw materials in exports fell from almost two-thirds to one-third, while the share of manufactures in exports rose from one-quarter to three-quarters.

Lall (1999) argues that this high export growth was based on a shift in the structure of the export sector, where complex activities began to replace simple production. The sector encompassed four types of technologies: resource based (food processing), low (textiles, leather, and plastics), medium (the automotive industry), and high (complex electronic and electrical products). Between 1985 and 1996, the share in exports of products manufactured using medium and high technology rose from among the lowest in the region (20 percent) to the highest (50 percent) (table

TABLE 6.8
Structure of Demand (percent of GDP)

	1980	1996
Private consumption	65.0	55.0
Government consumption	12.0	10.0
Gross domestic investment	29.0	41.0
Exports	24.0	39.0
Imports	30.0	44.0
Gross domestic savings	23.0	35.0

Note: Total GDP = private consumption + government consumption + investment + exports − imports.
Source: World Bank 1998.

TABLE 6.9
Integration with the Global Economy

	Trade (as percent of PPP GDP)		Gross private capital flows	
	1986	1996	1986	1996
Thailand	14.7	31.3	1.6	5.0
Korea	33.6	46.7	3.5	11.1
Indonesia	10.7	13.6	2.0	2.1
Malaysia	33.6	70.2	2.8	4.6
Philippines	8.0	21.3	2.3	4.8

Source: World Bank 1998.

6.10). Thailand's medium- and high-technology product export shares exceeded those of China, Hong Kong (China), and Indonesia, although those of Korea, Singapore, and Taiwan (China) were higher.

INVESTMENT AND INFLOWS. Gross domestic investment rose by 12 percent of GDP between 1980 and 1996, climbing from 29 to 41 percent (table 6.8). Its largest component, gross domestic savings, rose by 12 percent over this period, bringing its share of GDP up from 23 to 35 percent. These very high levels of investment and savings helped fuel growth in Thailand.

Capital inflows filled the gap between the domestic savings rate and the domestic investment rate. In the 1980s capital inflows doubled, rising to $4.5 billion per year, and between 1990 and 1996 they tripled to $14 billion per year. Thailand's private capital flows (5 percent of GDP) competed well with those of Indonesia, Malaysia, and the Philippines. Foreign direct investment as a proportion of inflows fell gradually over time from about two-thirds in 1988 to 17 percent by 1996. Portfolio investment and bank and trade lending became the major form of capital inflows. The increase in the volume of capital inflows raised the current account deficit. In 1980–85 the gap between domestic savings and domestic investment was filled by a current account deficit of 6 percent of GDP. This current account deficit had risen to approximately 8 percent by 1996, by one estimate (table 6.11).

Weaknesses in the Labor Market and the Economy

Even as Thailand's growth peaked in the mid 1990s, the sources of that growth were creating hidden weaknesses in the economy. The competi-

TABLE 6.10
Structure of Manufactured Exports (percent)

Economy	1985				1996			
	RB	LT	MT	HT	RB	LT	MT	HT
Argentina	67.5	15.6	11.8	5.1	49.1	18.8	28.8	3.3
Brazil	32.6	33.3	27.1	7.1	25.6	31.8	34.0	8.6
China	11.7	57.1	21.8	9.4	9.8	56.3	13.4	20.6
Hong Kong (China)	2.1	64.3	14.2	19.3	4.4	52.7	14.0	28.9
India	40.3	46.1	10.6	3.0	31.1	52.3	13.1	4.4
Indonesia	72.2	19.2	5.9	2.8	34.9	41.9	8.5	14.7
Korea	7.8	59.9	12.2	20.1	9.4	28.4	26.6	35.7
Malaysia	53.7	9.7	5.5	31.0	17.8	13.1	8.7	60.4
Mexico	20.2	15.0	29.2	35.6	7.1	20.9	35.2	36.9
Singapore	42.3	10.8	14.6	32.3	12.7	7.9	14.0	65.4
Taiwan (China)	8.7	57.3	13.3	20.7	5.1	33.9	20.2	40.9
Thailand	42.1	38.2	6.6	13.1	14.5	35.6	13.5	36.3
Turkey	22.0	62.3	13.4	2.3	17.5	63.9	12.8	5.7

Note: China's export structure for 1985 is based on 1990 figures.
RB = resource-based.
LT = low-technology.
MT = medium-technology.
HT = high-technology.
Source: Lall (1999).

tiveness in manufacturing that had fueled high export growth throughout the 1980s and early 1990s began to erode. The high levels of inflows and investment may even have helped disguise the decline in competitiveness. But when the currency crisis reversed the capital inflows, the decline in competitiveness became clear. Thailand's exports fell during the global trade slump and did not recover. The very high investment levels and capital inflows may also have led to inefficiencies in the use of capital, contributing to a decline in capital productivity throughout the 1990s.

LABOR PRODUCTIVITY AND THE EROSION OF COMPETITIVENESS. Manufactured exports grew at 23 percent in 1993–94 and at 26 percent in 1994–95. The value of manufactured exports was $46 billion in 1995. Of this amount medium- and high-technology products had the largest share ($24 billion) (table 6.11). These exports are considered critical to the transformation of the manufacturing base from simple to complex technology. The slump in world trade in 1995–96, from trend growth of 9 percent to 2 percent, reduced Thai manufactured exports to negative growth (Lall 1999). They have not recovered from that jolt. In 1996–97 manufactured exports grew by 5 percent, but in 1997–98 growth of these exports once again was negative.

What are the winners and losers among Thailand's exports? Thailand's medium- and high-technology manufactured exports appear to be more competitive than low-technology and resource-based products. Despite the global slump medium- and high-technology manufactured exports have grown on trend by 12 percent, rising from $24 billion in 1995 to $27 billion in 1998. In contrast low-technology exports declined from $12 billion in 1995 to $8 billion in 1998, and resource-based products have stagnated at $6 billion. Within medium- and high-technology exports, two important product groups—hard-disk drives and semiconductors—have continued growing throughout the crisis, albeit at a lower rate (Lall 1999).

If labor- and resource-intensive manufactured exports have been falling since the mid-1990s, then the competitiveness of Thailand's labor-based products has declined. While competitiveness has many dimensions—including costs, product types, and quality—essentially the problem of competitiveness is one of labor productivity. One important indicator of competitiveness (in this case, of labor-based products) is unit labor cost (ULC). In 1990 Thailand's ULCs were higher than those for China, Indonesia, Korea, Malaysia, or the Philippines (table 6.12). China and Indonesia had lower ULCs in virtually all product categories. ULCs for the Philippines were lower in all product categories except textiles, wood, and fabricated metals. And ULCs in Malaysia were lower for chemicals and metals.

Three major components determine the ULC. They can be written as follows:

$$ULC = f(wage\ rate,\ labor\ productivity,\ exchange\ rate)$$

The ULC increases as the real wage and exchange rate rise and decreases as labor productivity rises (Mahmood 1998).

Thailand's ULCs, which were not particularly competitive for labor-intensive products even at the end of the 1990s, were the result of wage increases that outstripped labor productivity increases throughout the decade (TDRI 1998). The real wage rate increased at the rate of about 3.5 percent annually throughout the 1990s (table 6.7). In comparison Korea had much higher wage growth, Malaysia about the same level of growth, and the Philippines lower wage growth. Labor productivity

TABLE 6.1
Recent Thai Manufactured Export Performance

	Values (US$million)					
	1993	1994	1995	1996	1997	1998
Low-technology	9,048.1	10,669.2	12,123.4	10,201.4	9,518.7	8,422.6
Medium-/ high-technology	15,067.0	17,830.5	23,680.4	24,573.9	26,611.9	26,557.5
Resource-based	3,970.2	4,668.2	5,758.8	6,351.0	6,632.7	5,692.3
Other manufactures	1,636.8	3,523.5	4,640.1	4,310.4	4,704.2	4,040.0
Total manufactures	29,722.2	36,691.5	46,202.7	45,436.7	47,467.5	44,712.4
	Growth rates (percent)					
	1993–94	1994–95	1995–96	1996–97	1997–98	1993–98
Low-technology	17.9	13.6	-15.9	-6.7	-11.5	-1.4
Medium-/ high-technology	18.3	32.8	3.8	8.3	-0.2	12.0
Resource-based	17.6	23.4	10.3	4.4	-14.2	7.5
Other manufactures	115.3	31.7	-7.1	9.1	-14.1	19.8
Total manufactures	23.4	25.9	-1.7	4.5	-5.8	8.5

Source: Lall (1999).

TABLE 6.12
Unit Labor Costs in Manufacturing, Selected Asian Economies, 1990

Economy	Total manufacturing	Food, beverages	Textiles, apparel, footwear	Wood products, furniture	Paper products, publishing, printing	Chemicals (including petroleum, rubber, plastics)	Pottery, china, glass products	Iron, steel, nonferrous metals	Fabricated metal products, machinery, equipment	Other manufacturing
East Asia										
China[a]	0.57	0.74	0.32	0.37	0.51	0.58	0.51	0.44	0.44	0.41
Hong Kong (China)	1.94	1.59	1.85	1.86	1.51	1.64	1.43	1.11	1.46	2.46
Korea, Rep. of	0.99	0.81	1.20	1.20	0.90	0.85	0.95	0.61	0.87	1.55
Singapore	1.12	1.58	1.57	1.57	1.04	0.99	0.94	0.73	1.07	1.80
Taiwan (China)	1.45	1.23	2.31	2.31	1.37	1.50	1.25	0.70	1.43	1.16
Southeast Asia										
Indonesia	0.71	1.15	0.79	0.84	0.80	1.01	0.83	0.16	0.68	1.15
Malaysia	0.95	1.04	1.35	1.31	1.03	0.69	0.80	0.65	0.79	1.41
Philippines	0.85	0.77	1.44	1.38	0.88	0.75	0.84	0.28	1.06	1.96
Thailand	1.00	1.00	1.00	1.00	1.00	1.00	1.00	1.00	1.00	1.00
South Asia										
Bangladesh	1.16	0.88	0.92	1.20	1.23	0.67	0.73	0.89	1.06	0.68
India	1.52	1.99	1.50	1.88	1.66	0.97	1.36	0.81	1.30	1.71
Pakistan	0.76	0.65	0.93	1.04	1.28	0.68	0.74	1.22	0.97	1.14
Sri Lanka	0.62	0.42	0.86	1.46	0.81	0.62	1.06	0.59	0.91	0.85

Note: Thailand = 1.
a. Data are for 1986.
Source: United Nations Industrial Development Organization industrial statistics database.

in manufacturing, which in the second half of the 1980s had risen by 40 percent, increased by much less in the second half of the 90s—only 15 percent (table 6.13).

Why did wage increases outstrip productivity increases in Thailand? The answer is that the economy turned the Lewisian corner in 1990 and ran straight into labor shortages (Warr 1998). In the 1980s agriculture had already experienced low labor productivity and a labor surplus that could be transferred to manufacturing, raising average productivity without a proportional increase in the wage rate. As the supply of surplus agricultural labor ran out in the early 1990s, peak season shortages developed and agricultural labor productivity increased. Soon the tighter labor market pushed up wages.

Labor productivity may also be constrained by a relative lack of skilled workers in Thailand. In 1995 Thailand had the second-lowest secondary school enrollment ratios in the region (only Indonesia's were lower) (table 6.14). Thailand's tertiary enrollment ratios were higher only than those in China, Indonesia, and Malaysia. Similarly tertiary enrollment in technical subjects like mathematics was the lowest in the region, and enrollments in engineering and technology were among the lowest.[4]

Another factor contributing to the rise in ULCs is real exchange rate appreciation. The real exchange rate (the rate at which commodities are traded) is strongly affected by movements in the nominal exchange rate. The standard argument is that the Thai baht appreciated because it was pegged to the U.S. dollar, which had appreciated against the yen. But this scenario occurred only after 1995. Between 1990 and 1995, the dollar did not appreciate against the yen. Evidence is now emerging that the real exchange rate appreciated because of the phenomenon known as Dutch Disease (Warr 1998). With a fixed exchange rate like Thailand's, the price of traded goods is determined by the international market price, even when demand increases. But the price of domestic nontraded goods is bid up when demand increases, reducing average competitiveness in the economy.

INEFFICIENCY IN THE USE OF CAPITAL. Investment peaked at 41 percent of GDP in 1996, domestic savings at 33 percent, and capital inflows at 8 percent. But weaknesses were emerging in the way capital was used. One measure of efficiency in the use of capital is the incremental capital output ratio (ICOR), which shows how much capital is needed to produce a unit of output. The smaller the amount needed, the lower the ICOR. A lower ICOR means increased efficiency in both the use of capital and the economy. Thailand's ICOR was 5 in 1980–85, but it dropped to 3 in

TABLE 6.13
Labor Productivity

Sector	1986	1987	1988	1989	1990	1991	1992	1993	1994	1995	1996
Average	88.6	93.5	100.0	110.8	112.1	130.1	135.8	143.3	161.0	169.2	178.0
Agriculture	97.8	100.4	100.0	111.9	92.0	124.9	128.0	123.7	148.2	151.0	165.0
Mining	86.1	98.9	100.0	144.0	136.7	135.2	148.8	166.8	203.0	193.1	227.6
Manufacturing	83.0	80.8	100.0	97.6	119.9	103.0	107.5	115.9	121.8	127.8	134.5
Construction	96.3	87.8	100.0	109.5	123.4	92.0	85.4	101.3	85.4	89.3	80.0
Utilities	87.1	88.2	100.0	121.6	144.7	142.4	153.8	143.4	131.2	146.4	168.1
Transport	88.9	84.8	100.0	104.8	114.0	104.5	114.7	119.8	129.4	134.9	147.7
Trade	85.8	84.6	100.0	111.1	133.1						
Public admin. and others			100.0								

Source: ILO (1998).

TABLE 6.14
Educational Enrollment, 1999 (or most recent years)

| Country | Enrollments (percent) | | Tertiary level technical enrollments | | | | | | | |
| | Secondary | Tertiary | Natural science | | Math/computing | | Engineering | | Total technology | |
			Number	%	Number	%	Number	%	Number	%
Argentina	67	36	69,727	0.21	...	...	96,205	0.29	165,932	0.49
Brazil	46	11	46,322	0.03	92,701	0.06	149,660	0.10	288,693	0.19
China	55	4	95,492	0.01	174,862	0.02	1,156,735	0.10	1,427,089	0.13
France	106	50	304,093	0.53	...	...	50,845	0.09	354,938	0.62
Germany	101	36	310,435	0.39	...	...	389,182	0.49	699,617	0.88
Hong Kong (China)	n.a.	21	5,503	0.09	6,441	0.11	14,788	0.25	26,732	0.46
India	49	6	869,119	0.10	...	...	216,837	0.02	1,085,956	0.12
Indonesia	45	10	22,394	0.01	13,117	0.01	205,086	0.11	240,597	0.13
Japan	98	29	59,030	0.05	20,391	0.02	488,699	0.39	568,620	0.46
Korea, Rep. of	99	55	81,222	0.18	171,147	0.38	437,537	0.98	689,906	1.55
Malaysia	61	10	8,776	0.05	4,557	0.02	12,693	0.07	26,026	0.14
Mexico	58	14	42,457	0.05	97,575	0.01	221,867	0.27	361,899	0.45
Philippines	79	27	27,200	0.04	121,300	0.18	225,700	0.33	373,900	0.55
Singapore[a]	68	46	1,281	0.05	1,420	0.05	13,029	0.47	15,730	0.56
Taiwan (China)	88	38	16,823	0.08	32,757	0.16	179,094	0.86	228,674	1.09
Thailand	49	21	77,098	0.14	1,292	0.00	105,149	0.19	183,539	0.32
UK	94	41	105,983	0.18	76,430	0.13	219,078	0.38	401,491	0.69
USA	97	81	496,415	0.19	525,067	0.20	801,126	0.31	1,822,608	0.70

Source: UNESCO, *Statistical Yearbook*, various years; Government of Taiwan *Statistical Yearbook* 1994; and Lall (1999).

a. Singapore's tertiary enrollment figures include polytechnics, which enroll 27 of the age group.

n.a. not available.

... not applicable (included in another discipline).

1985–90, rose again to 5 in 1990–95, and then peaked at 6 in 1996 (table 6.15). In other words, the Thai ICOR doubled during the 1990s, halving the efficiency of capital use and of the economy.

In 1985–90 Thailand had the lowest ICOR in the region and the highest GDP growth (10 percent annually). But in the latter half of the 1990s the situation reversed itself, and the Thai ICOR rose to 5—the highest in the region. Countries with lower levels of investment, including China, Malaysia, and Singapore, achieved higher or equivalent growth rates. The very high levels of investment and capital inflows in Thailand, which peaked in the 1990s, appear to be associated with this drop in the efficiency of capital use.

The high ICORs and inefficient use of capital reflect a substantial reduction in the rate of technical change in the economy. Technical change can be measured by total factor productivity (TFP), which shows the change in output for one unit of input. TFPs for Thailand follow the same pattern across time as ICORs (table 6.16). In the first half of the 1980s, when the ICOR was 5, the TFP stood at a low 0.5. In other words technical change was negative over this period, when a unit of capital and labor produced less than a unit of output. In the second half of the 1980s, when the ICOR fell to 3, the TFP was high (over 3). And from 1990 to 1995, when the ICOR doubled to 5 and then rose to 6, the TFP fell to near zero. The highly negative TFP of –4 in industry and manufacturing was largely responsible for the near-zero aggregate TFP.

The high level of capital inflows are also partly responsible for the high ICORs and falling TFPs. Paradoxically macroeconomic policies designed to deal with the inflows may have heightened their impact (Warr 1998). Macroeconomic policy deals with inflows by sterilizing them through the sale of central bank bonds. Sterilization offsets the impact of capital

TABLE 6.15
Savings, Investment, and Growth

	1980–85	1985–90	1990–95	1996
Output growth	5.4	10.3	8.0	6.4
ICOR	5.3	3.1	5.1	6.4
Investment/GDP	28.8	31.8	41.1	41.0
Domestic savings (% of GDP)	22.9	25.5	33.6	33.0
Current account deficit (% of GDP)	5.9	6.3	7.5	8.0

Source: Dwor-Frecaut (1998).

TABLE 6.16
Total Factor Productivity Growth Rates

		GDP	Land	Capital	Labor	TFP
Total	1981–85	5.45	0.16	3.39	1.37	0.53
	1986–90	10.34	−0.02	4.92	2.20	3.24
	1991–95	8.56	−0.04	6.73	1.84	0.03
	1981–95	8.12	0.03	5.01	1.80	1.27
Industry	1981–85	6.47	...	5.58	2.76	−1.87
	1986–90	14.42	...	7.07	3.83	3.52
	1991–95	10.62	...	8.97	5.30	−3.65
	1981–95	10.50	...	7.20	3.97	−0.67
Manufacturing	1981–85	4.99	...	3.41	2.85	−1.27
	1986–90	15.10	...	7.19	3.93	3.98
	1991–95	10.95	...	8.28	5.74	−3.07
	1981–95	10.35	...	6.29	4.18	−0.12
Services	1981–85	5.33	...	3.99	2.79	−1.45
	1986–90	10.01	...	5.22	3.26	1.53
	1991–95	8.15	...	6.71	2.73	−1.29
	1981–95	7.83	...	5.30	2.93	−0.40

... not applicable.
Source: TDRI 1998.

inflows and the resulting current account deficit on the money supply. As the public buys bonds, the money supply shrinks and interest rates rise. But another irony is at work: as rates of return rise, more portfolio capital flows into the economy. The added inflows increase the money supply, nullifying the sterilization and increasing demand (the Mundell-Flemming effect). Increased demand bids up the price of nontraded goods (Dutch Disease), attracting more resources to this sector than to the traded goods sector and decreasing the efficiency of the economy.

Certain macroeconomic conditions can help economies avoid the Dutch Disease dilemma. A current account deficit is more sustainable if capital inflows are invested in exports (Dwor-Frecaut 1998). Net export growth should be greater than the interest rate on foreign savings, or the high interest rate will simply attract more portfolio capital inflows to the nontradables sector (bypassing the tradables sector). In Thailand these macroeconomic conditions may have been violated, leading to major losses in efficiency and competitiveness. The interest rate spread—the difference between the lending and deposit rates, or the lending and London

Interbank Offer Rates (LIBOR)—is the incentive for foreign savings to flow into an economy. Thai spreads rose in 1990–96 from 4 to 6 percent. In comparison spreads in Korea ranged from 0–1 percent. Similarly Thai spreads in terms of the LIBOR also rose, climbing from 8 to 10 percent, while Korean spreads ranged between 2 and 3 percent. These high spreads competed with exports, increasing capital inflows to 8 percent of GDP. But these inflows were increasingly and predominantly portfolio capital, so that large amounts of both foreign and domestic savings were channeled into nontradables, especially real estate, resulting in a concomitant decline in capital efficiency, technical change, and competitiveness.

A macroeconomic policy that maintains high spreads and therefore even higher interest rates has a major impact on productivity and profitability through yet another channel. A survey of 1,227 Thai firms shows that the top 30 percent have a high TFP (approximately 175) while the bottom 70 percent have a very low TFP (approximately 30) (Dollar and Hallward-Driemeirer 1998). Small and medium-sized firms (SMEs) have low levels of productivity and technical change because of the high interest rates they face and are acknowledged to be starved for credit (Colaco 1998).

Finally, a survey of firms shows that their profitability had declined considerably prior to the crisis (Dollar and Hallword-Driemeirer 1998). Net profits relative to capital and retained earnings had dropped from 17 to 4 percent. The high real exchange rate was largely responsible for this decline, along with the high cost of capital. The tradable sector is unable to bid up prices in a fixed exchange rate regime in an open economy that allows international markets to set prices.

The Impact of the Crisis on the Labor Market

There are several ways to estimate the impact of the crisis on the labor market, but the methods vary according to the rigor of the estimation. We look at unadjusted estimates, including raw employment levels, and estimates adjusted for such factors as seasonal unemployment. In 1997 employment stood at 30.3 million, but it fell to 29.4 million in 1998 (table 6.17). Although the employment level rose again in 1999, it did not reach the 1997 level.

Unadjusted Estimates

Unemployment jumped from 0.7 million in 1997 to 1.7 million in 1999. Official statistics show that recorded layoffs increased from 5,000 in 1996 to 42,000 in 1997 and 52,000 in 1998 (ILO 1999). Women constituted a somewhat higher proportion of those laid off (53 percent). Because of the preponderance of women workers in the export sector and the decline in exports, women were severely hit in particular industries. Women as a proportion of all those retrenched equaled 95 percent in garments, 88 percent in toys, 80 percent in knitting and electrical appliances, 73 percent in jewelry, 71 percent in plastic products, and 68 percent in shoes and leather products.

The crisis has generated underemployment as well as unemployment. Employers wishing to avoid severance payments have an incentive to reduce working hours rather than laying workers off altogether. Labor Force Survey data show that underemployment increased from 2.43 million (7.6 percent of the labor force) in 1997 to 4.41 million (13.7 percent of the labor force) in 1998 (NSO 1999).

The unemployment and underemployment levels do not show the full impact of the crisis, however. Declines in the wage rate are an important indicator of the impact on income, because very low-income workers facing total loss of income will take jobs at even lower rates of pay. Labor Force Survey data show that between February 1997 and February 1998, the nominal wage rate dropped by 6 percent, while the real wage rate dropped by 4 percent (ILO 1999). The decline in urban areas (8.3 percent) was almost double the decline in rural areas (4.7 percent). At the aggregate level men and women seem to have experienced the same levels of decline. But in urban areas women's real wages eroded by 10.5 percent, more than the decline in men's wages. In rural areas, however, the drop in men's real wage rate was higher than it was for women's. In urban sectors the steepest declines in real wage rates were in manufacturing (13 percent) and construction (24 percent).

The unemployed had recourse not only to work at lower wages but also to work in the informal sector, self-employment, and migration to rural areas. Table 6.6 reflects the shift in the occupational structure prompted by the crisis. Of an employed labor force of 30 million in 1997, private sector employees constituted the largest group (11.6 million). By 1999 this group had shrunk by 1.4 million, but the number of self-employed workers had increased by 0.8 million. This shift out of wage employment into self-employment represents a shift primarily to the informal sector in urban areas and to the agricultural sector in rural areas.

Adjusted Estimates

Estimates made using data from the Labor Force Survey are based on one particular indicator (such as employment) at one point in time. Even

TABLE 6.17
Labor Force Status, 1994–99 (February)

	1994	1995	1996	1997	1998	1999
Total population	59034.9	59112.9	59750.4	60350.7	60949.0	61551.2
Total labor force	31049.9	31347.9	31898.4	32000.2	32143.1	32810.2
Employed	28233.5	29055.1	30099.2	30266.4	29412.9	30024.5
Unemployed	1244.4	723.5	641.3	697.9	1479.3	1715.7
Looking for work	200.1	167.8	119.6	179.6	402.8	475.8
Available for work	1044.2	555.7	521.7	518.3	1076.5	1239.8
Seasonally inactive	1571.9	1569.2	1157.8	1035.9	1250.8	1069.8
Unemployment rate (%)	4.0	2.3	2.0	2.2	4.6	5.2
Open unemployment rate (%)	0.6	0.5	0.4	0.6	1.3	1.5

Source: Labor Force Survey, ILO, CEPR.

comparisons of a single indicator at two points in time do not necessarily reflect a specific event such as the crisis. The change in the indicator over time must be adjusted for the internal dynamic of the economy. In Thailand's case two important factors integral to this internal dynamic that need to be considered are seasonality and the trend growth of the economy.

The impact of the seasons on labor market variables is high in Thailand. There are two distinct seasons— dry (winter and spring) and wet (summer and autumn). Kakwani (1998) estimates the seasonal impact on employment at a highly significant 10 percent—that is, employment in the dry season drops by 3 million (out of a labor force of 30 million). Women are the most seriously affected (2.2 million).

The second factor, the trend growth of the economy, shows us what would have happened to an indicator like employment had the crisis not occurred. Kakwani takes Labor Force Survey data for six wet and six dry seasons for the years 1992–98 and adjusts them for seasonality and trend growth. He then creates a "crisis index" for 1997–98 that estimates the impact of the crisis on the indicator. The estimates show that the trend growth of employment in Thailand resulted in 0.22 million jobs per year before the crisis. Calculating the immediate impact of the crisis involves comparing wet season data for 1997 to dry season data for 1998. The unadjusted data show that employment dropped by 3.8 million (from 33.2 million to 29.4 million). But adjusting for seasonality and trend growth, we find that employment dropped by only 0.7 million (from 31.7 million to 30.9 million).

Trend growth in unemployment was negative before the crisis, with the number of unemployed falling by 0.08 percent per year. The gender gap in unemployment rates was narrowing, with women's unemployment rates falling faster than men's (–0.18 percent compared with –0.1 percent). Seasonality accounted for a loss of 0.52 million jobs in each dry season. Given these variables the adjusted crisis index shows that the crisis generated unemployment of 2.6 percent (2.9 percent for men but only 2.2 percent for women). The result is an adjusted unemployment level for the first quarter of 1998 of 3.9 percent. Adjusted estimates of formal sector unemployment place the level higher, at 5.4 percent, twice as high as informal sector unemployment of 2.6 percent.

Growth in underemployment was also negative before the crisis, with underemployment falling at an annual rate of –0.01 percent. The adjusted estimates show that the crisis increased underemployment by 0.11 million, raising the underemployment level to 0.36 million (0.19 million men and 0.16 million women) in the first quarter of 1998.

Kakwani (1998) estimates that real wage growth was experiencing an upward trend before the crisis, rising at an annual average rate of TB 188 per month, with the gender gap decreasing over time. He also estimates that the adjusted average real wage dropped by TB 506 per month because of the crisis (at the basic rate) and by TB 629 per month (with overtime reductions). The impact on men's wages was more pronounced than the impact on women's wages.

Kakwani also estimates a standard-of-living index by adjusting for regional variation in prices. According to his estimates the standard of living was increasing at a rate of 6.8 percent annually before the crisis and dropped 21 percent after the crisis began. Disaggregating this figure shows that the largest contribution is a decline in income per earner of 19 percent. A less significant contribution (2.7 percent) is attributable to a drop in employment, and the least significant contribution (0.4 percent) can be traced to a drop in the LFPR. The crisis caused poverty to increase in 1998 by 2 percent, raising it to 13 percent (table 6.2).

The occupational impact of the crisis was especially severe on wage employees. Wage and salary employment dropped by an estimated 1.2 million, while farm employment picked up by 0.6 million. Wage income overall dropped by an estimated TB 768 per month. The impact was particularly profound in construction, manufacturing, trade, and banking, with the adjusted real wage in manufacturing dropping by an estimated TB 857 per month. The crisis did not significantly affect farm income, however, confirming that an occupational shift took place. Migration to rural areas became a significant strategy for maintaining income among the urban unemployed. The scope of internal migration is difficult to estimate, not the least because Thailand's population has always had migratory habits. Of the 47 million Thais older than 13 in 1998, approximately 2.3 million had migrated in the last year and 5.2 million in the last 5 years.

Recent migrants make up one of two groups that have been particularly vulnerable during the crisis. The unemployment rate for recent migrants has increased 13 percent since the crisis began, and their income has dropped from an average of TB 3,765 per month to TB 3,294. The other particularly vulnerable group is children. Kakwani (1998) estimates the incidence of child labor in Thailand at 15 percent in 1998. But even this high level represents a decline in the trend growth of child labor of over 5 percent per year. The adjusted crisis index shows that child labor increased by 0.4 million because of the crisis.

The Policy Response to the Crisis: A Matter of Causality

In essence there are four explanations for the Asian financial crisis, each with its own policy implications. We offer a fifth explanation based on a consensus that offers more comprehensive options for designing policy instruments.

The first position argues that the crisis was induced by currency policy (IMF 1998). An overvalued pegged exchange rate reduces export competitiveness, creates a current account deficit, and depletes foreign exchange reserves. In this situation tight monetary and fiscal policies, especially higher interest rates and tight credit controls, can help to prevent further exchange rate depreciation and inflation.

A second position characterizes the Asian crisis as a financial panic. Thai banks especially borrowed short-term, unhedged capital from international markets and lent it to the corporate sector on a long-term basis against inflated assets. The banks and the corporate sector were highly leveraged. When portfolio investors saw that the exchange rate regime was unsustainable, they panicked, reversing the huge inflows. The panic became a self-fulfilling prophecy created by investors withdrawing capital from indebted but solvent borrowers in a situation that offered no lenders of last resort to bail the borrowers out. The macroeconomic policy prescription in these cases is to protect the economy through lenders of last resort.

A third position holds that the Asian financial crisis was caused by moral hazard (Lee 1998; Krugman 1998). Moral hazard occurs when banks borrowing with public guarantees use the funds for overly risky ventures. These banks and their risky debtors are prone to failure, triggering downturns in economic activity. Since moral hazard is based on collusion among the government, banks, and the corporate sector, and government intervention has gone wrong, the policy position is to reduce government intervention.

The fourth explanation maintains that a lack of government intervention caused the crisis. The governments of the region had a solid 20-year track record of generating high growth and lowering poverty through judicious regulation and intervention. The problems underlying the crisis arose when the governments deviated from their successful policies, principally through poorly managed financial liberalization. The policy position suggested by this viewpoint, then, is a return to the regulatory policies of the past.

Our consensus-based explanation of the Asian crisis is grounded in the recognition that all three major markets—currency, capital, and labor—were experiencing problems simultaneously. All three had major imperfections. While the imperfections in the currency and capital markets have been widely discussed the problems of the labor market have not been stressed and therefore have been assigned a low priority in the process of policy reform.

THE CURRENCY AND CAPITAL MARKETS. The currency market suffered as the government attempted to maintain a pegged exchange rate with an open capital account. There were a number of capital market imperfections—for instance, the problem of moral hazard highlighted by Lee (1998) and Krugman (1998) and, perhaps most important, the inefficient patterns of investment. As we have seen, to a large extent the declining efficiency of capital was the result of a combination of the Mundell-Flemming effect and the Dutch Disease syndrome. Macroeconomic policy designed to sanitize inflows into Thailand reduced the money supply, increasing interest rates and paradoxically leading to higher inflows. As demand increased the prices of nontradables such as real estate rose, and more and more resources were channelled to the sector. The result was not only inefficient capital allocation but also a decline in competitiveness.

Further, high interest rates and spreads raised the opportunity cost of capital, reducing productivity, profitability, and technological development among SMEs, which account for 70 percent of all employment in Thailand. High spreads increased the inflows but at the same time created a disincentive against hedging. When the capital flows were suddenly reversed, the banks—which had borrowed short and lent long (in unhedged funds)—faced a liquidity crisis that flowed on to domestic firms, and both banks and firms faced closure.

THE LABOR MARKET. As we have argued, the labor market suffered from declining competitiveness in all categories of manufacturing, but especially in labor-intensive industries. Thailand's ULCs were not competitive in the region in the 1990s, in part because of growth in wages that outstripped growth in productivity. This weakness is also in part attributable to Dutch Disease syndrome during the first half of the 1990s. As an increasing volume of resources flowed into nontradables, aggregate productivity fell and the real exchange rate (and therefore ULCs) rose. And in the mid-1990s the nominal exchange rate, which was pegged to the U.S. dollar, appreciated against the yen, raising ULCs even more.

Because of these weaknesses, Thai exports never really recovered from the export recession in East Asia that began in 1995. Declining competitiveness in both traditional and technology-intensive industries left Thailand at a disadvantage. When the regional currencies depreciated in mid-1997 and capital flows reversed, the liquidity problems of Thai banks and firms brought economic growth to an immediate halt. Thailand's growth was unsustainable because its fundamentals were wrong. It was based on simple input increases rather than on increased productivity and technological advancement. At the time the crisis struck, the economy needed very high investment levels (financed through inflows) in order to continue growing.

The Debate over Policy Instruments

The financial crisis (and arguably the current reform package) has severely compressed demand. Liquidity problems have kept Thai firms from maintaining past levels of production. Without the goods to export, the competitive edge provided by the depreciation in the real exchange rate means little. Thus import compression rather than export expansion has reduced the current account deficits.

The crisis may have been deepened and prolonged by some of the domestic policies the Thai authorities followed. Monetary tightening may have accounted for as much as a quarter of the contraction in GDP between 1997 and 1998 (IMF 1999). Monetary tightening may also have exacerbated liquidity problems for firms, especially SMEs. But the key problem was the effectiveness of interest rates, the chosen policy instrument. The most recent studies show that the relationship between interest rates and the exchange rate (the variable that interest rates were supposed to influence) was not the predicted positive but instead was highly ambiguous. In other words raising interest rates did not raise the exchange rate.

Policy measures such as closing banks and raising interest rates could have increased the panic rather than stemming it. The authorities believed that tight money would attract capital. However the Kindleberger effect (which was operative here) introduced another element—the elasticity of investors' expectations. If interest rates rise and investors' expectations are not elastic (that is, investors do not expect a crisis), the higher interest rates will attract capital. But if interest rates rise and investors' expectations are elastic (that is, investors expect a change in prices or an exchange rate depreciation), capital will flee.

A New Macroeconomic Policy

A new macroeconomic policy designed to increase the growth of output and employment needs to be based on trends in both demand and supply. The Thai economy is experiencing a severe compression of demand. Reversing this situation requires reflation through expansionary fiscal and monetary policy and higher fiscal deficits to expand consumption.

In order to improve the supply of goods and services, policies must be designed to increase competitiveness, particularly of SMEs. A more expansionary monetary policy based on lower interest rates will help increase their survival rate, competitiveness, and employment capacity. Other policies must address training and education, research and development R&D, and labor productivity. Weaknesses in all these areas prevent Thailand from regaining its competitive standing. Given the credit bias against SMEs, a much higher proportion of credit needs to be directed to them. Improving the competitiveness of inefficient SMEs is more cost-effective than fostering marginal improvements in the competitiveness of larger enterprises that already have relatively high productivity levels. One institutional possibility would be to set up a trust fund to bail out the most vulnerable SMEs.

In order to regain its competitive edge, Thailand also needs to improve skills training, vocational education, and R&D. The lack of much-needed skills contributes to the country's low rates of productivity and technological change and low value added in medium- and high-technology manufacturing. Thailand has low enrollments in secondary and tertiary institutions as well as in technical areas and insufficient investment in R&D. Policies need to be designed to increase enrollments and technical training. To increase investment in R&D, the government must invest in capacity and provide incentives for private firms to increase funding for innovation.

Increasing labor productivity requires a number of enabling conditions. First, it requires a forum for cooperative dialogue with employers in order to prevent conflict. Next, it requires effective training for management as well as labor. It requires incentives for firms to provide training, including financial support. And finally, because employment and welfare are inextricably linked to productivity, it requires attention to the conditions of employment. The benefits of productivity increases can be reaped only if firms retain their skilled labor by providing job security and a safety net that includes unemployment insurance, accidental death and injury insurance, and a retirement system.

The Response to the Crisis

The government's actions in response to the crisis fall into three areas: employment generation, employment services, and vocational education and training. In 1998, as the recession worsened, the government launched a social safety net program. The program aimed to:

- Generate employment and stimulate the economy, especially through productive investment and labor-intensive job creation;
- Mitigate the short-run impact of the crisis by providing income support and social services for the unemployed, the vulnerable, and the poor;
- Develop the skills workers need to stay abreast of technological changes; and
- Implement the structural reforms necessary to increase economic competitiveness.

The government allocated a budget of approximately TB 20,000 million for the program. For the 1999 fiscal year, the allocation was TB 157,800 million, or 21 percent of the expenditure budget. Additional financial support from the World Bank, the Asian Development Bank (ADB), the Overseas Economic Cooperation Fund, and the Japanese Export-Import Bank has also been secured under various programs. These include a Social Sector Program ($500 million), a Social Investment Program ($462 million), and the Miyazawa Initiative ($1.5 billion).[5]

Job Creation and Employment Maintenance

To create jobs and encourage reverse migration from urban to rural areas, in 1999 the government allocated TB 51 billion from its regular budget to provide direct and indirect employment in rural areas. Of this amount TB 18 billion was to be used to employ 800,000 people. Direct employment initiatives include 68 rural job-creation projects involving public works. These projects rehabilitate and construct economic infrastructure (roads, drainage, dredging, weirs, bridges, dams, airports, tourism facilities, utilities, and offices), construct public health centers, build low-cost housing, and help conserve forests. Indirect job-creation projects involve vocational development (such as handicrafts, vocational education, and rubber tapping) for youth and women, agricultural irrigation projects, and livestock projects.

The Social Investment Program supports 5 main projects that generate 557,000 person-months of employment plus 16,375 road construction jobs. The work includes constructing village feeder roads, constructing and dredging weirs, rehabilitating and expanding small-scale irrigation networks, rehabilitating and constructing tourist facilities, rehabilitating and building schools, and upgrading civic amenities in the Bangkok urban area.

The Social Structure Program Loan funds a project that provides employment at village welfare centers for 13,000 unemployed and laid-off workers and new university graduates. Project participants assist welfare workers in improving services to villages. Of the TB 852 million budget approved for the project in December 1998, however, less than a quarter had been disbursed by March 1999.

Of the Miyazawa Initiative budget of TB 53 billion, just under half has been used to create direct employment for unskilled and educated workers. The unskilled workers upgrade rural irrigation systems and construct small infrastructure projects, while some 89,000 educated workers assist with government services. Ministry of Interior projects received approximately 35 percent of the total Miyazawa fund to generate employment for 24,000 educated workers and provide 50 million person-days of employment for unskilled workers.

Income-support Measures

Income-support measures have included severance pay, tax and utility price cuts, a price support program for rice, and extension of health care and educational subsidies. As Thailand has no unemployment insurance scheme, the first (and primary) income support workers receive is severance pay. The new Labor Protection Law (in effect since September 1997) raises the maximum severance pay rate to the equivalent of 10 months of the employee's salary. However, compliance is apparently low. Although official statistics on severance pay have not been available since the crisis, casual evidence from small enterprises indicates that none of the retrenched had been given any severance pay. Some reported that they were not even given their last paycheck. Most people do not consider the long court procedure entailed in recovering this money worthwhile, given the amounts involved. But the Ministry of Labor and Social Welfare closely monitors enterprises that look likely to shut down and warns management about its legal obligations to employees.

The government announced tax reductions in March 1999. The most significant reduction is in the value-added tax (VAT), which was reduced from

10 to 7 percent for two years. Income tax was waived on the first TB 50,000 of income, as was a corporate tax of 1.5 percent of sales levied on small-scale enterprises earning less than TB 1.2 million per year. And the excise tax on fuel oils was slashed from 17.5 percent to 5 percent. The government estimates that these tax cuts will cost TB 57 billion a year in lost revenue.

The government also reduced electricity tariffs as of March 1999 by an average of TB 0.26 per unit. This reduction will cost TB 19 billion per year in lost revenue. At the same time the government reduced the price of cooking gas by 10.5 percent, a move that will save consumers an estimated TB 229 million per month.

To help rice farmers affected by the crisis and by falling world paddy prices, in February 1999 the government initiated a price support program for rice at a level above the prevailing market price. TB 3,500 million will be used to buy 250,000 tons of rice at fixed prices, but the rice will be exported in order not to affect domestic prices.

Thailand has two public health insurance systems: a health-card scheme run by the Ministry of Public Health and a social security scheme run by the Social Security Office of the Department of Labor and Social Welfare. The health-card scheme is open to the general public. Thais pay a fee of TB 500 to obtain a health card for one year, with the government contributing another TB 500. The health card entitles the holder to health services at a designated health center and to emergency treatment at any public health center. In 1999 the number of subscribers was raised from 1.2 million to 2.4 million, and the government's contribution rose to TB 1,000 under the Social Safety Net Program.

The social security scheme is a form of health insurance, but it also includes compensation for hospitalized workers and a death benefit. Participation is mandatory for all workers in enterprises with a staff of 10 or more. The government, employers, and employees all contribute 1 percent of the employee's salary as the insurance premium. Workers receive free medical treatment at a designated hospital and, in case of prolonged treatment that causes them to miss work, 50 percent of their salary. Because of the crisis the government extended coverage to laid-off subscribers, who can receive hospitalization benefits for a year without having to pay monthly contributions. The retrenched can continue subscribing to the scheme after a year but must make monthly payments.

To improve educational opportunities for the underprivileged, the government gives education loans to households with incomes of less than TB 150,000 per year. The loans, which can be used up to the bachelor's degree level, enable borrowers to meet school fees and some living expenses. Repayment begins two years after students complete their education and can be extended for up to 15 years at an interest rate of 1 percent. As of the end of 1998, TB 13 billion had been loaned to about 638,000 students.

Additionally, the Miyazawa Initiative has provided TB 869 million to expand the school lunch and school uniform programs for poor students. And a TB 35 million loan from the ADB under the Social Structure Program provides milk and lunch to 15,000 disadvantaged children in urban areas and in child development centers. A loan of TB 480 million from the Miyazawa Initiative provides subsidies for 400,000 elderly poor and for 50,000 poor families needing to supplement their income.

Skill Development and Vocational Training

To upgrade the skills of the unemployed, in 1999 the Ministry of Labor and Social Welfare launched a skill development program targeting 123,000 people over three years. The program provides training in a range of skills, including truck driving, equipment maintenance, appliance repair, and computer programming. Approximately 10,000 unemployed workers are scheduled to undergo training in programming and system design and analysis. The ministry also provides training in managing home-based production networks for leaders of subcontracting groups in rural areas. Approximately 7,500 project leaders are expected to receive this training.

The Ministry of Industry provides occupational and vocational training for rural workers, and the Bangkok Metropolitan Administration services those residing in the capital. While rural workers receive training primarily in handicrafts, the Bangkok Metropolitan Administration aims at self-employment in the service industry. Under the Miyazawa Initiative, Thammasat University will train 10,000 unemployed university graduates to become computer programmers.

Capacity-building Schemes

In addition to skill development, the government offers programs to improve productivity and competitiveness in manufacturing. The Ministry of Industry, for instance, will train 4,500 people to act as advisors to some 2,000 export businesses on adopting the ISO 9000 standard.[6] In collaboration with the National Productivity Institute, the Thai Japanese Technological Promotion Association, and the Small Industrial Financial Corporation, the ministry has also set up a TB 72 million project to evaluate enterprises. The program aims to improve the competitiveness of SMEs by enhancing their management capabilities. Evaluators trained through the program will use an "enterprise diagnosis system" with an evaluating index to assess enterprises. By the end of 2000, the program will have certified an estimated 100 evaluators and assessed 2,000 SMEs.

SMEs can also receive assistance in creating jobs and improving productivity. The Department of Industrial Promotion in the Ministry of Industry, in collaboration with the Krung Thai Bank, has set up a loan facility for SMEs. The facility has funds totaling TB 10 billion and will lend to a projected 2,700 SMEs in 1999–2000. The program, which targets primarily rural enterprises, is expected to generate direct and indirect employment for about 120,000 persons. The Krung Thai Bank has also allocated TB 3 billion in loans for approximately 200 SMEs in 1999, and the Government Savings Bank has set aside TB 1 billion to support SMEs. In addition the Bank for Agriculture and Cooperatives is proposing to amend its operations to include lending to farmers in the off season to support income-generating activities. Once the change is approved, the Bank is expected to provide TB 2,000 million to support 10,000 microenterprises.

The Ministry of Industry is also providing venture capital for SMEs (approximately TB 3–5 billion) from the government budget, the Overseas Economic Cooperation Fund, the ADB, and private investors. These funds will be used to buy shares of less than 50 percent in targeted industries, including electrical appliances and vehicle parts and industries using local technologies and inventions. In addition, credit guarantee facilities for SMEs are being planned to assist enterprises that have good prospects but lack collateral.

Assessing Program Performance

The programs the government launched in response to the crisis have enjoyed only limited success. The job creation and maintenance programs suffered from delays in implementation and are only stopgap measures. Income-support measures such as the severance pay scheme bypass a large number of workers released by failing firms that lack the funds to make the payments. Securing the severance pay system is especially important in light of the fact that Thailand has no unemployment insurance system.

JOB CREATION AND MAINTENANCE PROGRAMS. Each of the employment generation projects creates a large number of jobs. The Ministry of the Interior alone expects to provide some 790,000 jobs using the regular government budget and approximately 2 million person-months of work under the loan from the Miyazawa Initiative and the World Bank (through the Social Investment Program). Under the Social Investment Program, the Ministry of Agriculture and Cooperatives is generating employment equivalent to 9 million person-months. Despite these encouraging numbers, the programs have a number of problems.

First, despite the fact that the programs may have tightened up the labor market to some extent, numerous projects have been delayed. For instance only 58 village feeder road projects out of 883 had been carried out under the Social Investment Program as of May 1999, although all the funds were scheduled for disbursal that year. The weir projects under the same program have had similar problems. By May 1999 only 662 of the planned 1,635 weirs had been dredged and only 11 were under construction.

Second, many of the projects—especially under the Miyazawa Initiative—require a large number of workers with secondary and college education. Ministry of Interior projects alone will generate employment for 24,338 educated workers. At the same time other agencies are also either hiring or training these workers. The National Election Committee plans to recruit 20,000 graduates to create greater awareness of the new constitution, and Thammasat University expects to train 10,000 as programmers. These projects are unlikely to be easy to implement in view of the small number of qualified workers, many of whom may not be willing to relocate.

Third, the jobs that are being created are in general temporary. The pay for educated workers is below the market rate, creating a disincentive for workers to stay and jeopardizing the projects. Because the work is temporary, it affords no job security—another disincentive to stick with a project through completion. The temporary nature of the jobs also reduces their multiplier effect. While the measures are meant to meet more than one objective (for instance, stimulating economic growth while providing assistance to the unemployed), the general outcome appears to be various forms of work sharing.

The emphasis thus far has been on direct job creation rather than self-employment. The Social Investment Fund, which provides assistance to communities, the Ministry of the Interior (under the Miyazawa Initiative), and the Ministry of Labor and Social Welfare have plans to encourage self-employment by providing funds for start-up investment. But with the credit crunch and high interest rates, unemployed workers need more assistance in training and equipping themselves to become self-employed.

INCOME-SUPPORT ACTIVITIES. As we have seen, the government's income-support activities take a variety of forms. Its activities include direct transfers, subsidies for school lunches and uniforms, price supports for rice and utilities, health insurance (through the health-card scheme and social security), tax reductions on income and excise taxes and VAT, and education and business loans.

The school lunch and uniform projects were in place before the crisis. The crisis has made it difficult to maintain these projects, especially since the budget deficit must be cut to meet the conditions of the IMF loan. Support from international donors allows the government to continue the projects and to step up the projects to accommodate more children.

Price support programs (such as the program for rice) have been invoked from time to time to lessen the consumption burden of the poor. To make these programs effective, however, the price support level must be above the market price, and the funding for the programs must be substantial. Otherwise the programs cannot be sustained and should be avoided.

Since the crisis the government has extended health insurance coverage to more people through both the health-card scheme and the social security program. While more people now have coverage, the composition of demand for services has changed. As incomes have fallen, public health centers rather than private health clinics and hospitals are increasingly in demand. The government has not addressed the problem of increased demand at public clinics, where long lines of people await care.

The absence of a nationwide unemployment insurance scheme leaves many workers with no income protection when they lose their jobs. The severance pay scheme and a provident fund program are limited to employees in the formal sector, leaving workers in the informal sector unprotected. As we have seen the severance pay system is often ineffective in times of crisis, as failing firms (both large and small) often lack the money to make the mandated payments. A severance pay guarantee scheme may be the only method of ensuring that workers have some form of social protection when they lose their jobs. One alternative scheme that has been under consideration is a public compensation fund for unpaid severance payments financed with fines on firms that violate the Labor Protection Act. But this scheme may be most feasible during times of relative normalcy. During a crisis of any magnitude, the funds generated by the fines would not be enough to pay the large number of unemployed workers. For this reason businesses may also need to contribute to such a fund. An unemployment insurance scheme could be instituted to ensure that workers are not left without some form of support.

The benefits of tax reductions should not be overstressed. Tax reductions (especially in the VAT) are often effective in increasing purchasing power. But the VAT does not apply to essential goods such as foods, limiting the impact of such a reduction. Moreover, an economy realizes the full impact of tax reductions only if the government maintains its expenditure levels and accepts a larger deficit. If it maintains the deficit at the existing level, the tax reduction represents expenditure switching (from the government to consumers). The effect of an increase in government expenditure on the economy is greater than the effect produced by a tax reduction.

Labor Market Services

Increased unemployment and underemployment have created a significant demand for labor market services. Both public and private market services are available in Thailand. The government provides services that include job matching, career counseling, and testing, but its effectiveness is limited by a weak labor market information system. Private employment agencies assist workers in finding employment domestically and abroad.

Public Employment Services

The Department of Employment provides services for both employers and job seekers through its 9 Bangkok and 76 provincial branches. Job seekers and employers needing workers are listed in a database for one year and matched on request. Periodic job fairs (over 800 in 1998 alone) bring prospective employers face to face with job seekers. The department provides job counseling and career guidance at job fairs, at educational institutions for graduates, and in villages, where people may seek subcontracting work from home. Some 894,000 members of the general public and 814,000 villagers received job counseling and career guidance in 1998.

Of the 1.5 million Thai workers who were unemployed in 1998, some 700,000 applied for 550,000 jobs through public placement services. However, only half the vacancies were filled. This low success rate underscores the importance of private placement services.

One method of boosting employment has been to reduce the number of foreign migrant workers in the country by increasing security at borders. While attempts to push out illegal migrant workers have been relatively successful, firms used to the cheaper wage rates of migrant labor have experienced problems as a result.

A second method of promoting employment has been to send workers abroad. This approach also creates problems, as the contagion effect of the crisis has reduced regional demand for labor. Overseas employment is expected to peak at just under 0.5 million in 1999, with new placements tapering off sharply from 200,000 per year to a quarter of that number. The Department of Employment provides some overseas placement services. Through its missions abroad the department identifies job vacancies, announces them, and processes applications for prospective employers. The department also provides skill testing to screen applicants and orientation sessions for newly hired workers, all free of charge. (In 1998 a quarter of a million workers were tested and over 100,000 workers going abroad received orientation.) But overall the department's placement rate for overseas jobs is low (table 6.18).

Private Employment Services

Private placement agencies, which operate temporary employment and permanent placement services, are under the supervision of the Ministry of Labor and Social Welfare through the Job Search and Worker Protection Act of 1985. The act allows the ministry to monitor the agencies to protect workers and to set fee levels.

Statistics on private agencies are not available. The Department of Employment's data on number of placements, applicants, and vacancies offer the best estimate of the magnitude of private employment services. These statistics provide only a residual, but the implication is significant—public employment services accounted for only half of job placements in 1998. Private agencies also accounted for almost 46 percent of foreign placements.[7]

The Department of Employment licenses private agencies as well as supervises them. The operating conditions include a deposit of TB 5 million with the department and registered minimum capital of TB 1 mil-

TABLE 6.18
Overseas Job Placement, 1998 (number of workers)

	Self-arranged	DOE	Employers	Private agencies	Total
Middle East	5,914	2	623	11,244	17,783
Africa	209	—	136	—	345
Asia	81,428	1,181	9,298	76,091	167,998
Others	4,661	87	537	324	5,609
Total	92,212	1,270	10,594	87,659	191,735

— not available.
Source: Department of Employment.

lion. Private agencies must submit work contracts to the department for approval and repatriate and reimburse job seekers whose contracts are withdrawn. In addition placement firms and overseas employers contribute to the Overseas Workers Aid Fund, which provides welfare and orientation training and skill testing for job seekers. Despite these safeguards the agencies are not trouble free. Some unscrupulous agencies charge exorbitant fees, and in some cases workers have been stranded abroad when promised jobs fell through.

Labor Market Support Services

The crisis has resulted in numerous business failures and the subsequent termination of employees. The Department of Labor Protection and Welfare provides assistance to the retrenched, especially in getting severance pay. The department inspects enterprises that are likely to close down and coordinates with other government agencies in determining the financial status of these businesses. When businesses close and the employees are terminated, the department examines documents such as wage and payroll accounts and employment agreements. The department also discusses with managers their obligations to their employees. When severance pay is not forthcoming, the department helps employees prepare legal documents (such as petitions) and joins in requests to sequester assets. It also coordinates with the Revenue Department to stop tax refunds to enterprises that shut down and leave their workers with no severance pay.

The Effectiveness of Labor Market Services

The Public Employment Service accounts for only a small share of job placements in Thailand. The service has trouble matching workers to jobs in part because it has limited contact with job seekers. In addition, Thailand has a weak labor market information system. This system is relatively new, and nationwide data are available, but the processing capacity is inadequate. The timeliness of the data is also an issue, as job opportunities change continually. The department has relied mainly on employers to provide information on vacancies, although it also initiates some contact with firms. It needs a more proactive strategy (based on ongoing contact with employers) in order to gather all the necessary information. A more dynamic information system will also provide the data needed to improve job counseling and career guidance services.

Vocational Education and Training

Both private and public vocational education and training are available in Thailand. Vocational education involves some years of formal schooling, while vocational training is generally relatively short term and skill specific. The institutions responsible for vocational education include the Department of Vocational Education of the Ministry of Education and various universities offering professional curricula as well as liberal arts. The major public institutions that provide vocational training are the Department of Skill Development (of the Ministry of Labor and Social Welfare) and the Bangkok Metropolitan Training Center (of the Bangkok Metropolitan Administration).

Vocational Education

The Department of Vocational Education offers a number of options ranging from short training courses to diplomas in five subject areas (industrial mechanics, handicrafts, home economics, commerce, and agriculture). The department has 413 schools and training centers around the country. The curricula include both formal education, which requires 2–3 years of study, and informal education, which requires anywhere from 45 to 225 hours. Enrollment in vocational education courses in 1997 was approximately 0.5 million, of which 54 percent was in industrial mechanics, 32 percent in commerce, 6 percent in agriculture, 5 percent in home economics, and 2 percent in handicrafts.

In July 1998 the department started a new project to provide vocational and technical education to retrain unemployed workers. In the first three months the 27,000 workers received training at 54 centers. Some 1,000 assistant trainers were also recruited from laid-off workers. The government urges workers who have completed the training to return to their hometowns—a strategy aimed at generating local income and reversing rural-urban migration. The project was deemed successful, with demand exceeding supply, and was repeated in 1999 with an additional budget of TB 35 million and 700 assistant trainers.

A project is also under way to upgrade the department's 413 training institutions. Under this project 2,200 new graduates or retrenched workers are setting up a database of enterprises and their occupational requirements. The government will use the database to estimate demand for vocational training. These workers will also execute an in-school job creation project designed to give students on-the-job training by subcontracting work from the private sector. The program will also supplement the income of both the school and the students.

Skill Development

The main role of the Department of Skill Development is to provide skill training to both new labor market entrants and employed workers from both the public and private sectors wanting to upgrade their skills. The service is also offered to the economically vulnerable, particularly in the agricultural sector, and the urban poor. The department has established skill standards and testing and provides training courses for trainers.

The department has sought greater private sector participation in skill development through a number of measures. In 1994 it set up a Skill Development Fund under the Vocational Training Promotion Act with initial capital of TB 400 million. Businesses can apply for loans from the fund at below-market interest rates to train their employees. Employers providing training for employees in the workplace can also deduct training costs from their taxes. The department supports the private sector in establishing Skill Standard Testing Centers. Training organizations registered under the Vocational Training Promotion Act are exempted from some labor regulations and statutes governing private schools. The department is also revising the Vocational Training Act of 1994 to further encourage private involvement in skill training.

In response to the economic crisis, the department has initiated a number of projects. The Thais Help Thais project provides vocational skills to retrenched and unemployed workers. Low-cost funding is available to unemployed workers to upgrade skills and prepare for self-employment. The Urban/Rural Employment project provides training in rural areas, particularly in subcontracting work such as rubber tapping and other forms of self-employment that can be carried out in villages. Finally, the Employment in the Industrial Sector project provides skill development to the general public and training for trainers. It also establishes test standards and encourages enterprises to train their own workers.

Metropolitan Vocational Training

The Bangkok Metropolitan Vocational Training Department of the Bangkok Metropolitan Administration offers short vocational and occupational training courses to the general public, but particularly to low-income groups and the vulnerable. Participants are trained in skills they can use in wage labor and in self-employment.

The department has 54 training centers in the Bangkok area. Courses offered include mechanics, electronics, small appliance repair (radio, television, computer, and air conditioner), stone cutting, dressmaking and tailoring, barbering, food preparation, typing, handicrafts, and music. The training takes from 48 to 600 hours, depending on the subject and the level, and carries a small tuition fee.

Private Vocational Training

Private businesses have made only limited efforts to provide training for employees beyond what is needed to perform job functions. Several disincentives—including training costs and the possibility of losing newly skilled workers—keep firms from expanding training possibilities. Crisis-induced declines in profits have also had a negative effect on workplace training. Only a small number of firms have taken advantage of the Skill Development Fund and the tax incentives.

The Vocational Training Promotion Act that created these incentives also allows private companies to set up training organizations as business enterprises. In 1998 Thailand had 268 such companies with 2,329 courses and 190,358 trainees, up from 2 companies with 2 courses and 132 trainees in 1996. In the first half of 1999, there were 125 training companies with 1,584 courses and over 150,000 trainees. Six skill-testing centers for overseas workers had also been established and had tested 14,543 workers, and 8 new licenses had been granted.

Meeting the Demand for Skills in the Labor Market

The Thai labor force comprises mainly unskilled workers with elementary-level schooling. In 1999 an estimated 73 percent of all workers had six years or less of education, and most of these had completed only four years of schooling (table 6.19). About 18 percent of the labor force has a secondary-level education and about 9 percent a university degree. The proportion of workers with a university degree is projected to increase to 14 percent of the total labor force by the year 2006, and the proportion with a secondary-level education is expected to rise to 24 percent (table 6.20). The percentage of the work force with only a primary-school education will shrink to 62 percent.

TABLE 6.19
Educational Levels of Thai Labor Force (in millions)

Year	Primary education	Lower secondary education	Upper secondary education	College education and above	Total
1997	25,258.8	3,359.3	2,074.9	2,530.2	33,223.3
1998	24,960.0	3,543.5	2,206.1	2,772.0	33,481.6
1999	24,624.7	3,747.7	2,343.2	3,014.3	33,730.0
2000	24,264.7	3,960.2	2,485.5	3,256.5	33,966.9
2001	23,854.7	4,180.5	2,636.1	3,503.7	34,174.9
2002	23,428.5	4,393.2	2,794.9	3,757.2	34,373.8
2003	23,007.0	4,589.2	2,959.8	4,046.2	34,572.2
2004	22,592.3	4,776.9	3,133.2	4,288.9	34,971.3
2005	22,191.6	4,954.4	3,310.3	4,569.6	35,025.9
2006	21,791.6	5,119.7	3,490.7	4,860.4	35,253.7

Source: Master Plan for Manpower Development in Thai Manufacturing and Service Sector: 1998-2206, Thailand Development Research Institute, September 1998.

The relatively low educational levels in Thailand mean that the country has a surplus of unskilled labor. The country has more workers than it has jobs, despite a labor shortage at the upper end of the educational scale. A surplus in the science and technology sector is projected to disappear by 2006, leaving a labor shortage in this area (table 6.21). The labor surplus is also shrinking rapidly in skill areas addressed by vocational education and in manufacturing engineering, raising the possibility of labor shortages in these areas by 2006. There may also be a shortage in managerial and entrepreneurial occupations.

Some Thoughts for the Future

The Thai economy is facing a policy dilemma. Prior to the crisis the economy had strong export-based growth, with medium- and high-technology products approximating a third of the total. But sluggish labor and capital productivities weakened the country's competitiveness in the 1990s. The government must now decide how to shift from crisis-oriented policies to policies designed to restore competitiveness and economic growth. The Thai economy needs to raise the share of medium- and high-technology products in exports from one-third to the two-thirds share that is the average in East Asian economies. The increase in labor and capital

TABLE 6.20
Estimated Labor Force Requirements According to Educational Level (in millions)

Year	Primary education	Lower secondary education	Upper secondary education	Vocational education	College liberal education	College professional education	Post-graduate education	Total
1997	24,026.7	3,371.1	1,061.3	856.2	1,736.2	658.0	120.0	31,829.5
1998	22,975.5	3,385.4	1,111.8	857.6	1,812.5	700.0	126.1	30,969.0
1999	22,377.0	3,481.6	1,190.1	880.3	1,915.6	762.5	134.1	30,741.3
2000	21,938.9	3,620.4	1,287.5	916.3	2,039.1	840.5	143.6	30,786.2
2001	21,507.4	3,769.1	1,394.8	955.7	2,172.2	928.1	153.8	30,881.1
2002	21,101.6	3,927.8	1,512.3	997.9	2,315.5	1,026.0	164.6	31,045.7
2003	20,682.1	4,087.1	1,636.3	1,040.0	2,465.1	1,132.7	175.8	31,218.9
2004	20,227.7	4,240.8	1,766.0	1,081.5	2,622.7	1,248.4	187.7	31,374.7
2005	19,763.4	4,393.1	1,901.3	1,122.3	2,783.7	1,372.9	199.6	31,536.4
2006	19,291.3	4,545.3	2,044.2	1,163.8	2,951.9	1,508.5	212.0	31,716.9

Source: Master Plan for Manpower Development in Thai Manufacturing and Service Sector: 1998 - 2206, Thailand Development Research Institute, September 1998.

TABLE 6.21
Shortage of Science and Technology Manpower, by Level of Education

	1998	1999	2000	2001	2002	2003	2004	2005	2006
Lower-level vocational education	−36,469	−19,711	−14,886	−11,010	−9,609	−6,667	−5,967	−4,749	−1,950
Upper-level vocational education	−51,835	−34,248	−25,513	−21,896	−19,104	−16,429	−15,596	−13,872	−10,761
University	−39,247	−21,800	−15,655	−15,051	−17,117	−16,594	−17,193	−16,585	−14,415
Engineering	−24,750	−11,176	−6,813	−5,414	4,234	−3,420	−3,489	−2,969	−1,632
Manufactoring	−7,595	−4,518	−2,517	−1,879	−1,379	−1,043	−1,200	−987	−410
Electrical and electronics	−8,743	4,903	−3,553	−3,119	−2,756	−2,594	−2,649	−2,654	−2,287
Infrastructure	−7,635	−1,656	−728	496	−226	51	243	508	820
Material science	−777	−199	−15	80	128	164	116	164	244
Science	−9,896	−6,799	−4,955	−5,518	−8,381	−8,078	−8,566	−8,315	−7,662
Engineering	−2,147	−1,476	−1,260	−1,243	−1,404	−1,329	−1,309	−1,332	−1,177
Science	−2,454	−2,349	−2,628	−2,877	−3,098	−3,766	−3,830	−3,969	−3,944

Source: Master Plan for Manpower Development in Thai Manufacturing and Service Sector: 1998–2206, Thailand Development Research Institute, September 1998.

productivities required to make this change entail increased investment in human capital and R&D. It also requires increased efficiency in the use of capital, in the form of significant restructuring of the corporate and banking sectors. Thailand, with its history of strong economic growth, can make this shift.

Notes

1. Like all markets the labor market is an abstraction. But it is a particularly difficult abstraction given the difficulty of separating the labor market from the macroeconomy. In classical models of the economy, the labor market is the core of the economy, and for some prototypes, like that of Lewis (1954), it *is* the economy. This chapter assumes that the labor market is inextricably embedded in the macroeconomy, so that the two must be viewed together.

2. Labor Protection and Welfare Department, Government of Thailand. Personal communication.

3. National Statistical Office, Labor Force Survey, Round 1, 1999.

4. Lall (1999) ranks 120 countries according to a skills index (tertiary plus technical enrollment multiplied by a factor of 10). On this scale, Thailand ranks 55 out of 120. But for the region it ranks above only three other countries— China, Indonesia, and Malaysia.

5. The Miyazawa Initiative refers to Japanese bilateral aid offered to East Asian economies affected by the crisis.

6. ISO 9000 is a set of quality management guidelines used by companies throughout the world to establish systems of continuous improvement (e.g., Total Quality Management).

7. The largest category (self-arranged placements) was made up of workers returning to jobs after an absence. Most of the workers private placement agencies send abroad and most returning workers are unskilled laborers and low-level technicians. Most of those recruited by employers, however, are white-collar workers.

References

The word *processed* describes informally reproduced works that may not be commonly available through libraries.

Asian Institute of Technology and ILO (International Labour Organization). 1999. "Gender Policy and the Economic Crisis." Working paper, processed. Bangkok, Thailand.

Colaco, F. X. 1998. "Thailand and International Competitiveness: A Framework for Increasing Productivity." Working paper, processed. Washington, D.C.: World Bank.

Dollar D., and M. Hallward-Driemeirer. 1998. "Competitiveness and the Industrial Sector." Working paper, processed. Washington, D.C.: World Bank.

Dwor-Frecaut, D. 1998. "Thailand's Balance of Payments and Financial Crisis: Export Competitiveness, Investment Efficiency, and Financial Fragility." Working paper, processed. Washington, D.C.: World Bank.

ILO (International Labour Organization). 1999a. *Key Indicators of Labor Markets.* Geneva.

———. 1999b. "Country Employment Policy Review for Thailand." Geneva. Processed.

IMF (International Monetary Fund). 1998. *World Economic Outlook.* Washington, D.C.

———. 1999. *World Economic Outlook.* Washington, D.C.

Kakwani, N. 1998. *Impact of the Economic Crisis on Employment, Unemployment, and Real Income.* National Economic and Social Development Board and Asian Development Bank.

Krugman, Paul. (1998) "Saving Asia: It's Time to Get Radical Part 1. Asia: What Went Wrong" *Fortune* Investor September (available online at http://www.fortune.com/fortune/investor/1998/980907/sol1.html.

Lall, S. 1999. *Raising Competitiveness in the Thai Economy.* Geneva: International Labor Office. Working paper. Processed.

Lee, Eddy. 1998. *The Asian Financial Crisis: The Challenge for Social Policy.* Geneva: International Labor Office.

Lewis, W. A. 1954. *Economic Development with an Unlimited Supply of Labour.* The Manchester School of Economic and Social Studies. Vol. 22, pp. 139–191.

Mahmood, M. 1998. *Establishing Some Determinants of Competitiveness in Thai Manufacturing.* Bangkok: International Labour Organization, Regional Office for Asia and the Pacific

NSO (National Statistical Office). 1999. Labor Force Survey, Round 1. Bangkok

TDRI (Thai Development Research Institute). 1998. Processed.

Warr, P.G. 1998. *Thailand—What Went Wrong?* Washington, D.C: World Bank.

World Bank. 1998. *World Development Indicators.* Washington, D.C.

———. 1999. *World Development Indicators.* Washington, D.C.

Labor Market Issues and Policies in the Region

7

Active Labor Market Policies: Issues for East Asia

Gordon Betcherman, Amit Dar,
Amy Luinstra, and Makoto Ogawa

O15
J24
J64
J68
J23
J65
J38

After 1960 active labor market policies emerged as an important employment policy tool, particularly in industrial countries. This policy envelope includes a wide range of measures intended to increase the quality of the labor supply through activities such as retraining, raise the demand for labor with direct job creation and related programs, and improve job matching for both workers and employers by expanding job search assistance. The objective of these measures is primarily economic. They are intended to increase the probability that the unemployed will find jobs and that the underemployed will increase their productivity and earnings.[1] More recently the case for active labor market policies has emphasized the potential social benefits (inclusion and participation) of productive employment.

The debate that surrounds these labor market policies is often formulated in terms of the relative value of active versus passive measures in combating unemployment. So-called passive programs, such as unemployment insurance or social transfers, mitigate the financial needs of the unemployed but are not designed to improve employability. Active programs are meant to directly increase unemployed workers' access to the workplace.

As the disincentives and dependencies inherent in passive programs receive more emphasis, active policies become increasingly attractive. The now-familiar safety net and trampoline metaphors for the passive and active approaches illustrate the growing interest in active measures. Not only are trampolines more politically acceptable, but they also have a theoretical rationale in models of the labor market that incorporate asymmetric information and market failures associated with investments in human capital. Active programs (specifically retraining) will become increasingly important as technological change raises skill requirements and quickens the pace of obsolescence. But as the experiences of the late 1980s and 1990s show, actually implementing active labor market policies poses many challenges.

The immediate question is whether these programs do any good. Evaluations of their impact are mixed, with many programs assessed as having little or no effect on the employability or earnings of participants. Even policymakers who judge the evidence favorably or feel compelled to introduce active policies for political reasons must address a host of complex design and implementation issues in order to maximize the probability of success. These issues include the complementarity of public and private roles, optimal resource allocation, targeting, delivery, monitoring and evaluation, and feedback. Further, effective and efficient active labor market programs require considerable capacity. For this reason most of what is known about them is based on experience in industrial countries. Clearly, however, the role and nature of active programming varies at different stages of development. And as the experiences of industrial countries show, culture and institutions matter a great deal as well.

This chapter reviews international experiences with active labor market policies and discusses their applicability to five East Asian countries: Indonesia, Korea, Malaysia, the Philippines, and Thailand. While several of these countries have some active policies, no country makes active measures an important policy instrument. But East Asian policymakers need to consider these policies carefully as these economies respond to the crisis and the long-term requirements of development.

Active Labor Market Programs: An Overview

Active labor market programs, including job creation (public works, support for self-employment, and wage subsidies), training, and employment services can affect both the supply of and the demand for labor, as well as the way the labor market matches the two.[2] The overall objective of these interventions is to increase employment and incomes. They can serve equity objectives as well, most obviously when they target vulnerable groups.

Active policies increase employment and incomes in various ways. Direct employment creation—for instance, temporary jobs through public works—has a stabilizing effect. Training and wage subsidies move supply and demand curves outward. Training, mobility incentives, and other employment services reduce structural imbalances by improving the match between workers and jobs. By decreasing the number of vacancies (and thus reducing both upward wage pressure and labor bottlenecks), these policies also increase employment. The employment and income effects are further transmitted through increases in skill levels and productivity. Even though the net employment effects may not be significant, some active labor market programs increase the attachment of the long-term unemployed to the labor force and decrease their dependence on unemployment benefits. By assisting the most disadvantaged workers, these policies break down the potentially negative consequences associated with "outsider" phenomena.

Active labor market programs can positively affect employment and incomes in many ways, then. But substitution, deadweight, and displacement effects can dissipate or even eliminate their potential benefits.[3] To minimize these losses policymakers must address various issues in designing and implementing active programs, including the overall strategy as well as specific details of program design. The overall strategy for active labor market programs involves identifying clear objectives, determining the composition of programs, targeting priorities, and establishing an effective balance with passive policies. As we have noted active programs can serve several objectives, and policymakers need to determine which of these are the most important. An active strategy can be designed to moderate cyclical downturns, reduce structural imbalances, or otherwise improve the functioning of the labor market. It may also aim to increase productivity, support disadvantaged or at-risk workers, assist at-risk employers or industries, or achieve more than one of these goals. These objectives have different client populations and call for a variety of policies (table 7.1).

The relationship between active and passive policies is an important strategic issue. As a general rule countries with active programs also have unemployment insurance or some other form of passive support. But for the most part coordination between the two types of policies is weak. A few countries, including Austria, Germany, Japan, Norway, and Spain, have integrated systems. Others, such as Canada, are moving toward integration by coordinating active program options with unemployment insurance. This trend is likely to continue, for two reasons. First, attempting to reintegrate unemployed workers into the labor market is more politically attractive than simply providing income support or insurance. Second, integrated systems may have positive economic outcomes. After a period with little labor market intervention in the United Kingdom, the public employment service began interviewing unemployment insurance claimants. The agency found that even minimal contact reduced the number of claims (OECD 1994). Furthermore, coordinating benefits distribution with job search assistance can save on administrative costs.

TABLE 7.1
Tailoring Programs to Objectives

Objective	Program orientation	Targeting orientation
Moderate cyclical downturns	• Direct job creation (for instance, public works) • Wage subsidies • Training (subsidies or grants to workers or employers) • Self-employment support	• Vulnerable groups (those with the least resiliency) • Hard-hit regions and industries
Reduce structural imbalances	• Employment services (information and search and mobility assistance, among others) • Training • Wage subsidies	• Proximate regions, industries, or occupations
Improve general labor market functioning	• Employment services • Training (such as apprenticeships)	• All
Enhance skills and productivity	• Training and retraining (including in-service and apprenticeships)	• At risk or disadvantaged worker categories (especially for retraining)
Support disadvantaged or at-risk workers	• Employment services (counseling and job search assistance) • Training (for instance, grants and subsidies) • Wage subsidies	• At-risk or disadvantaged worker categories

Types of Active Labor Market Programs

Policymakers involved in planning and implementing active labor market programs confront a variety of issues specific to the type of program (table 7.2). We discuss some of the key issues involved in the main types of labor market programs: employment services and job search assistance, training, job creation, microenterprise development and support for self-employment, and public works.

TABLE 7.2
Active and Passive Labor Market Programs: Some Key Features

Program	Objective and activities	Possible pros	Possible cons	Key issues
Job search assistance and employment services	To match jobs and job seekers through services such as initial interviews at employment offices, in-depth counseling, and job clubs.	1. Helps reduce the length of unemployment. 2. Generally is reasonably inexpensive. 3. Prescreens participants who may be receiving assistance from other programs.	1. Crowds out private services. 2. Results in deadweight losses. 3. Benefits only a fraction of job seekers.	1. Determining the roles of public and private job search agencies. 2. Providing integrated services. 3. Using monitoring and evaluation to improve effectiveness.
Training and retraining	To help new and redeployed workers (the long-term unemployed or those laid off during restructuring) accumulate employability skills.	1. Increases productivity and enhances workers' skills. 2. When well targeted may benefit groups such as the disadvantaged and women.	1. When poorly targeted results in deadweight losses. 2. Produces poor outcomes when the economy is flat. 3. Is one of the most costly programs (but is extremely popular).	1. Defining the roles of the government and private sector. 2. Improving linkages with the labor market. 3. Resolving costs.

(Table continues on the following page)

TABLE 7.2 (continued)

Program	Objective and activities	Possible pros	Possible cons	Key issues
Wage subsidies	To encourage employers to maintain employees and hire disadvantaged groups such as the long-term unemployed and youth by paying part of workers' salary for a period of time.	1. May lead to permanent employment by helping individuals develop work-related skills. 2. Helps individuals maintain contact with the labor market.	1. Can result in deadweight losses. 2. Can displace workers and cause a substitution effect if employers replace unsubsidized employees with subsidized workers. 3. May be viewed by employers as a source of cheap labor, with workers laid off once the subsidies end.	1. Determining the duration of the subsidies. 2. Determining the ideal level of the subsidies.
Microenterprise development and self-employment support	To create and promote small-scale businesses and self-employment activities with technical assistance, credit, and other support.	1. Can assist in creating entrepreneurial spirit.	1. May have high deadweight losses. 2. May displace other small businesses that do not get this assistance. 3. Has low take-up rate among the unemployed.	1. Identifying the kind of support to provide (financial, technical, or other). 2. Improving targeting to minimize deadweight losses. 3. Measuring the impact of programs, including

				the proportion of unemployed that use them, the proportion of businesses that survive, and the number of additional jobs created.
Public works and public service employment	To address poverty and nutrition objectives and create temporary employment by generating income through low-wage temporary work.	1. May assist disadvantaged groups to regain labor market contact. 2. Leads to production of public goods and develops infrastructure. 3. Can be self-targeting if wages are set effectively.	1. May crowd out private sector jobs, especially if targeting is ineffective. 2. May be perceived negatively and thus not increase participants' employability.	1. Setting the wage level and determining the proportion of wages in total program costs. 2. Determining whether these programs generate employment and higher wages and are cost-effective. 3. Choosing whether to hire private or public contractors to implement the projects.

Employment Services

Employment services serve brokerage functions, matching jobs with job seekers. This assistance includes many different types of activities—for example, initial interviews at employment offices, in-depth counseling during the unemployment spell, and job clubs. In Hungary and Poland in the mid-1990s, workers had access to job referrals, job counseling, skills assessment, job search training, resume preparation, and job clubs (O'Leary 1998a, 1998b). In New Zealand job seekers attended job screening interviews, workshops, and follow-up interviews and received personal case management (New Zealand Department of Labor 1995). Australia offered training in resume writing and interviewing techniques.

Such services are relatively inexpensive and can help shorten spells of unemployment by providing job seekers with up-to-date information on jobs. On the negative side these interventions usually have deadweight losses, since individuals who use them are generally more qualified than most job seekers and could probably find jobs on their own.[4] Policymakers designing such interventions must address three key issues: public-private sector complementarity, the integration of active and passive services, and monitoring and evaluation.

PUBLIC-PRIVATE SECTOR COMPLEMENTARITY. Increasingly, public and private services coexist in many countries. Public employment services are justified on the grounds that they benefit the disadvantaged, including the poor and the long-term unemployed (Fretwell and Goldberg 1994). Private fee-charging agencies typically provide labor exchange services to more favored segments of the labor force, such as the employed, skilled, and white-collar workers. Some countries ban or restrict private agencies, so that public employment services operate under near-monopoly conditions. While governments need to provide services to certain segments of the population, public employment offices should not be viewed as substitutes for private agencies. Private agencies can enhance the operation of the labor market, especially when they are appropriately regulated to ensure quality.

INTEGRATED SERVICE PROVISION. Optimally employment services are integrated with other active as well as passive programs. This integration is beneficial to the extent that it helps the unemployed acquire the skills and knowledge they need to fill available job vacancies. The benefits must be weighed against the administrative requirements such integration entails, however.

MONITORING AND EVALUATION. As with all active labor market policies, monitoring and evaluating the impact of this intervention are essential. Countries of the Organization for Economic Cooperation and Development (OECD) use a variety of methods to enhance the effectiveness of public employment services. Some countries use administrative data such as the number of registered job vacancies to set targets that measure the effectiveness of these services and then allocate budgets accordingly. For example in Sweden and Finland funds allocated to the employment service are disbursed to the regional and local levels based on the authorities' success in meeting performance targets (OECD 1997).

Labor Market Training

Public support for training can take the form of direct provision through public training institutes; financial support for trainees in the form of funds for training costs, subsidies for trainees, or both; and "infrastructure" services such as labor market information, licensing, monitoring, and credentialing. Most countries focus on three types of training programs:

- Retraining aimed at the long-term unemployed (12 months or longer);
- Retraining for displaced workers, especially those laid off as a result of enterprise or industrial restructuring; and
- Training programs targeting young people, often with special attention to school dropouts.

While these types of training programs can help increase productivity and employability, they have a number of limitations. First, they are relatively costly. Second, they often have little impact when the economy is not performing well and job opportunities are limited. Finally, training programs can also result in deadweight losses, as those participants who benefit the most may have more skills to begin with and could have found jobs even without training. In designing effective training programs, policymakers must consider three central issues: the government's role in training provision, the role of private providers, and the link between training and the labor market itself.

THE GOVERNMENT'S ROLE IN TRAINING PROVISION. Governments have a number of potentially important roles to play in the provision of labor market training. Governments may provide training directly, act in a regulatory capacity, collect and disseminate information, set standards, and provide financing. Many governments are moving away from the role of direct provider to focus on market failures in information and financing, leaving delivery in the hands of private providers. This approach may be the most successful way for governments to foster the development of a relevant and cost-effective training system.

THE ROLE OF PRIVATE PROVIDERS. To encourage private delivery of labor market training, governments must create a set of enabling conditions. First, they must ensure that the laws governing private provision are clear and do not discriminate against private providers. Second, they need to exercise caution in providing training directly in order to avoid crowding out private suppliers. Finally, they must let employment growth lead the demand for training. Countries that meet these requirements (including Australia and Indonesia) are rewarded with a growing, vibrant, and competitive private training sector. In these countries the public sector focuses on providing services to the most vulnerable groups (Gill, Fluitman, and Dar 2000).

LINKING TRAINING WITH THE LABOR MARKET. Creating strong linkages between the training system and the labor market requires governments to examine their own internal structures and operations. In some countries where training reform succeeded, governments developed strong institutional links with employers, making training institutions relatively flexible. In Chile, for example, groups comprising representatives of employers, workers, and the government govern vocational training institutes. This tripartism strengthens accountability while offering the institutes the autonomy necessary to respond to the needs of employers.

Job Creation

These programs are intended to maintain existing jobs as well as to support the creation of new ones. Three types of programs fall into this category: subsidies, public works, and self-employment support. Subsidies encourage employers to hire new workers or keep employees who might otherwise be laid off. These programs may offer direct wage subsidies (for either the employer or worker) or social security payment offsets and are always targeted to a particular category of worker or employer. Public works and related programs provide temporary jobs in the public or nonprofit sector. Typically these programs cover the costs of hiring previously unemployed workers. Support for self-employment often takes the form of assistance for unemployed workers willing to start their own enterprises.

This support can involve microfinancing for business start-ups or operating costs, extended unemployment benefits while claimants start their own business, grants, and business support services.

WAGE AND EMPLOYMENT SUBSIDIES. These subsidies support the long-term unemployed, those coming from severely disadvantaged areas (such as sectors with high unemployment), and special groups of workers (such as youth). The subsidies were instituted under varying economic conditions, though most often during slack periods. The programs often have a social objective, in that they encourage employment and thus the inclusion of disadvantaged individuals in productive activities. Detractors argue that designing subsidies that actually meet the goal of creating jobs in a cost-efficient manner is a difficult task and that in any case subsidies are also often associated with deadweight losses. Subsidies can also can have unintended effects—for example, firms may hire subsidized workers to replace unsubsidized staff or take on subsidized workers only to lay them off once the subsidy period ends. Good design, effective targeting, and careful monitoring can reduce these negative impacts. Subsidies may target individuals to promote hiring in industries with excess demand (or by individual firms). Monitoring employers' behavior minimizes program abuse.

DURATION AND LEVEL OF SUBSIDIES. Wage subsidy programs are most often payments to firms in the form of a wage offset—that is, they are an inducement to hire program participants. The level and duration of such subsidies vary significantly across programs and countries, and the optimum levels depend on specific conditions. For example under the U.S. Targeted Job Tax Credit, firms are paid 50 percent of the individual's wages for a period of up to two years. The job subsidy program in the United Kingdom provides up to 100 percent of wages for a period of six months. Careful monitoring and evaluation allows policymakers to arrive at an informed decision about the length and levels of subsidies.

Public Works

Some governments attempt to alleviate unemployment by creating jobs and hiring the unemployed directly; others contract with nonprofit organizations or private businesses to provide jobs. Most programs target the displaced and the long-term unemployed (that is, the workers who are hardest to place). Some programs target youth, providing a way to introduce young workers to the labor market.

The idea behind these programs is generally to help the unemployed reestablish contact with the labor market, minimizing the possibility that these workers will be stigmatized by long periods of unemployment and obsolete skills. Such programs can also produce public goods and develop basic infrastructure, and in many cases public works have exactly these goals and are not aimed primarily at creating jobs.[5] Another advantage of these programs is that with appropriate wage levels they can be self-targeting, attracting only those most in need. In some countries public works jobs have a major drawback, however: the jobs carry a stigma and may decrease participants' employability in the long term. Policymakers designing public works programs need to consider two important issues, then: targeting and management.

TARGETING. When the objective is to reduce poverty, the most successful form of targeting is an appropriate wage. The wage offered should be no higher than the prevailing market wage for unskilled manual labor in the area where the scheme is introduced. High wages can attract less disadvantaged workers, in effect crowding out private sector employment. Restrictions on eligibility are best avoided. Ideally the fact that workers are willing to accept low wages should be sufficient as an eligibility requirement. When the demand for jobs exceeds the budget, the projects can be targeted to poor areas using a credible "poverty map" and can focus on the assets that will be of most benefit to local residents. Flexibility in future budget allocations will allow the government to respond to demand from a variety of locales (Ravallion 1998).

MANAGEMENT. Tendering public employment activities through private contractors and nonprofit organizations enhances the effectiveness of public job creation schemes. An evaluation of public works programs in Hungary showed that those operated by private contractors tended to be the most cost-effective (Fretwell, Benus, and O'Leary 1999). Another lesson from experience is that programs need not be managed at national levels. Decentralization often increases administrative efficiency and facilitates appropriate targeting.

Microenterprise Development and Self-employment Assistance

Technical assistance, credit, and other support contribute to the creation and promotion of new small-scale businesses and self-employment. In countries with an embryonic financial infrastructure, private banks are often unable to conduct the comprehensive risk assessments necessary to offer credit to unemployed workers who want to create their own business. Public programs to support small business loans can help eliminate this distortion.

Microenterprise development assistance is offered on a universal basis to particular groups under varied economic conditions. These groups include the newly unemployed (in the U.S. state of Massachusetts in the early 1990s), the long-term unemployed (in Denmark in the 1980s), and displaced workers (in Hungary and Poland in the 1990s). The programs vary in design. Participants may receive a lump-sum payment or periodic allowances to set up their businesses. A screening mechanism often subjects potential beneficiaries to a rigorous assessment that evaluates the likelihood of success (for example, in Germany). But in other countries, such as the United States, screening is more cursory (Wilson and Adams 1994). In most cases participants also receive business advice and counseling.

Few among the unemployed (usually less than 5 percent) typically take up opportunities for self-employment (Wilson and Adams 1994). One explanation for this low figure may be that individuals are generally risk averse and, given a choice, will opt for unemployment benefits. These programs also have potential displacement effects, since small businesses that do not receive assistance are disadvantaged relative to those that do. The most important issues facing policymakers in designing these programs are determining the appropriate level of support, targeting, and screening.

How much support? The experience of successful microcredit schemes such as Bangladesh's Grameen Bank shows that successful credit programs have several common characteristics.[6] First, they offer small initial amounts of credit, with subsequent loans contingent on a good repayment record. Second, they charge market interest rates. They also use group lending with community guarantees rather than formal collateral, and they offer flexible repayment schedules. Finally, microenterprise credit programs start on a very small scale and grow gradually, allowing both the agency and the community to learn by doing and ensuring that supervision and training activities keep pace with the lending activities.

Screening participants. Screening is especially important in microenterprise development assistance and self-employment support programs. Instruments that improve screening include information sessions, detailed application forms, interviews, preentry business advisory services, training, and developing business plans. Using these instruments can sharply reduce deadweight losses and greatly enhance a project's chance of success.

FIGURE 7.1
OECD Average Active Labor Market Program Expenditures

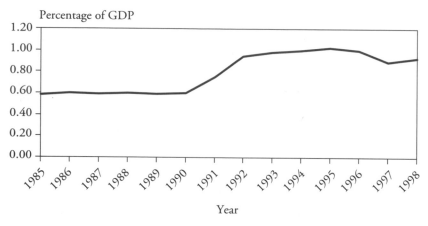

Source: OECD, *Employment Outlook,* various years.

The Cost of Active Labor Market Programs

The OECD collected statistics on its member countries' expenditures on active labor market programs from the mid-1980s until the late 1990s and compared them with expenditures on passive programs such as unemployment insurance (figure 7.1). Such comparisons provide a rough measure of the relative importance of the two types of labor market policies over time and across countries.

Relative spending levels on active labor market programs increased in the early 1990s and continued at that level throughout the decade (figure 7.2). This increase likely reflected both the increasing preference for active programs and high unemployment rates in most OECD countries compared with the 1980s. An OECD (1993) analysis confirms that spending on active programs increases when unemployment rises. In 1990, for example, a 1 percent increase in the unemployment rate was associated with a 0.6 percent increase in the share of expenditures in GDP allocated for these programs.

A second point emerging from the OECD expenditure data is that countries generally see active and passive programs as complements to rather than substitutes for each other. When spending for active programs is relatively high, it is also likely to be high for passive programs. In 1990 the correlation coefficient between national spending on active and passive programs was .60 (OECD 1993). After diverging in the early 1990s,

FIGURE 7.2
OECD Spending on Active Labor Market Policies

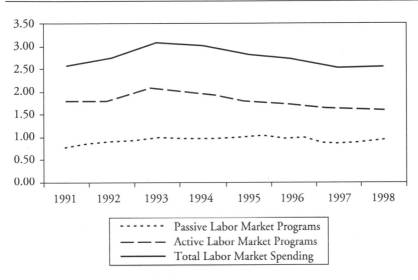

Source: OECD, Employment Outlook, various years.

when income support jumped to accommodate workers laid off in the recession, the correlation grew strong again in 1993. Spending on active programs then increased slightly relative to spending on passive programs (figure 7.1). Nonetheless spending on passive programs remains roughly 50 percent greater than spending on active programs in the OECD region. The level and composition of spending on active labor market programs also vary widely across OECD countries (table 7.3).

Evaluating the Impact of Active Labor Market Policies[7]

In spite of relatively large public expenditures on active labor market programs, rigorous evaluations of their impact are limited. Policymakers are increasingly realizing the importance of evaluation to improving program design, however. They want to know what programs accomplish, what they cost, and how they can be made cost-effective.

Impact Evaluation Techniques

Techniques for evaluating the effectiveness of programs can be either scientific or nonscientific. Scientific evaluations are of two types: experi-

TABLE 7.3
Expenditures on Labor Market Programs, Selected OECD Countries
(percent of GDP)

Program	Australia (1997–98)	Denmark (1998)	France (1997)	Germany (1998)	Italy (1996)	Japan (1997–98)	Spain (1998)	Sweden (1998)	United States (1997–98)
Public employment services and administration	**0.21**	**0.14**	**0.16**	**0.23**	**0.04**	**0.03**	**0.07**	**0.30**	**0.06**
Labor market training	**0.07**	**1.07**	**0.35**	**0.34**	**0.01**	**0.03**	**0.21**	**0.48**	**0.04**
Training unemployed adults and those at risk	0.06	0.73	0.31	0.35	—	0.03	0.10	0.47	0.04
Training employed adults	—	0.34	0.04	—	0.01	—	0.11	0.01	—
Youth measures	**0.06**	**0.08**	**0.26**	**0.07**	**0.42**	—	**0.07**	**0.03**	**0.03**
Measures for unemployed and disadvantaged youth	—	0.08	0.07	0.06	0.04	—	0.07	0.03	0.03
Apprenticeship and related forms of general youth training	0.05	—	0.19	0.01	0.38	—	—	—	—
Subsidized employment	**0.13**	**0.30**	**0.52**	**0.39**	**0.61**	**0.02**	**0.35**	**0.58**	**0.01**
Subsidies to employment in the private sector	0.04	0.03	0.32	0.03	0.56	0.02	0.24	0.15	—
Support of unemployed persons starting enterprises	0.02	0.04	0.20	0.03	—	—	0.03	0.09	—
Direct job creation (public or nonprofit)	0.07	0.23	0.20	0.32	0.04	—	0.07	0.35	0.01

TABLE 7.3 (continued)

Program	Australia (1997–98)	Denmark (1998)	France (1997)	Germany (1998)	Italy (1996)	Japan (1997–98)	Spain (1998)	Sweden (1998)	United States (1997–98)
Measures for the disabled	**0.06**	**0.30**	**0.08**	**0.25**	**—**	**—**	**0.02**	**0.62**	**0.04**
Vocational rehabilitation	0.02	0.30	0.02	0.10	—	—	—	0.04	0.04
Work for the disabled	0.04	—	0.06	0.15	—	—	0.02	0.58	—
Unemployment compensation	**1.17**	**1.86**	**4.50**	**2.29**	**0.68**	**0.43**	**1.64**	**1.91**	**0.25**
Early retirement for labor market reasons	**—**	**1.88**	**0.35**	**—**	**0.20**	**—**	**—**	**—**	**—**
TOTAL	**1.69**	**5.63**	**3.22**	**3.56**	**1.96**	**0.52**	**2.36**	**3.93**	**0.43**
Active measures	0.52	1.89	1.37	1.27	1.08	0.09	0.72	2.01	0.18
Passive measures	1.17	3.74	1.85	2.29	0.88	0.43	1.64	1.91	0.25

— Not available.
Source: OECD Employment Outlook, various years.

mental and quasi-experimental. Experimental evaluations require the selection of both treatment and control groups before the intervention. Treatment groups are made up of those receiving assistance; control groups include only nonrecipients. Quasi-experimental studies select these groups after the intervention.

Nonscientific techniques do not use control groups in evaluating the impact of interventions, relying instead on statistics compiled by program administrators. Since there is no counterfactual information detailing, for instance, what might have happened in the absence of the program, these evaluations are of little use in determining whether participants benefit. Nonscientific evaluations provide some information on deadweight losses and substitution and displacement effects.

EXPERIMENTAL (CLASSICALLY DESIGNED) EVALUATIONS. If large samples are randomly assigned to treatment and control groups, on average neither the observable or unobservable characteristics of the two groups should differ, and any difference in outcomes can be attributed to participation in the program. The main appeal of experimental evaluations, then, lies in the simplicity of interpreting results. The program impact is the simple difference between the means of the treatment group and control group members on the outcome of interest. Although experimental evaluations have many virtues, they have pitfalls as well. First, they require careful planning and design in advance of the experiment. In addition groups may not be assigned randomly owing to factors such as nepotism and the desire to exclude high-risk individuals in order to produce certain results. Participation in experimental analyses may affect participants' behavior (the Hawthorne effect). Further, such experiments typically incur high costs and can raise ethical questions if some people are excluded.

QUASI-EXPERIMENTAL TECHNIQUES. With these techniques the treatment and control groups are selected after the intervention. To isolate the effects of the program, econometric techniques correct for differences in the characteristics of the two groups. The main appeal of this technique lies in its relatively low cost and in the fact that evaluations can be done at any time after the intervention. The main drawbacks are statistical complexity and a failure to account for all differences in the two subsamples. Techniques for adjusting for differences in the observable attributes of a group (such as sex, education, and region) are relatively straightforward, although they are subject to specification errors. Correcting for unobservable characteristics (such as motivation) requires a complex procedure that can yield different results depending on the specification. Quasi-experimental evaluations are of three types: regression-adjusted for observables, selectivity-corrected, and matched pairs.

- Evaluations that are regression-adjusted for observables assess the impact of participation in a program when the observable characteristics (sex, age, and education, for example) of the participant and comparison groups differ. They are used when these differences explain variations in outcomes for the two groups.
- Evaluations that are regression-adjusted for observed and unobservable variables (selectivity-corrected) are used when treatment and control groups have unobservable differences. Such differences arise when selection is not random and participation is thus based on both types of characteristics. Unobservable differences (such as innate ability) can cause nonparticipants to respond differently than they would have if they been included in the program. In these cases evaluations that are regression adjusted for observables only are likely to be biased. The Heckman selectivity method is the most commonly used method of controlling for unobservables.
- Matched pairs are used to control for differences in the observable characteristics of the individuals in the control and treatment groups. Individual characteristics always differ, so that the groups are likely to have different success rates in finding employment even in the absence of active labor market programs. To control for these spurious differences, a synthetic control group is constructed using matched pairs. The synthetic control group, a subset of the entire control group, is composed of individuals whose observable characteristics closely match those of the treatment group.

Interpreting Evaluation Results

We now turn to the evidence on program impacts. While we include some results based on evaluations in developing countries, this evidence focuses primarily on the experiences of OECD countries. Here we merely review the main conclusions emerging from the literature (table 7.4).[8]

An important caveat with these evaluations concerns their summary nature. The studies treat the programs as "black boxes" by not evaluating issues relating to program design and implementation, staffing, and the intensity and quality of services. These factors are obviously important and will have an impact on a program's likelihood of success.

TABLE 7.4

Evaluation Results for Active Labor Market Programs

Program	Appear to help	Comments
Job-search assistance and employment services (19 evaluations)	Unemployed adults when economic conditions are improving; women may benefit more	Relatively more cost-effective than other labor market interventions (such as training) because of low costs. Possible deadweight losses if not effectively targeted.
Training for long-term unemployed (28 evaluations)	Women and other disadvantaged groups	No more effective than job-search assistance in increasing reemployment probabilities and postintervention earnings; two to four times more costly.
Retraining workers displaced in mass layoffs (12 evaluations)	Little positive impact; positive results mainly when economy is improving	No more effective than job-search assistance and significantly more expensive. Rate of return usually negative.
Training for youth (7 evaluations)	No positive impact	Employment and earnings prospects not improved. Negative real rate of return to these programs when costs are taken into account.
Employment and wage subsidies (22 evaluations)	Long-term unemployed	Benefits to treatment group not significant compared with control group. Sometimes used by firms as a permanent subsidy program. High deadweight and substitution effects.
Public works programs (17 evaluations)	Severely disadvantaged groups	Long-term employment prospects not helped. Program participants less likely to be hired for permanent jobs than control group and

TABLE 7.4 *(continued)*

Program	Appear to help	Comments
		less likely to earn the same wage. Not cost-effective if objective is to get people into gainful employment.
Microenterprise development programs (15 evaluations)	Relatively senior and more educated groups	Very low take-up rate among unemployed. Significant failure rate of small businesses. High deadweight and displacement effects. High costs— cost-benefit analyses rarely conducted but sometimes show higher costs than for control group.

Source: Dar and Tzannatos 1999.

JOB SEARCH ASSISTANCE AND EMPLOYMENT SERVICES. Expenditures on these programs range anywhere from 5 percent of the budget for active labor market programs (Denmark) to over 70 percent (the Czech Republic). On average OECD countries spend about a quarter of the funds budgeted for such programs on employment services, including job search assistance. These expenditures include not only the costs of financing job search assistance programs but also the administrative costs associated with operating the unemployment benefit system and other active labor market programs.

Of the 19 evaluations we examined, all except 1 are scientific. Six of the scientific evaluations are experimental and 12 quasi-experimental. The evaluations suggest that job search assistance is one of the most successful active labor market programs. In general the programs cost little and are as effective as other more expensive active labor market initiatives. However, much depends on whether the economy is growing and on the availability of public funds (which can be scarce during a recession).

Most results for job search assistance programs are positive, though not all. The least successful programs tend to operate during periods of recession and rising unemployment. For example job search assistance to workers displaced during mass layoffs in Canada in the late 1980s did not raise the probability of employment or increase earnings compared with the control group. In fact participants terminated during mass layoffs spent a significantly greater amount of time searching for jobs than nonparticipants (Fay 1996). At the time, however, unemployment was rising. The effectiveness of job search assistance seems to increase when economic conditions improve and when new jobs are being generated. When unemployment rates were falling in the Netherlands in the late 1980s, program participants were more likely to be employed than those in the control group (OECD 1993). Evaluations in Hungary and Poland show similar results (O'Leary 1998a, 1998b).

Studies that examine both cost and effectiveness data generally conclude that job search assistance is one of the most cost-effective of the active interventions. Leigh (1995) finds that training and retraining programs are two to four times more expensive than measures designed to help workers find jobs and that the interventions are equally effective. Job search assistance is not a substitute for training, however, especially since people who use such assistance may well be more "employment-ready" than individuals who get training. However, if job search assistance and training programs cater to roughly the same clientele, policymakers may prefer the less expensive option.

Overall, then, the evidence suggests that job search assistance can have some positive effects and is usually cost-effective relative to other active labor market interventions. A positive correlation exists between the likelihood that these initiatives will succeed and local labor market conditions. Finally, like other interventions job search assistance does not seem to help all types of workers equally—for example, these programs have little impact on youth.

TRAINING PROGRAMS. Training and retraining programs generally account for a significant share of expenditures on active labor market initiatives (between 40 and 60 percent in most countries, but over 75 percent in Denmark in the early 1990s). Training can reach many different groups. We concentrate on training for three groups: the long-term unemployed, those displaced by mass layoffs, and youth.

Training programs for the long-term unemployed. We reviewed 28 studies (6 experimental, 18 quasi-experimental, and 4 nonscientific) of training programs for the long-term unemployed. A few of these studies are longitudinal and thus provide evidence on the long-term impact of the programs. Scientific evaluations suggest that these programs can have a positive impact but that they sometimes do not. As we have seen in most cases training programs are generally no more effective than job search assistance in increasing the probability of reemployment and postintervention earnings.

As with job search assistance initiatives, the success of programs for the long-term unemployed tends to be heavily dependent on the business cycle. Programs perform better when they are instituted during times of economic expansion. In Hungary training outcomes improved as the economy grew (O'Leary 1995, 1998a). In general programs seem to be more effective for women (Puhani 1998; Friedlander, Greenberg, and Robins 1997; Goss, Gilroy, and Associates 1989). Longitudinal studies provide mixed results. While in some cases the positive effects of training dissipate within a year or two after the program ends, in some cases the impacts persist. For example in Sweden training for the unemployed raised earnings in the short term, but the long-term impact (more than two years) was somewhat negative (Meager and Evans 1998). Conversely the long-term unemployed trained as part of the New Jersey Reemployment Demonstration Project in the mid-1980s were earning more than the control group 30 months after program ended (Anderson, Corson, and Decker 1991).

Costs—when they are known—vary substantially. In most cases they are so high compared with the benefits of the program that social returns can remain negative (especially for males) even if the effects persist for 10 years (Friedlander, Greenberg, and Robins 1997).[9] The U.S. Job Training Partnership Act of 1982, which gave employers subsidies to hire workers for on-the-job training, offers a rare exception. Both male and female participants did significantly better than the control group, and the training was relatively inexpensive. However, single mothers benefited more than men (Bloom 1990). In spite of the positive results, some evaluators caution that the aggregate effects are likely to be modest, both for the target population and for the labor force as a whole (Friedlander, Greenberg, and Robins 1997).

One of the major implications emerging from our analysis is that training should not be seen as a panacea for securing jobs for the long-term unemployed, especially when demand is slack. Evaluations also show that tightly targeted on-the-job training programs, which are typically aimed at women and other similarly disadvantaged groups, often offer the best returns. Rigorous cost-benefit analyses are seldom performed, but the limited evidence that does exist shows that training programs are not usually cost-effective.

Retraining programs for workers displaced during mass layoffs. We summarized the results of 12 studies of retraining programs for displaced workers: 5 quasi-experimental, 6 nonscientific, and 1 mixed (using both techniques). The studies relate to retraining programs for workers displaced by mass layoffs during major enterprise restructuring and plant closures. Unfortunately none of the evaluations is longitudinal, so we lack insights into the long-term effects of these programs.

Scientific quasi-experimental evaluations find that though some retraining programs may result in a modest increase in reemployment, the result is often statistically insignificant (Corson, Long, and Maynard 1985). The results for postprogram earnings are even more discouraging. Wage effects on participants (compared with control group workers) are generally negative (OECD 1991). Evaluations seldom report the full costs of retraining. But the available evidence shows that direct costs (usually measured as total recurrent program costs) vary from US$3,500 to US$25,000 per participant (Dar and Gill 1998). As noted earlier given that retraining and job search assistance have roughly similar impacts, job search assistance can be more cost-effective than retraining. Some researchers claim that they can find no evidence of an incremental effect for retraining programs that exceeds the effects of job search assistance (Corson, Long, and Maynard 1985). As with some other initiatives, these programs may be serving different groups of unemployed workers and thus may not be direct substitutes for one another.

The experience of OECD countries with retraining programs for workers displaced in mass layoffs may be useful in designing assistance programs in transition countries and other economies that experience large-scale labor redundancies. The evidence on the expense and lack of effectiveness of these programs suggests that they should not be the principal source of support for individuals seeking gainful employment. Instead they should be relatively small and targeted toward the subgroups that will benefit the most from them.

Training programs for youth. We examined seven evaluations, five experimental and two quasi-experimental. These evaluations are mostly discouraging, even though the programs were often introduced during periods of relatively stable youth unemployment. We find that training rarely has an effect on the earnings or employment probabilities of program beneficiaries (Fay 1996). A more mixed (and more promising) picture arises from the evaluation of the Canadian Job Entry Program. A quasi-experimental evaluation of the program shows that while youth who received only classroom training did no better than the control group, those who undertook enterprise training did significantly better than the control group (OECD 1993). This positive effect was attributed to the fact that many of those trained in enterprises stayed on with the firms. Cost-benefit analyses of several of the youth training programs suggest that the social rates of return to these programs are typically negative in the short as well as the long run (Friedlander, Greenberg, and Robins 1997). Correcting the failures of the educational system with what is generally short-term training is very difficult.

WAGE AND EMPLOYMENT SUBSIDIES. We analyzed 22 evaluations, 6 of them experimental, 8 quasi-experimental, 7 nonscientific, and 1 mixed. Wage and employment subsidy programs are some of the most poorly funded active labor market initiatives in OECD countries, attracting less than 10 percent of expenditures on active labor market programs. Funding for these programs is also negligible in the United States and the United Kingdom.

Evaluations tend to agree that wage and employment subsidy programs have high deadweight losses and substitution effects. In the most extreme case, the losses from Ireland's wage subsidy program totaled over 95 percent, while the program's net incrementality was a meager 4 percent (OECD 1993). Evaluations of similar programs in Australia, The Netherlands, and the United Kingdom also show losses, though not as severe (table 7.5).

Equally disappointing are evaluations that compare wage and employment outcomes of participants with those of a control group. For example

TABLE 7.5
Losses from Wage Subsidy Programs (in percent)

Country	Deadweight and substitution effects	Additionality
Australia, mid-1980s (Jobstart Program)	65 D	35
Belgium, early 1990s (recruitment subsidy)	89 (53 D, 36 S)	11
England, 1986–90 (training grant)	69 D	31
England, late 1980s (Workstart I)	75 (45 D, 30 S)	25
England, mid-1970s (employment subsidy)	70 D	30
England, early 1980s	73 (63 D, 10 S)	27
Germany, mid-1970s (wage subsidy)	75 D	25
Ireland, 1980s (Employment Incentive Scheme)	91 (70 D, 21 S)	5–10
Netherlands, early 1980s (Vermeend-Moor Act)	75 (25 D, 50 S)	25
Netherlands, late 1980s (JOB scheme)	80 S	20
United States, mid-1980s (Targeted Job Tax Credit)	80 (70 D, 10 S)	20

Note: D = deadweight losses; S = substitution effect. Additionality is the employment effect after accounting for deadweight, displacement, and substitution effects.

a longitudinal study of the U.S. Targeted Job Tax Credit program found that participants earned significantly more than individuals in the control group for the first year. But this effect declined in the second year and disappeared after that (OECD 1993). Similarly evaluation results for Hungary show that participants were significantly less likely to be employed and earned less (though not significantly so) than those in the control group (O'Leary 1998a).

However, a few exceptions do exist. For example Australia's program experienced deadweight losses of around 30 percent, but the subsidies had a significant positive impact on postprogram employment. Participants were 15 percent more likely to be employed than members of the control group (Webster 1998). And as we have seen, the U.S. Job Training Partnership Act had positive effects for participants (Bloom 1994; Friedlander, Greenberg, and Robins 1997). Overall, however, the high deadweight losses and substitution effects strongly suggest that wage and employment subsidies are unlikely to have positive social returns that economists can measure, although these initiatives may help reduce social exclusion among older workers and single mothers.

PUBLIC WORKS PROGRAMS AND PUBLIC SERVICE EMPLOYMENT. Public works programs are among the most heavily funded active labor market interventions in OECD countries. We summarized the results of 17 evaluations of public works programs, 13 of them quasi-experimental and 4 nonscientific. These evaluations suggest some general conclusions.

First, nonexperimental evaluations show that these programs have some desirable short-run effects in the form of increases in employment and declines in unemployment. Second, some scientific evaluations suggest very high displacement effects (in Sweden they reached 100 percent) (Skedinger 1995). Third, workers who participate in these programs are less likely to find employment than their counterparts in the control group and tend to earn less. Finally, these programs do not significantly reduce long-term unemployment, and whatever small short-run impact they do have tends to diminish over time (Webster 1998).

These conclusions are to a large extent predictable. Unlike other active labor market initiatives, public works provide current benefits and are only temporary escape routes from unemployment. Irrespective of the merits of such projects, an economist's first impression is that public works are generally expensive and are not an effective instrument if the objective is to get people into long-term gainful employment (table 7.6).

TABLE 7.6
Annual Cost of Job Creation in Public Works

	Egypt	Honduras	Nicaragua	Madagascar	Bolivia	Senegal	Ghana
Cost per job (US$)	1,401	2,120	2,580	786	2,700	5,445	2,122
Cost per job (PPP)[a]	7,212	9,759	14,302	3,620	9,388	12,100	10,610
Per capita GDP (US$)	790	600	380	230	800	600	390
Ratio (1:3)	1.77	3.53	6.79	3.42	3.38	9.08	5.44

a. PPP = purchasing power parity.
Source: Subbarao (1997); World Bank (1997).

Public works can serve as a short-term antipoverty intervention. For this reason some developing countries use them extensively during periods of hardship. Keddeman (1998) suggests that labor-intensive infrastructure construction projects, if carefully targeted and properly designed and implemented, not only provide a valuable safety net but also contribute to further economic recovery and development. Increasing the involvement of local communities and the private sector in the design and implementation phases can lead to improved outcomes.

MICROENTERPRISE DEVELOPMENT AND SELF-EMPLOYMENT SCHEMES. We summarized the results of 15 evaluations of programs aimed at helping unemployed individuals start their own businesses. Two of these evaluations are experimental, seven are quasi-experimental, five are nonscientific, and one is mixed. These programs are described in various ways—as microenterprise or self-employment schemes, for example—but we refer to them as microenterprise development assistance.

These programs have high deadweight losses. Estimates of such losses range from about 30 percent (for the self-employment experiments in the U.S. states of Massachusetts and Washington) to over 50 percent (for Canada's self-employment assistance program and Denmark's enterprise start-up grant scheme) (Fay 1996; Graves and Gauthier 1995; Balakrishna 1998). Evaluations show that businesses started with assistance from these schemes are short-lived. Typically one-third to one-half of them close down in the first year of operation (table 7.7).[10] Even when businesses survive, the multiplier effect is small. Most surviving businesses create, on average, half an additional job. In Hungary each surviving enterprise created 0.3 additional jobs, in France 0.5, and in Australia (during a period of declining un-

TABLE 7.7
Failure Rates for Businesses Receiving
Microenterprise Development Assistance
(percent)

Program	Failure rate of businesses
Australia (New Enterprise Initiative, late 1980s)	58 (1 year), 71 (2 years)
Canada (Self-Employment Assistance Program, early 1990s)	20 (1 year)
Denmark (Enterprise Allowance Schemes, late 1980s)	60 (1 year)
France (Microenterprise Development, early 1980s)	50 (4.5 years)
Hungary (Microenterprise Development Assistance, mid-1990s)	20 (15 months)
Netherlands, early 1990s	50 (4 years)
Poland (Microenterprise Development Assistance, mid-1990s)	15 (2 years)
United States (state of Washington, Self-Employment Experiment, 1990)	37 (15 months)

employment) 0.7 (OECD 1993; Wilson and Adams 1994). Businesses that receive mentoring and business counseling are more likely to succeed, and even though a majority of them may close, the entrepreneurs are likely to move to employment in another industry rather than into unemployment.

Despite heavy deadweight losses and high rates of business failures, participants in these programs fare reasonably well in terms of employment outcomes compared with control groups. Scientific evaluations show that participants are more likely to be employed than individuals in the control group. However in this case employment does not necessarily translate into higher earnings. For example, in the Washington self-employment experiment, participants were more likely to find employment than the control group but earned significantly less (Fay 1996). In Hungary and the Czech Republic, participants were more likely to be employed than individuals in the control group but earned US$30 per month less. In Poland, however, participants were 25 percent more likely to be employed than the control group and earned significantly more. In the Hungarian and Polish programs, women and older workers generally had better outcomes than individuals in other subgroups (Fretwell, Benus, and O'Leary 1999).

The cost-benefit issue is rarely addressed. The available data indicate that the cost of starting up a small business varies from $4,500 in France to $13,000–14,000 in Canada and Denmark. The Canadian evaluation concludes that the long-term cost-effectiveness of these programs is uncertain. Preliminary analyses from Poland and Hungary indicate a loss to the unemployment insurance system. In both countries the duration and amount of benefits are greater for participants than for the control group. But drawing any conclusions on the cost-effectiveness of these programs would be premature given the small amount of evidence.

Overall the evaluations show that microenterprise development assistance programs work for only a small subset of the unemployed population and that they have high deadweight losses and displacement effects (as well as high rates of business failures). In the end, then, the net effects of these programs are small. As in the case of training, assistance targeted at particular groups, such as women and older individuals, shows the greatest likelihood of success.

The East Asian Experience with Active Labor Market Programs

East Asia does not have a strong tradition of active labor market programs. The one exception is the fairly widespread use of public works to create short-term earning opportunities. Other instruments, such as retraining and employment services, are not used on any significant scale to integrate unemployed workers into the labor force. In part this policy reflects the stage of development of most countries in the region and the prevailing ideologies regarding the role of public policy. It also reflects the low unemployment rates in most countries before 1997.

The potential for using active labor market initiatives in the region changed with the crisis. The increases in unemployment, the difficulties many laid-off workers face in finding new employment and earning an adequate salary, and the obstacles confronting young people trying to enter the labor force all underscored the need for policymakers to consider new options. While the crisis increased the need for new programs, however, fiscal pressures soon restricted the spending capacity of governments.

Even with these constraints governments in all countries are assessing how they can use active labor market interventions to help alleviate unemployment problems (table 7.8). These programs are particularly important because unemployment insurance exists only in Korea. But the governments of the region must address many problems if such initiatives are to make an important contribution, not only to the crisis but to the development of a long-term labor policy framework.

TABLE 7.8
Employment Services

	Services offered	Public-private provision	Labor market information	Crisis-specific interventions
Indonesia	1. Job search assistance, vacancy tracking, and placement 2. Voluntary registration of unemployed workers	1. Strict regulation of private agencies	1. Limited computer literacy among administrative clerks 2. Interagency overlap and communication problems	None
Korea, Rep. of	1. Registration and administration of unemployment benefits 2. Job search assistance, vacancy tracking, and placement 3. Career guidance and counseling	1. Recent easing of restrictions on private agencies	1. New Internet-based career guidance and job search system (Work-Net) 2. New "Worker Profiling System" 3. Major revisions in occupational classification	1. Increased number of public employment service agencies. 2. New one-stop "Employment Security Centers"
Malaysia	1. Job search assistance, vacancy tracking, and placement 2. Career guidance and counseling 3. Monitoring of labor mobility	1. Licensing requirements for private agencies	1. Computer-based Employment Service Automatic Reporting System	1. Tracking and monitoring of placements through task force

TABLE 7.8 (continued)

	Services offered	Public-private provision	Labor market information	Crisis-specific interventions
Philippines	1. Registration of unemployed, national skill registry 2. Referral for job placement locally and overseas 3. Career guidance, job fairs, and placement in other programs	1. Innovations in private provision (radio station airs job openings and takes calls from job seekers and employers) 2. Government regulation of private agencies 3. Growth of successful private agencies, especially for overseas placements	1. Long-term project under GATT Adjustment Program known as Systematization of Labor Market Information and Employment Counseling 2. Job-matching service (Phil-Jobnet)	1. 146 new Public Employment Service Offices (PESO) in 1998 2. National facilitation network in every province and key city
Thailand	1. Job search assistance, vacancy tracking, and placement 2. Job fairs and counseling	1. Monitoring and supervision of private agencies (under Ministry of Labor and Social Welfare)	1. Very little coordinated or comprehensive effort to collect data	1. No significant new initiatives

Employment Services

All the East Asian countries have public employment services that have two responsibilities: to gather information on job seekers and job vacancies and to provide access to services that will match the two. These services are delivered through a network of employment bureaus in each country. The Philippines has an extensive network of public employment service offices (1,825 across the country), buttressed by new offices opened since the crisis. Such offices also seem plentiful in the other countries (for example, Korea has about 120, Malaysia about 40, and Thailand 85). But the size, population, and topography of most of the countries make providing complete geographical coverage difficult.

Another constraint stems from what public employment services can offer in terms of services for the unemployed. In most industrial countries the public employment service is driven by three activities:

- Delivering unemployment insurance benefits (and validating job availability and other criteria);
- Serving as a point of access to labor market programs like retraining and job search assistance; and
- Disseminating labor market information to workers, employers, and service providers.

The lack of unemployment insurance, limited number of active labor market initiatives, and shortage of labor market information (and the fact that when it is available it is inadequately used) mean that public employment services in East Asia do not serve these functions. On the positive side, however, policymakers can take advantage of the experiences of effective employment services in industrial economies. We know, for instance, the importance of coordinating and integrating services, of providing complementary public and private service delivery, and of using technology effectively. But ultimately the value of public employment services as an element of active labor market policy depends on how well the services are integrated with other aspects of labor policy (active and passive). East Asian countries are making efforts to foster such integration. Korea and the Philippines (and possibly Indonesia) are transforming traditional employment offices into one-stop centers where job seekers can access unemployment benefits (in the case of Korea), job search assistance, and vocational training opportunities. Throughout the region committees, task forces, and government and tripartite bodies are examining how integrated and coordinated services can improve labor adjustment.

All the countries also allow private companies to provide employment services alongside the public systems, although in some cases (for instance, Indonesia), some concerns exist about the efficiency of government regulation. Currently private service providers are facing difficulties because of depressed business conditions (especially in Malaysia), while public systems are being forced to handle rapidly increasing loads. In Korea, for example, the number of job seekers using public employment services increased almost 10-fold between 1997 and 1998.

East Asian countries vary in their use of information technology, and its apparent effectiveness also varies throughout the region. In Malaysia and Korea employment offices in different geographic areas can share information about job seekers and vacancies on computerized networks and the Internet. In Malaysia the Employment Service Automatic Reporting System assists the Manpower Department in matching job seekers and job vacancies. In Korea the government has an electronic labor exchange system, "Work-Net," which provides information on job vacancies, vocational training, career guidance, employment policies, unemployment insurance, and labor market statistics. In the Philippines the public can search for job vacancies and find application information at selected government offices and on the Internet through "Phil-Jobnet," an electronic information system.

Deficiencies in training, networking, and the computers themselves continue to constrain the effectiveness of information technology in much of the region. The Philippines network, for example, registered only 1,500 vacancies and 6,000 workers in 1998, its first year of operation. In Indonesia computerized data in district employment service offices are not available in other regions. And because many staff do not have appropriate training or experience, much of the data is still collected and analyzed manually.

Some limited activity is taking place in the areas of counseling and placement services. Korea stepped up its placement and counseling services by rapidly increasing the number of counselors in the public employment service offices. In Thailand and the Philippines, the public employment service holds job fairs to bring prospective employers and job seekers together. Counseling is provided at the job fairs, as well as at educational institutions and other outreach venues.

How is the effectiveness of employment services in the region evaluated? Placement rates, the most commonly used indicator, fell once the crisis began. In Korea, for example, a survey on unemployment and welfare needs found that only 5.8 percent of the unemployed succeeded in finding jobs through the public employment services. This finding suggests that unemployed workers in Korea find jobs through other more important channels. Information from Thailand suggests various reasons for the difficulties registered workers have finding jobs through the public employment service, for two reasons. First, a mismatch exists between workers' qualifications and job requirements (and between workers' expectations and the available jobs). Second, employers continue to rely on other means of finding workers.

Labor Market Training

Training is an increasingly popular intervention in East Asia. The region is moving along a long-term development path toward industrial activities that require highly skilled workers. All the countries now have relatively complex systems of vocational training at the national level (table 7.9). For the most part these systems are funded by the public sector and operated by the government.

Not surprisingly the crisis changed the context for training. In general the increase in unemployment created pressure to step up training activities designed to reintegrate laid-off workers into the job market and provide social relief. In Korea, for example, the number of people participating in vocational training programs for the unemployed rose eightfold between 1997 and 1998. In Thailand the Department of Employment launched a special program of three-month courses in 1998 to retrain workers laid off because of the financial crisis that drew more than 27,000 unemployed workers. Vocational training and education in Indonesia, however, decreased once the crisis began because of the worsening fiscal situation.

Despite the growing popularity of training programs in the wake of the crisis, governments need to address a number of important challenges in order to improve job training in the long term. Some of these challenges are common across East Asia, including enhanced coordination and a stronger demand-side orientation. Coordination among the various arms of government responsible for vocational education and training is currently limited. For example, in the Philippines and Thailand three separate government agencies have overlapping responsibility for vocational educational and training activities. The situation in Indonesia is even more problematic: a recent report identified 19 different departments that were involved in 815 vocational training programs (see chapter 2).

Virtually all the East Asian countries need to make their vocational training programs more responsive to labor demand. Specifically they need to generate more high-technology training, and some governments have

Labor Market Training

	Vocational education system	Public and private provision	Training innovations	Crisis-specific interventions
Indonesia	1. 19 different government departments run 815 vocational training programs 2. Ministry of Manpower oversees 156 public training institutions	1. Estimated capacity of private training centers more than that of the public 2. Heavy regulation of private training and lack of public-private coordination	1. German-style dual education system operating in 11,000 SMEs	1. Public vocational education somewhat threatened by fiscal constraints of crisis
Korea	1. National training system since 1967 2. Ministries of Labor and Education responsible for programs 3. 3.3 million in training courses since 1967	1. Approximately 500 vocational training institutes, 237 in-plant centers, and 178 centers run by nonprofit organizations and private firms	1. Pilot program of training vouchers since 1998	1. Eightfold increase in training programs for the unemployed from 1997 to 1998
Malaysia	1. Vocational training policies overseen by Ministry of Human Resources and administered through the National Vocational Training Council (public training) and the Human Resource Development Council (private sector training)	1. Government promotion of private training but little coordination between public and private 2. Many agencies not accredited 3. Dearth of public instructors owing to low pay	1. Training fund for skill upgrading financed by levies on firms	None

(Table continues on the following page)

TABLE 7.9 (continued)

	Vocational education system	Public and private provision	Training innovations	Crisis-specific interventions
Philippines	1. Technical Education and Skill Development Authority responsible for programs since 1994 2. Programs smaller than in other East Asian countries	1. 723 public and 1,383 private vocational technical centers 2. 80 percent of trainees in private institutions	1. Government-funded scholarships for students in private training institutions 2. Dual-training system being tested	1. Expansion of scholarship program and shift toward private provision of services
Thailand	1. 413 training centers under the Department of Vocational Education (Ministry of Education) 2. New entrants and current employees under the Department of Skill Department (Ministry of Labor and Social Welfare)	1. Restrictions on private agencies relaxed 2. Tax deductions for company training expenses 3. Small but growing private training sector	1. Training institutions to be improved by hiring 2,155 new college graduates to set up national database on training needs by province, assist staff in training and supervision, and execute in-school job creation dual-training project for students	1. New 3-month training courses for laid-off workers (27,000 since July 1998) 2. Donor-financed training for groups such as entrepreneurs, rubber-tappers, electronics repair persons, and tailors

introduced initiatives in this area. The Malaysian government, for instance, established three centers for high-technology skills training and negotiated bilateral agreements with France and Germany for additional facilities.

Countries are also making attempts to increase the role of the private sector in training. Private training institutions represent one vehicle for getting the private sector involved in training. The Philippines and Thailand report increasing numbers of private providers, but public institutions continue to predominate in the region. Even in the Philippines, which probably has the highest number of private trainers, the private sector faces constraints in terms of access to credit and competition from highly subsidized public institutions. A more neutral policy environment or one that encourages the entry of private providers is likely to lead to a more efficient and responsive training sector.[11] Creating such an environment requires governments to set standards and develop accreditation arrangements.

Governments are introducing a number of innovations in financing for training. While there is no guarantee that all the innovations will be useful in the long run, policymakers need to try new ideas in this area, given the well-known financial market imperfections associated with human capital. In Korea the Employment Insurance System provides financial incentives both for employers to provide training and for employees to take it. Employers can apply for money from a special fund to implement various educational and training activities, including offering paid leave for workers who participate. Korea launched a pilot program for training vouchers in 1998 with the objective of providing more choice in the training system. The Philippines also introduced a voucher-style scholarship program through the government-sponsored Private Education Student Finance Assistance program. In Malaysia the Human Resources Development Council encourages retraining and skill upgrading for current employees in part by requiring firms registered with the council to contribute to a training fund.

A number of countries in the region are now considering German-style vocational education systems that integrate vocational and technical education with work experience. In 1994 the Indonesian government introduced a "dual" system, and all the public institutions offering vocational education, plus a higher-than-expected number of small and medium-size enterprises (SMEs), are participating. The Philippines is testing an apprenticeship program modeled on the German system. The program lasts 30–36 months, with trainees spending 70 percent of their time in the firm and 30 percent at a training center. Trainees receive 75 percent of the minimum wage but retain only 30 percent of their wages after paying the training centers.[12] While such dual systems have strong features, they have been criticized for a lack of flexibility, and some firms are unwilling to involve themselves in these programs.

Job-Creation Activities

Traditionally job creation is the major active labor market policy in all the East Asian countries (table 7.10). Most job-creation activities take the form of public works, but these projects are generally motivated by social relief objectives rather than by employment development goals. Two other activities used in East Asia fall under the rubric of job creation programs. Both Malaysia and Korea have employment subsidies to firms to encourage new hiring and maintain existing jobs. And all East Asian countries have some type of initiative to support the self-employed and SMEs.

Public Works

All five countries implemented substantial public works programs as a social safety net provision in the wake of the 1997 financial crisis. While these countries had offered similar programs before, the extraordinary growth of the mid-1990s substantially reduced the need to create infrastructure and provide jobs. In Indonesia, for example, labor-intensive job creation programs officially ended in 1994, only to be resurrected in 1997 following an extreme drought, the economic crisis, and political turmoil.

Design flaws can limit the effectiveness of public works programs, and these flaws are issues in East Asian countries. Some are the result of the haste with which the projects were put together or expanded. In Indonesia, Korea, and the Philippines, public works programs struggled to reach their target populations because wages were set too high. Other design flaws in Indonesia included a low wage bill (as a percentage of total project costs) and the absence of women in most public works projects. Projects in the Philippines suffered from insufficient monitoring and a failure to identify those areas most in need of antipoverty initiatives.

The rush to respond to the crisis before all the recent gains in economic, social, and human development were lost created numerous problems in policy coordination and follow-through on public works projects. The Thai government, for example, hurried to design and implement new public works projects by soliciting input from various ministries. The resulting menagerie of programs included a number that had previously been dismissed or rated as low priorities but that were implemented any-

TABLE 7.10
Job Creation Activities

	Public works	Employment subsidies	Self-employment and SME support
Indonesia	1. A 4-month, RP 42 billion-program targeting retrenched construction and manufacturing workers (implemented December 1997) 2. Massive public works program with 16 subprograms targeting various groups in all provinces (implemented April 1993)	None	1. Percentage of commercial lending set aside for small borrowers, subsidized credit for cooperatives 2. At least 24 credit programs for groups such as farmers, trans-migrants, and women (micro-entrepreneurs and SMEs)
Korea	1. Major focus of postcrisis policy (400,000 participants in 1998) 2. Internship programs for high school and college graduates expected to create 10,000 and 57,000 jobs, respectively	1. Subsidies offered to firms that maintain employment by reducing work hours, offering paid leave, training employees, temporarily shutting down, or dispatching workers to weaker affiliates	1. Postcrisis support through new Korea Venture and Investment Fund Cooperative, a public fund of 100 billion won 2. "Business incubators" offering management training, technolo-gical capacity, and office space

(Table continues on the following page)

TABLE 7.10 (continued)

	Public works	Employment subsidies	Self-employment and SME support
Malaysia	1. Public works programs in infrastructure and agricultural and rural development	1. Primary labor market strategy that encourages employers to use pay cuts, temporary layoffs, flexible work hours, and part-time work rather than retrenchment	1. Industrial linkages, technology development and acquisition, enterprise development, financial support, and skill upgrading provided by Small and Medium Industries Development Corporation
Philippines	1. Public works projects (with multiple objectives) in transportation, agriculture, environment, communications, and housing departments	1. Wage subsidy program for students (children of displaced workers) during school vacations	1. Over 100 "livelihood" programs administered by government 2. Multiple credit and guarantee facilities for SMEs
Thailand	1. Primary labor market policy response to crisis, with Ministry of Interior projects for 1999 creating an estimated 788,799 jobs 2. Additional 11 million person-months provided by donor-financed projects	None	None

way in lieu of expanding existing high-priority public works projects. The numerous public works programs implemented in 1998 in Indonesia suffered from a lack of conceptual clarity about objectives and beneficiaries, in part because of inadequate labor market information. As in Thailand there were numerous problems of overlap and lack of coordination among implementing agencies and a virtual absence of program monitoring.

Wage and Employment Subsidies

Providing incentives to employers to maintain current employment and create new jobs is not a major policy tool among East Asian governments. The exceptions are Malaysia, where such subsidies are the primary labor market strategy, and Korea, which implemented subsidies in the immediate aftermath of the crisis. The Philippines has two small wage subsidy programs targeted to young people.

In Malaysia the government launched efforts to encourage the private sector to choose pay cuts, temporary layoffs, flexible work hours, and part-time employment for workers rather than retrenchment. Initial evaluations of government incentives report that these measures are having some success in preventing unemployment. In particular employers are choosing to cut pay rather than instituting voluntary retrenchment or simply retrenching workers. In Korea employment stabilization programs immediately following the crisis took several approaches. The government offered subsidies to firms that agreed to maintain their current workforce using any of the following measures: shutting down temporarily, reducing working hours, offering in-firm training or paid leave, reassigning workers, and even taking up a new line of business while retaining at least 60 percent of the staff. The employment effects of this program appear positive. In a survey of 533 firms receiving government support, managers estimated that they would have had to layoff 22.3 percent more workers in the absence of subsidies (see chapter 3).

Support for the Self-employed and SMEs

Many programs in the region support the self-employed and SMEs with a variety of technical services and, most prominently, financial assistance. A number of the programs are not driven by immediate labor market concerns but are part of the overall industrial policy envelope. Because governments now view them as instruments for encouraging employment, we include them here.

Financing can be an obstacle for microentrepreneurs and small enterprises, and governments everywhere have responded by introducing programs designed to increase access to credit for these groups and in some cases to improve the terms of financing. After the East Asian crisis began, declines in product demand, increases in production costs, and a credit squeeze exacerbated the financing issue, raising demand for further government intervention to protect SMEs and their employees. Most of the programs existed prior to the crisis but received no additional funding afterward.

In the Philippines SMEs had access to credit through government programs long before the crisis. According to a World Bank evaluation, participating firms perform better in many dimensions than other small firms, but the magnitude of this job-creation effort and its effectiveness as a poverty reduction tool are relatively minor (World Bank 1998). The Philippines also offers self-employment initiatives through various government departments. The Self-Employment Assistance livelihood program offers access to credit as well as social services delivered at the community level and targeted to poverty reduction goals.

In Malaysia the government created a number of schemes for entrepreneurs that are expected to assist about 12,000 traders and small businesses in setting up or expanding their businesses. Indonesia currently has at least 24 credit programs for microentrepreneurs and SMEs. Some target special groups such as farmers and transmigrants or subsidize credit for cooperatives (typically groups of SMEs with common interests). The latter programs have come under criticism for allowing cooperatives to profit at the government's expense by borrowing cheaply and investing the money at higher interest rates. A recent assessment of credit programs for SMEs in Indonesia argues that the best government intervention in support of SMEs is the development of an environment conducive to the efficient operation and development of the commercial financial institutions serving them (Wieland 1998).

Various technical assistance programs are also available in these five countries. The Korean government is developing "business incubators" to assist entrepreneurs with management training, technological capacity, and office space. The Malaysian government provides opportunities for self-employment not only through financing assistance but also through franchise development, various farming extension services, and basic business training for unemployed graduates. Indonesia provides technical assistance through different channels. For example prior to the crisis the government had established the Small and Medium Industries Development Corporation (SMIDEC) to assist industries with issues such as industrial linkage, technology development, technology acquisition, market development, enterprise development, financial support, and skill development and upgrading.

The Future of Active Labor Market Policies

What can policymakers in East Asia conclude from our review of active labor market programs? First, the OECD experience illustrates the range of programs industrial countries have undertaken and the issues that are involved in this area of public policy. While various types of interventions exist that address different policy objectives, our review of the evidence from evaluations certainly sends out cautionary signals. Ultimately active labor market programs are judged by their performance in improving the employability and earnings of workers, and the evaluations reviewed here suggest that these programs often have little or no impact on these outcomes.

However in putting forward this evidence, we are not arguing that policymakers in countries that have not made major investments in active labor market programs should avoid this area in the future. First, active labor market programs can serve social as well as economic objectives. Researchers have not addressed the question of the programs' social impacts, which may be more positive. Second, work-force development, the social and economic integration of marginalized and at-risk groups, and the status of unemployed workers are central concerns for policymakers. Active labor market programs are obvious instruments for addressing these issues. Third, the disappointing performance of these programs in the aggregate masks the fact that some program designs do seem to lead to positive outcomes for some types of workers. Moreover in the 1990s policymakers in some countries utilized novel and promising approaches to active labor market programs, including finding new roles for the private sector and instituting innovative tripartite arrangements. The challenge is to learn from experiences such as these and to design future programming along lines that appear to work.

The evidence from the evaluations suggests that policymakers should exercise caution in two areas. First, policymakers should be realistic about what active labor market programs can do. Second, they should make only careful and modest investments in this area. As policymakers in the East Asian countries look toward the future, we recommend that they carefully consider the following issues related to active labor market policies.

Priority setting. As we have noted, active labor market programs can have multiple policy objectives, including reducing unemployment during cyclical downturns, correcting structural imbalances, improving labor market functioning, and assisting disadvantaged groups of workers. In designing an overall strategy, policymakers need to identify which of these objectives will have top priority and therefore determine the choice and design of programs. We do advocate the use of private placement agencies. But because these businesses serve only relatively skilled white-collar workers, they are no substitute for public employment services. Regardless of the specific objectives, one immediate and high priority is to develop a strong employment service—the first link in the chain of active labor market policies.

The roles of the public and private sectors. This consideration is key both to developing an overall strategy and to designing and implementing programs. At one time OECD governments developed and delivered virtually all active labor market programs, but increasingly governments are reconsidering the role of the private and nonprofit sectors in program delivery. In many countries these sectors now play important roles in the delivery of services. This development can lead to more diverse, innovative, and cost-efficient services and to programs that respond to demand. But even in countries where the scope for private sector involvement is considerable, governments still play the central role. They must remain responsible for the overall system, ensuring that it remains focused on public priorities. They must also address distributional issues (for instance, ensuring that all types of workers receive adequate services) and provide public goods. They also must be the catalysts in the process of harnessing private sector involvement in retraining and other active labor market programs.[13]

Partnerships and dialogue. The process of identifying priorities for active labor market policy and program choices can benefit from ongoing dialogue among government, business, labor, and other relevant organizations (such as private and nonprofit service providers). When this dialogue is conducted effectively, policymakers understand the needs of the labor market and can maximize support for active programs and policies. The dialogue needs to be carried out both at the national level, where priorities are set, and at the local level, where programs are delivered. Governments typically must be the leaders and catalysts of this process.

"Infrastructure" for the labor market. Infrastructure services are essential if active labor market programs are to be useful policy instruments. By infrastructure we mean labor market information, a viable and complete network of employment service offices, and certification and accreditation systems. These services are the cornerstones of an effective system, informing the program choices that should be made. They provide the bridges among the labor market, service deliverers, workers, and employers. And

they ensure quality throughout the system. As largely public goods, they are inevitably the responsibility of governments. In countries where the development of active labor market policies is at an early stage, these infrastructure services should be the first priority.

Coordination within government. In many countries (including those in East Asia), a number of government agencies share the responsibility for administering active labor market programs. In these cases overlapping responsibilities and a lack of coordination complicate service delivery. Too often mechanisms to ensure that the various departments are working together are not in place. In addition overall economic planning does not take into account the need to set priorities and design effective active labor market programs. Coordination within the government needs to be improved to ensure the relevance and efficiency of active labor market programming.

Policy and administrative and operational capacity. Designing and implementing active labor market programs requires considerable capacity within the government itself. In many ways active programming is more complicated than passive income support programming, especially since capacity needs differ significantly by program. Public works can be relatively straightforward to design and implement—so much so that these programs are often the primary active labor market intervention in many developing countries. Employment services, however, require a network of facilities with extensive geographic coverage, skilled counselors, reliable connections with employers and the educational communities, and the technological resources and know-how to generate and disseminate accurate and timely labor market information. Training programs also require labor market information, training and occupational standards, monitoring and evaluation capabilities, and capacity (increasingly in the private or nonprofit sectors) to deliver good programs. Governments must recognize that capacity building is a slow but necessary process.

Financing. The most important question in this area concerns the balance of public and private financing. Clearly the rationale for public spending is strong: market failures exist with respect to human capital investments, and active labor market policies have some elements of public goods. But there are also private gains to employers and employees as a result of training and other interventions, and governments need to think about how financing can reflect such gains. They can consider the applicability of innovative financing arrangements (such as income-contingent loans) that address market imperfections but reflect the fact that active labor market programs offer some private returns. In terms of public financing the essential choice for policymakers is drawing from general revenues or creating a fund financed by employer and (perhaps) employee contributions. Each option involves important considerations, including fungibility, assumptions about responsibility for labor programs, funding integrity, and incentives for formal employment creation. OECD countries, which use a full range of funding arrangements, offer useful lessons for countries in East Asia.

Monitoring and evaluation. In spite of large public expenditures on active labor market programs, OECD countries generally have not undertaken rigorous evaluations. In an effort to improve the targeting and efficiency of social programs, governments need to conduct sound impact evaluations. These evaluations can compare labor market outcomes for program participants with those of a control group. Data on program costs can be used to determine the impact on individuals, the net social gains, and the outcomes—that is, to determine whether the programs provide the optimum results for the money spent.

Clearly many considerations are involved in developing a strong active labor market policy. The experience of the OECD countries and the extensive resources such programs require suggest that East Asian countries should move slowly to build on what already exists. Over the long run building the capacity to implement active labor market programs will be important as formal labor markets grow and the need for a skilled workforce increases. Countries now need to think about priorities, the role of government, and a range of issues related to how these programs are best carried out. Given its significance, labor market "infrastructure" demands immediate attention. As the East Asian economies continue to develop, active labor market policies will need to become part of the overall policy tool kit.

Notes

1. Objectives can focus on the needs of employers as well—for example, the need for an adequate supply of trained (and trainable) workers. These needs may take priority in times of rapid expansion, when vacant jobs rather than unemployed workers are the predominant form of labor market imbalance, as they were in the 1960s when active labor market programs were first introduced on a significant scale.

2. For an extensive listing of active labor market programs, see OECD (1993).

3. Displacement effects usually occur in the product market. A firm with subsidized workers increases output, displacing output from firms with no subsidized workers. Displacement effects also occur when some individuals receive support for self-employment activities and others do not. The substitution effect

occurs when a subsidized worker replaces an unsubsidized worker who would otherwise have been hired, for a zero net employment effect.

4. Deadweight losses occur when program outcomes are no different from what would have happened in the absence of the program. In this case the workers receiving job search assistance would have found jobs on their own. Similarly, wage subsidies may go to support workers who would have been hired without them.

5. We count as active labor market policies only public works designed specifically to alleviate unemployment and poverty, not those routinely planned to construct infrastructure.

6. Grameen Bank, which has more than 2 million members (94 percent of them women) has become a successful mechanism for reducing poverty. Over time it has demonstrated its ability to operate with market resources and to reduce its dependency on subsidized funds. Its loan recovery rates are consistently higher than 90 percent.

7. This section is based on Dar and Tzannatos (1999) and Dar and Gill (1998).

8. For a more detailed review, see Dar and Tzannatos (1999).

9. Social returns are based on a comparison of measurable economic costs and benefits that do not take into account either possible externalities associated with the reintegration of the long-term unemployed into the labor force or reductions in high levels of unemployment in specific regions.

10. We do not have data on the failure rate of small businesses that do not take part in these programs. But anecdotal evidence suggests that these rates are usually similar. While businesses receiving assistance, then, do no worse in terms of survival rates than businesses not receiving assistance, they do not appear to do any better.

11. Assessments in the region have identified problems with the quality and efficiency of public institutions. In Malaysia, for example, low salaries resulted in a shortage of qualified instructors. A World Bank evaluation of public training institutions in Indonesia found low levels of efficiency and capacity utilization (World Bank 1997b).

12. Another apprenticeship initiative in the Philippines allows firms to pay wages considerably below market levels to apprentices receiving on-the-job training for up to six months. But the law that allows this exemption does not require firms to establish a specific training program. Thus a recent government review suggests that firms use the law as a means of exploiting workers (see chapter 5).

13. For discussions of these aspects of government roles, see ILO (1998) and Betcherman, McMullen, and Davidman (1998).

References

Anderson, P., and B. D. Meyer. 1994. "Unemployment Insurance Benefits and Take-up Rates." NBER Working Paper 4787. Cambridge, Mass.: National Bureau of Economic Research.

Anderson, P., W. Corson, and P. Decker. 1991. "The New Jersey Unemployment Insurance Re-employment Demonstration Project Follow-up Report." Unemployment Insurance Occasional Paper 91-1, U.S. Department of Labor, Washington, D.C.

Balakrishna, R. 1998. "An International Review of Active Labor Market Policies and the Lessons for the GCC Countries." Discussion paper. London: London School of Economics.

Betcherman, G., K. McMullen, and K. Davidman. 1998. *Training for the New Economy.* Ottawa: Canadian Policy Research Networks.

Bloom, H. 1990. "Back to Work: Testing Re-employment Services for Displaced Workers." Working paper. Kalamazoo, Michigan: W.E. Upjohn Institute for Employment Research.

Corson, W., S. Long, and R. Maynard. 1985. "An Impact Evaluation of the Buffalo Dislocated Worker Demonstration Program." Working Paper. Princeton: Mathematica Policy Research.

Dar, A., and I. Gill. 1998. "Evaluating Retraining Programs in OECD Countries: Lessons Learned." *World Bank Research Observer* 13(1): 79–101.

Dar, A., and Z. Tzannatos. 1999. "Active Labor Market Programs: A Review of the Evidence from Evaluations." Social Protection Discussion Paper Series 9901. Washington, D.C.: World Bank.

Fay, R. 1996. "Enhancing the Effectiveness of Active Labour Market Policies: Evidence From Program Evaluations in OECD Countries." OECD Labor Market and Social Policy Occasional Paper 8. Paris.

Fretwell, D., and S. Goldberg. 1994. "Developing Effective Employment Services" in "Equity, Efficiency and Adjustment in Labor Markets." Discussion Paper 208. Washington, D.C.: World Bank.

Fretwell, D., J. Benus, and C. J. O'Leary. 1999. *Evaluating the Impact of Active Labor Programs: Results of Cross Country Studies in Europe and Central Asia.* Social Protection Discussion Paper Series 9915. Washington, D.C.: World Bank.

Friedlander, D., D. Greenberg, and P. Robins. 1997. "Evaluating Government Training Programs for the Economically Disadvantaged." *Journal of Economic Literature* 35(4).

Gill, I., F. Fluitman, and A. Dar. 2000. *Vocational Education and Training Reforms: Matching Skills to Markets and Budgets.* New York: Oxford University Press.

Goss, Gilroy, and Associates. 1989. "Evaluation of the Job Development Program: Final Report." Report prepared for the Program Evaluation Branch, Employment and Immigration Office, Canada.

Graves, F., and B. Gauthier. 1995. "Evaluation of the Self-Employment Assistance Program." HRDC Working Paper. Ottawa, Canada.

Heckman, J. 1992. "Randomization and Social Policy Evaluation." In C. Manski and I. Garfinkel, eds., *Evaluating Welfare and Training Programs.* Cambridge, Mass.: Harvard University Press.

ILO (International Labour Office). 1998. *World Employment Report: Employability in the Global Economy: How Training Matters.* Geneva.

Keddeman, W. 1998. "Of Nets and Assets: Effects and Impacts of Employment-Intensive Programmes—A Review of ILO Experience." Development Policies Department, International Labour Organization. Geneva: International Labour Office.

Leigh, D. 1995. *Assisting Workers Displaced by Structural Change: An International Perspective.* Kalamazoo, Mich.: W. E. Upjohn Institute for Employment Research.

Mangan, J. 1988. "Wage Subsidies for the Disabled: A Discussion of Their Impact in Australia." *International Journal of Manpower* 11(1).

Meager, N., and C. Evans. 1998. "The Evaluation of Active Labor Market Measures for the Long-Term Unemployed." Employment and Training Papers 16. Geneva: International Labor Office.

New Zealand Department of Labor. 1995. "Evaluation of Job Action." New Zealand Employment Service Report. Wellington, New Zealand.

OECD (Organization for Economic Cooperation and Development). 1997. *OECD Employment Outlook.* Paris.

———. 1994. *The OECD Jobs Study: Evidence and Explanations.* Paris.

———. 1993. *OECD Employment Outlook.* Paris.

———. 1991. *Evaluating Labor Market and Social Programs: The State of a Complex Art.* Paris.

O'Leary, C. 1998a. "Evaluating the Effectiveness of Active Labor Programs in Hungary." Draft Working Paper. W. E. Upjohn Institute for Employment Research.

———. 1998b. *Evaluating the Effectiveness of Active Labor Programs in Poland.* Draft Working Paper. W. E. Upjohn Institute for Employment Research.

———. 1995. "An Impact Analysis of Employment Programs in Hungary." Research Working Paper 95-30. W. E. Upjohn Institute for Employment Research.

Puhani, P. 1998. "Advantage Through Training? A Microeconometric Evaluation of the Employment Effects of Active Labor Market Programs in Poland." ZEW Discussion Paper 98-25. Warsaw, Poland.

Ravallion, M. 1998. "Appraising Workfare Programs." Working Paper Series 1955. Washington, D.C.: The World Bank.

Skedinger, P. 1995. "Employment Policies and Displacement in the Youth Labor Market." *Swedish Economic Policy Review* 2(1).

Subbarao, K. 1997. "Public Works as an Anti-Poverty Program: An Overview of Cross-Country Experience." *American Journal of Agricultural Economics.*

Webster, E. 1998. "Microeconomic Evaluations of Australian Labor Market Programs." *Australian Economic Review* 3(12): 189–201.

Weiland, R. 1998. "SME Finance in Indonesia: An Assessment." Discussion paper prepared for the Trade and Industry Strategy project (BAPPENAS) and the Indonesian Ministry of Industry and Trade, Jakarta.

Wilson, S., and A. V. Adams. 1994. "Self-Employment for the Unemployed: Experience in OECD and Transitional Economies." Discussion Paper 263. Washington, D.C.: World Bank.

World Bank. 1997a. *World Development Report: The State in a Changing World.* Washington, D.C.: World Bank.

———. 1997b. *Training and the Labor Market in Indonesia: Productivity Gains and Employment Growth.* Washington, D.C.

———. 1998. "World Bank Support for Small and Medium Industries in the Phillipines: An Import Evaluation." Operations Evaluation Department Report 18041. Washington, D.C.

8 The Economics of Employment Protection and Unemployment Insurance Schemes: Policy Options for Indonesia, Malaysia, the Philippines, and Thailand

Alejandra Cox Edwards
and Chris Manning[1]

THIS CHAPTER EXAMINES the current systems of income protection in place in Indonesia, Malaysia, the Philippines, and Thailand and looks at policy options for protecting workers in both the formal and informal sectors. While acknowledging the problems that have arisen because of the Asian financial crisis, we take as our main focus future institutions. We start from the assumption that employment stability, and more precisely *income* stability, is the preferred state for individuals. At the same time employment creation and destruction are normal and permanent features of market-oriented systems. It follows, then, that private employment contracts must deal with the finite nature of employment relations in some way. But it is also clear that legislation establishing rules for terminating employment or restricting fixed-term contracts affects contract negotiations between employers and workers.

All economies offer a continuum of employment opportunities, from self-employment within the household to formal employment in registered enterprises. Part of a household's strategy for allocating its labor time—that is, choosing activities from this continuum—involves dealing with the risks surrounding temporary and permanent declines in income. Some of the risks households face are crop failure, unemployment, ill health, and incapacity in old age. Managing these risks is often intimately tied up with decisions affecting labor supply. Households make decisions about the allocation of labor to different activities (working at home, in other towns, or abroad, for instance) based on whether the activities reduce or increase potential risks.[2]

The expansion of formal labor and financial markets does not entirely replace traditional forms of dealing with risk, but these wider markets offer households alternative mechanisms for managing it. Knowing that workers are concerned with a variety of risks, firms interested in a stable and loyal labor force compete in the labor market using not only wages but also the overall labor contract, which includes important benefits such as health insurance. Similarly, well-developed financial and insurance markets offer households the opportunity to earn a return on even small savings and the option of spreading their risks more broadly, lowering the unit cost of insurance.

Labor Market Policy in Developing Countries

In developing countries informal and formal jobs together usually provide some form of employment for the entire labor force. A large number of rural workers are in the informal sector and may not be fully employed. Some work only part of the year, while others average fewer hours than they would like or find themselves performing low-productivity activities and earning meager wages. But the nature of production in agricultural economies is such that open unemployment is relatively rare. Poor households cannot afford to be without any income at all, and sharing low-productivity work is a common practice. The result is widespread underemployment.

As developing countries seek to transform themselves from traditional to modern economies, open unemployment rises. The transition from widespread underemployment to open unemployment in these economies is in part an income effect. As countries grow and household incomes rise, jobless workers are able to endure periods without work while waiting for a job to open. Rising open unemployment is also in part a result of urbanization and the shift to modern forms of production, since modern economies organize work in ways that do not lend themselves as easily as agricultural arrangements to work sharing. Realistic policy interventions, then, must recognize the need for an approach that includes economic activities appropriate to both types of economies. Ideally such policies will lend themselves to a smooth transition between traditional and modern forms of production.

One important policy issue is loss of income during the transformation. Two kinds of policy interventions address the problems associated with income loss. The first includes poverty-targeted emergency programs. Not necessarily focused on the unemployed (since unemployment is not the most important characteristic of the poor and may not be the most appropriate targeting mechanism), these programs are considered effective mechanisms for reaching households severely affected by income loss. The second set of policies, which we focus on here, includes all permanent labor market interventions that focus on dismissals and the unemployed.

Labor market interventions can address the risk of income loss associated with formal employment during the normal operations of a growing economy as well as in times of recession. Such labor policy interventions may help households deal with the risks associated with employment. But if labor policy overlooks the role of wages and working conditions as incentives and market signals, it will end up closing the formal labor market to the influence of market forces and discouraging the formalization of labor contracts.

Ideally policy interventions reduce the transaction costs associated with employer-employee negotiations and help workers manage job-to-job transitions. The central question is how employers and employees conduct themselves in the event of job termination and what to do in these situations. Legislation can simply require that all employment contracts include a clause on termination, potentially preventing disputes and reducing transaction costs. Alternatively legislation can impose specific rules concerning job dismissals, establishing property rights and liabilities such as severance payments. Legislation can also create a program of transfers for the unemployed. But such transfers rely on some source of funding, usually a payroll tax, and are likely to alter some or all of the following: job creation, job search incentives, labor costs, and net wages.

The existing evidence indicates that firing costs deter hiring, reduce labor demand, and hamper the economy's ability to deal with uncertainty and structural change (OECD 1995; Saint-Paul 1999). In general unemployment insurance lowers the incentives to look for work, but the relative size of this effect is a function of the program's design and thus varies across countries. European unemployment insurance programs pay benefits according to certain preestablished rules and collect the same tax rate from all employers, generating large cross-subsidies from some taxpayers to program beneficiaries. In contrast the unemployment insurance program in the United States is financed by an experience-rated payroll tax (box 8.1). In this case the employers that dismiss the most workers pay the

---

BOX 8.1

Experience Rating as a Means of Financing Unemployment Insurance

Experience rating is unique to the U.S. unemployment insurance system. Employers finance the system with payments that are essentially a state-level tax. Firms pay a percentage of the earnings of each employee, up to a relatively low maximum level that varies across states. (The maximum taxable wage was only $7,000 in most states in 1999.) In California, for example, new employers are assigned a rate of 3.4 percent. After an employer has made payments for three years, the company's rate is adjusted according to its "reserve ratio"—the sum of all contributions minus the benefits paid to former employees, divided by the total base payroll. Based on the 1999 schedule of tax rates, an employer could see the tax rate fall as low as 0.7 percent or rise as high as 5.4 percent. The rate continues to be adjusted yearly as new information on the employer accumulates. Employers receive a yearly summary of their account and can contest items that are inconsistent with their records.

The experience-rating system can make the marginal cost of firing more than zero and is intended to force firms to internalize the cost of unemployment benefits for its employees. However, because the tax rates have both lower and upper limits, many firms are in effect not experience rated—that is, an additional layoff or week of unemployment by a former employee has no effect on the firm's unemployment insurance tax bill. Feldstein (1976) was the first to note the frequency with which laid-off workers were recalled, citing it as evidence that many workers do not search for alternative employment while receiving unemployment insurance but simply wait for their previous employer to recall them. Topel (1983) argued that most of the impact unemployment insurance systems have on layoffs is caused by the fact that current methods of experience rating are incomplete. In other words, in spite of experience rating, in a large number of cases the marginal cost of layoffs for the firm is zero or negligible. Unemployment insurance systems can create an incentive for employers to rely on unemployment benefits to adjust cyclical labor costs.

highest tax rate, especially if these workers collect from the unemployment insurance system.

When looking at the impact of job security legislation or unemployment insurance programs, we must keep in mind the possible interaction between the two types of programs. European unemployment insurance programs coexist with job security legislation. Such legislation tends to reduce the number of dismissals, but once employees are terminated they have a difficult time finding new jobs because of the "slowing" effect of job security on job creation. In the United States employment at will prevails, making the event of dismissal more likely but easing the process of reemployment. The employment-at-will doctrine allows employers to dismiss workers for a just reason, an economic reason, or no reason at all, as long as the dismissal does not violate federal antidiscrimination legislation (such as the Civil Rights Act of 1964) or the National Labor Relations Act. Not surprisingly one of the key differences between the labor markets in Europe and the United States is that in Europe workers experience much longer periods of unemployment (Blanchard and Portugal 1998).

Informal Employment Protection Arrangements

The four countries discussed here differ not only in per capita incomes but also in the organizational features that characterize their economies (table 8.1). According to the World Bank's classification system, Indonesia is a low-income country, the Philippines and Thailand are lower-middle-income economies, and Malaysia is in the upper-middle-income category (World Bank 1999).

At the beginning of the 21st century, these countries are undergoing a rapid transformation. The share of overall employment in agriculture fell on the order of 10 points between 1985 and 1997 (table 8.2). Traditional forms of production coexist with modern methods in economies that, in spite of vast regional differences, have well-integrated labor markets. Internal migration and the ongoing reallocation of labor from the least productive to the most productive activities have contributed to more than two decades of sustained growth and an impressive trend of real wage growth. These achievements are particularly striking compared with the situation in developing countries outside the East Asia region (World Bank 1995).

The labor markets of these countries have three distinct features. The first is their size. The large numbers of active workers, especially in Indonesia, require decentralized programs in order to make administering labor market regulations a manageable task. Second, unemployment rates

TABLE 8.1
Basic Indicators, 1998

Country	Population (millions)	Population density (per km^2)	Per capita GNP (US$)	Per capita GNP (PPP)
Indonesia	204	112	680	2,790
Philippines	75	252	1,050	6,740
Thailand	61	120	2,200	5,840
Malaysia	22	68	3,600	6,990
World	5.9	45	4,890	6,200
Low income	3.5	85	520	2,130
Lower middle	908	25	1,710	4,080
Upper middle	588	27	4,860	7,830

Note: PPP = purchasing power parity.
Source: World Bank (1999).

have been modest, suggesting that focusing income security policy on the unemployed may not be appropriate (table 8.3). Third, with the exception of Malaysia more than half the workers in these countries are self-employed. For this reason programs focused on wage employees miss a significant proportion of the labor force.

Wiebe (1996) argues that income insecurity in Indonesia stems from a combination of low earnings and seasonal unemployment. Households have two types of protection against the possible consequences of these fluctuations—private strategies and government welfare programs. Private transfers flow among rural households and from urban to rural areas. Cox and Jimenez (1990) report that these types of transfers are also important in Malaysia and the Philippines (table 8.4). At the community level, Indonesian neighborhood associations *(Rukun Tetangga)* collect an informal tax to provide welfare assistance in emergencies.

Employers sometimes provide a third form of private insurance, even in the informal sector. Studies of labor markets in developing countries find that implicit contracts capture a number of social and economic forces (Hopenhayn and Nicolini 1997). Employers typically put in place systems of incentives that link compensation to productivity and reduce monitoring costs. Employers also make widespread use of fringe benefits in an attempt to make jobs more attractive and to secure workers' loyalty. These benefits include meals, transportation, some form of medical cov-

TABLE 8.2
Distribution of Employment by Major Sector, 1985–97
(percent)

	Malaysia[a]	Thailand[b]	Philippines[c]	Indonesia[d]
Agriculture				
1985	30.5	63.5	49.6	54.7
1990	26.0	64.0	45.2	56.0
1997	17.3	50.3	40.4	41.2
Industry				
1985	23.9	13.0	13.8	13.4
1990	27.5	14.0	15.0	13.8
1997	33.7	19.7	16.7	19.0
Manufacturing				
1985	15.1	9.4	9.5	9.3
1990	19.9	10.2	9.7	10.2
1997	23.4	12.9	9.9	12.9
Services				
1985	45.6	23.5	36.5	31.8
1990	46.5	22.0	39.7	30.3
1997	49.0	29.9	42.9	39.8

Note: Data are based on annual or quarterly labor force surveys (August round in Thailand, October/fourth round in the Philippines). Data for 1985 for Indonesia are taken from the National Intercensal Survey.

a. Ages 15–64 years.
b. Ages 11 and above (1985); ages 13 and above (1990 and 1997).
c. Ages 15 and above.
d. Ages 10 years and above.
Source: ILO (1998).

erage, and some form of income smoothing or employment continuity. In agriculture, for example, wages often vary by task. Tasks are specific to seasons but do not directly reflect the value of marginal productivity in each season. Instead the most productive workers tend to be employed more steadily than less productive workers, who are likely to be hired during peak seasons only (Dreze and Mukherjee 1997; Hart 1984; Otsuka, Chuma, and Hayami 1992).

A relatively large number of wage workers are on fixed-term contracts and move easily among jobs in search of the best working conditions. In

TABLE 8.3
Basic Labor Market Indicators

Country	Labor force (millions) 1997	Unemployment rate (percent) 1990–1996	1997	1998[a]	Agriculture Wage	Other wage	Industry Wage	Other wage	Services Wage	Other wage
Indonesia	91.3	2.5	4.7	5.5	6.5	43.9	10.0	5.8	14.3	19.5
Philippines	30.3	8.1	7.9	—	9.6	35.7	12.3	3.7	23.6	15.1
Thailand	33.3		2.2	4.6	6.6	59.7	8.7	3.2	11.6	10.2
Malaysia	8.6		2.5	6.4	8.8	21.8	19.0	3.6	34.0	12.7

(Distribution of labor force by sector (percent))

Note: Labor force statistics are based on quarterly or annual labor force surveys and cover those ages 15 and above, except for Indonesia (ages 10 and above), Thailand 1997 (ages 13 and above), and Malaysia (ages 15–64).

a. Indonesia, August 1998; Thailand, February 1998; Malaysia, projected (Economic Planning Unit).

Source: World Bank (1995); Economic Planning Unit, *National Economic Recovery Plan* 1998; Department of Statistics, *Labor Force Survey 1996;* NSO (1998); various press reports, January–March 1999.

TABLE 8.4
Private Transfers among Households

Country	Year	Per capita GNP[a]	Percentage of households receiving or sending transfers		Average transfer as a percentage of average income	
			Receiving households	Sending households	Receiving households	Sending households
Indonesia (Java)	1982	490				
Rural			31	72	10	8
Urban			44	45	20	3
Malaysia	1977–78	1,830	19–30[b]	33–47[b]	11[c]	—
Philippines[d]	1978	560	47	—	9	—

a. In 1986 dollars.
b. Average not available. Figures denote upper and lower bounds.
c. The average transfer was 46 percent of income for households in the lowest income quintile.
d. Cash gifts in a large informal housing area.
Source: World Bank (1995).

the Indonesian garment districts worker mobility is very high, reflecting instability in the placement of sales orders and the continuous entry and exit of workers to and from the labor market. This mobility can be interpreted as a form of negotiation, where workers who find conditions unfavorable simply leave the job rather than voice a complaint. It also reflects the uncertain nature of production contracts in that sector of economic activity—an uncertainty that discourages employers from engaging workers on long-term contracts.

When hiring costs become relatively high, employers are willing to pay for workers' "waiting time" in an effort to avoid high rotation rates. In fact in a very tight labor market employers must offer incentives to retain workers. For example in 1995 a growing number of Indonesian construction workers in Medan were reportedly being hired on weekly contracts. These contracts set a daily wage and a bonus for workers who remained at the work site continuously for the week (Edwards 1996).

Should the legal system enforce such implicit understandings? The key to contract enforcement is the expected penalty associated with a breach of contract, and the existence of penalties does not necessarily depend on a formal legal system. In traditional communities, for example, a person's reputation may be a more binding guarantee. In either a formal or an informal system, however, local authorities who are genuinely respected by the population are in the best position to deal with disputes over failures to comply with such contracts. A formal legal system based on written agreements is unlikely to be able to deal appropriately with informal contracts. But in order for the legal system to take part in the conflict resolution process, contracts that are acceptable to employers and employees must also be recognized as legal agreements. Policymakers must pay attention to the reality of the traditional or informal sector and encourage the coexistence of traditional and modern forms of conflict resolution.

Formal Employment Protection Arrangements

In most countries existing legislation establishes rules and procedures governing employment termination. This legislation is particularly important in the four countries under review in light of the fact that none of them has an unemployment insurance system. (A few self-financed private schemes do exist, but they cover only a small proportion of highly paid employees.[3]) Provident funds (described in box 8.2) and severance pay are the two forms of income support available to workers dismissed from formal-sector jobs. Severance pay is the centerpiece of employment protection legislation.

BOX 8.2
Provident Funds and Worker Security

Along with severance pay, provident funds are available to workers in the formal sector in Indonesia, Malaysia, the Philippines, and Thailand. These funds provide pensions, disability, health, and severance payments based on years of service with a firm. Employers and employees contribute to the funds in relatively equal amounts. Workers generally withdraw the money as a lump sum at retirement (age 55).

Total contributions in Thailand, which introduced the funds in 1990, amount to 4.5 percent of wages. In Indonesia, where the funds were put in place since 1992, contributions equal 5.7 percent of wages. Malaysia's funds began operating much earlier, and contributions amounted to a much higher 22 percent of monthly wages following reforms in 1993.

Coverage extends to approximately 12–16 percent of the employed population in Indonesia and Thailand, 24 percent in the Philippines, and a much higher 48 percent in Malaysia (Lee 1998). Contributions are mandatory for all firms with 10 or more employees in Thailand and Indonesia, but in practice those firms enrolled in the scheme tend to be large establishments (100 employees or more). In the mid-1990s in Indonesia, the average enterprise in the scheme had 165 employees, although the average manufacturing enterprise had only 50. At the same time employer-financed contributions amounted to 0.52 percent of wages for accident insurance and 36 percent (individual and family coverage, respectively) for health insurance.

The Malaysian Employment Act of 1955 established a minimum level of severance pay. Workers with 1–2 years of tenure would get 10 days of pay per year of service. Workers with 2–5 years of tenure are entitled to 15 days and workers with more than 5 years of tenure to 20 days. The Indonesian law (12/1964) and its implementing regulations control termination of employment. After discussing termination with the employee or the union, the employer must seek permission to dismiss the employee from a regional committee set up to resolve labor disputes, even if the employee consents to the dismissal. Severance pay is set at a minimum level of one month's pay for less than one year of service, two months' pay for one to two years of service, three months' pay for two to three years of service, and four months' pay for more than three years of service. The same regulation sets merit allowances, which are added to severance pay, in effect doubling it.

Severance pay in Indonesia does not apply to fixed-term contracts. Fixed-term contracts make the contracting parties more aware of the finite nature of employment relationships and are a desirable aspect of the system. In countries where employers do not have the legal option to establish fixed-term contracts, job security legislation becomes binding on all employment contracts. For example in Latin America (with the notable exception of Mexico) the law restricts the use of temporary contracts. Formal contracts become indefinite after a probationary period, which can be as short as three months. Once contracts become indefinite under the law, they are subject to a minimum severance in case of dismissals. Similar conditions used to apply in many European countries, but during the 1990s fixed-term contracts became more available.

Job security is traditionally an important component of labor legislation in Africa, the Middle East, Latin America, and South Asia. In general laws in these regions establish limits on employers' freedom to hire workers on fixed-term contracts and to dismiss employees. These types of restrictions are also common in European countries, but not in the United States, as we have seen. However in the United States the experience-rated payroll tax that finances the unemployment insurance program is designed to reflect the costs employers impose on the program (see box 8.1).

Protection against dismissal (or termination) may take any of several forms: mandatory advance notice, mandatory severance pay, or the option to question what appears to be wrongful termination. In Indonesia the mandatory formal authorization is intended to prevent wrongful terminations. In Latin America the law establishes a set of legal causes for dismissal, and workers have the right to appeal any firing. Employers unable to provide proof of due cause may be required to reemploy workers or to pay increased severance monies—either a predetermined sum or an amount set by the judge.

The relative weights of severance payment rules and wrongful termination hurdles are important features of employment protection systems. The reality of market forces tells us that job terminations are necessary. Legally mandated severance pay may coexist with employment at will and may well serve the function of unemployment insurance systems in developing countries that lack them. But the emphasis on wrongful termination distorts the functioning of the labor market. It delays access to severance payments and makes voluntary job separations a rare occurrence, because workers who leave voluntarily do not receive it. Arguably these rules do exactly the opposite of what is intended, creating conflicts and increasing transaction costs.

Employment Protection and Severance Pay

The simplified model proposed by Lazear (1990) considers a government-ordered severance payment equal to Q (a fixed amount). Assuming that newly hired workers are willing and able to make an up-front payment equal to Q, the rule will have no efficiency effect. Lazear concludes that in the absence of constraints on borrowing or lending, any state-mandated severance pay can be seen as a delayed payment scheme, with no efficiency effect. Lazear's conclusions extend to severance payments that are based on a defined-contribution plan. In this case, just as in the case of a fixed amount Q, we can think of the severance payment as a payoff based on the accumulated value of periodic employee contributions. Countries such as Brazil have a system that requires employers to contribute a fraction of workers' monthly salary to a fund that covers severance pay (*Fondo de garantia do tempo de servicio*). The state guarantees this fund, which is indexed and earns a minimum yield. It is portable, and workers may withdraw funds from it in case of involuntary separations. The nominal incidence of the contribution (employee or employer) does not determine its economic impact.

Three sets of issues arise here. First, severance schemes are generally defined-benefit rather than defined-contribution plans—that is, they pay a multiple of the employee's salary at the time of separation. Second, legislation governing job security not only defines a minimum level of severance pay but also makes the payments a function of two factors: the party that initiates the separation and the cause. Third, to say that a defined-contribution benefit has no efficiency effect is an oversimplification. As Lazear recognizes, lack of liquidity (imperfections in the capital market) or lack of confidence in the system's viability (the absence of guarantees on defined-contribution funds) may hurt workers required to pay the amount Q. If capital markets are limited, poor workers do not have the option of making an advance payment for the minimum amount and are blocked from accepting permanent contracts. Furthermore, if there are no credible guarantees on the defined-contribution funds, the mandated severance payments have a nontrivial tax component and labor costs increase relative to the initial equilibrium, inducing inefficiency.

WHY IS THE BENEFITS FORMULA IMPORTANT? Mandated severance pay defined as a function of workers' final salary and number of years on the job has two effects. First, it causes the employer's liability to vary with changes in the prevailing wage. Second, it means that employers must make relatively high payments to employees with many years of service. A useful way to look at the effects of this type of formula on labor contracts is to consider a situation in which a contract worker pays a marginal contribution to a severance fund. We assume that all workers receive severance pay at the end of their contract and that they are willing to accept a reduction in their current cash wages in return for a future payoff. Given this assumption workers receive compensation composed of a cash wage (W_t) and a contribution to a severance fund (α). The other variables are T, the worker's years on the job; L, the employer's liability for severance pay when the worker is dismissed (equal to a factor α times the formal wage FW_t times the years of tenure T); and A, the present value of the accumulated contributions to the worker's severance pay fund.

In one portion of the labor market, the cash economy, severance payments are not required. In Indonesia this part of the labor market includes all workers on fixed-term contracts. The presence of this alternative sector affects competitiveness in the formal sector—that is, total compensation in the formal sector must be at least equal to the cash wage, since workers can easily move to the cash economy. Starting from a situation where L exactly equals A, we posit an increase in the level of wages in the cash economy. Market competition then forces an increase in compensation in the formal sector. From the point of view of both employers and workers, the compensation increase has two components: an increase in the wage in the current period $d(FWt)$, plus an increase in the liability dL, a multiple of $d(FW_t)$. Assuming that $L = \alpha(FW_t)*T$ and that initially $A = \alpha(FWt)*T$, then:

$$d L = d(FW_t)* T*\alpha.$$

But the marginal condition for labor employment is:

$$d\ VALUE\ MARGINAL\ PRODUCT = d\ MARGINAL\ COST,$$

or:

$$d\ VALUE\ MARGINAL\ PRODUCT = d(FW_t) + dA.$$

A financially sound policy that allows a firm to honor its liabilities when employees are terminated requires that $dL = dA$. For this relationship to be true, however, the following must also hold:

$$d\ VALUE\ MARGINAL\ PRODUCT =$$
$$d(FW_t) + d(FW_t)*T*\alpha = d(FW_t)(1+T*\alpha).$$

This relationship implies that the formal wage adjustment required to maintain competitiveness is a function of a worker's years of experience and the factor α. If the firm's employees have relatively few years of service, the wage adjustment will be close to the change in cash wages. But if the firm's employees have more experience, the wage adjustment will be much smaller. Since most firms are likely to have a combination of newly hired and experienced workers, this financially sound policy poses a difficult management challenge.

How does the formal sector react to a reduction in real wages in the cash economy? Employers in the formal sector may choose to reduce current wages, simultaneously reducing the amount of severance they will have to pay the most experienced workers. Assuming that all workers are dismissed at some point and receive the severance payment, a current wage reduction represents a much larger reduction in permanent income. The more years an employee has spent on the job, the larger the reduction in permanent income will be relative to the reduction in current wages. Workers will oppose the wage reduction, but they will have a very weak case. First, the threat of quitting is not very credible, since it entails giving up the right to severance. Second, alternative sources of employment will force them to accept lower market wages. In short a wage reduction in the cash economy poses an enormous threat to formal sector workers with many years of experience.

Employers can try to reduce the cost of severance payments by maintaining a very young work force with a high turnover rate or simply by trying never to dismiss workers, thus avoiding the issue altogether. These choices have further efficiency effects. In the first case the type of workers the firm employs affects its activities.[4] In the second labor is treated as a fixed factor. Hiring decisions are delayed and unfavorable market conditions make severance payments realized losses for employers and a bonus for employees. Since employers prefer to avoid losses, this system of protection against dismissals is likely to offer long-term employees a high degree of job security. Employers are also likely to be reluctant to offer wage incentives for loyalty and performance. Instead, they are likely to offer bonuses or other one-time awards that do not permanently affect wages in order to keep severance payments as low as possible. Pagés and Montenegro (1998) found that relaxing job security regulations in Chile increased hiring and encouraged firms to move away from the traditional policy of firing younger workers. Stricter employment security legislation, however, reduced the rate of labor market participation among the young.

Severance payments based on a multiple of final wages conspire against good labor relationships, the use of long-term contracts, and competitiveness.[5] In particular, changes in market conditions that result in variations in current wages have an asymmetrical effect on firms and workers, depending on whether real wages increase or decline. Wage increases have a magnified effect on firms' costs as a function of workers' tenure, and wage reductions have a magnified effect on workers' permanent income. These problems can be avoided if severance payments required by law are defined in terms of explicit contributions to a fund—that is, if severance payments become a forced savings program. The exact amount individual workers receive at termination (voluntary and involuntary) equals the amount of funds in the account.

SEVERANCE PAY AND WRONGFUL TERMINATION. Employers generally do not have to make severance payments when employees are dismissed for due cause. Due causes for dismissal are spelled out in labor codes and typically include mutual agreement, voluntary retirement with minimum notice, death of the employee, termination of fixed-period contracts, and behavioral problems such as bad conduct, intoxication, and excessive absences. Dismissals for economic reasons (financial problems of the enterprise) are not always included in this list. Argentina and Chile are among the exceptions to this rule. The laws of both countries treat dismissals for economic reasons (redundancies), requiring employers to pay severance based on years with the firm, but subject to a cap. Such dismissals entitle workers to 50 percent of the allowable severance pay for unjust dismissals in Argentina and to severance pay equaling one month per year of service (to a maximum of 11 months) in Chile.

How different is job security legislation in industrial countries? Grubb and Wells (1994) ranked the countries of the European Union according to the strictness of regulations protecting regular and fixed-term workers against dismissal. According to their assessment employment protection is relatively low in Denmark, Ireland, and the United Kingdom and high in Italy, Portugal, and Spain (see also OECD [1994]). The study shows that Finland, Norway, and Sweden also restrict fixed-term contracts and that the latter two restrict temporary work agencies significantly.

The United States has no federal policy mandating severance payments. Employers that pay severance do so in response to collective bargaining agreements, individual contracts, or market incentives. Survey data indicate that of those companies offering severance, most provide payments to workers who are dismissed permanently for economic reasons. The most common payment schemes use functions of tenure to determine the benefit level, typically one week's salary per year of service. Schedules based on age and length of service are also common.[6]

Despite the prevalence of the employment-at-will doctrine throughout the United States, in the 1980s various state court rulings weakened employers' right to dismiss workers at will. By 1987, when Montana passed landmark legislation requiring firms to have "just reason" to fire a worker, nine other states had introduced similar legislation. These statutes include economic cause as just cause for dismissal. Kruger (1991) argues that such legislation has been introduced to limit employer liability, expedite dispute settlements, reduce legal costs, and clarify property rights. But a study by Dertouzos and Karoly (1992) provides evidence that making employers liable for wrongful termination creates substantial costs beyond those directly attributable to lawsuits. When such legislation in is in place, they argue, firms hire fewer workers, causing a decline in aggregate employment of 2–5 percent. They also found that the decline in employment is greater in large firms, suggesting that costs vary on a per-employee basis.

Why do some countries adopt wrongful termination doctrines? Dertouzos and Karoly look at supply and demand as they relate to the willingness of state governments in the United States to adopt such legislation. They argue that declines in union membership increase the number of workers without employment protection under collective bargaining agreements, increasing the demand for common-law remedies to wrongful discharge. When the unemployment rate rises, the number of potential litigants increases, leading courts to look for ways to lighten their workload. An increase in the lawyer-to-population ratio, as a proxy for litigiousness, also increases the demand for wrongful termination legislation and coincidentally the likelihood that states will recognize a new doctrine.

In the United States an increased awareness of workers' rights, particularly the advent of civil rights legislation at the federal and state levels, may have contributed to the general belief that workers can use the justice system to pursue claims of unfair treatment from their employers. Ideological factors may also explain the willingness of state judiciaries to provide increased job protection. All of the reasons that Dertouzos and Karoly offer could apply to developing countries, except for the fact that in most of these countries state or provincial governments do not have jurisdiction over labor legislation. Many labor laws in developing countries date to the 1950s and 1960s and the technical assistance provided by the International Labour Organization (ILO) in response to individual governments' attempts to improve labor practices.

Extreme job security was imposed in Zimbabwe and in India in 1980. Fallon and Lucas (1991) determine (after controlling for other factors) that these laws significantly reduced the demand for labor. The weighted-average estimate of the impact of this legislation on jobs, given output, is on the order of 20 percent. Moreover the data for India show an interesting pattern across industries. Those industries with the most public enterprises were the least affected by the legislative change. The authors interpret this finding as a sign that job security was already high within the public sector. But the authors find no evidence that the legislative changes affected the speed with which employment adjusted to changing market conditions.

Lazear (1990) found that mandatory severance payments reduced employment across countries of the Organization for Economic Cooperation and Development (OECD), although the results were not robust. Alba-Ramirez (1991) reported that the introduction of fixed-term contracts in Spain in 1980 spurred employment growth. Marshall (1991) noted that temporary and part-time employment became more common in Lima than in Buenos Aires when Peru began encouraging temporary contracts in an effort to reduce unemployment (Argentina did not follow such a policy).

Improving the Design of State-Mandated Severance Schemes

Experience shows that different types of severance and pension schemes are successful when they are largely self-financed, when contributions and benefits correspond to each other, and when they are designed to minimize incentives for workers to leave the labor force or shift to informal or casual contracts. Severance payments defined as multiples of prevailing salaries at the moment of separation (as in East Asia, most of Latin America, and Europe) are not defined-contribution programs. As we have seen workers who have been on the same job for different lengths of time need to be compensated differently. This fact creates personnel management conflicts and limits employers in their efforts to improve working conditions and induce cooperation. Given the long tradition of severance payments in many countries, improving on the existing systems makes more political sense than adding an unemployment insurance plan. Alternatively a system can be designed that requires all workers (through their employers) to establish a "job termination account" that is accessible at the time of dismissal or voluntary separation.

In some countries severance pay is entirely the responsibility of employers. The advantage of this design is that it avoids the problems posed by employers unable (or unwilling) to pay severance benefits. If severance payments are financed through employer-paid premiums, firms need not be reinsured or granted public guarantees in the event of insolvency. In Bolivia, for example, workers have access to the same severance payments regardless of the conditions surrounding their separation (which may be voluntary or involuntary) after five years on the job. Some countries, including Brazil, Colombia, and Peru, replaced the traditional mode of severance pay (a specified amount, such as a month's pay, for each year of service) for a Time of Service Fund—the *Fondo de Garantia do Tempo de Servicio* (FGTS) in Brazil and *Compensacion por Tiempo de Servicio* (CTS) in Peru. Employers pay a percentage of workers' salaries (8 percent in Brazil, 8.33 percent in Peru) into the fund, which is available in case of justified layoffs or voluntary separation. Chilean law allows workers to choose this type of arrangement instead of the traditional severance payment scheme after seven years on the job. Employers are required to deposit the equivalent of one-twelfth of the worker's annual salary in a savings account (Edwards 1993).

This type of system is likely to operate smoothly in an economy that has introduced a social security system based on individual accounts, allowing the same institutions that manage pension funds to manage the funds. Such systems can also be indexed, so that all deposits are shielded from the inflation tax. But contribution rates, like those in Brazil and Chile, can be too high relative to what is needed for the program. Feldstein and Altman (1998) provide a full calculation of the contributions necessary to finance a system with the level of benefits that the current system in the United States offers. They argue that 4 percent of salaries, up to a maximum, is sufficient.

In the cases described above, employees will receive severance payments some time in the future. In the meantime employers treat the amounts they deposit as an expense for tax purposes. At the time of separation workers receive severance payments equal to the amount that has accumulated in the fund (in real terms plus interest). This type of system has many advantages over the traditional method. First, workers receive severance pay equal to what has accumulated in their funds in all cases of termination—whether they quit, are fired, or are laid off. Second, the funds are portable, so workers do not lose the accumulated amounts when they move to a new job. Third, these funds help firms avoid the liquidity problems that making severance payments can create. Fourth, the system is very transparent. Employers see it as part of the current cost of labor. For employees it is a deferred payment, since the funds are portable and payment is not conditional on the circumstances of termination.

The specifics of the benefits program may vary. For example, benefits can be a multiple of individual salaries. The benefit period and replacement ratio can also be defined in advance. Since workers will use employment transition funds to look for new jobs, and the typical job search lasts six months or less, the mandated contributions can be subject to a maximum relative to the income level of the individual worker. Thus, as earnings increase, the maximum contribution employers must pay into the fund will increase as well.

The fact that employers cannot use the funds as working capital is the most important aspect of this system. But this change is the price of moving to a system that guarantees employees some security if they find themselves unemployed. The alternative is a system of compulsory insurance, which is administratively complex and in any case is unlikely to be sufficient during an event such as the 1997 East Asian crisis. In such cases the government is left to make up the deficit (in the Republic of Korea the authorities created a special fund for this purpose in 1997). Since those laid off from the formal sector in a crisis are likely to be better off than those outside the sector, governments are likely to want to avoid relying on a public guarantee.

Unemployment Insurance Systems

Is an unemployment insurance system financed by both employees and employers a superior method of providing income security to terminated employees? What are the advantages and disadvantages of the U.S. system, which is financed by taxes on employers? What other alternatives (such as subsidized savings plans and welfare-for-work schemes) should be considered in order to improve the income security of employees in the formal sector?

Unemployment insurance programs are intended to protect workers from income losses associated with involuntary and unanticipated interruptions of employment. These programs are managed by the public sector, because two characteristics of unemployment risk discourage private insurance. First, unemployment is associated with business cycles. As a result some types of workers regularly experience unemployment at certain periods in the business cycle. Second, unemployment insurance systems require significant institutional capacity, much like income tax systems, in order to operate properly. In fact taxpayer numbers (such as Social Security numbers in the United States) can be used to identify employers and employees and to maintain records of contributions.

The Problem of Moral Hazard

The frequency and duration of periods of unemployment are to a degree the result of employment decisions made by both firms and workers. The existence of unemployment insurance makes retrenchment more attractive to employers. To the extent that employment contracts do not perfectly internalize the costs of unemployment insurance, the incidence of unemployment increases. Becker (1972) points out that the method of financing an unemployment insurance system is of key importance, because it affects firms' decisions to keep or lay off employees.

For workers unemployment insurance makes longer spells of joblessness more attractive, creating problems of moral hazard. Unemployment insurance affects search strategies by raising reservation wages and therefore increasing the average period of unemployment (McCall 1970; Mortensen 1970). Holen (1977) and Ehrenberg and Oaxaca (1971) find that relatively liberal unemployment insurance payments result in extended periods of unemployment for those eligible for compensation. To eliminate the problem of moral hazard, unemployment insurance plans must be designed so that the insured share some of the costs. A self-financing program of social insurance, for instance, can offer partial insurance and benefits that decline over the period of unemployment.

Coverage and Funding

Self-financed unemployment insurance systems pay benefits only to workers who have made contributions to the system either directly or indirectly (through their employers). Such systems generally exclude informal-sector workers. In the United States employers make mandatory payments that are essentially a tax (see box 8.1). Because employers fund the system, eligibility for benefits depends on a worker's having a substantial attachment to the labor force. One of the methods used to measure this attachment is a minimum earnings test that requires a certain level of earnings in a 12-month period.[7] Obviously, informal-sector earnings do not help a worker meet the minimum earnings test, since employers are not making contributions on those earnings.

All self-financing unemployment insurance systems must be experience rated in an aggregate sense. Tax rates must be high enough so that inflows equal outflows over a period of time long enough to meet demand during recessions as well as ordinary business cycles. Most European countries use a flat tax rate to finance unemployment insurance programs and other policy instruments to discourage firings. But average unemployment rates are very different across industries, so with this system firms with relatively few terminations subsidize the benefit payments of firms with more layoffs and firings. In the United States firing practices are considered liberal compared with other countries, and experience rating is intended to force employers to subsidize the employees they terminate.

What are the effects of the unemployment insurance payroll tax? The U.S. state of Washington provides a natural experiment that tells us much about the impact of methods of funding unemployment insurance systems. From 1972 to 1984 unemployment insurance taxes were not experience rated in Washington state. Instead all firms paid the same payroll tax (either 3 or 3.3 percent, depending on the year). Changes in federal legislation prompted the state to introduce experience rating in 1985. Between 1984 and 1985 some firms saw their tax rate increase from 3.0 to 5.4 percent, while others saw it fall from 3.0 to 2.5 percent. Anderson and Meyer (1998) compared wages and labor market outcomes before and after the change and were able to draw conclusions regarding the impact of experience rating. Overall the results suggest that experience rating reduces claims for unemployment insurance and stabilizes employment. But the experiment sheds light on the behavioral changes experience rating induces. In particular Anderson and Meyer find a significant decrease in the level and seasonality of claims and an increase in the number of benefit denials because firms have an incentive to "police the system" and contest invalid claims.

Anderson and Meyer are also able to tackle the question of who bears the cost of the unemployment insurance tax. They separate the payroll tax into two parts: a base tax that applies to a "market" or industry, and the remainder, which they descibe as "firm based." Their hypothesis is that the market part of the tax is internalized in the wage determination process and reappears in the form of lower market wages. But the firm absorbs the firm-based portion of the tax in the form of higher costs. Although the authors are limited to imprecise estimates, they present two emerging patterns from the data that are consistent with the theory. Firms seem to be able to pass on a substantial part of the market part of the payroll tax but none of the firm-specific portion.

Perfect experience rating means that each firm pays (over time) a tax rate proportional to the differential between its rate of insured layoffs and the industry average. The firm-based part of the premium is thus analogous to the extra costs incurred by a firm that is required to make severance payments and that lays off more employees than the average, raising labor costs. The main difference, of course, is that while unemployment insurance entitlements usually increase with duration of employment, they are rarely proportional. Entitlements are generally greater than the value of contributions for those with a short employment record and less than accumulated contributions for long-term employees. These systems tend to support those with short-term employment tenure at the cost of premiums paid on behalf of long-term employees. Employers and employees are therefore encouraged to make their contracts shorter than they would in the absence of unemployment insurance. This bias is systematic in such unemployment insurance arrangements. Experience rating will reduce the opportunistic use of the system to subsidize short-term turnover but will not eliminate the general bias toward shorter contracts.

Unemployment insurance systems therefore have the same bias as severance payment systems based on workers' final salaries. Both systems create an incentive for employers to move to short-term contracts. The distortions such systems impose lead to administrative controls, such as denying eligibility for voluntary separations and requiring those receiving benefits to actively look for work, so that benefits are not used to subsidize leisure or other pursuits. The same reasoning that argues for a more "neutral" system of severance payments has led to recent proposals for income security systems that eliminate these short-term biases.

Alternatives to Unemployment Insurance

Is an improved severance payment system a viable alternative to unemployment insurance? Taking into consideration conditions in developing countries, this option may be the most reasonable approach to providing income insecurity. As we have seen unemployment insurance systems require an administrative capacity that is often lacking in these economies. Existing severance pay systems can be the basis for more functional arrangements, such as the defined-contribution system, that help workers who are between jobs and also make formal contracts more transparent. Employers must recognize that a formal contract involves obligations that employees value, such as severance pay (or, in industrial countries, unemployment insurance). A system of severance payments based on accumulated contributions to individual funds is equivalent to an unemployment insurance system in which benefits are proportional to contributions. However, unemployment insurance systems do not pay benefits in cases of voluntary separation, while defined-contribution systems do.

UNEMPLOYMENT INSURANCE SAVINGS ACCOUNTS. The key feature of these accounts is that they are defined-contribution funds (Feldstein and Altman 1998; Cortazar 1994). Each individual, or the individual's employer, is required to contribute 4 percent of the employee's wage income to an unemployment insurance savings account (UISA).[8] Unemployed workers receive benefits according to the U.S. system—that is, equal to 50 percent of the worker's salary, or a replacement rate of 50 percent, up to a maximum amount for six months. As individuals withdraw benefits, their accounts are debited. Individuals whose account balances are insufficient to pay the benefits to which they are entitled can borrow from the government at the same rate they earn on their account.

The wages on which contributions are based are limited to a maximum level that may be slightly above the median wage. This level is roughly equal to the level of wages on which unemployment insurance benefits in the United States are based. An individual or employer is exempted from making UISA contributions after the employee's fund reaches a certain amount. Since benefits are 50 percent of wages (up to the ceiling) and last for no more than six months at a time, the maximum benefit the employee can draw during a single period of unemployment is one-quarter of annual wage income from the previous year. Most periods of unemployment are substantially shorter than six months, the median being less than 10 weeks in almost all years. (These episodes would be even shorter with the change in incentives the savings accounts would provide.) Contributions stop, then, when the accumulated balance in an account reaches 50 percent of the individual's wage income in the previous year or 50 percent of the ceiling, whichever is smaller.

Like employer payments to the U.S. unemployment system, the funds deposited in UISAs are from pretax income and accumulate tax free. If a worker withdraws funds, the money would be considered taxable income, again like unemployment benefits in the United States. The tax would also apply to funds withdrawn in retirement or by heirs. Alternatively the funds deposited in UISAs can come from after-tax income, so that subsequent withdrawals are not taxed.[9]

Does such a system in the formal sector raise labor costs and drive some employers into the informal sector, or do employees absorb the costs in the form of lower wage rates? The impact on wages and employment is a function of the program design. A tight link between contributions and benefits at the individual level creates a kind of forced savings program, and the impact on wages is insignificant. But for low-wage workers, a forced savings program may be equivalent to a tax. Thus the self-employed can be exempted, providing room for choosing between formal and informal methods of income security.

Evidence on the coexistence of formal systems of income security and informal employment is already available from almost two decades of experience with social security reform in Chile (Edwards 1999). The Chilean law requires wage employees to make contributions to their personal retirement accounts. The self-employed may make voluntary contributions to the pension system. In urban areas, for example, employees account for around 72 percent of working men and 60 percent of working women. Within this group, 82 percent of males and 85 percent of females have fixed-term or permanent contracts, and among those with contracts, 95 percent of both men and women make contributions. The decision to become an employee with a contract is not independent of the decision to contribute to social security. Up to 25 percent of individuals not required to contribute (the self-employed and employees without contracts) do make contributions. This proportion increases with age and schooling and does not vary much with salary level or sector.

Enforcement and UISA Accounts

Even if an individual holds informal jobs while drawing UISA benefits, eligibility is limited by the worker's attachment to the formal sector, and the level of benefits is a function of the individual history of contributions. Payments continue until the recipient finds a new job in the formal sector (that is, one that pays premiums into the system) or for up to the maximum benefit period. Because the benefits stream consists of withdrawals from workers' own funds, the system offers no incentive for workers to continue receiving funds. Workers want to find a job quickly so they can stop withdrawing funds from their account. Workers with a negative savings balance understand the consequences of extending the job search. Administrative remedies such as requiring workers to visit employment offices weekly to document the job search are not necessary.

The reality of the job search is complex. One worker may limit the search to newspaper advertisements. Another may prefer to obtain informal employment. Still others may work at casual jobs or attend a training program. These choices should not affect eligibility for benefits. The key actor is the unemployed worker, who is not receiving encouragement to stay unemployed. For the same reason unemployed workers do not need the incentive of a bonus when they find a formal job (the practice in Japan and Korea). Individuals do not receive a free transfer under the UISA system.

Government Programs and Income Security in the Informal Sector

Instituting UISAs in lieu of severance pay systems would still leave a large proportion of the labor force with no income security coverage. What measures should be put in place (if any) to provide some income security for day laborers and other nonpermanent employees who are not eligible for severance payments under present legislation and would not be covered by UISAs? Unemployment insurance would not help those affected by the East Asian financial crisis, making some form of direct assistance more appropriate. How should such a scheme be designed? If eligibility is based on family deprivation, how is it determined in societies with a large informal sector?

First, complementary programs are best designed to alleviate poverty rather than to mitigate unemployment, since income- and wage-replacement programs are impossible to administer in the absence of effective verification procedures. A number of food-for-work programs or employment guarantee schemes are in place that focus on the unemployed (Ravallion, Datt, and Chaudhuri 1993). But the targeting method is primarily wages (or their equivalent in food and other transfers). Without other verification methods, low wages become a self-targeting mechanism. Poverty alleviation programs, even when they are set up in response to a recession or major employment reduction, should not be funded from the same source as unemployment insurance or UISAs. Separate funding for these programs is an important condition if the unemployment insurance program is not to distort labor market incentives.

EMERGENCY EMPLOYMENT PROGRAMS. Through the antipoverty program IDT (Impres Desa Tertinggal), Thailand and Indonesia adopted public works programs (*Padat Karya*) and revolving credit schemes. These programs are considered cost-effective given the limited resources available. Latin American countries developed a few large-scale employment programs after the mid-1970s, including the Minimum Employment Plan and the Employment Program for Heads of Families in Chile and the Temporary Income Support Program in Peru. The Chilean programs covered about 500,000 people in 1983 and the Peruvian program about 375,000 at its peak. Mexico developed an array of public works and community employment programs that provide training, credit, emergency employment, and public services.

Flexible approaches and a large degree of local autonomy in the disbursement of funds characterize emergency employment programs. Some impose stringent eligibility requirements. Others pay wages below the legal minimum, and others require participants to work. These restrictions are a function of the availability of funds relative to the number of potential beneficiaries. For example, the proportion of the labor force employed in the Chilean emergency program was virtually constant from 1977 to 1981 in spite of the economic recovery and a decline in real compensation. The explanation lies in increasingly flexible entry restrictions that allowed large numbers of potential workers to qualify.

Response to the Economic Crisis: Social Safety Nets in Indonesia and Thailand

Thailand and Indonesia, the countries worst hit by the economic crisis in 1997–98, sought to dampen the effects on labor through public sector spending on social safety net schemes, including employment creation (public works) and education and health subsidies (see chapters 2 and 6). Both countries abandoned initial balanced budget policies in favor of a fiscal deficit, a significant proportion of which was allocated to social expenditures (Lee 1998).[10] While unemployment rose as a result of the crisis, only 4–6 percent of the labor force in both countries had been affected by late 1998 (Manning 1999a). The government saw its main priority as stimulating spending and economic activity in order to support jobs in the flexible informal sector, where many displaced workers had sought work.

INDONESIA. Confronted with spiraling food prices, Indonesia allocated a substantial amount to rice subsidies in 1998 and 1999.[11] It was also forced to retain subsidies to other goods and services, most notably kerosene and electricity. The rice subsidies (60–70 percent of the market price) were expected to benefit around one-third of the total population in the first half of 1999.

The employment support schemes involved three sets of activities in budget year 1998–99: special labor-intensive programs, regular labor-intensive programs, and public works programs (through local governments). Outside of the rice subsidy the government allocated by far the largest part of the social safety net budget in 1998–99 to credit subsidies for small-scale industries and cooperatives at interest rates of 6–16 percent (market rates were above 50 percent). A budget of Rp 20 trillion (US$2.67 billion, or close to 10 percent of all public expenditure) was allocated for distribution by the Department of Cooperatives and Small Enterprises to small-scale firms and cooperatives throughout the country.

The government sought to protect the education budget from the effects of inflation by maintaining expenditures in real terms in 1998–99. The main concern was dropouts who failed to make the transition from primary to lower secondary school. Intervention involved scholarships for needy primary and junior secondary students in their final years (with the support of the World Bank and Asian Development Bank).[12] In the area of health, the main form of assistance was subsidies for imported inputs used in the manufacture of basic drugs. Emergency procedures were also put in place to combat shortages of major drugs at the district level.

THAILAND. Thailand faced a similar sharp cutback in labor demand, although in several ways it was better placed to deal with the crisis than Indonesia (Somsak 1999; Sussangkarn, Flatters, and Kittiprapas 1999). The country had put several social support programs in place prior to the crisis in response to lagging performance in key social indicators. Prices remained relatively stable despite the large drop in the exchange rate. Although substantial the declines in the exchange rate and GDP were much smaller than in Indonesia, and by late 1999 the economy showed strong signs of recovery in two successive quarters.

Major efforts were taken early on to help displaced workers. These included the creation of a center that offered assistance to displaced workers, including help in obtaining severance pay and social security, plus counseling and job-matching services. A National Committee on Employment Alleviation introduced measures designed to increase rural employment and help displaced workers find employment at home and abroad. These measures set up loan and training programs and provided support for employment-creation programs through Government Savings Bank branches throughout the country. As in Indonesia these efforts were supplemented by social sector loans through the World Bank and Asian Development Bank. In particular, the government program set up several years earlier to provide interest-free educational loans was extended (and much more widely accessed) after the crisis began. A health card system for the poor and a medical assistance program for the elderly were also quickly expanded and helped cushion the effects of the crisis on the poor. In addition the government sought to dampen the effect of layoffs by increasing severance pay from 6 to 10 months and extending social security and health coverage from 6 to 12 months for 100,000 retrenched workers who were contributing to the social security fund.

Some Final Thoughts

As the 21st century begins, Indonesia, Malaysia, the Philippines, and Thailand are making the transition from traditional to modern economies. A realistic approach to policy interventions aimed at improving income security must include both ends of the spectrum and help smooth the transition between traditional and modern forms of production. Two types of policy interventions address the problems associated with income loss. Poverty-targeted emergency programs do not necessarily focus on the unemployed, since unemployment is not the most important characteristic of the poor and may not be the most appropriate targeting mechanism.

These programs are considered effective mechanisms for reaching households severely affected by income loss. The second set of policies includes all permanent labor market interventions focused on dismissals and the unemployed. Labor market interventions can address the risk of income loss associated with formal employment not only in a recession but also during the normal operation of a growing economy.

In most developing countries, including the four cases specifically addressed here, legislation is in place that deals with procedures and responsibilities surrounding dismissals. The existing evidence indicates that firing costs deter hiring, reduce labor demand, and hamper the economy's ability to deal with uncertainty and structural change (OECD 1994; Saint-Paul 1999). Unemployment insurance systems are not necessarily a better alternative. In general unemployment insurance reduces the incentive to seek work, but the relative size of this effect is a design function and varies from program to program. European unemployment insurance programs pay benefits according to certain preestablished rules and collect the same tax rate from all employers, generating large cross-subsidies from some taxpayers to other program beneficiaries. In contrast the U.S. program is designed so that employers dismissing the most workers pay the highest tax rate, especially if the workers collect from the unemployment insurance system.

Severance pay based on final salaries is an inefficient method of providing income support and smoothing. Severance payments serve welfare and efficiency objectives best if they are designed around defined-contribution funds workers can access without any reference to the cause of separation. Similar unemployment savings accounts are an optimum form of unemployment insurance but require a well-developed institutional setting. At the very least the system must be able to generate numbers for employers and employees that can be used to track contributions and benefit payments. Furthermore a system that relies on self-controls requires a very efficient and relatively up-to-date flow of information. The administrative capacity that ultimately makes these information flows possible takes time to establish. But the type of information system needed to manage a defined-contribution system of unemployment benefits is much like the one needed to administer a defined-contribution system of old-age benefits. Both types of programs can be designed to cover part of the labor force, and coverage can be extended as the degree of formalization and their relative value increases.

A program designed to help workers transition from job to job, be it unemployment insurance based on individual accounts or a severance pay system that replaces existing programs, still leaves out the large proportion of the labor force in the informal sector. The most appropriate focus of a complementary program is poverty alleviation rather than unemployment, primarily because an alternative program of income or wage replacement is impossible to administer in the absence of verification methods. Flexible approaches and a large degree of local autonomy in the disbursement of funds characterize effective poverty alleviation and emergency employment programs. Some programs impose eligibility requirements and other restrictions that are very much a function of the availability of funds relative to the number of potential beneficiaries.

Notes

1. Alejandra Cox Edwards is a professor in the Department of Economics at California State University, Long Beach. Chris Manning is Head, Indonesia Project, Economics Division, at the Australian National University, Canberra. The authors are grateful to Peter Scherer for his detailed comments and suggestions.

2. Despite these strategies even poor working households succeed in having much less variation in consumption than in income. They use a variety of mechanisms to maintain their consumption level—financial savings, transfers from other members of the family or the community, and borrowing.

3. See, for example McLeod (1993), Nayyar (1995), Khoman (1998), Betcherman and Ogawa (1999). Among the East Asian countries affected by the crisis, only Korea had an unemployment insurance scheme in 1997.

4. With a young and inexperienced work force and high turnover, assembly-type activities that require little or no training become relatively more attractive. Fine crafts and industrial activities that require a high degree of training and that incur high costs when employees leave become relatively less attractive, all other things remaining constant.

5. These issues are similar to the distortions that result from defined-benefit pension schemes based on workers' final salary.

6. See Bureau of National Affairs, Inc., *Personnel Policies Forum* (various surveys, 1985–90).

7. Workers who have not earned the minimum are not eligible for benefits, on the assumption that low earnings indicate a short or temporary attachment to the labor force. The 12-month base period comprises 4 quarters, and the quarter with the highest earnings determines the weekly benefit amount.

8. The nominal incidence of current unemployment insurance taxes is on employers, but the economic incidence of the tax would presumably be the same if the nominal incidence were on employees. Similarly, gross wages are adjusted downward if employers rather than employees make the contributions, since these deposits are the property of individual workers and thus are similar to tax-deferred cash compensation.

9. Feldstein and Altman (1998) consider several options for managing UISA funds.

10. Thailand projected a budget deficit of 3 percent in 1998, and Indonesia projected a deficit of 6 percent for the financial year 1998–99.

11. See Manning (1999b) for a discussion of the main programs.

12. Block grants were also provided to the poorest 60 percent of schools.

References

Alba-Ramirez, A. 1991. "Fixed Term Contracts in Spain: Labor Market Flexibility or Segmentation" Unpublished disucssion paper.

Anderson, Patricia M., and Bruce D. Meyer. 1998. "Using a Natural Experiment to Estimate the Effects of the Unemployment Insurance Payroll Tax on Wages, Employment, and Denials." NBER Working Paper 6808. Cambridge, Mass.: National Bureau of Economic Research.

Becker, Joseph. 1972. *Experience Rating in Unemployment Insurance: An Experiment in Competitive Socialism.* Baltimore and London: John Hopkins University Press.

Betcherman, Gordon, and Makoto Ogawa. 1999. "Labor Market Institutions and Structures in Indonesia: Reforms to Labor Legislation and to Social Security." Social Protection Department. Washington, D.C.: World Bank. Draft paper.

Blanchard, Olivier, and Pedro Portugal. 1998. "What Hides Behind an Unemployment Rate: Comparing Portuguese and U.S. Unemployment." NBER Working Paper 6635. Cambridge, Mass.: National Bureau of Economic Research.

Cortazar, Rene. 1994. "Labor Policy in a Democratic Chile." Paper presented at the International Forum on the Latin America Perspective, Paris, November 2–4.

Cox, Donald, and Emanuel Jimenez. 1990. "Achieving Social Objectives Through Private Transfers: A Review." *The World Bank Research Observer* 5(2): 205–18.

Cox, James, and Ronald Oaxaca. 1990. "Unemployment Insurance and the Job Search." *Research in Labor Economics* 11: 223–40.

Dertouzos, James, and Lynn Karoly. 1992. *Labor Market Responses to Employer Liability.* Santa Monica: Rand Corporation, Institute for Civil Justice.

Dreze, Jean, and Anindita Mukherjee. 1987. "Labor Contracts in Rural India: Theories and Evidence." Discussion Paper 7, Development Research Programme, London School of Economics.

Edwards, Alejandra Cox. 1993. "Labor Market Legislation in Latin America and the Caribbean." Regional Studies Program Report 31, Latin America and the Caribbean Technical Department. Washington, D.C.: World Bank.

_____. 1996. "Labor Markets in Indonesia." Washington, D.C.: World Bank. Unpublished paper.

_____. 1999. "Are Social Security Reforms Gender Neutral? Evidence from Chile." Economics Department, California State University, Long Beach. Unpublished manuscript.

Ehrenberg, Ronald, and Ronald Oaxaca. 1971. "Unemployment Insurance, Duration of Unemployment, and Subsequent Wage Gain." *American Economic Review* 66(5).

Fallon, Peter, and R.E.B. Lucas. 1991. "The Impact of Changes in Job Security Legislation in India and Zimbabwe." *The World Bank Economic Review* 5(3): 395–413.

Feldstein, Martin. 1976. "Temporary Layoffs in the Theory of Unemployment," *Journal of Political Economy* 84(5):937–57.

_____. 1978. "The Effect of Unemployment Insurance on Temporary Layoff Unemployment." *American Economic Review* 68(December): 834–46.

Feldstein, Martin, and Daniel Altman. 1998. "Unemployment Insurance Savings Accounts." NBER Working Paper 6860. Cambridge, Mass.: National Bureau of Economic Research.

Grubb, D., and W. Wells. 1994. "Employment Regulation and Patterns of Work in EC Countries." *OECD Economic Studies* 21 (Winter): 7–58.

Hamermesh, Daniel. 1991. "Unemployment Insurance: Goals, Structure, Economic Impacts, and Transferability to Developing Countries." Population and Human Resources Department. Washington, D.C.: World Bank. Unpublished working paper.

Hart, W. 1984. "Agrarian Labor Arrangements and Structural Change: Lessons from Java and Bangladesh." Working Paper 67, World Employment Programme Research. Geneva: International Labor Office.

Holen, Arlene. 1977. "Effects of Unemployment Insurance Entitlement on Duration and Job Search Activity." *Industrial and Labor Relations Review* 30(4).

Hopenhayn, Hugo, and Juan Pablo Nicolini. 1997. "Optimal Unemployment Insurance." *Journal of Political Economy* 105(2): 412–38.

Khoman, S. 1998. "Social Policy in Thailand: Issues and Policy Actions." In United Nations Development Program, *Social Implications of the Asian Financial Crisis*. EDAP Joint Policy Series. Seoul: Korean Development Institute.

Kruger, Alan. 1991. "The Evolution of Unjust-Dismissal Legislation in the United States," *Industrial and Labor Relations Review V* 4(2): 123–45.

Kuruvilla, Saroth. 1996. "Linkages between Industrialization Strategies and Industrial Relations/Human Resources Policies." *Industrial and Labor Relations Review* 49(4): 635–57.

Lazear, Edward. 1990. "Job Security Provisions and Employment." *Quarterly Journal of Economics* 105(3):699–726.

Lee, E. 1998. The Asian Financial Crisis: *The Challenge of Social Policy.* Geneva: International Labor Office.

McCall, John. 1970. "Economics of Information and Job Search." *Quarterly Journal of Economics* 84(1).

McLeod, R. 1993. "Workers' Social Security Legislation." In Chris Manning and Joan Hardjono, eds., *Indonesia Assessment 1993—Labor: Sharing in Growth?*

Political and Social Change Monograph 20, Australian National University, Canberra, 88–107.

Manning, Chris. 1999a. "Labor Market Trends in the NIEs and the ASEAN-4." *Asian-Pacific Economic Literature* 13(1): 50–68.

———. 1999b. "The Economic Crisis and Child Labor in Indonesia." Paper prepared for the International Labour Organization, Canberra.

Manning, C., and S. Jayasuriya. 1996. "Survey of Recent Economic Developments." *Bulletin of Indonesian Economic Studies* 32(2) 3–43.

Marshall, A. 1991. "The Impact of Labor Law and Employment Practices: Temporary and Part-time Employment in Argentina and Peru." Labor Market Programme DC/38/1991. Geneva: International Labor Office.

Miller, Paul W., and Paul A Volcker. 1985. "Unemployment Insurance Eligibility Rights: Evidence from a Comparison of Australia and Canada. *Journal of Macroeconomics* 7(2): 223–35.

Mortensen, Dale. 1970. "Job Search, the Duration of Unemployment, and the Phillips Curve." *American Economic Review* 60(5).

———. 1994. "Reducing Supply-side Disincentives to Job Creation." In *Reducing Unemployment: Current Issues and Policy Options.* Kansas City: Federal Reserve Bank.

NSO (National Statistical Office). 1998. *The Impact of the Economic Crisis on Employment, Unemployment and Labor Migration.* Bangkok.

Nayyar, R. 1995. "Indonesian Labor Legislation in Comparative Perspective: A Study of Six APEC Countries," Unpublished paper, World Bank, Washington, D.C.

Nickell, Stephen. 1997. "Unemployment and Labor Market Rigidities: Europe vs. North America." *Journal of Economic Perspectives* 11(3), 55–74.

OECD (Organization for Economic Cooperation and Development). 1994. *The OECD Jobs Study. Evidence and Explanations.* Vol. II: *The Adjustment Potential of the Labor Market.* Paris.

———. 1995. Employment Outlook. Paris.

Ofreneo, R. 1995. "Philippine Industrialization and Industrial Relations." In A. Verma, T. A. Kochan, and R. D. Lansbury, eds., *Employment Relations in the Growing Asian Economies.* Londen: Routledge.

Otsuka, Keijiro, Hiroyuki Chuma, and Yujiro Hayami. 1992. "Land and Labor Contracts in Agrarian Economies." *Journal of Economic Literature* 30(4): 1965–2051.

Pagés, Carmen, and Claudio Montenegro. 1998. "Job Security, Tenure and Employment Dynamics: Theory and Evidence from Chile." Paper presented at the 72nd Western Economic Association Conference, Lake Tahoe, July.

Ravallion, Martin, Gauran Datt, and Shubham Chaudhuri. 1993. "Does Maharashtra's Employment Guarantee Scheme Guarantee Employment? Effects of the 1988 Wage Increase." *Economic Development and Cultural Change* 41(2).

Saint-Paul, Gilles. 1999. "The Political Economy of Employment Protection." Economics WP No. 355, National Center for Research Science, Universitat Pompeu Fabra Delta. Barcelona, Spain.

Somsak, Tambunlertchai. 1999. "The Social Impact of the Financial Crisis in Thailand and Policy Responses." In United Nations Development Program, *Social Implications of the Asian Financial Crisis*. EDAP Joint Policy Series. Seoul: Korean Development Institute.

Sussangkarn, C., F. Flatters and S. Kittiprapas. 1999. "Comparative Social Impacts of the Asian Economic Crisis in Thailand, Indonesia, and Malaysia." *TDRI Quarterly Review* 14(1): 3–9.

Topel, Robert. 1983. "On Layoffs and Unemployment Insurance." *American Economic Review* 73(4): 541–59.

U.S. Department of Labor. Various years. *Foreign Labor Trends*. Washington D.C.

Verma, Anil, Thomas A. Kochan, and R. D. Lansbury, eds. *Employment Relations in the Growing Asian Economie*. London: Routledge.

Warr, P. G. "Thailand." In R. H. McLeod and R. Garnaut, eds., *East Asia in Crisis: From Being a Miracle to Needing One*. London: Routledge.

Welch, Finis. 1977. "What Have We Learned from Empirical Studies of Unemployment Insurance?" *Industrial and Labor Relations Review* 4(July): 451–61.

Wiebe, Frank. 1996. "Income Insecurity and Underemployment in the Indonesian Informal Sector." Paper presented at the Indonesian Workers in the 21st Century Workshop for Economic Reforms and Labor Market Restructuring for Indonesia, Jakarta, April 2–4.

World Bank. 1995. *World Development Report*. Washington, D.C.

_____. 1998. *East Asia: The Road to Recovery* Washington, D.C.

_____. 1999. *World Development Report*. Washington, D.C.

9 Vulnerable Groups and the Labor Market: The Aftermath of the Asian Financial Crisis

Susan Horton and Dipak Mazumdar[1]

THE ASIAN FINANCIAL crisis has had severe repercussions for labor markets in the most seriously affected countries of East and Southeast Asia (Indonesia, the Republic of Korea, Malaysia, the Philippines, and Thailand). This chapter traces some of the consequences of the crisis for what we call *vulnerable groups*—young workers, women, workers with the lowest educational and skill levels, and migrant laborers. The crisis has played out differently in each of the five countries, in part because the magnitude and timing of events differed and in part because labor markets operated differently in each country before the crisis. For this reason the groups that are most vulnerable also differ across countries.

The affected countries implemented a variety of measures in response to the crisis. Labor market interventions included expanded severance pay, public works programs, labor market information, and enhanced skill and vocational training, among others. Because of the relative lack of government intervention in labor markets in East and Southeast Asia prior to the crisis, the countries of the region had been held up as models of successful laissez-faire strategies. The crisis showed that while these strategies presented few problems when the economy was growing rapidly, they were not effective during the downturn that followed the crisis. Thus we argue that Asian countries may wish to use the experience of the crisis to strengthen aspects of their social safety nets such as labor market policies. This chapter presents experiences from other regions (primarily Latin

379

America and South Asia, but also Eastern Europe) that may help guide such reforms.

Labor Markets Prior to the Crisis

We begin by examining labor market functioning in the five countries prior to the crisis, focusing particularly on vulnerable groups. The five countries were at different stages of development, with per capita income in the most developed (Korea) almost 10 times higher than in the least developed (Indonesia). Several issues are pertinent here: labor supply, inequality, the structure of employment, and educational levels. The exhaustion of the labor surplus in the traditional sector (agriculture) was particularly important to the situation of the labor markets in the 1990s. Both Korea and Malaysia passed this point before 1990 and from then on exhibited tight labor markets with very low unemployment. Thailand also reached this point in the 1990s, although unemployment had been creeping up for some time because of emerging structural problems. Indonesia and the Philippines had substantial levels of unemployment and underemployment before 1997.

The level of inequality is also an important background factor. According to the Gini coefficients, Malaysia, the Philippines, and Thailand had higher levels of inequality than the other two countries (table 9.1). Inequality had been increasing in Thailand but decreasing in Korea (Kakwani and Son 1999). Wage differentials had been narrowing in Korea since the 1980s, and the country had experienced increasing income dispersion during the period of heavy industrialization (Lee and You 1999).

Employment structures also differed across the five countries prior to the crisis. Korea had made the most complete transition out of agriculture,

TABLE 9.1
Per Capita GDP Growth in Five Asian Countries
(percent)

Year	Indonesia	Korea	Malaysia	Philippines	Thailand
1996	8.0	7.1	8.6	5.7	5.5
1997	4.0	5.0	7.8	5.2	−0.5
1998	−13.6	−5.8	−6.1	−0.4	−9.9
1999 (estimated)	−4.0	2.0	0.9	2.0	1.0
Gini coefficient	34.2	36.3	48.4	44.9	46.2

Source: Mahmoud (1999); Gini coefficient for Korea: Lee and Kim (1999).

TABLE 9.2
Selected Labor Market Variables for Five Asian Countries

Variable	Indonesia	Korea	Malaysia	Philippines	Thailand
Real wage growth (%)					
1996[a]	6.6	6.8	5.8	3.3	2.3
1997[a]	4.2	4.3	4.2	7.7	−1.4
1998[a]	−37.8	−5.7	−1.1	−2.0	−7.4
% labor force in agriculture, 1990[b]	57	18	27	64	45
% labor force in industry, 1990[b]	14	35	23	15	14
Foreign workers precrisis (millions)[c]	few	0.2	1.7[d]	few	0.8
Workers overseas precrisis (millions)[c]	1.1	few	few	0.75	0.3

a. Mahmoud 1999.

b. World Bank 1993.

c. Estimates, from country studies (estimates only); for Thailand: personal communication with Chris Manning.

d. An estimated two-thirds were in the country legally.

followed by Malaysia (table 9.2). Thailand had more of its GDP and labor force in agriculture than might have been expected given the country's per capita GDP. This fact has important implications, since countries where rural-urban migration occurred closest to the crisis were the most likely to experience reverse migration (urban-rural) during the crisis itself. These countries also had higher levels of remittances between urban and rural areas, something that tends to diversify risks.

Employment structures are related to educational levels. As educational levels increase with development, participation rates fall for younger workers, and the vulnerable age for recent labor market entrants increases.[2] We can observe the effects of educational enrollment on the labor market participation rates for young East Asian workers. The participation rate for children ages 10–14 was zero or virtually zero in Korea and Malaysia before the crisis, 7–9 percent in Indonesia and the Philippines, and as high as 15 percent in Thailand (table 9.3). A similar pattern occurred in the 15–24 age group. Two-thirds of the young men in this age group were in the labor force in Indonesia, the Philippines, and Thailand, but only one-third were in the labor force in Korea. We therefore see workers as young

TABLE 9.3
Participation Rates before and after the Crisis
(percent)

	Indonesia 1996	Indonesia 1998	Korea 1994
Male, total	84.8	83.2	76.4
Male, youth (15–24)	61.4	59.8	31.0
Female total	51.3	51.2	47.9
Female, youth (15–24)	42.9	41.1	42.3

Source: World Bank 1999.

as 10–14 as vulnerable groups (new labor market entrants) in Thailand, but this group extends into the 25–34 age cohort in Korea, where educational levels are much higher.

Levels and patterns of female participation differed across the five countries (Horton 1996). Women in the Philippines and Thailand were the most strongly attached to the labor force, with a pattern of participation similar to men's in both urban and rural areas. This pattern, which is typical of many rural economies, was also found in Indonesia. In contrast Malaysia exhibited the highest participation rates prior to marriage and childbearing. Korea displayed the pattern characteristic of industrial countries, with women leaving the labor market when their children are born and returning later. (In countries where labor market participation is interrupted by childbearing, women tend to receive less on-the-job training and smaller investments in skills training.)

Wage differentials between genders also differed across the five countries before the crisis. Data on these differentials are hard to find. Sources such as the International Labour Organization (ILO) provide information only on manufacturing and are thus not sufficiently representative. Data from labor force surveys (Horton 1996) suggest that gender differentials were largest in Korea, followed by Indonesia, where women earned only 50–60 percent of what men earned. The smallest differentials were in Thailand, where women earned almost 90 percent of what men earned. These data must be used cautiously, since they include hourly, quarterly, and annual wages and some are for employees only, excluding the self-employed. However the data do confirm that the two countries where women had the strongest attachment to the labor force (the Philippines and Thailand)

Korea 1998	Philippines 1997	Philippines 1998	Thailand 1996	Thailand 1998
75.2	82.4	82.9	82.5	71.5
26.4	60.6	61.9	64.4	58.9
46.9	48.9	48.7	66.9	63.8
35.8	35.9	37.1	56.6	50.1

tended to have the narrowest wage differentials between genders. In the Philippines the wage differential was further affected by the fact that women in the labor force had more education than their male counterparts.

Migrant workers were (and remain) an important part of the labor market in all five countries (table 9.2). Indonesia and the Philippines, the two countries with a labor surplus, had a substantial number of overseas contract workers (an estimated 1.1 million from Indonesia and 0.75 million from the Philippines before the crisis). Korea and Malaysia had sizable populations of foreign workers (0.2 million and an estimated 1.7 million, respectively). Thailand is an intermediate case. About 0.3 million Thais worked abroad in relatively skilled jobs in 1996, and about 0.8 million foreign workers from low-income countries worked in Thailand. About one-third of the Philippine's overseas workers were in other Asian countries in 1997 and were thus affected by the Asian crisis. Similarly, many foreign workers in Malaysia came from Indonesia and the Philippines, leading to the transmission of shocks within the region. Internal migration was also important, particularly in Indonesia and Thailand, which experienced significant rural-urban migration.

The Labor Market Response to the Crisis

How did the Asian crisis affect the labor markets, and in particular the most vulnerable groups? Our response to this question is restricted by data limitations. The most readily available data by age, sex, and educational and skill levels are for unemployment and participation rates. Unemployment rates alone can be misleading, since women and secondary workers (young workers) are more likely than prime-age men to drop out of the labor force when labor demand is weak. Participation rates are useful, since they provide some guidance as to the extent of this discouraged worker effect or its opposite, the added worker effect. The discouraged worker effect occurs when workers give up looking for jobs and leave the work force. The added worker effect occurs when, in some crises, additional workers enter the labor force because the main household earners experience a decline in income. Data on hours worked are also useful (estimates of underemployment often rely on hours worked) but are rarely available by age and sex. Real wage data are even more difficult to come by.

The figures that are most readily available—real wages for workers in manufacturing or for employees (as opposed to the self-employed)—are misleading at a time when employment levels are changing rapidly, since the skill composition of the labor force is also changing. Typically the least-experienced and least-skilled workers are the first to be retrenched, making it difficult to interpret gender and age differentials. For example in Korea the gender gap in wages (for employees) appears to have narrowed following the crisis, almost certainly because those women who remained as employees were disproportionately skilled or experienced. One final and serious limitation is that data for Malaysia are not available for this discussion. The Malaysian Labor Force Survey data present information on the composition of the unemployed but not population-based rates, with breakdowns only for the registered unemployed, a small and unrepresentative proportion of the total (Mansor and others 1999).

The estimates in table 9.4 on labor market responses to the crisis should be taken as orders of magnitude rather than precise estimates, since figures on (for example) job losses are hard to come by. The labor force in 1997 totaled 94 million in Indonesia, 22 million in Korea, 8 million in Malaysia, 30 million in the Philippines, and 35 million in Thailand (World Bank 1996). The data suggest that the Philippines was the least affected by the crisis and that in Malaysia the brunt of the adjustment was borne by migrant workers. Malaysia is unusual in its very large proportion of foreign workers (close to 20 percent of the labor force). That, plus the large fall in participation rates, left relatively little of the adjustment in Malaysia to open unemployment and real wage declines. Neither Malaysia nor the Philippines engaged in intensive efforts to cushion the adjustment, unlike Indonesia, Korea, and Thailand.

The scale of labor market adjustment has been staggering in Indonesia and of course has been accompanied by tremendous social unrest. Even before the crisis Indonesia was having difficulty absorbing new labor mar-

TABLE 9.4
Estimated Magnitudes of Labor Market Response to the Crisis

Effect	Indonesia	Korea	Malaysia	Philippines	Thailand
Job losses (millions) 1997/98	2.5	0.1[a]	0.1	n.a.	0.8
Usual labor force growth (annual)	3.5	0.4	0.4	n.a.	0.2
Unemployment[b] increases (millions) 1997/98	0.9	0.8	0.2	n.a.	1.2
Underemployment increases (millions) 1997/98	3.7	n.a.	n.a.	n.a.	up 1 m (defined as < 20 hours/wk)
Change in labor force participation (millions) 1997/98	+0.7	+0.1 (men) −0.3 (women)	−0.2	n.a.	−0.9 m[c]
Change in migration (millions) 1997/98	overseas work +0.8	n.a.	legal foreign workers −0.3	overseas work +0.8	n.a.
Real wage growth (percent)					
1996	6.6	6.8	5.8	3.3	2.3
1997	4.2	4.3	4.2	7.7	−1.4
1998	−37.8	−5.7	−1.1	−2.0	−7.4

n.a. not available.

Source: Country studies; real wages from Mahmoud (1999).

a. Data are for permanent job losses only; temporary job losses were much higher.

b. Underemployment is defined as less than 35 hours per week for Indonesia and less than 20 hours in Thailand.

c. First quarter to first quarter.

ket entrants, and unemployment rates were relatively high (table 9.5). Even a large shift in labor to agriculture after the crisis—5 million workers—was not enough to prevent unemployment and underemployment from increasing or real wages from decreasing (by around 38 percent in one year). Participation *increased* during the crisis, largely because the number of women in the work force grew. As more women went to work, secondary school students were pulled out of school, an occurrence that is indicative of the desperate economic situation. These labor market responses typify those of a low-income country where formal safety nets are completely inadequate to deal with the scale of a crisis.

The response in Thailand was a larger proportionate increase in the open unemployment rate than in Indonesia and a significant decline in participation. The data used here compare August 1997 and November 1998 and overstate the decline somewhat, since there are seasonal effects, but the overall effects are still significant. Thailand also experienced substantial internal migration that led to job losses in Bangkok and rising unemployment rates in rural areas, particularly the northeast. (Urban migration in Thailand is a relatively recent phenomenon, and many individuals still retain ties to their original rural communities.)

The response in Korea was more typical of an industrial country, with open unemployment increasing substantially and the participation rate of women in the labor force decreasing (the discouraged worker effect). Job losses affected casual rather than permanent workers. Many firms undertook multiple adjustments—shorter hours, temporary leave, and temporary shutdowns (Shin 1999). Korea also exhibited the problems of industrial countries, with a growing proportion of long-term unemployed and difficulty reallocating the most senior workers, since firms customarily keep permanent workers whenever possible.

The Crisis and Vulnerable Groups in the Labor Market

The groups we have identified as vulnerable include young workers, who are vulnerable in all countries, women and their households, less educated workers, and migrants. Labor market concerns vary across these groups. With young workers the issue is generally not their immediate welfare (except for those young workers who do not live with their parents but are themselves household heads or live on the streets), but their long-term prospects for entering the labor market. Female-headed households in countries such as Indonesia, Korea, and Malaysia, where women receive low relative wages and tend to be seen as temporary workers, are especially

TABLE 9.5
Unemployment Rates before and after the Crisis
(percent)

	Indonesia 1996	Indonesia 1998	Korea 1995	Korea 1998	Philippines 1995	Philippines 1998	Thailand 1996	Thailand 1998
Male, total	4.0	5.5	2.3	7.7	7.0	9.5	1.0	4.3
Male, 15–24	12.2	15.7	9.3	20.8	25.9	17.9	2.6	11.2
Male, 35–54	1.0[a]	2.3[a]	1.7	6.2	5.6[b]	5.2[b]	0.3	1.9
Male, 50+	n/a	n/a	0.9	5.4	7.6[b]	6.6[b]	0.4	2.5
Female, total	3.3	5.0	1.6	5.6	8.2	9.8	1.1	4.6
Female, 15–24	15.0	19.1	6.0	12.8	33.9	22.1	2.3	8.6
Female, 35–54	1.8[a]	2.3[a]	0.7	4.5	6.7[b]	4.5[b]	0.5	3.2
Female, 50+	n/a	n/a	0.3	2.4	6.9[b]	5.7[b]	0.8	2.7

a. Age 25+ for Indonesia.
b. Age groups for Philippines are 35–54 and 55+.
n/a not available.
Source: BPS (1998); NSOP (1999); NSOT (1998); ILO (various years).

vulnerable. Households where women are not well educated are also vulnerable. Beegle, Frankenberg, and Thomas (1999) found that female education in Indonesia and Peru, respectively, was an important factor in ameliorating the impact of crises on household welfare. Less educated workers, who are also at risk in all countries, are particularly vulnerable in areas where the option of going back to work in agriculture is not viable. Finally, migrant workers, such as low-skill foreigners in Malaysia and internal migrants in Thailand, are an important vulnerable group, as are internal migrants in Indonesia, although no data are available on these workers.

Young Workers

Young workers (new labor market entrants) have less labor market experience, little firm-specific training, and (usually) low productivity rates. Unemployment rates for the young are higher than they are for prime-age workers even during normal times, and this group is one of the first affected during a crisis, when new hiring slows down or halts. Among countries of the Organization for Economic Cooperation and Development (OECD), unemployment rates for the young have climbed as high as 75 percent in particularly depressed regions. This level of unemployment is a recipe for social problems. Even if the majority of young workers still live with their parents and are not under imminent threat of starvation, there are negative welfare effects. "Scarring" is an issue, as these workers do not develop a long-run attachment to the labor force. And some young workers are household heads and may have children.

Graduate unemployment, a special type of youth unemployment, has been a long-term problem in a number of developing countries. The problem became acute in the 1980s in countries where a university degree had traditionally been the ticket to a government job. As government hiring slowed, some graduates opted to remain unemployed for several years and wait for their place in the job queue. The wait was often long—up to four years in Egypt, for example (Assad and Commander 1994).

The Asian crisis had dramatic effects on youth unemployment (table 9.5). In Indonesia the unemployment rate for young workers (ages 15–24) is normally about 7–8 times as high as for older workers (25 and above) of the same sex. In Korea, the Philippines, and Thailand, it is around 4–5 times that of prime-age workers—that is, workers ages 35–49 in Korea and Thailand and ages 35–54 in the Philippines. In Korea, where tertiary education is widespread, unemployment in the 25–34 age group is also about twice that of prime-age workers, as it is in the Philippines and Thailand.[3]

Although the ratio of youth unemployment to that of older workers did not change much with the crisis, absolute rates went up to very high levels. Rates in subgroups, such as the 15–19 age group, were even higher.

Participation rates for young workers declined by more than the average in absolute terms. In all four countries participation rates decreased more in both absolute and relative terms for vulnerable groups (young workers, women, and older workers) than for prime-age males. The decreases for young workers were 1–2 percent in Indonesia, 2–4 percent in Korea, and 4 percent in Thailand. Participation increased by just over 1 percent in the Philippines (table 9.3). Participation rates did not decrease because young workers were staying longer in school. In Indonesia, for instance, school participation for those ages 7–12 and 13–19 also decreased (Frankenberg, Thomas, and Beegle 1999), although falling school enrollments were not particularly noticeable in the other four countries. Preliminary results from Beegle, Frankenberg, and Thomas (1999) for Indonesia suggest that the presence of young women ages 15–19 in the household was one factor helping to maintain income. These girls may have assumed household responsibilities in order to free their mothers to participate in the labor market.

Women

A sizable literature exists on the question of whether structural adjustment in Latin America and Africa during the 1980s adversely affected women (Cox-Edwards and Roberts 1994; Bardan 1994). To some extent the outcomes were specific to country situations. In Bolivia, for example, the first large layoffs were in mining, a sector dominated by men. In other Latin American countries, cuts in public sector employment disproportionately affected women, who made up a smaller share of private formal sector employment. In Africa relatively few women were in urban formal sector employment (which shrank), and women working in food-crop agriculture could benefit from improved terms of trade from agriculture. But crises and recessions that slow (or reverse) the transition from the informal to the formal sector put women in all countries at a disadvantage, since women tend to shift relatively slowly out of unpaid family work into formal employee status.[4]

Do developments that disadvantage women in the labor market translate into disadvantages in terms of welfare? If most adult women live in households that also contain male adults, the effects of changes in total household income are of first-order importance. But there are second-order effects if women's earned incomes decrease relative to men's. The literature on intrahousehold spending suggests that decreases in women's relative contributions to household income are associated with a decrease in household expenditures on both children and basic needs. Depending on the country, the share of female-headed households may also be so large that adverse welfare effects result when women are disadvantaged in the labor market. If women have to work longer hours in poorly paid jobs in the informal sector following a crisis, for instance, their ability to provide childcare is reduced.

The unemployment data do not suggest strong gender differentials in unemployment (table 9.5). In both the Philippines and Thailand, female unemployment is consistently higher than male unemployment, although the differential has been narrowing over time. The opposite is true in Indonesia and Korea, where male unemployment rose relative to female after the crisis. The most likely reason for the apparent increase is that female participation rates fell more than male participation rates in all countries except Indonesia. Participation rates for women are consistently lower than for men in virtually all age groups, with the exception of the youngest (15–24) in Korea, where men receive more education (table 9.3). As noted earlier, declines in the participation rates of women of all ages exceeded those for prime-age men after the crisis, with the sole exception of Indonesia, where participation rates for women over 25 increased.

Data on hours worked by sex are not available for all the countries, but data from a smaller sample survey for Indonesia (the Indonesia Family Life Survey) suggest that the number of hours worked declined for both genders following the crisis. The decline in hours worked was greater for women than for men, especially in the formal sector. The hours men in the formal sector worked dropped by 1.4 per week, while the hours worked by their female counterparts fell 2.9 per week.[5] At the other extreme, the incidence of long hours (defined as more than 45 hours per week) for women increased, rising from 20 percent in 1994 to 22.9 percent in 1997 and 24.9 percent in 1998. For men it fell following the crisis, although about twice as many men as women work long hours (Islam and others 1999). This situation is consistent with the view that women entered the labor force in Indonesia to try to offset the drastic falls in household income. Jobs open to women are more frequently in the informal sector, where the poorest work very long hours at jobs with very low returns.

Data on sectoral employment are available by sex only for Korea (table 9.6). The main sectoral shift in Korea after the crisis was out of employ-

TABLE 9.5
Sectoral Employment before and after the Crisis
(percent)

	Indonesia 1996	Indonesia 1998	Korea 1994	Korea 1998	Philippines 1997	Philippines 1998	Thailand 1996	Thailand 1998
Total								
Employee	34.2	38.2	62.0	61.2	47.7	49.0	46.4	42.8
Self-employed	21.4	22.7	27.8	28.8	37.5	37.6	33.3	36.7
Unpaid family	44.4	39.2	10.2	10.0	14.8	13.4	20.3	20.4
Male								
Employee	n.a.	n.a.	64.2	63.1	n.a.	n.a.	n.a.	n.a.
Self-employed	n.a.	n.a.	34.0	35.1	n.a.	n.a.	n.a.	n.a.
Unpaid family	n.a.	n.a.	1.8	1.7	n.a.	n.a.	n.a.	n.a.
Female								
Employee	n.a.	n.a.	58.7	58.3	n.a.	n.a.	n.a.	n.a.
Self-employed	n.a.	n.a.	18.8	19.4	n.a.	n.a.	n.a.	n.a.
Unpaid family	n.a.	n.a.	22.6	22.3	n.a.	n.a.	n.a.	n.a.

n.a. not available.
Source: NSOT (date) (key tables 1996–98.)

ment and into self-employment (with no other employees). The data also show that women are more likely than men to be unpaid family workers in Korea and less likely to be employees or self-employed. Data on relative wages by gender following the crisis are not readily available, especially household survey data, which would be more useful than establishment survey data.

Workers with Low Educational and Skill Levels

Workers with few skills and little education are vulnerable to economic downturns for two major reasons. First, many of them work in construction, a highly cyclical industry, or agriculture, where they are susceptible to a variety of developments. (In Asia, for instance, the adverse effects of El Niño reduced demand for agricultural labor.) Second, they have less training and less firm-specific capital and thus are the group most likely to be retrenched.

In Asia wage differentials between skilled and unskilled workers have traditionally been high owing to the relative scarcity of skilled workers. However, the gap has been narrowing as educational levels rise. In Korea wages for middle school graduates have increased steadily, rising from 33 percent of those of university graduates in 1980 to 60 percent in 1997. Relative wages for high school graduates also rose from 46 percent of university graduates' to 68 percent over the same period. And the ratio of earnings for wage earners in the 90th percentile to earnings for workers in the 10th percentile fell from 4.7 to 3.7. These trends are unlike those in industrial countries, where wage differentials between skilled and unskilled workers are on the rise.[6]

Information on the effects of the Asian crisis on relative wages broken down by skill level is not yet available for most countries. A little information can be gleaned from data on unemployment rates that are disaggregated by skill level. In Korea relative wages fell for the least educated and for those in production jobs after the crisis, and distribution by quintiles also worsened. In fact the only wage gap that did not worsen was the differential between genders, which continued to narrow. Unemployment among those with a high school education or less had traditionally been lower than among college graduates, but after the crisis the unemployment rate for those with less education began to exceed the rate for those with a college education (Shin 1999). In Thailand, where the average educational level is lower, the highest unemployment rates are usually in the group with either a lower or upper secondary education, and this trend remained unchanged during the crisis (TDRI 1999). Indonesia experienced a small increase in the proportion of unemployed with a lower secondary education (Islam and others 1999). Thus Korea offers the clearest evidence of weakening demand for the unskilled.

Migrants

Recent migrants are among those most likely to lose their jobs in an economic downturn because they have less local labor market experience and often work as temporary laborers (a group that, as we have seen, is among the most vulnerable when the economy slackens). We do not have comparable data on this vulnerable group for all five countries, but at least one source (Abubakar 1999) provides information about foreign migrant workers in Malaysia and data on internal migration for Thailand. The Philippines collects more extensive data on its overseas workers than most other countries, but the results of the 1998 survey of overseas workers were not available to the authors at the time of writing.

FOREIGN MIGRANTS. Abubakar (1999) discusses the extent to which the situation of foreign migrants in Malaysia became increasingly desperate after the crisis. Employers began to skimp on housing costs by crowding more migrant workers into each housing unit. Bonuses for foreign workers disappeared, and hours of work increased. Abubakar suggests that in some cases domestic workers were retrenched because they were more expensive than migrants and that migrants were forced to work longer hours. The government also increased the cost of renewing permits for foreign workers to 140 ringgit (RM) per month, a substantial sum for service workers who may only earn RM 350–400 monthly. The Malaysian government stopped issuing new permits for foreign workers in the service sector and even considered trying to repatriate as many as a million foreign workers whose work permits expired or who entered the country illegally. This scheme created so much concern that the government decided instead to redeploy foreign workers from services and construction to sectors unable to recruit enough nationals (plantations and parts of manufacturing, for instance). But according to Abubakar, of the 1.7 million foreign workers in Malaysia, only 1,000 had been formally redeployed as of 1998, and only 2,382 had applied to change sectors (table 9.2).

INTERNAL MIGRANTS. In periods of economic downturn, when regional disparities tend to increase, we can expect internal migrants to bear the brunt of the recession. In developing countries generally, including those in Asia, labor markets are less integrated than those in industrial economies, in part because urbanization rates are lower. For this reason income dispersion and wage differentials among regions tend to be higher in developing countries. During periods of strong growth, a sizable number of workers migrate from low- to high-income regions, but to a large degree this internal migration is temporary. The cost of this type of migration tends to be relatively low, and temporary migrants from rural areas do not give up their stake in the land or family farm. Such temporary migrants are disproportionately represented in the lower echelons of workers in high-income regions (the informal sector, casual labor, and the non-tenured segment of the formal labor force).[7] Typically such migrants return to their regions of origin, where incomes are generally lower.

Thailand offers a good example of the effects of the crisis on internal migration. Data from the National Migration Survey of Thailand from 1995 suggest that the country enjoys considerable interregional labor mobility, largely from richer regions to poorer ones.[8] About a third of all internal migrants have moved more than once in a two-year period, and about half of these were seasonal migrants who moved to urban areas in the dry season, returning to agricultural work (most often in the north and northeast) in the wet season. Short-term population flows are strongly affected by this trend. Net losses as a result of seasonal and other temporary migration were nearly 150 per 1,000 for Bangkok in the 1995 wet season and 50 per 1,000 for the central region. At the receiving end, net gains of 33 and 68 people per 1,000 were recorded for the north and northeast, respectively. Rates of net permanent inmigration, however, are generally small, with gains ranging from 4.1 per 1,000 for Bangkok to 12.8 per 1,000 for the southern region over the two-year period.

In the 1980s and early 1990s, Bangkok and the surrounding vicinity formed Thailand's major growth center. Because of this growth the region enjoyed some of the highest incomes in the country. In 1992–97, however, incomes in the northeast grew at more than three times the rate of Bangkok and its surrounds. But the crisis interrupted this strong favorable trend toward increased income equality across regions. Financial crises and foreign investment flows arguably impact the modern sectors of an economy much more than the traditional farming sectors—and in fact the rise in unemployment was proportionately higher in Bangkok than in other regions (NSOT 1998). But this hypothesis does not take into account the impact on regional economies of disrupted flows of labor migration. Traditional labor flows from the north and northeast to Bangkok raised incomes through remittances. As unemployment in the Bangkok area increased, the flow of migrants slowed and incomes in the northern regions fell, reversing the trend toward more income equality across regions. We can say, then, that while the direct impact of the crisis in the poorer northern and northeastern regions of Thailand may have been smaller than it was in Bangkok, the net effect was greater.

Kakwani calculated the trends in per capita incomes for different regions in 1992–98, with seasonal adjustments (NESDB 1998) (table 9.7). He then goes on to calculate the deviations from the trend line for income, which he terms "crisis indices." The crisis indices thus show not just actual declines in incomes in the postcrisis period but declines relative to the levels incomes would have reached if the crisis had not interrupted the trends.

Labor Market Interventions

Governments in East and Southeast Asia tend to intervene in labor markets less than developing country governments in other regions. Despite the crisis, for instance, four of the countries studied here still have no unemployment insurance scheme (the exception is Korea; see table 9.8). The crisis has forced governments to intervene to some extent to protect workers, largely in the areas of income support and training.

Labor Market Institutions before the Crisis

Payroll taxes in the region traditionally tended to be somewhat lower than in Latin American countries, largely because individuals and households rather than the state provided social services such as health, education, and pensions (World Bank 1996).[9] Those payroll taxes that were levied frequently support individual provident funds (in Malaysia and Singapore), individual health accounts (for instance, Medisave and Medishield in Singapore), and severance pay (in Korea, Malaysia, the Philippines, and Thailand). Contributions to general (rather than individual) pension funds were also less common than in regions such as Latin America. In Korea a national pension scheme began in 1988, but it covered only 58 percent of the working population (Lee and You 1999). Other labor market institutions were also weak before the crisis.

PUBLIC WORKS. Public works had been phased out as an employment protection strategy in all five countries as a result of burgeoning growth.

TABLE 9.7
Per Capita Income Measures, Thailand

Region	Per capita income Q1 1998 (baht per month)	Per capita income Q3 1998 (baht per month)	Long-term growth rate (percent)	Kakwani's crisis index, Q1 1998	Kakwani's crisis index, Q3 1998
Central	2,791	2,791	6.8	-20.4	-26.1
Eastern	2,791	2,791	7.1	-29.6	-31.7
Western	2,569	2,518	5.1	-18.8	-22.1
Northern	2,096	1,896	6.0	-19.3	-26.0
Northeastern	1,488	1,166	10.2	132.4	-37.4
Southern	2,339	2,195	8.1	-22.7	-31.3
Bangkok and vicinity	5,439	5,147	2.9	-8.1	-14.5
Country	2,633	2,402	6.3	-19.2	-24.8

Source: NESDB (1998).

TABLE 9.8
Labor Market Institutions Prior to Crisis

Institution	Indonesia	Korea	Malaysia	Philippines	Thailand
Unemployment insurance	None	Began 1995 for firms >30 employees; requires 6 months of contributions	None	None	None (but can access some of pension fund when unemployed)
Severance pay	No information	Dismissal only for cause prior to 1997; severance pay progressive with experience; dismissal of senior workers costly	Those employed for >12 months receive 10–20 days' pay per year of experience	1 month per year of service	Yes (no details)
Skills/vocational training	712 public, 3,000 private schools	140 public, 178 private, 237 in-plant providers; firms required to pay levy or provide in-plant training	No information	TESDA began 1994: 80% of training private, 20% public; PEFSA provides vouchers to individuals	Public training under Ministry of Labor, Ministry of Industry and Bangkok Metro Training Centre; few private institutions

(Table continues on the following page)

TABLE 9.8
Labor Market Institutions Prior to Crisis (*continued*)

Institution	Indonesia	Korea	Malaysia	Philippines	Thailand
Labor market information	System not well developed; offices not computerized, and not linked	Network of centers, not heavily utilized	Network of centers	No information	7 branches in Bangkok, 76 in provinces, computerized and linked, but access is slow (hardware problems)
Other		Low minimum wages		Minimum wages relatively higher than rest of Asia, but exemptions permitted	Minimum wages, nonbinding

Sources: Country studies; Abubakan (1999).

Indonesia was the last to phase out its program in 1994 (for more on labor market strategies before the crisis, see chapter 7).

TRAINING AND VOCATIONAL EDUCATION. All five countries had training and vocational education systems before the crisis (table 9.8). These systems utilized both private and public institutions. The Philippines, for example, instituted the Technical Education and Skill Development Authority (TESDA) in 1994. TESDA still operates as a regulatory agency and also runs most of the public training institutions (other than state universities and colleges). The Philippines had a voucher system that permitted trainees to shop around for a suitable institution, either private or public. However outright competition between public and private providers was restricted, since public institutions continued to receive block grants, and the number of vouchers was fairly limited (around 10,000 in 1999). Prior to the crisis Korea had begun making the transition from a system of compulsory training that required firms to provide in-plant training or pay a levy to a voluntary system that would provide firms with incentives to offer training.

UNEMPLOYMENT INSURANCE AND SEVERANCE PAY. Unemployment insurance tends to exist only in high-income countries, as it requires not only extensive record keeping but also a reasonably large formal sector to support it. Korea began an unemployment insurance scheme in 1995 that covers firms with more than 30 employees. Employees must make contributions for six months in order to file a claim. None of the other countries had an unemployment insurance scheme prior to the crisis.

Severance pay has long been widespread in the formal sector in Asia. Both employers and employees contribute to a fund that guarantees dismissed workers a certain amount of severance pay based on years of service. In Korea all firms with more than five employees are required to provide severance pay. Dismissal (other than for cause) was not permissible for formal sector workers in Korea prior to 1997. These precrisis systems were not necessarily ideal. In Korea, as we have seen, severance pay accumulated with experience, making it almost prohibitively expensive to terminate senior workers while providing an incentive to dismiss workers in the middle of their careers. In other cases access to funds intended for severance pay encouraged workers to leave their jobs.

OTHER LABOR MARKET POLICIES. Traditionally other labor market policies have been relatively noninterventionist in Asia. Minimum wages were not emphasized and in many cases were not binding in Asia before the crisis (with the possible exception of the Philippines). Korea, the Philippines, and Thailand all had minimum wages. In Thailand minimum wages rose 17 percent in real terms during the 1980s, but this increase meant that they declined sharply relative to average wages (Squire and Suthiwart-Narueput 1996).

As of January 1, 1991, each of the 151 members of the ILO had ratified an average of 36 of its conventions. But Indonesia had ratified only 9, Malaysia (including component regions) 12, the Philippines 21, and Thailand 11. Korea was not even an ILO member at the time. In Asia only Sri Lanka and the Philippines ratified the 1990 ILO convention on the Protection of Rights of All Migrant Workers and Their Families. Enforcement of labor legislation was also an issue in the years before the crisis. The Philippines made fairly strenuous efforts to improve enforcement, dramatically increasing the number of staff available to conduct inspections. But Thailand lagged in this respect, and Malaysia did not make domestic labor legislation binding in export processing zones.[10]

Changes in Labor Market Institutions Following the Crisis

East Asian governments were forced to intervene in the labor markets following the crisis. The most significant changes occurred in the three countries with the greatest adjustment problems—Indonesia, Korea, and Thailand (table 9.9). However in Indonesia these changes were concentrated in two areas: public works and self-employment. Thailand also made changes to its policies on severance pay and its vocational training schemes. Korea made the largest number of changes, expanding its programs in every category. The Philippines made no major changes, as it had been dealing with high unemployment for some time. Malaysia shifted much of the adjustment onto the migrant workforce, blocking new recruitment in certain sectors, increasing the penalties for citizens aiding illegal immigrants, undertaking a limited amount of redeployment, and raising some levies on migrants. The government also considered but did not implement repatriation.

PUBLIC WORKS. Since 1997 Indonesia, Korea, and Thailand have all implemented large public works schemes that have created millions of person-days of employment. In Indonesia the Padat Karya programs were revived in Java for 4 months, followed by a second phase implemented as 16 subprograms by different ministries and institutions across the coun-

TABLE 9.9

Changes in Labor Market Institutions Following the Crisis

Institution	Indonesia	Korea	Malaysia	Philippines	Thailand
Public works	Large public works schemes	Large public works schemes; some targeted to women	No change	No change	Large public works schemes
Unemployment insurance	None	Extended to firms >5 Mar 98, to all firms Oct 98, but only to those contributing >6 months; only covers 20–25% of job losers	None	None	None
Severance pay	No change	Allow employees to received severance for voluntary quits	No change	No change	Increased maximum benefits to 10 months salary; set up public fund for workers whose firms go bankrupt

(Table continues on the following page)

TABLE 9.9
Changes in Labor Market Institutions Following the Crisis (continued)

Institution	Indonesia	Korea	Malaysia	Philippines	Thailand
Skills/vocational training	No change	103 bn won additional; shifting from compulsory levy to incentives for voluntary training	Graduate entrepreneurial training scheme, with business loans	TESDA trained only 1545 displaced workers in 1998	Funds for skills development for new entrants, unemployed; considering making skills development fund mandatory; loans to businesses for training
Labor market information	No change	Government set up "Employment Security Centres"; large rise in usage; "Work-Net" begins	No change	No change	No change
Other	Subsidized loans to co-ops	6.4 trn won in wage subsidies, some targeted to youth and women; loans for venture business	New immigrant recruitment blocked in some sectors; efforts to redeploy existing migrants; levies on migrants raised		Self-employment loans

try. The second phase created around 225 million person-days of employment between April 1998 and December 1999 (Islam and others 1999). The program suffers from some problems, however. It has a top-down management structure, so that the involvement of community organizations is weak. Detailed background information on vulnerable groups is lacking, corruption and nepotism abound, and the scheme pays wages in excess of market levels.

Thailand has several public works schemes. The Social Investment Program operates a Social Investment Fund for small projects originating or implemented at the community level. The Regional Urban Development Fund supports local governments seeking to expand urban infrastructure. The program, which started in September 1998 and is scheduled to run for at least 40 months, is expected to provide 557,000 person-months of employment. The projects experienced some initial difficulties. As of May 10, 1999, some seven months after the program commenced, only 2 percent of the funds under the Social Investment Fund had been dispersed, and only 4 percent (comprising two projects) under the Regional Urban Development Fund had been approved. Most of the proposed projects did not meet the program's approval requirements (Arya 1999).

Thailand's Miyazawa program expects to fund newly created jobs for 86,000 educated workers and 400,000 unskilled workers in activities such as rural infrastructure. The program was implemented through local authorities in March 1999 and should provide 50 million person-days of work. In addition funds have been earmarked in the regular government budget to support the employment of almost 800,000 people in rural areas.

In Korea public works projects benefited 440,000 workers in 1998 and were expected to benefit 1.2 million in 1999, peaking in the second quarter. Local governments use 10 percent of the general public works budget to implement projects that employ daily labor. The government has also allocated funds to help employ the highly educated by instituting an internship program for graduates. The program is in such high demand that the government is introducing a similar one for high school graduates. Korea also has a venture capital fund, although the fund's restrictive conditions have prevented it from being used to create employment to any great extent.

SELF-EMPLOYMENT. Indonesia, Korea, and Thailand have implemented schemes to encourage self-employment. The Indonesian government provides subsidized loans to cooperatives. However, the cooperatives can get a safe return by depositing these funds at banks (which are offering higher

interest rates), diminishing the effect of the loans on employment generation. Thailand has also earmarked funds for self-employment loans, as has
Korea with its venture capital loan scheme (for further discussion of these
programs, see chapter 7).

WAGE SUBSIDIES. Korea has implemented a large wage subsidy program. The program pays as much as two-thirds of a worker's wage if a firm
can demonstrate its need to adjust by shutting down two or more days a
month, cutting hours by more than 10 percent, placing employees on
leave for a month or more, transferring workers to affiliates, or switching
to a new line of business while retaining at least 60 percent of existing employees. In 1998 the program covered 800,000 workers, and in 1999 the
government expanded it and increased the duration of the subsidy from 6
to 8 months. A survey of enterprises suggests that without the subsidies,
22.3 percent of all jobs would have been lost (the figure is higher in the
nonmanufacturing sector).

TRAINING AND VOCATIONAL EDUCATION. In Thailand some funding was
included in the various programs for skills development for new job market entrants and the unemployed. Malaysia instituted a graduate entrepreneurial training scheme as well as business loans. Korea increased its budget for training by 103 billion won. Lee and Kim (1999) argue that the
change from a compulsory to a voluntary system "mostly extends what has
been proven ineffective" (p. 12). The changes do not offer training providers incentives to meet market needs, and private providers continue to
overemphasize skills for manufacturing, where demand has been declining.

UNEMPLOYMENT INSURANCE AND SEVERANCE PAY. Korea broadened its
unemployment insurance scheme following the crisis, extending it first to
firms with more than five workers and subsequently to all firms. However
the requirement that workers contribute for six months to establish eligibility limits coverage to only 20–25 percent of job losers. None of the
other countries discussed here has instituted an unemployment insurance
scheme since the crisis, and all still rely primarily on severance pay. Thailand extended the maximum amount of severance pay to 10 months and
set up a fund to make the legislated severance payments to workers whose
firms go bankrupt (the fund is supported by fines on firms that break
labor laws). Malaysia has also extended its severance pay scheme since the
crisis to cover workers who quit voluntarily.

LABOR MARKET INFORMATION SYSTEMS. Labor market information systems in the region tend to vary with the level of development and were extremely limited before the crisis. Public employment offices in Indonesia, for instance, are seen as limited in their offerings because they are not computerized (and therefore not linked). Those in Thailand are computerized and linked, but some of the equipment is old, and access is slow. Malaysia and Korea have networks of public employment offices, but they are not widely used, and job seekers do not see them as a major strategy in the job search. Korea has made major changes in its labor market information systems, setting up "employment security centers" that combine payment facilities for unemployment insurance with information on work applicants and vacancies. The government has also instituted a system (modeled after systems in the United States and Canada) that allows workers to check vacancies via the Internet. The number of people using the centers increased enormously in 1997–98, rising by a factor of nearly 10, and the number of vacancies posted doubled. The ratio of the unemployed registered with the centers went from 4.8 percent in 1996 to 22.5 percent in 1998. But only 5.8 percent of those who found a job found it through the public system (Keum 1999).

The Effects of Labor Market Interventions on Vulnerable Groups

Information about the effects of the interventions on vulnerable groups is limited, but we can make some observations based on program design. For instance, successful public works programs can be designed to include women. In Bangladesh food-for-work programs include projects aimed specifically at women and pay attention to issues such as childcare for participants.

In Indonesia, however, the limited evidence available suggests that women have not participated heavily in public works projects, for three reasons. First, 70 percent of the factory workers (both male and female) surveyed by AKATIGA (1999) were reluctant to join the Padat Karya program. They felt the work provided was not appropriate for factory workers and preferred instead to start their own businesses. Women interviewed in Java further felt that the tasks involved in the public works projects were not appropriate for women and proposed instead work involving "women's skills" (including cleaning community facilities such as schools and parks, sewing, and cooking). A final factor deterring women in Indonesia was the location of the projects, which were implemented in areas far from people's homes.[11] A local initiative in Surabaya did have some success in involving women. The local government negotiated with businesses and workers, encouraging local firms that had not been seriously affected by the crisis to hire unemployed factory workers as daily workers. Although the program was not targeted by gender, the main beneficiaries were women.

In Korea one disincentive to incorporating women and young workers in public works is that compensation on the projects is 50 percent higher than the minimum wage. As a result the projects attract new participants from outside the labor force and draw workers away from small businesses. In fact the higher the project wage offered, the less likely that women and young workers will obtain jobs. Some schemes have been targeted specifically to women and young workers, and women's participation in these projects increased markedly between 1998 and 1999. Some schemes are specifically designed to provide women from poor households with short-term employment opportunities in the areas of social services and childcare. The government also specifically subsidizes new jobs (in existing firms) for women who are household heads, subsidizing wages by one-third to one-half. Another scheme provides internships for unemployed college graduates—for example setting up electronic network systems in public institutions or working in private companies. However companies are permitted to hire new subsidized workers only if they are not laying off workers, a restriction that substantially limits the number of potential employers.

In Thailand, where women's labor market participation is high, women also undertake heavy agricultural work. For this reason there may be fewer barriers to women's participation in public works projects.

The majority of wage-support policies, including severance pay and unemployment insurance, are biased in favor of prime-age male workers. Severance pay, in particular, favors workers who have worked steadily in permanent jobs, those who have been employed in large firms (small firms can be exempt from the scheme), and those who have worked in the formal sector. Unemployment insurance tends to have similar effects. Linking unemployment insurance payment locations to job information centers, as in Korea, is likely to make the centers more useful and available to males who have worked in the formal sector, since they are the ones eligible for payments. Minimum wages are also biased against vulnerable groups, unless separate lower wages are set for these groups. Both Canada and the United States, for example, have separate minimum wages for young workers. And finally wage subsidies of the kind implemented in Korea benefit mostly men. In Korea the smallest firms (which employ a disproportionate number of women) are too financially risky to benefit from wage subsidies.

Lessons from Other Regions

We focus here on the experience of other developing countries, particularly those in South Asia and Latin America, with some reference to East European economies. There are also many lessons to be learned from the OECD experience that are more applicable to Korea than to the other Asian countries, given current incomes levels (Betcherman and others 1999). We focus more on income support policies than on labor market information and training, since more information is available on the effect of income support on vulnerable groups.

Public Works

Developing countries have used public works widely as income-support measures. The Maharashtra Employment Guarantee Scheme in India employed roughly half a million workers, or around 2.5 percent of the labor force, each month between 1975 and 1989. The Bangladesh Food for Work schemes created 100 million person-days of employment per year in 1987–8 (Ravallion 1991).

Latin American countries have implemented many public works schemes (Marquez undated). In Argentina, for instance, large public works projects employed up to 9 percent of the labor force. The majority of these workers participated in two large schemes, one operated by the social security agency and state governments (*Programa de Asistencia Solidaria*), the other by local governments and nongovernmental organizations (NGOs) (*Programa Trabajar*). In Chile during the 1970s and 1980s, public works employed up to 10 percent of the labor force during the painful adjustment period, although these projects have now disappeared. In Mexico about 5 percent of the labor force has been included in two programs: the Program to Maintain Rural Roads [*Programa de Conservación de Caminos Rurales*], financed by the federal government and implemented by state and local governments, and a similar but smaller program designed to improve social infrastructure (Marquez undated; Marquez and Martinez 1998). In Bolivia the Emergency Social Fund helped ease the plight of the poor during the adjustment that followed the adoption of the New Economic Policy in 1985 (Jorgensen, Grosch, and Schacter 1991). At the end of 1988 about 2 percent of the labor force were participating in the fund.

LESSONS FROM LATIN AMERICA. Discussing the Latin American experience, Marquez (undated) notes that "labor-intensive public works have been the tools of choice to deal with economy-wide shocks" (p. 16). In fact Latin American governments spend more on public works than on other mechanisms for income support. For this reason observers have been able to draw a number of lessons about such projects. Marquez, for instance, cites three characteristics of good programs:

- First, they are financed by the central government but implemented by a local agency—either a local government (as in Mexico and Argentina) or local NGO (as in Bolivia). The relationship between the central government and the executing agency is well structured and appropriate to the political structure of the country.[12]
- Second, wage levels and selection criteria for beneficiaries are set centrally, but local agencies do the actual selecting. Community oversight ensures that there is no favoritism and is complemented with a nontrivial expenditure of central resources on monitoring.
- Third, the wage level is lower than the prevailing market wage to ensure self-targeting, even at the cost of stigmatizing participants.

Marquez also counsels against the danger of allowing public works to become entrenched and lose their important countercyclical properties. In Bolivia the Emergency Social Fund was deliberately cut off after four years of operation, despite the expense. Generating a pipeline of adequate proposals takes about a year, so that programs may be cut off just as they are beginning to run smoothly.

LESSONS FROM OTHER REGIONS. Ravallion (1999) makes several recommendations for successful projects. First, he maintains that work should not be rationed (the Maharashtra model) but notes that if rationing is necessary, it should be done geographically as well as temporally. He also argues that a project's labor intensity (the share of labor in total project cost) must be at least as great as the average for similar projects in the same setting. Finally he counsels that projects should be aimed at poor areas to ensure that the assets created are of maximum value to poor people. In the event that they are not, then local cofinancing is required.

Ravallion further calculates benefit-cost ratios for public works in both a middle-income country (based loosely on Argentina) and a low-income country (based on South Asia). He suggests that under plausible assumptions, $1 of government spending in the middle-income country leads to a transfer of $0.20 to the poor. He assumes that the labor share of the cost of public works is 33 percent, that the wage is low enough to prevent leakage to the nonpoor in employment, and that foregone income by participants is $0.40 per $1.00. The same calculation for the low-income country suggests that $1 of government expenditure leads to $0.28 for the poor. This calculation is based on a labor share in the project cost of 50 percent, a leakage of 25 percent of the employment created to the nonpoor, and forgone earnings of $0.25 on $1.00.

At first sight, then, public works are hardly more attractive than uniform untargeted transfers (assuming that poverty rates are 20 percent and 50 percent in the two countries, respectively). Adding future returns to the assets created raises the benefits to the poor to around $0.40 per $1.00 of government spending in both low- and middle-income countries. This figure makes public works more attractive than untargeted transfers in the richer country but still not as attractive in the poorer country. One possible reason for continuing to use public works in low-income countries may be that external funds cannot be mobilized for untargeted income transfers. Geographically targeted public works projects are also likely to be politically more acceptable than similarly targeted cash transfers.

PUBLIC WORKS AND VULNERABLE GROUPS. Public works are generally successful at reaching unskilled workers but less so at reaching women. The effect on migrants is more difficult to gauge. Ravallion (1991) cites three studies of the Maharashtra scheme and one of the Bangladesh Food-for-Work scheme showing that these programs successfully reach the poor. One survey of Maharashtra participants found that 90 percent remained below the poverty line even when calculations of their income included project earnings (around 49 percent of the overall population lives below this level). Ravallion's estimates suggest that 60 percent of the participants in the Bangladesh project came from the poorest 25 percent of households. Jorgensen, Grosh, and Schacter (1991) do a counterfactual analysis for Bolivia and find that 25 percent of the workers in the Emergency Social Fund would have been in the poorest decile without it. With it none were in this decile, because mean monthly earnings, while below average wages for construction work, were actually above the average for low-skilled construction workers with the same characteristics and only slightly below the average for all workers in the population.

Public works may reach poor male workers, but experience suggests that unless projects are specifically designed for women and youth, these groups will not benefit. In Bolivia, for instance, 91 percent of the program participants were men, and 93 percent were heads of households. The Latin American projects tend to service prime-age men who are household heads, in part because these projects are designed to employ household heads during crises. A few schemes have been aimed specifically at women and youth. Two examples are the Mexican rural roads program for youth and a small program for female heads of household in Argentina, the Program for Community Service [*Programa de Servicio Comunitario*]. In Latin America programs aimed at women and youth have focused primarily on training and labor market insertion, including *Chile Joven, Proyecto Joven* (Argentina), and *PROJOVEN* (Peru). Programs in Chile and Costa Rica have also been designed to promote employment for those with handicaps. In general, though, public works leave out those who are poor but who have restrictions on their ability to work.

The South Asian schemes have had comparatively high levels of female participation. In Maharashtra men and women have participated at around the same rate. In Bangladesh, where employment has been created primarily for men, some projects have specifically targeted women workers. The Maharashtra scheme has encouraged women by siting projects near villages, not discriminating by gender in wages (piece rates are often the norm), and by providing childcare (usually by hiring women to provide it).

Because few studies are available that provide poverty profiles or that examine the location of projects, information on migrants and public works projects is almost nonexistent. In Bolivia targeting by location was not based on formal data; rather, administrators would go out and look at sites to see if they were in poor neighborhoods. Given the prevalence of this type of targeting, the poorest and most remote locations—where migrants often live—are likely to be left out of public works projects.

Wage Subsidies

Wage subsidies have not been widely used in developing countries, partly because of the difficulties of monitoring and enforcement (Marquez undated). Governments can use subsidies to promote the employment of particular subgroups (women, youth, and former combatants, for instance) by creating promotional contracts that allow firms to hire workers without the usual social benefits. However, unions tend to oppose these contracts, which they see as promoting less desirable forms of employment. Argentina adopted a voucher system that eased the tax burden on firms hiring unemployed workers in the target groups (workers turned the vouchers over to employers, who submitted the paperwork to the government). Firms willing to hire particular groups of workers could also get tax rebates. Canadian employers using "coop" students (students in programs combining work and study) are eligible for tax rebates.

Korea's experience with wage subsidies illustrates three potential pitfalls. First, as we have seen, only firms that were not laying off workers could hire subsidized workers, a condition that substantially reduced the number of eligible firms. Second, the wage subsidies created large displacement effects. One survey suggests that 78 percent of jobs would have been maintained even without the subsidies (chapter 3). Third, because it is politically effective to tie wage subsidies to apprenticeship schemes and training programs, wage subsidies in Korea disproportionately benefited men.

Severance Pay and Unemployment Insurance

Severance pay is a much more widespread institution than unemployment insurance in developing countries, though not in the industrial world. Both schemes have their merits and their problems. Severance pay exists in much of Asia, Eastern Europe, and Latin America, although it is restricted to the formal sector. Severance schemes are fairly straightforward. Employers withhold a specific amount from employees' paychecks, depositing it in a fund that is available to the worker upon dismissal. If not well designed, however, these schemes can generate undesirable incentives. In Brazil, for instance, the very high fluidity of the labor market (which inhibits firm-specific training) is in part the result of workers' ability to access their severance funds (Camargo 1997).[13] As we have seen, in Korea severance pay accumulates with seniority, making it difficult to dismiss senior employees. But in other countries (like Brazil) severance pay creates incentives for employees to force their own dismissal. Further, regulations regarding severance pay assume that firms (and the state) have the capability to maintain records. And as we have noted, severance pay tends to benefit prime-age males more than other groups, since these men are more likely to work in large firms and maintain steady employment.

Severance pay can be inferior to unemployment insurance in a more mature economy. Unemployment insurance covers a broader range of workers, though it also requires the state to keep detailed records and monitor firms. Unlike severance pay systems, which provide individual benefits, unemployment insurance typically involves some pooling of risk. In the United States unemployment insurance schemes use experience rating, levying higher premiums on high-risk industries or firms. Canada offers more generous benefits (less stringent eligibility requirements and a longer benefit period) in regions of relatively high unemployment. This kind of fine tuning helps discourage migration to those regions with the best employment prospects.

In Eastern Europe firms have switched from severance pay schemes to unemployment insurance but have not abolished severance pay for existing workers. Dismissed workers can therefore access both types of benefits, although some workers (specifically in the Czech and Slovak Republics) exhaust their severance benefits before claiming unemployment insurance (Ham, Svejnar, and Terrell 1998). All the Central and East European countries had established unemployment insurance schemes by the end of 1991, with benefits that were initially generous compared with those in Western Europe. But these benefits were gradually reduced because of budget considerations. In the Czech Republic, for instance, individuals who had not worked but had in the last three years taken care of children or sick relatives, left the military, or spent time in prison were initially eligible. In 1991 benefits lasted one year, but in 1992 that period was reduced to six months.

Ham, Svejnar, and Terrell (1998) find that unemployment insurance has only a moderate disincentive effect on workers. A 10 percent increase in benefits raises the time the average worker is unemployed by only 0.61 weeks in the Czech Republic. This result indicates an elasticity of duration with respect to benefits of 0.34; the corresponding elasticity in Slovakia is 0.14. Even drastic experiments, such as switching individuals from recipient to nonrecipient status, increase duration only by 10–20 percent. The main factor in how long workers are unemployed is labor demand conditions. The authors conclude that there is latitude for governments to provide social protection without unduly affecting the incentive to work.

In Latin America experience with unemployment insurance is limited. The length of time unemployed workers can receive benefits is typically restricted to four months, and the number of beneficiaries is small because the schemes are restricted to those with full-time employment in the formal sector. Argentina has only 100,000–125,000 recipients at a time, and Brazil, which has the largest scheme, has only 300,000–400,000. Venezuela never implemented the legislation it enacted on unemployment insurance, and Mexico permits workers only to draw against the pensions they have accumulated. In Latin America, as in Eastern Europe, unemployment insurance tends to be a complement to severance pay rather than a substitute for it (Marquez undated).

Retraining Schemes

Betcherman and others (1999) provide a comprehensive overview of re-training schemes in OECD countries. They conclude that more scientific evaluations (those with controls) belie the overly optimistic nonscientific assessments of training programs for workers who have lost jobs in mass layoffs. They also conclude that retraining programs do little to raise either the long-term earnings or employment prospects of such workers. The authors conclude that it is more cost-effective to provide job search assistance for these workers, especially since the costs of such assistance may be as little as one-tenth of the costs of retraining.

Training and job insertion programs may be more cost-effective for young workers, however. Chile Joven is one example of a successful reform of training programs for youth. The previous compulsory system of train-ing in Chile (with mandatory payroll taxes) had led to complaints that public sector training programs were not well suited to the needs of the labor force. Under Chile Joven governments provide scholarships for in-classroom training, with a three-month paid internship in a private firm (Marquez undated). The central government agency requests bids for projects, describing the content of courses and including a commitment form for firms willing to provide apprenticeships. This interaction with firms helps ensure that the training provided is relevant. Argentina and Peru have also followed this model. Brazil's scheme uses competitive bid-ding between the public and private sector, so that the national training institution must also bid. Some of the reforms of the Philippine training system (Esguerra, Balisacan, and Confessor 1999) have been made along similar lines, although the quantities of workers trained are much too low to be considered a significant response to the crisis.

The success of the Mexican PROBECAT scheme (a job training and labor market insertion program) may also have been a liability. As partic-ipation rates rose, so did youth unemployment, raising concerns that the program was causing students to leave school in order to join (Marquez undated).

Policy Considerations and Lessons from Experience

From the information presented here, we draw three policy considerations and present some lessons regarding labor market interventions and vul-nerable groups. The policy considerations apply not just to vulnerable groups but to the labor markets of which these groups form an integral part. While it is true that some very vulnerable groups cannot be reached through the labor market interventions alone, effective targeting improves the chances that members of such groups will remain employable during crisis periods.

Policy Considerations

• *Safety nets must be in place even in times of strong economic growth.*

At the onset of the financial crisis, the five Asian countries considered here were at different stages in the evolution of their labor markets and labor market institutions. One general characteristic was that public institutions were not in place to provide social support during such a crisis, perhaps because these countries had experienced such extraordinary growth. With very little experience to back them up, the governments were then faced with the need to design and implement very rapid labor market interventions. Their responses tended to be short term, designed primarily to respond to the immediate needs of laid-off prime-age male workers who were household heads. Concerns about vulnerable groups (other than unskilled workers) were of secondary importance.

These countries now have the opportunity to begin making some long-term changes in their labor market institutions. These institutions need to be able to meet the needs of an urbanized economy that faces the income variability associated with increased integration into the international economy. Marquez (undated) provides a useful agenda for reform in Latin America that is also applicable in Asia.

• *Up-to-date labor market information and the means to disseminate it are essential to effective policy responses during crises and beyond.*

During the Asian crisis the lack of up-to-date information on the distribution of poverty hampered policy responses. Siting public works programs in the neediest areas would have been easier if data on the distribution of poverty had been available early in the crisis, for example. There is no substitute for timely analysis of such tools as labor force and income and expenditure surveys. In response to the crisis some governments undertook useful initiatives in this direction. For instance, the Economic and Social Development Board in Thailand began publishing a newsletter analyzing economic trends in the country. Indonesia initiated the Social Monitoring and Early Response Unit, which includes NGOs that post information on an Internet website.

- *In order to prevent inequalities from worsening during crises, social safety nets must make special provisions for vulnerable groups.*

The crisis in Asia worsened inequalities among economic groups. Although the crisis initially affected the formal sector (leading to employment losses, including in exporting firms), it was transmitted quickly to the informal sector in at least three of the five countries studied here. In both Korea and Thailand the crisis exacerbated inequalities by reversing the trends toward narrower skill and age differentials (Korea) and more regional equality (Thailand). This result is consistent with what is known about crises in Latin America, but it is very unlike the situation in sub-Saharan Africa, where crises and structural adjustment in the 1980s narrowed urban-rural inequality (Jamal and Weeks 1987).

This result also suggests a hypothesis about the degree of market integration that can benefit vulnerable groups. When these groups are not integrated into the national market, they will not be as adversely affected by crises—but they will also not benefit as much from growth. However while vulnerable groups that are tied into the market can benefit disproportionately from growth, they suffer relatively more during crises. This fact lies behind our recommendation that policies concerning safety nets should take vulnerable groups particularly into account.

Lessons from Experience

Experience provides us with policy lessons to be learned about specific labor market interventions. We have discussed some of these experiences, which provide lessons in best practices for various activities.

- *Public works need to be well designed, encouraging suitable proposals, setting appropriate wages, and targeting vulnerable groups such as women, young workers, and migrants.*

Public works have been a mainstay of income support in three of the countries studied here. Since none had recent experience with such programs, there were inevitable difficulties in design. In Thailand for example, efforts to involve community organizations and NGOs in proposing projects resulted in very few suitable proposals during the first year (Arya 1999). In such cases central agencies need to be more proactive, developing "templates" for projects and actively encouraging suitable proposals.

Public works programs in Indonesia were not successful in attracting women participants. To do so these programs must keep wages moderate in order not to attract men who are self-employed. Setting project wages below the minimum wage may not be appropriate, however, if minimum wages are already very low. Nevertheless, wages that are too high will displace workers rather than reaching those most in need of work. In addition projects must provide work that is considered appropriate for women in the locale, and project sites must be accessible and childcare available. Finally, effective monitoring helps ensure that a project runs well.

- *Wage subsidies should be temporary and preferably directed to specific groups of workers.*

Of the countries discussed here, only Korea used wage subsidies to any extent. International experience (for example, in Argentina) with this measure suggests that temporary, targeted subsidies are best used in conjunction with training and labor market insertion programs. Otherwise deadweight losses will be high.

- *Because severance pay favors older male workers in permanent jobs, unemployment insurance schemes are an important addition to social safety nets, especially for vulnerable groups.*

The crisis exposed the weakness of severance pay schemes, which tend to cover few workers and are of little use when firms go bankrupt. Among the countries discussed here, only Korea has an unemployment insurance scheme in place. Although it had been expanded before the crisis, it had not been operating long enough to cover many workers when the crisis came. Reforming severance pay schemes or implementing unemployment insurance is a long-term effort, but it is one that will provide large benefits in future crises and recessions.

Only the relatively high-income Asian countries are likely to follow the Latin American model and shift to unemployment insurance systems. Experience with shifting out of severance pay schemes and into unemployment insurance is limited. The East European and Latin American countries, and even Canada and the United States (for those workers whose contracts include severance pay), have simply imposed one system on top of the other. Nevertheless, having only one mandatory system offers certain advantages. (Although having two systems can provide workers with benefits for a longer period, it can also worsen income distribution.) A period of economic recovery, with a young and growing labor force, can be used to make the shift from one system to the other. From the point of view of vulnerable groups, unemployment insurance is certainly preferable, as long as coverage is reasonably broad.

• *Training programs are valuable for specific vulnerable groups, particularly women, and for young people needing assistance in labor market insertion, but most existing programs need to be reformed to be effective.*

Here Latin America offers useful experience (with similarities to the German dual model) of shifting to systems of training provision that involve competition among providers and encourage strong links with employers. Government agencies still retain an important role in setting standards, however. These again are the kinds of reforms that cannot be undertaken during a moment of crisis but are important to have in place for the future. Several countries brought in training programs as a component of crisis response (internships for high school and college graduates in Korea, for instance, and skill development for the unemployed and new labor market entrants in Thailand). Training is not especially useful for mass layoffs, and alone it is not a cost-effective substitute for formal education for young workers.

Finally we repeat one important point. Not all vulnerable groups can be reached by labor market interventions. Some groups, such as the very low-skilled working poor who will never earn enough to be able to save for retirement, single parents with young children, and those with chronic health problems that make it difficult for them to work, must be reached through other social measures.

Notes

1. The authors work with the Centre for International Studies at the University of Toronto. Their analysis in this chapter (especially the first two sections) draws heavily on a number of country studies prepared as background, namely Arya (1999), Esguerra and others (1999), Islam and others (1999), Kang (1999), Keum (1999), Kim (1999), Mahmood (1999), Mansor and others (1999), and Shin (1999). The authors would also like to thank Suying Hugh for excellent research assistance.

2. Again, Thailand had lower secondary enrollments than per capita income alone would predict. Observers frequently comment on this issue, as this fact is generally expected to make Thailand's transition from low-wage to high-skill, high-productivity manufacturing more difficult.

3. Data are not available for Indonesia.

4. For data on this transition in Asia, see Horton (1996).

5. Personal communication with K. Beegle.

6. The most commonly accepted explanation for the widening differentials in industrial countries is that changing technology has given skilled workers the advantage in the labor market—an advantage that is buttressed by the skill intensity of the traded goods sector. Widening differentials would also be the norm in developing countries if technology were the main factor driving wages. Trade effects that narrow these differentials would offset this trend, however.

7. In Asian formal sectors, large firms employ a substantial number of temporaries along with a tenured core of workers who enjoy job security and other benefits. In the Indian textile industry such laborers, or *badlis*, account for 25–30 percent of the labor force. This type of labor structure has also been a continuing part of the Japanese industrial scene.

8. In fact the gap in income levels among the country's regions is enormous. In 1998 per capita income in Bangkok and the surrounding area (the country's richest region) was four times the average for the northeast (the country's poorest region). Part of the reason for these income disparities is the relatively low urbanization rate of poorer regions, since incomes tend to be higher in urban areas in all regions.

9. Some observers argue that the interventions of Latin American governments in labor markets has in part been responsible for the relatively large informal labor force there (World Bank 1996).

10. See Horton (1996) for a discussion of labor market legislation affecting women in Asian countries.

11. AKATIGA undertook a second study, which found that women are affected negatively when husbands are laid off. Women must continue working to supplement the household's income, but husbands do not increase their share of domestic chores or childcare.

12. Jorgensen, Grosh, and Schacter (1991) provide specific lessons for good program design from Bolivia, a country with limited local government capability.

13. But Brazil's very slow judicial mechanisms for enforcement often lead workers to accept less severance pay than is their right in order to get some money without a long wait. The slow judicial system also leads both employers and employees to prefer informal rather than formal contracts, undermining statutory mandates for severance pay.

References

Abubakar, Syarisa Yanti. 1999. "Migrant Labor in Malaysia: Impacts and Implications of the Asian Economic Crisis. Malaysia Institute of Economic Research. Mimeo.

AKATIGA. 1999. "Factory Unemployment: Gender Issues and Impacts." Jakarta. Mimeo.

Arya, Gosah. 1999. "Economic Crisis, Employment, and the Labor Market in Thailand." Paper prepared for the joint World Bank-International Labour Organization seminar on Economic Crisis, Employment and Labor Markets in East and Southeast Asia, Tokyo, October. Japanese Ministry of Labor, Japan Institute of Labor.

Assad, R., and S. Commander. 1994. "Egypt." In S. Horton, R. Kanbur, and D. Mazumdar, eds., *Labor Markets in an Era of Adjustment*, vol 2, *Case Studies*. Economic Development Institute, Development Studies series. Washington, D.C.: World Bank.

BPS (Badan Pusat Statistik). 1998. *The Labor Force Situation in Indonesia*, August 1998. Jakarta.

Bardan, K. 1994. "Gender and Labor Allocation in Structural Adjustment in South Asia." In S. Horton, R. Kanbur, and D. Mazumdar, eds., *Labor Markets in an Era of Adjustment*, Vol. 1. Washington, D.C.: World Bank.

Beegle, K., E. Frankenberg, and D. Thomas. 1999. "Economy in Crisis: Labor Market Outcomes and Human Capital Investments in Indonesia." Santa Monica, CA: RAND. Mimeo.

Betcherman, G., A. Dar, A. Luinstra, and M. Ogawa. 1999. "Active Labor Market Policies: Policy Issues for East Asia." Paper prepared for the joint World Bank-International Labour Organization seminar on Economic Crisis, Employment and Labor Markets in East and Southeast Asia, Tokyo, October 10–13, 1999. Japanese Ministry of Labor, Japan Institute of Labor.

Camargo, J. M. 1997. "Brazil: Labor Market Flexibility and Productivity, with Many Poor Jobs." In E. Amadeo and S. Horton, eds., *Labor Productivity and Flexibility*. Houndmills, UK: MacMillan.

Collier, P. 1994. "A Theoretical Framework and the Africa Experience." In S. Horton, R. Kanbur, and D. Mazumdar, eds., *Labor Markets in an Era of Adjustment*, Vol. 1. Washington, D.C.: World Bank.

Cox-Edwards, A., and J. Roberts. 1994. "The Effects of Structural Adjustment on Women in Latin America." In S. Horton, R. Kanbur, and D. Mazumdar, eds., *Labor Markets in an Era of Adjustment*, Vol. 1. Washington, D.C.: World Bank.

Esguerra, J., A. Balisacan, and N. Confessor. 1999. "Philippines Country Paper." Paper prepared for the joint World Bank-International Labour Organization seminar on Economic Crisis, Employment and Labor Markets in East and Southeast Asia, Tokyo, October 23–25. Japanese Ministry of Labor, Japan Institute of Labor.

Frankenberg, E., D. Thomas, and K. Beegle. 1999. "The Real Costs Of Indonesia's Economic Crisis: Preliminary Findings from the Indonesia Family Life Surveys." Labor and Population Program Working Paper Series 99-04. Santa Monica, CA: RAND.

Ham, J., J. Svejnar, and K. Terrell. 1998. "Unemployment and The Social Safety Net During Transitions to a Market Economy: Evidence from the Czech and Slovak Republics." American Economic Review 88:1117–42.

Horton, S. 1996. *Women and Industrialization in Asia.* London: Routledge.

ILO (International Labour Office). Various years. *Yearbook of Labor Statistics.* Geneva.

Islam, R., with G. Bhattacharya, S. Dhanani, M. Iacono, F. Mehran, W. Mukhopadhyay, and P. Thuy. 1999. "Indonesia Country Paper." Paper prepared for the joint World Bank-International Labour Organization seminar on Economic Crisis, Employment and Labor Markets in East and Southeast Asia, Tokyo, October. Japanese Ministry of Labor, Japan Institute of Labor.

Jamal, V. and J. Weeks. 1987. "Rural-Urban Income Trends in Sub-Saharan Africa." World Employment Program Labor Market Analysis and Employment Planning Working Paper 18 (WEP2-43/WP.18). Geneva: International Labor Office.

Jorgensen, S., M. Grosh and M. Schacter. 1991. "Easing the Poor through Economic Crisis and Adjustment." Regional Studies Program Report 3, Latin America and the Caribbean Technical Department. Washington D.C.: World Bank

Kakwani, N. and H.H. Son. 1999. "Economic Growth, Inequality, and Poverty: Korea and Thailand." Sydney, Australia: University of New South Wales. Mimeo.

Kang, Soon-Hie. 1999. "Vocational Education and Training in Korea." Paper prepared for the joint World Bank-International Labour Organization seminar on Economic Crisis, Employment and Labor Markets in East and Southeast Asia, Tokyo, October. Japanese Ministry of Labor, Japan Institute of Labor.

Keum, Jaeho. 1999. "The Financial Crisis and Labor Market Services in Korea." Paper prepared for the joint World Bank-International Labour Organization seminar on Economic Crisis, Employment and Labor Markets in East and Southeast Asia, Tokyo, October. Japanese Ministry of Labor, Japan Institute of Labor.

Kim, Dong-Heo. 1999. "Employment Creation/Maintenance and Income Support Activities in Korea." Paper prepared for the joint World Bank-International Labour Organization seminar on Economic Crisis, Employment and Labor Markets in East and Southeast Asia, Tokyo, October. Japanese Ministry of Labor, Japan Institute of Labor.

Lee, Ju-Ho, and Dae-Il Kim. 1999. "Crisis and Reforms in Korea's Labor Market." Seoul: KDI (Korean Development Institute) School of International Policy and Management. Mimeo.

Lee, Ju-Ho, and Jong-Il You. 1999. "Globalization and Social Policy: the Case of South Korea." Paper prepared for Conference on Globalization and Social Policy at the Centre for Economic Policy Analysis, New School for Social Research University in Seoul, October.

Mahmood, Moazam. 1999. "Thailand Country Paper: A Macro Appraisal of the Economy and the Labor Market: Growth, Crisis, and Competitiveness." Paper prepared for the joint World Bank-International Labour Organization seminar on Economic Crisis, Employment and Labor Markets in East and Southeast Asia, Tokyo, October. Japanese Ministry of Labor, Japan Institute of Labor.

Mansor, N., T. E. Chye, A. Boerhanordin, F. Said and Saad Said. 1999. "Malaysia Country Paper." Paper prepared for the joint World Bank-International Labour Organization seminar on Economic Crisis, Employment and Labor Markets in East and Southeast Asia, Tokyo, October. Japanese Ministry of Labor, Japan Institute of Labor.

Marquez, G. Undated. "Labor Markets and Income Support: What Did We Learn from the Crises?" Washington, D.C.: Inter-American Development Bank. Mimeo.

Marquez, G., and D. Martinez. 1998. *Programas de empleo e ingreso en America Latina y el Caribe.* Lima, Peru: Inter-American Development Bank and the International Labour Office.

Mazumdar, D. 1999. "Trends in the Labor Market: The Last Quarter in the Perspective of the 1998 Experience." University of Toronto, Center for International Studies. Mimeo.

NESDB (National Economic and Social Development Board). 1998. Indicators of Well-Being and Policy Analysis 2(4). Bangkok.

_____. 1999. Indicators of Well-Being and Policy Analysis 3(1). Bangkok.

NSOK (National Statistics Office, Korea). Various years. *Annual Report on the Economically Active Population Survey.* Seoul.

NSOP (National Statistics Office, Philippines). 1999. *Labor Force Survey.* Income and Employment Statistics Division, Household Statistics Department, Manila. Available at http://www.census.gov.ph

NSOT (National Statistics Office, Thailand). 1998. "Report of the Labor Force Survey, Whole Kingdom, Round 5." Bangkok: Office of the Prime Minister.

Ravallion, M. 1991. "Reaching the Rural Poor through Public Employment: Arguments, Evidence and Lessons from South Asia." *World Bank Research Observer,* 6:153–175, 1991.

_____. 1998. "Appraising Workfare." *World Bank Research Observer* 14:31–48.

Scarpetta, S. 1998. "Labor Market Reforms and Unemployment: Lessons from the Experience of the OECD Countries." Working Paper 382. Washington, D.C.: Inter-American Development Bank, Office of the Chief Economist.

Shin, Donggyun. 1999. "Statistical Overview of Current Labor Market Conditions and Trends." Paper prepared for the joint World Bank-International Labour Organization seminar on Economic Crisis, Employment and Labor Markets in East and Southeast Asia, Tokyo, October. Japanese Ministry of Labor, Japan Institute of Labor.

Squire, L., and S. Suthiwart-Narueput. 1996. "The Impact of Labor Market Regulations." *World Bank Research Observer* 11.

TDRI (Thailand Development Research Institute). 1999. *Social Impacts of the Asian Economic Crisis in Thailand, Indonesia, Malaysia and the Philippines.* Bangkok.

Thomas, D., E. Frankenberg, K. Beedle, and G. Teruel. 1999. "Household Budgets, Household Composition and the Crisis in Indonesia: Evidence from Longitudinal Household Survey Data." Paper presented at the Population Association of America meetings, New York, March.

World Bank. 1995. *World Development Report 1995.* Washington D.C.

_____. 1996. *World Development Report 1996.* Washington, D.C.

_____. 1998. *World Development Report 1998/99.* Washington, D.C.

_____. 1999. *Coping with the Crisis in Education and Health.* Thailand Social Monitor, issue 2. Bangkok: World Bank Thailand Office.

10 Social Dialogue and Labor Market Adjustment in East Asia after the Crisis

Duncan Campbell[1]

Relatively undeveloped worker and employer organizations and weak formal institutions for social dialogue in the labor market characterize much of East Asia. Both are a part of the legacy of ambivalence regarding freedom of association that persists in many countries of the region. It is all the more noteworthy, then, that in the past two years a number of tripartite initiatives have emerged in East Asia. A more participatory approach is clearly evident in attempts to address the economic and social havoc wrought by the collapse of the baht in July 1997 and the contagious aftermath.

In at least three ways, the emergence of this social dialogue represents a break with the past. First, the search for solutions has resulted in the creation of entirely new tripartite approaches in Cambodia, the Republic of Korea, Malaysia, the Philippines, Singapore, and Thailand. Second, some of the tripartite initiatives have included government participation at the highest level. In Malaysia, for instance, the Prime Minister himself headed the tripartite mechanism set up to address the economic crisis.[2] Third, in some instances, the agenda for dialogue has extended well beyond issues dealing solely with the labor market to include a range of macroeconomic policy choices.

This chapter focuses on the most institutionalized modalities for dialogue—those associated with a country's formal industrial relations sys-

423

tem. We look at the East Asian countries most affected by the recent financial crisis: Korea, Malaysia, the Philippines, and Thailand.

Good Governance Equals Participation—A New Equation?

Why does the East Asian economic crisis seem to have increased not only interest in but the general willingness to experiment with participatory approaches? The answer appears to lie in the political fallout from the crisis. The effect has been substantial, most obviously in Indonesia, where cronyism and an autocratic polity fell victim to popular protest. In fact, however, in all three of the countries most affected by the crisis, political transformation has been widespread. Popular resentment over the deterioration of the Korean economy galvanized support for the presidential candidacy of the country's best-known opposition leader and democracy advocate. In Thailand the crisis coincided with the culmination in August 1997 of a process of constitutional reform characterized by an unusually high degree of popular support and participation. The cornerstone of the Thai Constitution itself is an emphasis on openness, participation, and the consolidation of democracy. Even prior to the baht's collapse, moreover, Thailand's Eighth Development Plan had veered away from previous plans with its emphasis on community and "people-centered development." (NESDB 1997)

Malaysia's unorthodox response to the crisis extends well beyond capital controls and exchange rate policy and cannot be fully appreciated without reference to the rise of a credible political opposition. This opposition was personified by a former deputy prime minister and finance minister whose policy views were considerably more orthodox than the government's. While the press noted concerns over the resurgence of cronyism in the aftermath of the Philippine presidential election, there can be little doubt of the president's populist appeal, particularly among the poor. In both Malaysia and the Philippines, moreover, response to the crisis has raised the stature of the labor federations at the national level. In Malaysia this development is most evident in the inclusion of the country's largest worker organization, the Malaysian Trade Union Congress (MTUC), in decisionmaking at the national level. In the Philippines it is evident in the conclusion of the national tripartite social accords. And in Indonesia and Cambodia the ratification of the core standards of the International Labour Organization (ILO) on freedom of association signals the radically altered political climate.

To varying degrees, but consistently, political trends in the countries affected by the crisis underscore a rising demand for openness and popular participation in economic and social policy choices. While pressure for democratic reform has long been a secular trend in the region, the crisis appears to have given it new impetus. The increase in tripartite initiatives is one reflection of this greater momentum.

The demand for greater popular participation is a reaction to the origins of the crisis itself, since the weakness or absence of democratic mechanisms is generally seen as one of the causative factors. Thus the crisis has been the catalyst for changes such as an ambitious project of legal reform in Thailand. The link between political institutions and economic and social outcomes is worth probing more deeply, for it implies that economic and social costs may be associated with the absence of well-functioning democratic mechanisms. This point is debatable, of course. The Asian "miracle" occurred without strong democratic mechanisms. But a compelling link exists between democracy and economic performance over the long run, so that strengthening channels for dialogue may well have economic benefits. Here, then, is a view that fortifies what had been a purely normative trend, and justified as such (democratic participation as a human right) with a utilitarian motivation. Beyond its moral justification, participation also appears to pay economic dividends.

The Economics of Dialogue

When commentators on the Asian financial crisis cite as one of its causes a lack of transparency or accountability, they are evoking underlying problems, one of which is the inadequacy of information. For example, because international financial markets are dogged by the problem of asymmetrical information (that is, the extreme difficulty of obtaining accurate and timely information on the risks and rewards of distant investments), foreign portfolio investors failed to see the crisis coming. Because information on business dealings was often closely held and shared only among a select, few—one of the defining features of "crony capitalism"—investors were further prevented from obtaining a true picture of just how risky some of the soon-to-be-nonperforming ventures were (Lee 1999).

Markets, of course, run on information, and the lesson reinforced by the crisis is that information conveys economic benefits, whereas ignorance has economic costs. This principle underpins the economic value of mechanisms for dialogue. In fact, when looked at in narrowly economic terms, dialogue or participation through "voice mechanisms" offers two main advantages. First, it is a tool for solving the problem of asymmetrical information. And second, it is a mechanism through which commitment is instilled and resistance minimized. Each of these advantages is briefly reviewed below.

The Role of Information in the Quality of Decisionmaking

One economic value of dialogue lies in the fact that dialogue generates information, and information improves the quality of decisionmaking, increasing the likelihood that decisions will be successfully implemented. Both improved quality and better implementation are likely to increase efficiency, since bad decisions are costly. The problem of assymetrical information means that these benefits are rarely available in the absence of well-functioning mechanisms for dialogue. Asymmetries arise from the probability that no one person or interest group is likely to possess all the relevant information needed to make complex decisions. More information is likely to become available when enough concerned, knowledgeable players are involved in the decisionmaking process.[3]

The field of industrial relations offers some of the best examples of just how useful (and also how difficult) information exchange can be. In market economies the interests of various stakeholders in the labor market are not identical. Industrial relations systems in market economies must address a common problem: while cooperation is essential to production, the interests of labor, management, and the state are not fully convergent. Many implications flow from this simple point. But as regards the first proposition—that information has economic value—we can draw one conclusion: when *interests* are not thoroughly convergent, all parties are unlikely to share *information* equally. Nor are the parties likely to perceive the relevance of information identically. In consequence, some mechanism promoting dialogue needs to be devised for obtaining the information needed to improve a given decision—again, on the assumption that the greater the amount of relevant information, the better the decision is likely to be.

Much thinking in industrial relations has always been directed to questions of designing what we might call *information-* and *commitment-generating mechanisms*. For example, one key question much in vogue in recent years is the construction of trust. Parties that do not trust each other have incentives to withhold information, and withholding information leads to bad decisions. A manager, for instance, may react to a high rate of unexplained resignations by guessing that frequent unscheduled overtime is the source of the problem. The manager accordingly curtails overtime use but observes no change in the rate of departures. Finally the manager learns from the employees themselves that a particularly abusive supervisor is the source of the problem. The moral of this simple tale is that an informed decision is better (for example, less costly) than a trial-and-error approach.

The Role of Voice Mechanisms in Implementing Decisions[4]

The previous example illustrates a second economic advantage of participation. Beyond getting the decision right is the matter of implementing it. Substantial empirical evidence shows that voice, or a well-functioning mechanism for information exchange, is a less costly alternative to other adjustment behaviors such as worker resignations. Evidence shows that the major advantage of unionized over nonunionized workplaces is that the voice mechanism available in unionized settings provides an effective means of channeling the facts required to make an informed decision. Absent this channel, adjustment occurs in more costly ways—through employee turnover, for example. But there are other potentially costly reactions to a decision in the form of noncompliance of various sorts, such as resistance to change and reductions in work effort, motivation, and commitment. Both theory and experience show that when the decisionmaking process internalizes the concerns of those who will be affected by the decisions, it results in more effective compliance. In other words participation promotes compliance.

These two main positive outcomes of the "economics of participation" have significance at both the macro- and microeconomic levels of social dialogue (box 10.1). At the societal level, in a world of increasing interdependence and rising external shocks, no one ministry or organization is likely to possess all the information required to make difficult decisions. The participation of specialized interest groups in the labor market has improved the decisionmaking process. Although employers and workers have separate interests, they also have separate information pools that can be invaluable to all parties. At the same time, despite episodes of social unrest, it can be plausibly asserted that effective voice mechanisms have prevented disputes, as we will show. In the countries under review here, the recent financial crisis has increased communications and efforts at cooperation. In the country most affected by the crisis, Indonesia, the collapse of nonparticipatory institutions and the inevitable institutional void their absence has created is related to the considerable social and political unrest the crisis has occasioned.

BOX 10.1
Social Dialogue and Macroeconomic Performance

The ability to maintain macroeconomic stability in the face of turbulent external conditions is the single most important factor accounting for the diversity in post-1975 economic performance in the developing world. The countries that were unable to adjust their macroeconomic policies to the shocks of the late 1970s and early 1980s ended up experiencing a dramatic collapse in productivity growth. The countries that fell apart did so because their social and political institutions were inadequate to bring about the bargains required for macroeconomic adjustment—they were societies with weak institutions of conflict management. In the absence of institutions that mediate conflict among social groups, the policy adjustments needed to reestablish macroeconomic balance are delayed, as labor, business, and other social groups block the implementation of fiscal and exchange rate policies . . . [To overcome policy paralysis and social divides], evidence shows that participatory political institutions, civil and political liberties, high-quality bureaucracies, the rule of law, and mechanisms of social insurance . . . can bridge these cleavages.

Source: Rodrik 1999, pp. 2–3.

Recent work by Rodrik (1999) supports the notion that democratic mechanisms of participation play an important role in improving economic performance and minimizing social instability. Democratic societies perform better because they are able to resolve conflicts that otherwise impede adjustment to external shocks.

Over the several years that globalization has been discussed, interest in labor-management cooperation has increased, largely because of its "fit" with the changing nature of competitive advantage. Two examples illustrate this point. First, the most globally competitive firms in many industries increasingly rely on the skills and decisionmaking abilities of their employees—that is, on the employees' knowledge and information.[5] In fact, the greater the value placed on nonprice competitive assets such as speed, quality, and innovation, the greater the reliance on employees' capabilities. Enterprises cannot hope to harness the skills of their employees, tap their knowledge, and institute a culture of commitment and adaptability to change without strongly developed participative mechanisms.[6] Second, globalization has increased the rate at which enterprises need to adapt to change in both technologies and product markets. This factor is what underlies corporate interest in flexibility. Businesses are unlikely to adapt to change, however (or at least are likely to resist it) in the absence of extensive mechanisms promoting communication and the exchange of information.

Ultimately, however, it is design that matters to economic outcomes, not just the presence or absence of mechanisms for dialogue. Such mechanisms affect more than distributional outcomes. They also affect measurable indicators of performance—that is, variables such as the speed at which recovery occurs and the costs associated with reform. At present, there are grounds for guarded optimism about the awakening interest in social dialogue in the countries affected by the East Asian financial crisis. But these countries must still overcome a number of obstacles if social dialogue is to play a more substantial role in the policy debate.

The Institutional Framework for Social Dialogue

In most Asian countries, weak trade unionism and underrepresentation of the labor force are the rule, for many reasons. Among these are the legacy of overt repression of labor organizations. All the countries under consideration have experienced periods of such repression, with the possible exception of the Philippines (although efforts to curb labor organizations are not unknown even there). In all the countries under review, then, organized labor constitutes only a small minority of the total work force and an equally small minority of the modern, formal sector work force (table 10.1).

The full brunt of the crisis, meanwhile, has of course fallen squarely on the individual—individual workers and their families and individual enterprises. Absent collective agreements or social accords outside the enterprise that commit it to a particular adjustment path, the individual bears the cost of adjustment. The simple fact in all countries is that social dialogue over labor market adjustment during the crisis at the level at which that adjustment ultimately occurs has been largely absent—at least through any formal channels that would allow labor and management to interact.

Weakly organized labor markets have become weaker still in Malaysia and Thailand as a result of the economic downturn. In Malaysia trade union membership in 1995 stood at 708,253, or approximately 9 percent of the work force. As a result of the financial crisis, union membership fell an estimated 1 percent (about 7,100 members), for a decline in union density of about .10 percent (Peetz and Todd 1999). Table 10.2 shows the trend in trade union membership for Thailand.

TABLE 10.1
Estimated Union Densities
(percent)

Thailand	1.0
Philippines	11.0
Republic of Korea	11.2
Malaysia	9.0
Indonesia	—

— not available.
Source: ILO and author's estimate.

Recent data for the Philippines show that trade union membership has continued to inch upward throughout the recession, despite the increase in registered unemployment. In 1996 membership stood at an estimated 3,611,000. By the end of the first quarter of 1998, that figure had grown to 3,670,000. In Indonesia, as well, new trade unions have emerged with the changed political climate.

Collective Bargaining Coverage

Aggregate membership figures, of course, do not show the actual influence of trade unions on the economic and social choices made during adjustment. In all of the countries under review, however, collective bargaining takes place either solely or predominantly at the enterprise level. One mea-

TABLE 10.2
Trends in Trade Union Membership in Thailand

1991	169,424
1992	190,142
1993	231,480
1994	242,730
1995	261,348
1996	280,963
1997	270,276
1998	265,982

Source: Ministry of Labor and Social Welfare.

sure of the extent of social dialogue at the microeconomic level, then, is the number of collective agreements.

In Malaysia most trade unions are involved in collective bargaining, although as Peetz and Todd (1999) report, the number of workers covered by collective agreements varies from industry to industry. For example, well-established bargaining processes exist in the plantation industry at the enterprise level. But the construction industry registered only two collective agreements covering just 1,400 workers in the 1994–96 period (most collective agreements have a duration of three years). Overall just 434,000 workers (6 percent of all employees) were covered by new collective agreements during the same period. Still, collective bargaining coverage in Malaysia is greater than union density, since the agreements also apply to nonunion workers who fall within their scope.

Considerable disparity exists in the Philippines between estimates of trade union membership and the actual number of workers covered by collective bargaining agreements. In 1997 approximately 524,000 workers, a mere one-seventh of total trade union membership, were covered by collective agreements. As Kuruvilla and others (1999, p. 45) observe, "absent the ability to expand collective bargaining beyond these small numbers, the ability of unions to significantly voice the concerns of labor in the economic development process is seriously compromised."

In Thailand collective bargaining and employee committees constitute the two main formal channels for labor-management dialogue at the enterprise level. [7] In Thailand the number of trade unions greatly exceeds the number of collective bargaining agreements, since collective bargaining occurs between a single employer or enterprise and a single industrial union. Since trade union membership covers only a small share of the total work force, collective bargaining coverage is even smaller (and with the crisis has become smaller still). The number of collective agreements fell sharply in the recession year of 1997, dropping from the 1996 level of 381 to 271 in December 1997. Data related to trade union demands include the number of workers the demands will affect. Over the past three years, each demand for collective negotiation has affected an average of 450 workers (MOLSW, various years). Overall, then, just under 122,000 workers, or around 1.2 percent of the formal private sector work force, were actually covered by collective agreements in December 1997.

The Labor Relations Act of 1975 also allows for (but does not mandate) the creation of employee committees in enterprises with more than 50 employees.[8] Like trade unions, the number of employee committees grew over the 1990s, and their decline in 1997 may also be a reflection of the impact of the crisis. Thailand has 24,830 establishments employing more than 50 persons, and employee committees exist in only 2 percent of them. Moreover, the vast majority of employee committees exist in establishments that also have trade unions (Piriyangsan 1998). The two participatory mechanisms are therefore not substitutes for each other. If they were, a larger share of the work force would be covered by at least one voice mechanism.

A Changing Climate for Labor Organizations?

The data above allow us to make the simple proposition that, with the possible exception of Malaysia, little social dialogue in the context of the crisis is likely to have occurred at the microeconomic level in the countries under discussion—at least through any formal channels. While it is a safe bet that weak labor market organization will continue to characterize these countries in the near future, some positive signs have emerged, for the most part in response to the crisis.

In the three countries most affected by the crisis—Indonesia, Korea, and Thailand—the right to freedom of association has been affirmed in various ways. Indonesia, for example, ratified ILO Convention No. 87 on freedom of association in June 1998, with the strong encouragement of the International Monetary Fund (IMF). New freedoms of association are clearly evident in that country, where the number of trade unions and labor federations is growing. At the same time a new framework labor law and laws on trade unions and dispute resolution are well advanced in the legislative process. Similarly in Korea one outcome of the tripartite social accord process was the accelerated acceptance of the Korean Confederation of Trade Unions (KCTU) as a participant in collective bargaining not only at the national but also at the enterprise level. The KCTU's inclusion could help reverse the downward trend in labor market organization in that country. Freedom of association, formerly withheld from Korean teachers, has now been granted them: as of July 1999 Korean teachers also have the right to organize trade unions and bargain collectively.

In Thailand the new constitution explicitly reaffirms the right to freedom of association. Thailand's labor federations and major employer confederations recognize that bipartite labor-management relations remain underdeveloped and need to be strengthened. The two main pieces of industrial relations legislation in Thailand (covering state-owned enterprises and the private sector) are both well advanced in the legislative process.

Trade union membership had been cut in half in 1991 in the wake of a military coup and the subsequent banning of trade union membership in the state-owned enterprises. The country's ongoing legal reforms would reverse this ban. The current version of the bill would mandate social dialogue at the enterprise level in the private sector through compulsory labor-management councils. While many of these developments do not translate directly into strengthened institutions for social dialogue at the enterprise and other levels, they are all necessary if such strengthening is to occur.

As argued at the outset, global economic integration brings with it an increasing degree of external influence on national economies and domestic institutional arrangements. Coping with integration requires strong, resilient, and well-designed institutions of domestic governance if countries are to reap the advantages of globalization at minimal social cost. The need for effective labor market institutions is no less great. Reducing unemployment and equitably sharing the burdens requires national negotiations that create arrangements among firms, governments, and social actors, along with strong organizations and channels for dialogue. For the countries under review the formal channels for social dialogue at the enterprise level are, as we have seen, often rather weak and limited in coverage. One consequence of this situation is that initiatives undertaken at the national level become all the more important for addressing the social and economic consequences of the crisis. Otherwise, the costs continue to be disproportionately borne by the individual.

The Social Dialogue in Malaysia

Malaysia has experienced far fewer retrenchments than might have been expected during a crisis of such magnitude. From an impressive growth rate prior to the crisis, the Malaysian economy contracted in 1998, with the growth rate of GDP declining by 13 percent. Yet the Ministry of Human Resources estimates that the country experienced a total of only 80,000 retrenchments between the onset of the crisis in late 1997 and February 1999. Of these workers, moreover, the overwhelming majority were placed in new jobs, although sometimes at lower wages.[9]

A Participatory Approach

There can be little doubt that Malaysia's approach to "crisis management" has been characterized by a strengthening of tripartite dialogue at the national level. When the crisis erupted in late 1997, the government responded by creating the National Economic Action Council (NEAC), which was charged with developing a National Economic Recovery Plan. The plan, released in July 1998, had six main elements, including several unorthodox prescriptions for foreign-exchange transactions, capital controls, and fiscal stimulus. As a decisionmaking apparatus, the NEAC was an entirely new institution, born of the crisis. Chaired by the prime minister, it comprises 12 ministers, representatives of various industries, and representatives from the MTUC and the Congress of Union of Employees in the Public Administration and Civil Service. The new council marked a significant change in the sometimes uneasy relations between the government and the MTUC and a substantial elevation of the labor movement's stature in the economic and social policymaking apparatus. Two other indications of the MTUC's rising stature in terms of managing the crisis were the prime minister's well-publicized public recognition of trade union support for the recovery process and the appointment of the MTUC secretary-general to the senate.

There are at least some indications that giving the MTUC a voice in the management of the crisis has been effective. First, as the crisis deepened, the government recommended a freeze on wages and a suspension of collective bargaining over wages. At the MTUC's urging, however, the government drew back from this approach and accepted the proposal that collective bargaining over wages should continue and that wage outcomes should be a function of ability to pay.

Second, the absence of widespread systems of social protection, including unemployment insurance, exacerbated the costs of the crisis in the region. In the summer of 1998, the MTUC proposed the creation of a "one dollar" retrenchment fund to be capitalized by contributions of one ringgit per worker from both employers and employees. The fund would provide replacement income for retrenched workers not eligible for severance pay. Initially the idea met with a cold reception from both the Malaysian Employers' Federation as well as the government. Over the intervening months, however, the government's position changed, and the "dollar fund" concept remains under review.

Encouraging Alternatives to Retrenchment

Efforts to stem job loss have also been channeled through long-established mechanisms for dialogue. The National Labor Advisory Council, a tripartite consultative body dealing with a range of labor policy matters, drew up guidelines on retrenchment with a view not only to ensuring that procedures are equitable but also to highlighting alternatives to retrenchment.

In their emphasis on layoffs as a last resort, the guidelines reflect the strong aversion most Malaysian employers have to retrenchments. While drawing firm empirical conclusions about the effect of the guidelines is difficult, they are likely to have had some influence on the behavior of enterprises, for several reasons.

First, there can be little doubt that the regulatory framework for industrial relations in Malaysia is clearly harnessed to the state's objective of promoting industrialization and attracting foreign direct investment. Strong workplace unionism remains weakly developed in Malaysia because of the regulatory framework. For example, it is procedurally difficult to conduct a legal strike. The state is more likely to step in and resolve disputes, leaving negotiated compromise weakly developed. Second, in keeping with the government's "look east" emphasis of the 1980s, policy has strongly favored the development of in-house unions, which are prohibited from federating across industries. In export-oriented pioneer industries, unions are not allowed to use collective bargaining to improve on the terms and conditions of the employment laws. Finally, relative to other countries in Southeast Asia, Malaysian law is characterized by a distinctly narrow legal scope for bargaining. For example, hiring, promotions, transfers, and dismissals are the prerogatives of management and remain outside the legal scope of bargaining.

Despite the nominal constraints the law imposes, regulatory incentives encourage enterprises to avoid retrenchments. Malaysia's basic industrial relations law includes the Code of Conduct on Industrial Harmony. The code stipulates that enterprises seek alternatives to retrenchment before dismissing workers. It further states that sacrifice—for example, by lowering wages and salaries—must be equitable across the hierarchy of the enterprise. The code is technically a voluntary prescription of good conduct, but when dismissals have been challenged through the Industrial Court system, the courts have routinely based their judgments on the enterprise's adherence to the code. As a result the legal constraints on the scope of bargaining have been somewhat eroded.

In response to the crisis, the Ministry of Human Resources now requires enterprises to give one month's advance notice before resorting to collective dismissals. This requirement allows various reemployment initiatives to be put into place. It also opens a window for considering negotiated alternatives to retrenchment. Malaysia's severance pay requirement, which is relatively generous for the region, also affects the behavior of enterprises. Because of the cost of retrenching workers, employers are more inclined to retain labor, particularly when they view a downturn as temporary.

Innovation at the Sectoral and Enterprise Levels

Labor market adjustment is affected by other factors in addition to the regulatory environment and national tripartite dialogue. Important initiatives have taken place at the sectoral level, where substantial cooperation exists between trade unions and employers trying to lessen the effects of the crisis on jobs. Prior to the crisis, the Federation of Malaysian Manufacturers became the first employer organization to establish a joint committee with the MTUC. With the crisis, the joint committee has become a task force on retrenchments and vacancies, in essence functioning as a private employment service. It keeps a list of companies planning to retrench staff and then liaises with other companies to see whether they can take on workers about to lose their jobs. The MTUC is also part of the information conduit and seeks vacancies for the list of retrenched workers it maintains.

While there are no firm indications that employee participation at the enterprise level has increased in response to the crisis, trade unions, individual employers, and employer organizations all report an increase in cooperation and communication during the downturn. ILO-sponsored research on enterprise adjustment during the crisis, while neither comprehensive nor necessarily representative, reveals a pattern of labor retention beyond what might have been expected in the nadir of the downturn (Siengthai 1999a). Some of the alternatives to retrenchment that have been put in place are clearly innovative. One example from the automobile industry received substantial national media attention, especially when the Minister of Human Resources visited the enterprise (box 10.2).

Companies have put a variety of measures in place to avoid retrenchments (box 10.3). In most instances these measures are outcomes negotiated with the union. One exception was the largely nonunion electronics industry, which avoided retrenchments for two reasons. First, many corporations had explicit no-layoff policies. Second, the multinational enterprises in the industry had extensive financial resources to tide them over a downturn they viewed as temporary.

Peetz and Todd (1999, p. 184) observe that:

> Retrenchments could not be avoided altogether. But retrenchments were much less likely to occur where the downturn in demand was not severe, where the firm was unionized, where the firm was in some way linked with the State (including as a supplier to government), or where the firm was from an Asian-based [multinational corporations].

BOX 10.2
One Enterprise Responds to the Crisis

Quality Assembly assembles, sells, and provides after-sales service for motor vehicles that are designed overseas but built locally. The company was seriously hit
by the financial crisis. In 1997–98 sales of the Korean and Japanese vehicles it
assembles virtually halted, while sales of its European vehicles fell by over 60 percent. In total, monthly sales fell by 70 percent between July 1997 and November 1998. Since 1994 a new chief executive officer (CEO) has been trying to
create a culture of commonality. The firm's new motto is "if we sink, we sink
together; if we float, we float together." Union representatives find this culture
very different from the culture promoted under earlier CEOs and endorse the
new approach.

How has the company stayed afloat? It has taken a number of carefully thought
out steps:

- In August 1997, when the first signs of a downturn appeared, hiring was
  frozen, employees were encouraged to conserve on utilities such as power
  and water, and incidental expenses were cut (for instance, the annual dinner
  and sports meet were cancelled).
- In September 1997 overtime was reduced and assembly activities slowed.
- In October 1997 overtime was abolished. Cuts were made in petrol allowances paid to employees with company cars and in expenditures on business
  travel and outstation allowances.
- In November 1997 the company stopped importing some parts.
- In December 1997, with still further reductions in assembly, excess employees were redeployed to other departments or to maintenance.
- On April 1, 1998, the assembly plant was closed for three months, and 435
  employees were temporarily laid off at 75 percent of their base salary, with
  no reduction of other benefits in the collective bargaining agreement, including the contractual bonus and 100 percent holiday pay. This arrangement was less costly than retrenchment for employees with an average of
  three to four years of tenure with the enterprise. The three-month layoff was
  negotiated with the union, and employees were encouraged to accept temporary employment elsewhere (at no loss of layoff pay). The personnel director took an active role in identifying vacancies.
- At the end of the three-month period, all but 10 employees returned to the
  company.

When retrenchments could not be avoided, job losses tended to be shared equally throughout enterprises and were not concentrated in the unionized work force.

The Social Dialogue in Thailand

Thailand has lost a substantial number of jobs—860,000 as of the end of 1998. But these losses are far fewer than might have been anticipated given the magnitude of the downturn. The Thai labor market has experienced significant downward wage flexibility, as well as numerical flexibility (mostly through reductions in hours worked). Numerical flexibility, which is defined as adjustments in the quantity of labor inputs, occurs primarily through two channels: adjustments in the number of persons working or in the number of hours worked. Enterprises appear to have hoarded labor, retaining workers but reducing the hours they work and their pay. Substantial underemployment and loss of earnings have resulted from this practice (box 10.4).

The Extent of the Dialogue

The formal channels through which social dialogue can occur are relatively underdeveloped in Thailand. In fact, Thailand's labor market is the least or-

---

BOX 10.3
Alternatives to Retrenchment

1. Insourcing of previously outsourced activities.
2. Increased employee training during the slack time.
3. Temporary transfer of redundant employees to other unaffiliated enterprises.
4. Temporary layoffs, during which employees are paid a proportion of their usual wages and even allowed to work elsewhere.
5. Adjustments in pay through overtime cuts or freezes and the deferral or non-payment of *contingent* bonuses. Infrequent: Cuts in *contractual* bonuses, especially in the unionized sector, despite renogotiated payment schedules, and reductions in base pay (cuts in managerial salaries were the most significant of these—up to 50 percent in the hardest-hit firms).
6. Postponement of negotiations on new collective agreements on wages.
7. Reductions in profit and even losses.

BOX 10.4
Labor Market Adjustment in Thailand

Methods of
promoting
numerical
flexibility

Macroeconomic level

- Measures to reduce excess labor supply, including the repatriation of illegal migrant workers and promotion of overseas employment for Thai workers.
- Measures to stimulate labor demand, including fiscal stimulus, targeted job creation schemes (some funded by the social sector loan programs of World Bank and Asian Development Bank), and employment of graduates on public stipends.
- Measures to match workers with jobs by coordinating labor market information from provincial employment service centers and disseminating labor market information through the Mass Layoff Center of the Ministry of Labor and Social Work's (MOLSW) Employment Department.
- The dissemination of various alternatives to retrenchment through the MOLSW.
- Reform of the Labor Protection Act that increases the cost of dismissing workers with long tenure as a further incentive to avoid retrenchment.

Microeconomic level

- Reductions in number of hours employees work as an alternative to layoff.

Measures to
encourage wage
flexibility

Macroeconomic level

- No adjustment in the minimum wage in 1998 (and possibly in 1999) by decision of the tripartite National Wage Committee.
- Reform of the Labor Protection Act to stipulate gradual decentralization of minimum wage fixing to the

(Box continues on the following page)

BOX 10.4   *(continued)*

Measures to
encourage wage
flexibility
(continued)

provincial level. Ten pilot provinces in the process of
forming tripartite provincial wage committees.
- Devaluation of the Thai baht and subsequent exchange rate policy, leading to a de facto decline in real
incomes and shoring up export competitiveness of
Thai industry.

Microeconomic level

- Reductions in number of hours worked, leading to
pay decreases (and lower payroll costs), reductions in
overtime, nominal declines in base pay, and the reduction or elimination of annual bonuses.

Methods of
encouraging
functional
flexibility

Macroeconomic level

- De facto market-driven (rather than policy-driven)
functional flexibility through changes in the composition of employment such as reverse (urban-to-rural)
migration and growth of urban informal sector activities that help absorb displaced formal sector workers. Policy has supported this recomposition through
employment-generation schemes targeted to persons
returning to rural areas.
- A review of labor policy, including policy relating to
wages and competitiveness (for example, productivity
and skill development), spurred by the conditionalities
of Asian Development Bank assistance.

Microeconomic level

- Possible rethinking of human resource basis of productivity improvement; unknown whether labor market
slack has been used for retraining or skills upgrading or
if work reorganization to increase productivity has been
a feature of the downturn.

BOX 10.4   *(continued)*

Measures promoting flexibility in industrial relations

Macroeconomic level

- The seven-point program for the alleviation of unemployment under the chairmanship of the prime minister (one outcome of the tripartite process, albeit one in which government representation was dominant).
- Efforts to encourage greater direct, popular participation in the Eighth Plan (preceding the onset of the crisis), especially in the focus on community-based organizations as recipients of social sector loan grants and in a variety of electoral reform measures arising from the expansion of democratic rights in the August 1997 constitution.
- Two pieces of industrial relations legislation, the Labor Relations Act and the State Enterprise Relations Act, that are well advanced in a parliamentary process of reform.
- National promotion of bipartism through 1996 Code of Conduct on Labor Relations and 1998 Code of Practice on the Promotion of Labor Relations.

Microeconomic level

- In aggregate quantitative terms, some weakening of trade unions and of labor-management institutions (such as collective bargaining and employee committees).
- Despite crisis-related increase in the number of individual disputes (over wages, severance pay, and dismissals), greater labor-management communication during the crisis.

ganized of the four under review. Moreover, any dialogue on labor market adjustment at the enterprise level covers only a minority of Thai workers—those in the formal or modern sector. It covers an even smaller share of the work force when the rural and urban informal sectors are included. Extensive flexibility of the market-driven sort is the rule for the majority of workers in Thailand, where informal jobs and incomes are not even protected by law, let alone subject to social dialogue. And in the modern sector, the already low level of worker representation has fallen still further during the crisis.

The first year in the decade that saw the number of trade unions decline was 1997, most likely because of the initial effects of the crisis, which began in July of that year. The greatest share of the decline occurred in the industrial province of Pathum Thani, where the number of registered unions decreased from 148 to 87 over the 12-month period leading up to December 1997. In addition, the relative shares of different types of trade unions have shifted as a result of the downturn and the business closures associated with it. Most of Thailand's unions are at the enterprise level and are thus more vulnerable to downturns than other types of labor unions. The share of industry unions in the total had been increasing gradually in the 1990s, rising from 43–44 percent of all unions in the first half of the decade to 46 percent in 1996 and 48 percent in 1997. The number of enterprise unions declined by 9 percent in 1997, while the number of industry unions held almost constant.

Tripartism and the Crisis

Chief among the weaknesses of tripartism in Thailand is the fact that it is only as strong as its constituent parts. Fragmented interest groups with low membership levels risk being unable either to command the credibility or to develop the voice they need to become effective representatives of the country's work force. In practice this weakness is often reflected by the government's domination of tripartite consultations, as well as by the unsound criteria that are used to appoint worker representatives to tripartite bodies. Both weaken the effectiveness of tripartism. The Thai trade unions' own evaluation of the weakness of tripartism is shown in box 10.5.

As noted earlier, at least in quantitative terms the crisis seems to have weakened some of the building blocks on which social dialogue is founded, such as union membership. At the same time, however, the crisis has served to reinvigorate or add momentum to joint approaches to problem solving. Two tripartite mechanisms—the National Wage Committee (NWC), which sets the minimum wage, and the National Labor Development Advisory Council, which provides policy advice on matters relating to the labor market—have the most influence on employment policy.

BOX 10.5
Tripartism in Labor Affairs: Problems from a Labor Perspective

1. Workers and trade union members continue to be unaware of their legal rights.
2. Worker representatives to tripartite bodies are elected regardless of their qualifications, resulting in a low level of competence and easy domination by employers and government representatives.
3. Many tripartite mechanisms contain too many government appointees. Government appointees should not be allowed to serve concurrently on more than two tripartite committees.
4. Some worker representatives are not honest. A transparent monitoring process needs to be developed to ensure that these individuals act in the interests of the members they represent.
5. Rivalry exists among worker representatives on tripartite bodies, weakening labor's ability to speak with one voice.
6. The number of votes cast is not proportionate to the size of the membership but to the number of unions, further fragmenting labor's voice in the tripartite machinery.

Source: Labour Congress of Thailand seminar, March 18, 1999, Chaingrai, as reported in *The Labor Chronicle*, Series 272 (June 1999), p. 7.

The Minimum Wage

An important instance of the influence of social dialogue on employment policy in Thailand is the mechanism for determining wages. Wages in Thailand are guided by a nationally determined, three-tier minimum wage that is adjusted frequently. The NWC, which comprises equal numbers of worker, employer, and government representatives, recommends these adjustments. The government has endorsed virtually every one of the NWC's recommendations. At the microeconomic level, wage setting in Thai enterprises can be thought of as the outcome of the ways market forces are mediated—that is, through individual bargaining power and unilateral employer decisionmaking. This interpretation is logical in light of the scant coverage provided by collective bargaining. But it is also misleading, as the existence of the NWC shows.

The NWC is Thailand's primary vehicle for social dialogue related to macroeconomic policy choices. The crisis in Malaysia and Korea has led to national social dialogue over a broad range of macroeconomic policy variables, including fiscal and monetary policies. But social dialogue in Thailand does not embrace this full range of macroeconomic policy variables and is instead confined to minimum wage adjustments. As a tool of employment policy, moreover, the NWC cannot be considered a full-blown incomes policy mechanism. By law a minimum wage adjustment must take into account inflationary effects and anticipate employment impacts, among other factors, but it is not within the NWC's mandate to set inflation targets or employment objectives.

During the crisis period, Thailand has entered into various loan commitments from international financial institutions to be directed toward social programs. One of these is a loan from the Asian Development Bank (ADB) that is to be disbursed in tranches on fulfillment of certain conditions to which the Thai government has committed itself. One such commitment is to review labor policy, including wage policy. To this end, the ADB commissioned a study by an independent consultant (Brooker Group 1999). Concurrently the NWC formed the Subcommittee on Wage Policy and commissioned its own study, in this case, from the ILO (ILO forthcoming).

Both studies found that increases in the minimum wage during the 1990s may have been excessive and were one of the factors—or perhaps the only factor—behind the erosion of export competitiveness of labor-intensive industry in Thailand.[10] Three aspects of the minimum wage trend in the 1990s are of particular relevance here. First, the real minimum wage trend in the 1990s was generally in line with trend growth of the economy as a whole, especially as minimum wage growth lagged behind economic growth rates during the 1980s. To the extent that a problem existed, it lay in the rate of productivity growth. Thailand's high overall productivity growth rate reflected a shift in labor resources away from relatively low-productivity activities (such as rural agriculture) into more productive ones (such as manufacturing). Within sectors, however, the growth of labor productivity varied substantially. It was lowest in manufacturing.

The second aspect concerns the effect of minimum wage adjustments on earnings distribution in the 1990s. The largest increases in real wages were concentrated at the low end of the earnings distribution ladder. In effect minimum wage policy was compressing the wage structure. This compression was in turn reflected in a gradual increase in the ratio of the minimum to the average wage. Because a high percentage of the Thai work force is concentrated at or around the minimum wage rate, the adjustments affected a sizable share of the work force. Workers earning the minimum wage were affected directly, while workers at enterprises that adjusted the prevailing wage structure felt the indirect effects.

Third, the minimum wage in Thailand clearly applies to far more people than just new entrants to the work force and unskilled laborers. Trade union officials complained that workers with both tenure and skill acquisition were stuck at the minimum wage. Employers complained that they could not reward employees through an internal, enterprise wage policy, because adjustments to minimum wage displaced the capacity of companies to offer enterprise-based wage increases. A substantial share of workers remains at the minimum wage despite three or four years of on-the-job experience.

One unintended outcome may perhaps have been the displacement of enterprise-based mechanisms for wage determination. Wage setting at the national level may have supplanted a role that workers would otherwise seek through enterprise-based social dialogue via trade unions and collective bargaining. This displacement could be undermining efforts to organize labor by making unions less attractive. But as we have seen minimum wage adjustments have also partly displaced employers' efforts to develop more comprehensive, enterprise-based wage policies. Minimum wage policy can also work against the development of performance-based personnel policies that seek to build commitment and improve productivity, among other things.

In response to the crisis, the minimum wage remained at its 1997 level in 1998 and 1999. The crisis also prompted a legal reform of the minimum wage-fixing mechanism with a view to decentralizing responsibility for setting the minimum wage to the provincial level. While the NWC retains its responsibility for setting a national basic minimum age as the lowest threshold or wage floor, the provinces themselves recommend, on the basis of several statutory criteria, a provincial minimum wage. The NWC accepts, amends, or rejects the provincial recommendation. Local minimum wage fixing is intended not only to help fine-tune adjustment, bringing costs in line with capacity to pay, but also to help attract investment capital.

The Thai trade unions have voiced much of the concern over this decentralization. The provincial wage committees would be, like the NWC, tripartite. But trade union organization is particularly thin outside the Bangkok metropolitan area and the contiguous five provinces.[11] Finding legitimate, competent workers to sit on the provincial committees will be difficult.[12] The new system is as yet untried, but decentralization will be piloted in ten provinces. While it is too early to claim that the trade unions' concerns will prove unjustified, the opposite scenario also remains a possibility—that is, the growth of provincial wage committees may become an opportunity to extend and strengthen tripartism in Thailand.

In addition to these ongoing mechanisms, other instances of tripartite consultation have occurred, often of some significance. One of these was the process of formulating the comprehensive government response to the crisis. The prime minister undertook this initiative in December 1997 by forming the Committee on the Alleviation of Unemployment. Irrespective of the substance of the seven-point plan that emerged, the process itself cannot be described as a truly robust example of tripartite social dialogue. Worker and employer representation on the committee was minimal, and it is unclear what contribution their presence made to the final shape of initiatives proposed. Each of these initiatives was government driven, with various ministries given responsibilities for each point. Program implementation did not specify a role for the social actors, nor has the process of implementation been an explicitly tripartite or dialogic one.

Bipartism and the Crisis

The crisis has altered at least some of the underlying conditions that previously hindered the development of sound industrial relations at the enterprise level. In 1996 and again in 1998, Thailand's worker and employer organizations committed themselves to two codes of conduct. The 1996 Code of Conduct on Labor Relations stipulated that the parties find ways to reduce industrial conflict and set up mechanisms for bipartite dialogue. The 1998 Code of Practice to Promote Labor Relations outlined ways of reducing workplace costs and committed parties to the principle that bipartite social dialogue is a necessary prerequisite to any decision affecting employees' welfare in the workplace. The legal reforms under way for both the private and public sector labor relations frameworks are also a positive sign.

One of Thailand's most important employer organizations, the Employer Confederation of Thai Industries (ECONTHAI), has noted that one effect of the crisis has been to improve the flow of information and communication in the workplace. Box 10.6 provides a few examples of such improvements.

There is a growing awareness in Thailand of the need to improve social dialogue at the enterprise level, for three reasons. An argument can be made that the climate for industrial democracy is strongly shaped by attitudes toward democratic governance in society at large. The process of constitutional reform in Thailand enjoyed wide popular support and par-

BOX 10.6
Social Dialogue, the Enterprise, and Adjusting to the Economic Downturn: Some Examples[a]

Banking

Background

Unionized. 26,000 employees, 60 percent union members. Affected by crisis, but less severely than other major banks.

Effect of the crisis on labor-management dialogue

Marked increase in communication and information exchange through joint consultations. High degree of cooperation reported (first institutionalized by an abrupt 1984 business downturn in the bank).

Adjustment measures reached through dialogue

- No involuntary layoffs.
- Bankwide restructuring and negotiated internal redeployment.
- Reduction of bonus from 5–6 months to 3 months.
- Early retirement package:
    Minimum age 45 + 15 years' tenure for employees
    Minimum age 50 + 20 years' tenure for supervisors
- Reduction in salary increase from 8–10 to 3 percent.
- Union withholds new demands for the present time.
- Increased skills training for employees and labor law training (paid for by bank) for union officials.

Automotive

Background

Unionized. 4,000 employees. 70 percent union members. Sharp decline in business during the crisis.

Effects of crisis on labor-management dialogue

Marked increase in communication and information exchange through joint consultative committees.

Adjustment measures reached through dialogue

- Ongoing negotiations over wages and reductions in bonus.

(Box continues on the following page)

BOX 10.6   *(continued)*

- 1996 no-strike declaration in return for greater company support for union.
- No involuntary layoffs.
- Increased job rotation.
- Increased company-funded training in parent company.

Automotive

Background
Unionized. 380 employees, 65 percent union members
Sharp decline in business. (No new work from May 1997 until May 1999.)

Effect of crisis on labor-management dialogue
Marked increase in communication and information exchange through joint consultative committees.

Adjustment measures reached through dialogue
- No involuntary layoffs thus far.
- 3 months' leave at statutory pay reduction (Nov. 1998–Jan. 1999)
- Hiring freeze.
- Elimination of bonus.
- 10 percent wage reduction for those earning over 5,000 baht per month.

Garment

Background
Unionized. 1,200 employees.
Export oriented. Crisis has had no effect on business.

Effect of crisis on labor-management dialogue
Collective bargaining takes place each year. Because business has been stable throughout the crisis, the frequency of labor-management dialogue has not changed.

Adjustment measures reached through dialogue
- No layoffs. No additional measures.

BOX 10.6   *(continued)*

Garment

Background
Nonunion. 700 employees.
Export oriented. Crisis has had only slight impact on business.

Effect of crisis on labor-management dialogue
No effect reported. Company practices high degree of communication through informal channels, including frequent management meetings with employee groups and frequent meetings between supervisors and subordinates.

Adjustment measures reached through dialogue
- Current hiring freeze.
- No involuntary layoffs.
- Staff reduction through attrition.
- Units asked to reduce production costs.
- Efforts increased to find new product markets.

a. Names of enterprises have been withheld by request.
Source: Siengthai 1999b.

ticipation, and the new Constitution of 1997 is unambiguous in its support for freedom of association and democratic governance. If anything, the crisis has reinforced these trends.

Social Dialogue in the Philippines

Several features distinguish labor market adjustment in the Philippines. First, at least in terms of GDP growth during the crisis, the Philippines has fared better than the other countries. Growth prior to the crisis was proceeding at an impressive rate but was still lower than elsewhere in East Asia, reaching an estimated 5–6 percent in 1995–96. The Philippine economy did not contract with the crisis like economies elsewhere in the region. Instead, it stagnated. The social impact has nevertheless been severe: the peso's devaluation resulted in a 25 percent decline in per capita income in dollar terms, and the Department of Labor and Employment (DOLE) recorded over 120,000 layoffs in the first 10 months of 1998.

Second, as in Thailand, the number of unionized workers in the Philippines is extremely low—11 percent of all workers. Further, collective bargaining agreements cover only around one-seventh of this small group of unionized workers. "Real" union representation thus covers only about 1.5 percent of the total work force.

The third distinctive feature of the Philippine labor market is the weak growth of manufacturing employment during the precrisis years. Despite steady increases in foreign direct investment, employment in manufacturing held constant in the years prior to the crisis and declined when the crisis struck. Among the factors at work here is the effect of trade and investment liberalization on enterprise strategies. Downsizing (or *rightsizing*) had become very much a part of the vocabulary of adjustment even before the crisis. While the fear of retrenchments has become generalized in many countries since the crisis, the fear—and the factual basis for it—were already present in the Philippines.

The focus of dialogue at the enterprise level (and the subject of most recent disputes) has therefore been on employers' interest in greater numerical flexibility. In addition to retrenchments, employers have sought numerical flexibility through increased use of nonregular employees. The share of nonregular employees in total employment rose from 20 percent in 1992 to 28 percent in 1997.[13] Employers subcontract, hire casual labor (temporary or fixed-term contract workers), and in what has been a contentious matter throughout the 1990s, use labor-only contracting, leasing rather than hiring employees.

Two issues are of particular concern with labor-only contracting. First, wages and other terms of employment are then left up to the contractor and thus are often less favorable to workers than they would be if the workers were employed directly by the leasing firm. Second, such workers are largely unorganized. Trade unions attached to enterprises generally cannot recruit them because leased workers are not employees.

In effect the Philippines now has two tiers of workers: *core* and *periphery*. Core workers have permanent employment, receive training and other investments in human resource development, and are continually upgrading their skills. But the number of periphery workers is increasing because of the financial crisis, and this group of casual, temporary workers is bearing the brunt of the adjustment effort. In the environment of increasing casualization and subcontracting that characterizes the Philippine labor market, labor laws are often violated (Kuruvilla and others 1999).

A fourth feature of industrial relations in the Philippines (but one that it arguably shares with Korea) is its adversarial tradition. Legalism pervades labor-management relations and manifests itself in a variety of ways. Traditionally arbitration has been required to resolve disputes the parties themselves cannot conclude. Delays in dispute resolution impede the development of closer, more cooperative labor-management relations, and opposing parties simply become more firmly entrenched. Legalism, inherited in part from the U.S. model on which Philippine labor law is based, breeds mistrust.

Finally, labor-management relations at the enterprise level are poorly developed in the Philippines. Like Thailand, the Philippines has a fragmented trade union movement, with federations and individual unions vying with each other for members and thus unable to speak with a unified voice. There are seven national labor centers, a number of unaffiliated independent unions, and one workers' mutual aid society. At the national political level, one indication of the disadvantages of such fragmentation is that trade unions have been unable to advance the candidacies of all but one of their choices in the recent legislative elections. At the enterprise level, interunion rivalry has often resulted in an inability even to elect a union to represent employees.

Signs of Crisis-Induced Change in Philippine Industrial Relations

The recession may be changing industrial relations in the Philippines, moving it toward a more cooperative model. Perhaps the most significant sign of this change lies in the growing recognition that existing practices are inadequate. In this regard, the well-publicized dispute surrounding Philippine Airlines (PAL) in 1998 is an excellent example of this new awareness (box 10.7).

As noted, sensitivity to the negative effects of numerical flexibility appears to have been increasing in the Philippines even prior to the crisis. Kuruvilla and others (1999) find that for a small sample of enterprises, the crisis has induced a change of attitudes among trade unions and that unions have become more accepting of the need for retrenchments—or at least more accepting of the inevitability of job loss. In some instances, the trade union bargaining agenda has shifted away from simple resistance to discussing severance pay and retraining opportunities. The pattern has not been uniform, however, and in some instances acceptance has not meant acquiescence. This lack of agreement is reflected in at least some workers'

BOX 10.7
The Philippine Airlines Dispute

Philippine Airlines' (PAL) service was disrupted by a major dispute in mid-1998. Both domestic and overseas flights largely ceased for three weeks in June during a strike by the pilots' union over the issue of retrenchment. PAL management summarily fired over 600 pilots when they failed to respond to a return-to-work order issued by the Secretary of Labor and Employment. The courts have not ruled definitively on the legality of either the pilots' strike or the management's sweeping layoffs, although the pilots' union has filed suit to have its pilots reinstated. PAL was able to hire enough replacement pilots to restore limited service. In June the company filed for protection from its creditors under procedures similar to Chapter 11 in the United States. When the 1998 PAL labor dispute widened in July to involve the ground crew and support staff, it became a landmark labor relations event. Newly elected President Joseph Estrada took a direct hand in dispute mediation efforts in order to save the financially troubled carrier. Through his involvement, an unprecedented agreement was reached that required the union leaders to suspend their collective bargaining agreement for 10 years in exchange for employee stock shares and seats on the PAL board. . . . The union also agreed to a limited layoff plan (many fewer than management first announced). Although a strike was averted, a dissident faction within the ground crew union soon challenged the agreement in court as an illegal infringement of worker rights.

Source: U.S.D.O.L. 1999, p. 10.

---

disaffection with their organizations, as the increase in wildcat strike actions shows.

Evidence from the Kururvilla study suggests that both labor and management have become more willing to negotiate and cooperate because of the crisis. In the small sample of enterprises in the study, management has often tried to improve communications and cooperation in the workplace. This change complements the unions' greater realism when it comes to job losses and competitiveness concerns. In particular, the crisis appears to have galvanized greater support for labor-management councils (LMCs), originally initiated under the administration of Corazon Aquino. LMCs have since become vehicles for improving labor-management relations with less conflict. Effective LMCs may even be able to defuse workplace tensions, quicken the pace of collective bargaining, and improve the quality of enterprise industrial relations. But LMCs also pose a danger: non-union enterprises can use them as a strategy to avoid allowing unions in the workplace.

Efforts at the National Level

The fragmentation of the Philippine labor movement among competing labor federations has impeded the development of a clear and comprehensive labor strategy that addresses the effects of the East Asian financial crisis and other workplace issues. There have nonetheless been some positive signs of change here, too.

First, the DOLE joined in a national tripartite process involving employers' organizations and two labor federations that in February 1998 produced a national social accord. The fact that the accord was initiated by the employers themselves rather than by the government is a particularly healthy sign. The accord committed trade unions to forgoing strikes during the economic downturn in return for an employer pledge to avoid retrenchments as often as possible. After a six-month trial period, the tripartite process and accord were renewed, and the process was replicated at the regional level, resulting in a number of regional accords.

While the accords mark an important instance of a shift in the national mood toward greater social cooperation, gauging their effect in more concrete terms is difficult. The number of industrial disputes has decreased in the Philippines, but the trend has been secular and during the crisis more likely reflects a loss of bargaining power than anything else. Some indications suggest that a number of small and medium-size enterprises see themselves as exempt from the national social accord. These firms have used layoffs, pay cuts, and the elimination of benefits as emergency measures (U.S. Department of State 1999). In an effort to ensure that the accord is more than just a statement of good intentions, in late 1998 the DOLE established a monitoring program to evaluate and promote compliance. Other changes have occurred within existing tripartite mechanisms. The administration of Joseph Estrada broadened worker representation on the national Tripartite Industrial Peace Council to include representatives from six labor federations instead of just two.[14] The result could be greater cooperation among trade union federations.

Efforts to overcome labor fragmentation are evident among trade unions as well. The Brotherhood of Union Presidents in the Philippines, which was formed in 1996 to promote unity among trade unions, groups together union presidents from both independent local unions and labor federations. Another group, SULOG, is a loose coalition of unions representing workers in several industries. The group has developed a bargaining procedure for unions to use when faced with retrenchments and closures and also lobbies at the national level for lower interest rates to protect local industries (Kuruvilla and others 1999).

Responsibility for setting a minimum wage in the Philippines has been decentralized since 1999 and now rests with tripartite regional wage boards. As in Thailand, adjustments to the minimum wage can be influential, since the minimum wage approximates the average wage for a large share of the formal work force. When the crisis made itself felt in 1997, employer and government pressure to keep wage adjustments low prompted the major labor federations to boycott the tripartite process. By 1998, however, the labor federations had not only rejoined the tripartite process but had agreed to delay demands for higher wages in view of the recession and rising number of layoffs.

A final and hopeful indication of the changing mood in labor-management relations in the Philippines is the continuing trend toward finding alternatives to litigious, third-party dispute resolution. The DOLE has shown less eagerness to intervene directly in disputes on the grounds that such intervention crowds out the development of bipartite dispute resolution. It has increasingly promoted voluntary mediation and conciliation through the National Mediation and Conciliation Board and other less legalistic private and public alternatives to dispute resolution.

Social Dialogue in the Republic of Korea

The crisis in Korea has been characterized by two developments. First, there has been a marked increase in the number of industrial disputes, almost all of them over the issue of retrenchment. Second, the country has undertaken a historic and largely successful experiment in national tripartite social dialogue on solving the economic and social problems the crisis has caused.

Strikes increased from 78 in 1997 to 129 in 1998, and because the 1998 strikes were concentrated in large enterprises undertaking restructuring, the number of employees involved was substantially more—232 percent—than in 1997. In part in response to this increase, the Tripartite Commission and the Tripartite Social Agreement were established, and by early 1998 Korea had become the region's best example of the effectiveness of social dialogue in managing economic crises. Several factors lie behind this initiative. First, the election to the presidency of the country's foremost democracy advocate signalled the beginning of broad social participation in national decisionmaking.. Second, the new administration knew that making choices would be difficult in the middle of the country's worst postwar economic crisis. A crippling general strike under the previous administration in December 1996 had been largely triggered by the absence of dialogue (last-minute, late-night reforms were made to the labor law over the unions' objections). The strike was a pointed reminder of the consequences of excluding organized labor from discussions of reform.

Third, an immediate catalyst for dialogue was a condition of the US$57 billion IMF loan that mandated improved labor market flexibility. This condition meant simply that layoffs should be made easier so that enterprise restructuring could occur.[15] In Korea, however, lifetime employment is the cultural norm and is strongly protected by labor laws. Anticipating that widespread social unrest would arise from any attempt to violate this cultural and legal norm, the IMF urged the Korean government to enter into dialogue with the trade unions.

As of January 2000 the Korean economy has staged a rather stunning recovery. Despite a contraction in 1998, it grew at over 7 percent in 1999. By the end of 1999 unemployment had declined from its peak of 8.7 percent to just over 6 percent in May 1999. However, enterprise adjustment may not have gone far enough, and with growth resuming, the pressure to undertake further restructuring may have eased.

The Tripartite Process

The early accomplishments of the tripartite process in Korea are unique among the experiences we have seen, for several reasons. First, as in Malaysia, the Korean tripartite discussions have involved private actors in the full range of macroeconomic and macrosocial decisionmaking. But the Korean Tripartite Commission, unlike tripartite Malaysian groups, is characterized by the balanced participation of workers, employers, and the government. On the worker side, the Tripartite Commission includes not only the well-established Federation of Korean Trade Unions (FKTU), but also the more militant Korean Confederation of Trade Unions (KCTU). Inclusion on the committee provided the KCTU with substantial support in its ongoing process of establishing itself in Korean political and economic life.

Second, the tripartite mechanism, inaugurated by then President-elect Kim Dae-Jung in January 1998, explicitly staked Korea's chances for recovery on the tripartite process itself. Recognizing both that substantial sacrifices would be required and that the various economic reforms envisaged would be unlikely to succeed in the absence of cooperation, the commission initially produced the Tripartite Joint Statement on Fair Burden-Sharing in the Process of Overcoming the Economic Crisis. A third and related distinguishing feature of the process was the contentiousness surrounding the issue of layoffs. These would be required not only as an adjustment response to the recession, but also in the context of what was anticipated to be widespread restructuring—all in a labor market unused to retrenchment.

A fourth feature of the tripartite process was that it rapidly became an institution. The Tripartite Commission became a permanent feature of the industrial relations landscape, backed by legislation and strengthened by its own secretariat. It would involve government participation at high levels and would include the main economics and labor ministries. And finally, the outcome of the dialogue was quickly and concretely legislated into action. The Social Agreement reached on February 7, 1998, resulted in no fewer than 90 recommended actions, many of which have been acted upon (box 10.8).

Indicators of Success

The first round of the accord process resulted in a trade-off, with each side giving up something to gain something more. The labor federations acceded to legal reforms that make dismissals "on managerial grounds" easier and expand the use of temporary and fixed-term workers. In return the government expanded workers' rights to freedom of association (most notably to teachers) and undertook to increase the amount of unemployment benefits, the length of time workers can collect them, and the number of workers they cover. While employers gained the labor market flexibility they sought, they also committed themselves to greater managerial transparency, a reform of accounting practices, and to enterprise restructuring that would continue to use dismissals as a measure of last resort requiring consultations with employee representatives. The government played a catalytic role in the process of promoting one of the new administration's priority objectives—the reform of industrial relations.

In view of the magnitude of the economic downturn, and despite the increase in labor disputes, both the process and the outcome of the Tripartite Commission have played important roles in promoting economic reform while maintaining relative social stability. At the very least, the parties themselves credit the initiative with having played such a role. The Korean Employers' Federation (KEF) observed in August 1999:

BOX 10.8
Highlights of the 90-point Agreement of
the First Tripartite Commission

Management transparency and business restructuring
- Promote management transparency
- Improve the corporate financial structure
- Establish a responsible management system
- Promote business competitiveness

Price stabilization

Employment stabilization and unemployment policy
- Expand and improve the unemployment insurance system and extend coverage
- Provide support for retired and unemployed workers
- Strengthen employment services
- Expand vocational training
- Promote job creation
- Foster employer efforts to stabilize employment
- Reduce the number of migrant workers
- Increase necessary financial resources

Extension and consolidation of the social security system

Wage stabilization and the enhancement of labor-management cooperation

The crisis was a big shock to both labor and management. Over the last year, 23,000 enterprises have gone bankrupt because of high interest rates and stagnation of sales. Workers were faced with huge wage reductions (a minus 2.5 percent wage increase) and severe unemployment. The unemployment rate of 2 percent soared to 8.7 percent and the number of unemployed amounted to 1.8 million. *However, industrial relations remained relatively stable because of sustained social dialogue* [emphasis added] (Kim 1999).

If the process can be credited with having contributed to social stability during the crisis, a related question is whether it can also be credited with having improved the economic climate. Recent research has explored the possibility of an empirical relationship between indicators of successful dialogue (such as the resumption of participation in the tripartite dialogue and the successful resolution of industrial disputes) and indicators of macroeconomic performance (such as stock market performance and foreign direct investment) (Hayter 1999). Preliminary results show a convincing positive correlation between the indicators of social stability and economic performance. Investors appear to respond positively to indications of social stability and therefore to the mechanisms that generate such stability.

The tripartite discussions have included a number of procedural matters in industrial relations at the enterprise level, particularly the need to improve labor-management cooperation. One of the 90 specific points from the commission's first round involved the establishment of an organization designed to monitor labor disputes at enterprises, eliminate unfair labor practices, and promote cooperation between labor and management.

Some Continuing Challenges

The Korean dialogue has not been uniformly smooth or consistently productive. At various points over the past 19 months, one or both of the labor federations have withdrawn from the process, complaining that the pace of economic restructuring and retrenchments was proceeding without consultations with trade unions. Employers have also withdrawn, charging that the government was trying to make a deal with the trade unions that excludes the employers. The government too has either berated the major enterprises for dragging their feet on restructuring or sought legal penalties against trade union officials for engaging in legal strikes. As of January 2000 the FKTU has made a commitment to continue the dialogue with the government and employers to promote recovery and avoid industrial disputes. The KCTU, however, remains outside of the process.

Labor federations in Korea very clearly derive their power from the large industry- and enterprise-based unions that bargain at the enterprise level, where retrenchments occur. A very early consequence of the first round of tripartite dialogue—when the deal was struck that made layoffs easier—was that the rank and file of the KCTU, angered by the agreement, forced the top leadership to resign. The agreement was reached in the first half of 1998, when the number of retrenchments had reached its peak. The first real test case of the agreement occurred in the context of projected mass layoffs at one of Korea's *chaebols*, Hyundai. As with the PAL strike in the Philippines, the 1998 strike at Hyundai Motors was widely publicized. It became symbolic of the challenges of enterprise restructuring, a litmus test of the economic reforms of Kim Dae-Jung's government. In May of 1998 the company announced its plans to cut 4,830 jobs and sent layoff notices to 1,538 workers. Sporadic strike action began in late May and culminated in a plant occupation and 36-day strike in July and August. The KEF (1998b, p. 2) commented:

> The final agreement reached by the union and Hyundai stipulated that there would be only 277 retrenchments. On the face of it, the trade union appeared to have gained the advantage, as the majority of those affected were female cafeteria workers whose jobs had been secured by another company. The Korean Employers federation took a dim view of the government's conduct, the agreement, and the trade union's right to strike in the first place. It condemned the government for having what it called a "double standard" on labor reform—that is, urging businesses to restructure to remain competitive while at the same time urging them to minimize layoffs. The KEF saw the agreement as a dangerous precedent that threw into doubt the government's ability to make the labor market more flexible and that rewarded union militancy, especially since the employers believed that the strike had been illegal.

For the government, however, the significance of the strike lay elsewhere. The trade union had officially acceded to the principle of layoffs (box 10.9).

With the worst of the recession apparently behind it, Korea may find that economic growth will help to relieve some of the destabilizing tensions in the tripartite process. As a result of the first social agreement, replacement in the event of unemployment now applies to about 40 percent of the Korean work force instead of 9 percent (the prevailing level when the crisis struck), a factor that may encourage labor market flexibility. Discussions within the tripartite commission have clearly slowed, yet the agenda of reform measures to be discussed is lengthy and includes issues such as flexibility in hours of work and the activation of labor-management consultations at the regional and industry levels. While the mood in regard to increasing the momentum of dialogue is relatively optimistic, no clear steps have been taken in this regard. Plans to anchor the tripartite process firmly within Korean legislation will likely serve as a catalyst to stabilize and strengthen the social dialogue.

Looking to the Future

Interest in creating and maintaining mechanisms that allow popular participation in political and social institutions is clearly rising. These institutions include those pertaining to labor market governance at both the

---

BOX 10.9
Highlights of the Agreement in
the Hyundai Motor Company Dispute

1. Of the 1,538 workers who had been officially notified that they would be dismissed, only 277 would be retrenched "for managerial reasons."
2. The company would give consolation bonuses to the dismissed workers according to the following schedule: workers employed for less than 5 years, 7 months' pay; workers employed from 5 to 10 years, 8 months' pay; and those with more than 10 years, 9 months' pay.
3. The 1,261 workers exempted from dismissal would take 18 months of unpaid vacation leave. After one year, they would receive retraining courses from an external organization.
4. The government would be asked to take measures to cover the living expenses, reemployment, and job training of the dismissed workers. The company would try its best to see that the dismissed workers were employed by other Hyundai subsidiaries.
5. Redundancy dismissals would not be made for two years. The union would prepare a Joint Declaration on Industrial Harmony and the Avoidance of Disputes that focused on industrial peace.

---

national and enterprise levels and in some instances (Korea and Malaysia, for example) at the sectoral level. This interest is evident not only in the various examples of "crisis management" discussed here, but also in the important legal reforms that have either been completed (Korea and Indonesia) or are well under way (Thailand) (box 10.10).

These signs are also evident in the emergence of entirely new dialogue mechanisms in Cambodia, Indonesia, Korea, Malaysia, the Philippines, and Thailand.

It remains unclear whether every country can maintain the momentum of the shift toward greater political openness and dialogue. There is some concern that the momentum is inversely related to the pace of economic recovery—that with a return to growth, some of the pressure to keep channels of dialogue open will diminish and the incentive to improve labor-management institutions will slow. This risk is perhaps greatest in those countries where efforts at social dialogue during the crisis have been one-time events rather than ongoing institutionalized mechanisms. The risk is

BOX 10.10
Trade-offs Resulting from Social Dialogue at the National Level

Korea
- The *Tripartite Social Accord* (February 1998) made layoffs easier to promote economic restructuring and at the same time improved social protection by expanding social security.
- Layoffs are an adjustment measure of last resort and require negotiation.
- Second Tripartite Commission is examining the possibility of making adjustments in working time as an alternative to retrenchment.

Philippines
- Social Accord on Industrial Harmony and Stability (February 1998) between Employers' Confederation of the Philippines and two major labor federations provided for six months' mutual restraint on layoffs and industrial disputes.
- At regional level, the Department of Labor and Employment (DOLE) organized tripartite conferences on saving jobs and industries that culminated in regional social accords.

Singapore
- Tripartite Panel on Retrenched Workers (February 1998) provides for the development of a network for information on potential retrenchments in order to match those being dismissed with job vacancies. Also explores alternatives such as redeployment, adjustments in working time and wages, and training possibilities; access to advice on training opportunities.
- The Skills Redevelopment Program (December 1996) is being used as an alternative to layoff. The program, spearheaded by the National Trade Union Congress (NTUC) and funded by the government, allocates training subsidies of up to 80 percent of course fees and 70 percent of the absentee payroll for training conducted during normal hours of work.

Malaysia
- Tripartite Committee on Retrenchment set up to monitor retrenchment. Encourages reference to Malaysia' Code of Conduct for Industrial Harmony—in particular, the passages relating to retrenchment that stipulate a range of alternatives.

(Box continues on the following page)

BOX 10.10   *(continued)*

Malaysia   • Government introduces legislation (following consultations
(continued)   with the National Labor Advisory Council) requiring em-
                     ployers to notify the Labor Department of prospective layoffs
                     one month in advance. New law also to expand married
                     women's participation in the labor force by making hours of
                     work more flexible.
                   • Malaysian Trades Union Congress (MTUC) and Malaysian
                     manufacturing employers establish databank on job vacan-
                     cies for retrenched workers.

---

smallest in economies where reforms strengthening relevant social institutions have been legally sustained (such as Indonesia, Korea, and Thailand).

Social dialogue and sound economic outcomes are positively related and
thus move together. Arguably, the examples in this chapter have demonstrated that fact. Korea provides the most extensive and influential example
of tripartite management of the effects of the East Asian financial crisis, and
it is the Korean economy that has shown the strongest recovery. Yet as with
most research topics, much remains to be learned about the causal relationship between effective social dialogue and recovery from exogenous
shocks such as the 1997–98 crisis. Finally, the institutions on which formal
social dialogue are based in the countries under review are weak, sometimes
profoundly so. Collective bargaining coverage is very slight—smaller even
than trade union representation, which itself is often exceedingly weak.
Trade unions themselves are inadequately financed, and in most cases their
already small membership has been further weakened by the financial crisis. Labor movements are fragmented in the Philippines, Thailand, and increasingly in Indonesia. This weakness impedes the development of a coherent voice for workers and their employers that could influence the social
dialogue. Thus, while this chapter has maintained a tone of guarded optimism, it also makes clear that worker and employer organizations must be
strengthened if social dialogue is to progress beyond the "crisis" stage.

Notes

1. Duncan Campell is a Senior Industrial Relations Specialist with the International Labour Organization's East Asia Multidisciplinary Team in Bangkok.

2. So, too, in other countries. In the Republic of Korea, three-way dialogue is a primary government objective, and key economics ministries also participate. In the still-indeterminate case of Indonesia, the tripartite machinery is expected to extend beyond the Manpower Department to include government departments in commercial sectors. The composition of Cambodia's new National Labor Advisory Committee has similarly broad government participation.

3. One can be concerned about (that is, affected by) a decision but thoroughly ignorant of the information on which the decision can and ought to be made. For this reason, effective three-way dialogue relies on the competence and knowledge of the participants.

4. Much of the vocabulary and many of the concepts in this section are based on Hirschman (1970) and Freeman and Medoff (1984).

5. In the process, traditional notions of hierarchy are being eroded, since hierarchies can be barriers to the flow of information. See, for example, Hirschhorn (1998).

6. In the immediacy of the crisis, of course, the value of participation lies in the search for least-cost adjustment paths and ways to minimize the chance for social unrest.

7. Formal in the sense of provided for and regulated by law (unlike, for example, quality circles).

8. The Labor Protection Act of 1998 also mandates the establishment of employee welfare committees and promotes tripartite mechanisms.

9. One factor that helped keep retrenchments low was the buffer provided by the 11–12 percent of the Malaysian work force that is foreign. Repatriating foreign workers to safeguard the jobs of Malaysian citizens became explicit policy. Foreign workers were concentrated in particularly hard-hit sectors, such as construction. Job losses there, however, as well as for foreign workers generally, typically resulted from unrenewed contracts rather than from retrenchment. One implication of this scenario is that the number of jobs lost in the recession was a multiple of the number of those actually retrenched.

10. The ILO study also finds that this explanation is not entirely satisfactory, for a number of reasons. For example, capital-intensive exports in which labor accounts for a small share of total costs also saw a decline in export performance. In addition, the United States, as a major market for garment exports, has been reducing its reliance on Asian (not just Thai) sourcing in favor of closer-to-home, intraregional trade arrangements. And Thai exchange rate policy (rather than wage policy) greatly inflated real wage increases in Thailand when denominated in dollars.

11. The regional distribution of Thailand's trade unions suggests that they are geographically dispersed. In fact, however, when we look at Bangkok and the five industrial provinces surrounding it, we can see clearly that trade unions continue to be highly concentrated in the greater Bangkok metropolitan area.

12. Employers, on the other hand, have sometimes expressed concern that in the absence of effective worker voice on the provincial committees, the govern-

ment will be compelled to adopt the workers' viewpoint on wage setting, to the detriment of employers' concerns about labor costs.

13. Perhaps in part because in 1997 the DOLE further eased restrictions on hiring short-term contractual workers.

14. Two representatives had been the norm under the two previous administrations.

15. As might be expected, there is debate over the degree to which Korean *chaebols* are overstaffed. The Korean Employers' Federation (KEF) estimated in late 1998 (well after the legal reforms making layoffs easier had taken effect) that large enterprises continued to retain about 20 percent redundant labor (338,000 jobs), while the banking industry was hoarding 33 percent of employees it did not need (132,000). At the same time, the KEF estimated the labor shortages in small- and medium-sized enterprises at 120,000 (KEF 1998a).

References

Brooker Group. 1999. "Labor Policy in Thailand." Bangkok.

Freeman, R., and J. Medoff. 1984. *What Do Unions Do?* New York: Basic Books.

Hayter, S. 1999. "Social Fundamentals and the Asian Financial Crisis." Geneva: International Labor Office.

Hirschhorn, L. 1998. *Reworking Authority: Leading and Following in a Post-Modern Organization.* Cambridge: MIT Press.

Hirschman, A. 1970. *Exit, Voice, and Loyalty.* New York: Oxford University Press.

ILO (International Labour Organization). Forthcoming. "Minimum Wage Policy in Thailand." Bangkok. Working paper.

_____. 1999. "Evolution of the Asian Financial Crisis and Determination of Policy Needs and Responses." Governing Body Document 274/4/2. Geneva.

Kim, Jung-Tae. 1999. "Globalization and Industrial Relations: Employers' Perspective." Note prepared for the Asian Regional Tripartite Seminar on Globalization and Industrial Relations, Bangkok, August.

KEF (Korean Employers' Federation). 1998a. *Industrial Relations and the Labor Market.* Seoul.

_____. 1998b. *Quarterly Review* XV(III).

KLI (Korea Labor Institute). Various years. *Quarterly Labor Review.*

Kuruvilla, S., Erickson, C. 1999. "Industrial Relations and Globalization in the Philippines." Bangkok: International Labour Organization, East Asia Multidisciplinary Team. Unpublished manuscript.

Lee, E. 1999. *The Asian Financial Crisis: The Challenge for Social Policy,* (Geneva: International Labour Organization.

MOLSW (Ministry of Labor and Social Welfare). Various years. *Yearbook of Labor Statistics.* Bangkok.

NESDB (National Economic and Social Development Board). 1997. The Eighth National Economic and Social Development Plan, 1997–2001. Available at www.nesdb.go.th/New_menu/plan 8e/content_page.html.

Peetz, D., and T. Todd. 1999. "Industrial Relations and Globalization in Malaysia." Bangkok: International Labour Organization, East Asia Multidisciplinary Team. Unpublished manuscript.

Piriyangsan, S. 1998. "Bipartite Systems: Workplace Relations in Thailand." Paper prepared for International Labour Organization, East Asia Multidisciplinary Team, Bangkok.

Rodrik, D. 1999. *The New Global Economy and Developing Countries: Making Openness Work.* Washington, D.C.: Overseas Development Council.

Siengthai, Sununta. 1999a. *Employee Relations during the Crisis.* Bangkok: International Labour Organization, East Asia Multidisciplinary Team.

_____. 1999b. *Industrial Relations and the Recession in Thailand.* Bangkok: International Labour Organization, East Asia Multidisciplinary Team. *Foreign Labor Trends, Philippines.* FLT 99-4.

U.S.D.O.L. (United States Department of Labor). 1999. *Foreign Labor Trends, the Philippines.* FLT 99-4. Washington, D.C.

11 Japan's Experience with Employment Policy

Naoyuki Kameyama

E24
J64 J65
J68 J26

THROUGHOUT THE 1990s the Asian economies were caught up in a whirlwind of change, moving from stagnation to rapid growth, collapse, and recovery. During this period virtually all the Asian governments sought to construct an effective employment policy. These efforts inform our analysis of Japanese employment policy since World War II.

The East Asian economies are closely linked. But at the beginning of the 21st century they have reached separate stages of development and face very different employment (and unemployment) problems. Cultural differences and historical experiences have affected industrial relations in the region, making comparisons difficult. For this reason our analysis of the Japanese experience does not advocate best practices in employment policy. Instead we offer—in their historical context—lessons learned over the course of the last half-century. During the past 50 years Japan has experienced a number of economic scenarios that have required the government to respond to a variety of employment problems. We hope that other Asian countries will be able to draw on this experience as they struggle to cope with their own employment issues.[1]

In 2000 Japan is enduring a serious recession. The country has experienced periods of economic adjustment and stagnation before, even during the era of high economic growth era that lasted from the early 1960s to the mid-1970s. But the length and severity of the most recent recession, which began in 1992 with the collapse of the bubble economy, are unlike anything Japan has experienced before. The unemployment rate has reached nearly 5 percent. The collapse of lifetime employment, traditionally considered a fact of life for Japanese workers, is widely discussed. This chapter does not address the accuracy of such a claim, but the fact that it is being put forth at all is indicative of the degree to which the current recession has prompted new thinking about employment policies.

Understanding the new direction Japanese labor policy must take requires us first to systematically reassess the employment policies of the last half-century. These policies are best examined as a group rather than individually. We emphasize the systemic aspects of employment policy, since developing effective policies in East Asia requires thinking systemically and making coordination and consistency the top priorities. Our approach to post–World War II employment measures and policies also supports the development of effective targeting, a key component for policymakers to consider.

We evaluate Japanese employment policy for each of the five distinct economic periods the country has experienced since World War II:

- The immediate postwar recession (1945–60);
- The period of high economic growth (1960–73);
- The downturn induced by the oil crisis from the mid-1970s until the mid-1980s;
- The "bubble economy" of the late 1980s;[2] and
- The Heisei recession, which began in 1992.

The Postwar Recession (1945–60)

World War II destroyed the industrial base of the Japanese economy. The economic and labor resources that had been devoted to the war industry were no longer needed, and strategic bombing by the Allied Forces destroyed a vast number of industrial facilities and disrupted urban functions near the end of the war. The Economic Stabilization Board estimated the economic damage Japan sustained as a result of the war at 65.3 billion yen (as of August 1945)—approximately one-fourth of the country's production capability.

The Postwar Labor Market [3]

At the end of the war, Japan had a huge population of unemployed and underemployed workers, in part because of the vast number of people returning from overseas and the demobilization of the country's soldiers. This rapid increase in the productive population was noted in the 1950 census, which found that the number of people ages 15–59 had risen sharply during the previous decade, climbing from 40.7 million in 1940 to 44.7 million in 1947 and to 47.4 million in 1950. Further complicating the situation was the exodus of workers from war-damaged cities to farming and fishing villages. This internal migration resulted in population overflows and stagnation in the rural sector. In addition a large number of people were forced to stop working because of injuries suffered during the war or because they had been discharged from war industries.

Statistics Bureau data from a survey conducted in April 1946 found that 1.6 million people who could and wanted to work could not find a job. Among those working, underemployment was a major concern. The number of employees, self-employed individuals, and family business workers who worked only 1–7 days per month was 1.96 million. Another 4.32 million worked only 8–19 days each month. These figures indicate that one out of every four Japanese laborers was unemployed or underemployed immediately following the end of the war.

The employment situation continued to deteriorate in 1948, when the government adopted the Dodge Plan to counter inflation. This plan involved large-scale administrative readjustments and corporate consolidations that resulted in massive retrenchments. As many as 155,000 employees in administrative organizations and 435,000 employees in private companies were discharged. The Japanese economy did not begin to grow substantially until June 1950 and the start of the Korean War. The war effort meant huge orders for "special procurements" and an increase in exports. The manufacturing production index, which had been assigned a value of 100 for June 1950, had expanded to 135 by December of that year. Private investment also gained momentum. Ultimately the Japanese economy would grow at more than 10 percent annually for the three years of the Korean War. By 1954 manufacturing production had expanded by 225 percent, and after 1954 Japan enjoyed a long period of sustained economic prosperity, interrupted by brief periods of economic adjustment.

Unfortunately the renewed growth did not immediately eliminate the unemployment and underemployment problems, for a number of reasons. First, dramatic demographic changes in 1950–53 resulted in a growth rate of 10.9 percent in the labor force, which expanded from 65.5 to 68.3 percent of the total population. Second, although manufacturing production expanded, productivity also increased, holding down the demand for additional workers. Furthermore, those firms that did hire additional workers did so on a temporary basis because they feared that wartime procurements would not continue. Third, some underemployed people gradually became unemployed, raising the number of unemployed workers from 0.44 million in 1950 to 0.47 million in 1952. By March 1952 some 30 percent of the total workforce was underemployed.[4]

Postwar Employment Policy

The common belief in every industrial nation after World War II was that the ultimate objective of a national employment policy should be to achieve full employment. Japan was no exception. The definition of full employment, however, was unclear, and policymakers soon narrowed the scope of employment policy to address the issue of underemployment. The government's policy had a number of objectives:

- To reduce the need for underemployment, which exists to supplement inadequate household income;
- To reduce the possibility that unemployment could be disguised as underemployment and thus remain invisible;
- To reduce the scope for employer practices that encouraged underemployment through self-employment and family work; and
- To absorb underemployed people as the economy developed.

In addition to these efforts to address underemployment, the government created jobs directly (through public works programs), provided job-matching services, and offered training through public employment services.

PUBLIC WORKS. Large-scale public works programs were initiated in late 1946 for the purpose of recovering national lands, developing social capital, and absorbing the unemployed. The projects were not well targeted, however, and the projects absorbed only about half as many unemployed people as had originally been planned. The main problem was that the regions where public works were undertaken were not the areas where unemployment had increased dramatically. More than 70 percent of public works projects in those days were concentrated in farming villages and mountain areas in order to meet the urgent need to expand food production and improve the infrastructure around mountains and rivers. Although the top priority was eliminating unemployment, local farmers who were not among the unemployed were hired for these public works jobs.

The deflationary Dodge Plan in 1948 cut government spending and shrank the public works programs. Tight economic policy and corporate restructuring led to considerable layoffs in the private sector and increased unemployment. The Emergency Unemployment Countermeasures Law was established in May 1949 to address this problem. These emergency measures created new work relief projects to absorb unemployment. This time, however, the unemployed were required to register at a Public Employment Security Office (PESO), which then dispatched them to work sites. At their peak in the early 1960s, these public works projects employed 350,000 people.

Although they were much better than earlier programs at reaching truly unemployed workers, this generation of public works programs was not successful in providing only temporary employment. Those employed at work relief projects included large numbers of middle-aged and senior workers for whom reemployment was difficult, self-employed people who were having a hard time making a living, and women who had never worked before. Many of these workers tended to stay in public works jobs for a long time. Accordingly various changes were made to the projects, including establishing eligibility criteria that would screen out certain groups, enhancing work supervision, and setting wage differentials according to performance and skills, among others. These revisions met with limited success. As the workers got older, their capabilities declined, and the tendency to remain longer with the projects increased. Worker profiles collected in 1960 revealed the average age to be 50 and the length of service to be six years (MOL 1960).

Another problem with the public works projects was that most of the jobs did not require many skills, and the wages were low. This problem was in part the result of the prevailing thinking on employment policy. One of the main objectives of postwar macroeconomic policy was resolving what was called the "employment problem."[5] The main purpose of the economic policies designed to meet this goal was to produce and expand overall demand for goods and services. As demand for goods and services increased, the demand for labor would increase along with it. The policies did not target certain groups among the unemployed or certain jobs or industries, and the programs were not aimed at any particular category of unemployed worker. The goal of such general manpower policies was to provide a job for every worker, regardless of technical skills, knowledge, or physical or mental condition.

JOB-MATCHING SERVICES. The government of Japan also sought to reduce unemployment by matching job seekers and employers through the PESOs.[6] These offices were also responsible for dispatching workers to the public works programs and were preparing to implement the newly established unemployment insurance system. Given the very high numbers of unemployed persons at this time and these additional responsibilities, Japan's public job-brokering services were not nearly as successful as had been envisioned. The Ministry of Labor provided guidelines and training for staff in these offices in order to improve operational techniques.

The Period of Rapid Economic Growth (1960–73)

Full-scale economic growth did not begin until the 1960s, when the government developed the National Income Doubling Plan. The goal of the plan was to improve living standards substantially and work toward full employment. To meet these goals, the plan identified five core needs:

- To improve social capital;
- To provide guidance in the establishment of an advanced industrial structure;
- To promote trade and international cooperation;
- To improve worker skill levels and promote science and technology;
- To put an end to the "dual industry" economic structure and enhance social stability.[7]

The second issue merits particular attention. The basic idea was to improve productivity at the industry or individual firm level and to revamp the industrial structure by emphasizing high-productivity rather than low-productivity sectors.

Planning for a High-Growth Labor Market

In order to create an advanced industrial structure, the labor force distribution across industries would have to be changed. The plan projected that the total number of workers would expand by 7.15 million during the 1960s. That estimate assumed the following shifts among industries: a decline in the number of workers in primary industries of 4.91 million; an expansion of workers in secondary industries of 5.62 million; and an expansion in tertiary industries of 5.32 million workers. In addition, the plan forecast annual average real economic growth of 7.8 percent during the decade, resulting in annual average economic growth of 10.9 percent.

The number of workers in primary industry declined almost in accordance with the plan, with an actual drop of 4.5 million (table 11-1). This decline had been expected to occur as older workers retired and a shift in

TABLE 11.1

Employment by Sector, millions[a]

	Employed persons					
	Total (A)	Primary industry	Secondary industry	Tertiary industry	Employees (B)	B/A
1950	36.0 (100)	17.5 (48.6)	7.8 (21.7)	10.7 (29.7)		
1955	41.0 (100)	15.4 (37.6)	10.0 (24.4)	15.6 (38.4)	17.8	(43.4)
1960	44.3 (100)	13.4 (30.2)	12.4 (28.0)	18.5 (41.8)	23.7	(53.5)
1965	47.3 (100)	11.1 (23.5)	15.1 (31.9)	21.1 (44.6)	28.8	(60.9)
1970	50.9 (100)	8.9 (17.5)	17.9 (35.2)	24.1 (47.3)	33.1	(65.0)
1973	52.6 (100)	7.1 (13.5)	19.3 (36.7)	26.2 (49.8)	36.2	(68.8)
1975	52.1 (100)	6.6 (12.7)	18.4 (35.3)	27.1 (52.0)	36.5	(70.1)
1980	54.7 (100)	5.3 (9.7)	19.2 (35.1)	30.2 (55.2)	39.7	(72.6)
1985	57.8 (100)	5.1 (8.8)	19.9 (34.4)	32.8 (56.7)	43.1	(74.6)
1990	62.2 (100)	4.5 (7.2)	21.0 (33.8)	36.7 (59.0)	48.4	(77.8)
1991	63.3 (100)	4.2 (6.6)	21.6 (34.1)	37.5 (59.2)	50.0	(79.0)
1992	64.0 (100)	4.1 (6.4)	21.9 (34.2)	38.0 (59.4)	51.2	(80.0)
1993	64.3 (100)	3.8 (5.9)	21.7 (33.7)	38.8 (60.3)	52.0	(80.9)
1994	64.0 (100)	3.5 (5.5)	21.5 (33.6)	39.0 (60.9)	52.4	(81.9)
1995	64.1 (100)	3.4 (5.3)	21.3 (33.2)	39.4 (61.5)	52.6	(82.1)
1996	64.9 (100)	3.3 (5.1)	21.2 (32.7)	40.4 (62.2)	53.2	(82.0)
1997	65.2 (100)	3.5 (5.4)	21.3 (32.7)	40.4 (62.0)	53.9	(82.7)
1998	65.1 (100)	3.4 (5.2)	20.5 (31.5)	40.8 (62.7)	53.7	(82.5)

[a]Figures in parentheses are percentages of total labor force.

Source: Bureau of Statistics, Annual Report on the Labor Force Survey.

labor occurred between the agricultural and industrial sectors. In the end, however, the decline was the result primarily of improvements in productivity brought on by mechanization and a drop in off-farm jobs among rural households. In fact a large idle workforce was created in farming villages, and these unemployed workers eventually drifted into manufacturing and construction industries as migrant workers, creating a new employment problem. In secondary industries, the number of workers expanded by 5.62 million. Employment also rose in tertiary industries by 5.32 million, nearly in line with the plan. Importantly, no major social friction occurred during these shifts, thanks to the supply of new graduates during this period—over 20 million.

This period was not without its employment problems, however. Facilitating the movement of the workforce among regions became a priority, as did coping with the structural unemployment that developed as certain industries declined. Furthermore, near the end of the period of rapid economic growth the supply of labor slowed. New employment policies were needed to address this problem, which had begun to hinder economic growth.

Employment Policy during the High-Growth Period

Rapid economic growth during this period meant a gradual reduction in unemployment and underemployment, but it soon created a new problem—a labor shortage. The Employment Measures Law enacted in July 1966 addressed this issue by attempting to lift restrictions on the labor supply. Based on this law, the First Employment Measures Basic Plan was drawn up in March 1966 with the subtitle "Preparation for Full Employment" (JMOL 1966). The Basic Plan stated that:

> . . . . the objective of employment policy is to enable everyone to hold a job that is suitable to their aptitude and fully utilizes their capabilities, as well as to improve the economic and social position of these workers in order to contribute to the development of the national economy.

Although it incorporated qualitative aspects into the objectives, the policy was primarily intended to facilitate economic growth—the "development of the national economy."

The concept of full employment in Japanese labor policy continued to be expanded and modified. The Second Employment Measures Basic Plan (January 1973), subtitled "For a Rewarding and Comfortable Working

Life," recognized both a quantitative and qualitative dimension to the concept of full employment and began to incorporate qualitative objectives into employment policy:

> Amid high economic growth, employment conditions improved significantly in terms of volume. However, not all workers were given the opportunity to develop their abilities throughout their lives, hold jobs suitable to their capabilities, or to find something they could live for at the workplace. The reality is a long way from true full employment, both in terms of quality and quantity.

Despite reduced unemployment, the public works programs initiated in the aftermath of World War II continued to employ significant numbers of workers. In order to phase out this reliance on work relief projects, the Employment Security Law was revised in 1963. The government also shifted its employment policy priority from absorbing unemployment to promoting employment growth in other sectors. The PESOs focused on placing the unemployed in existing jobs whenever possible, falling back on public works jobs as a last resort.

Thanks to these measures and the long-lasting economic prosperity that had begun in 1964, the number of workers participating in public works projects declined. In 1971 the Promotion of Employment of Middle and Older Workers Special Measures Law had prohibited the absorption of any additional unemployed people, marking the beginning of the end of public works projects.[8] Although the existing projects did not take on any new workers, people who were already employed tended not to leave, resulting in a decline in capabilities and skills and more work-related accidents as the workers aged.

The job-brokering role of the PESOs increased in importance as demand for labor grew. The offices were required to help reallocate the labor force among industries, jobs, and regions. In particular, demand for labor concentrated on new graduates, mainly junior high school graduates.[9] The goal was to direct these new graduates to growth industries in accordance with their abilities, aptitudes, and desires. An amendment to Article 19 in the Employment Security Law allowing PESO staff to guide job seekers to positions in other regions was important in meeting the growing demand for labor.[10]

As labor shortages developed in some regions—either because of a lack of workers or because of a lack of workers with certain skills—companies diversified their recruiting activities to cover a wider area. Accordingly, in

1964 the government established the Labor Market Center. This center was intended to serve a number of purposes:

- To integrate PESO functions nationwide;
- To provide broad information on job vacancies and required skills in a timely and efficient manner;
- To facilitate job placement outside local areas; and
- To enhance clerical functions in areas such as the administration of unemployment insurance.

The opening of the Labor Market Center made it possible to quickly identify job seekers whose skills match specific job openings. The center also implemented a system to calculate the unemployment insurance eligibility period for job seekers with more than one former employer. In the 1990s an on-line system was established to link employment organizations all over the country and facilitate data transfers.

Employment programs of this era did not fail to target older workers. The economy was growing and the employment situation had improved substantially, but many older workers were still unemployed. The government introduced unique measures for this group instead of handling older workers as average job seekers. The Employment Security Law, which was substantially revised in 1963, contained new provisions for unemployed workers ages 35 and older. Five types of employment promotion measures were made available to these workers: long-term vocational training (six months to a year), short-term vocational training (about three months), occupational adjustment training (about six months), vocational courses (about two months), and job search courses (two to six months).

One of the first selective manpower policies designed to target a particular group of displaced workers was the 1959 Displaced Coal Mine Workers Temporary Measures Law (box 11-1). Other targeted initiatives were implemented during this period, including the 1958 Temporary Measures Law for Displaced Workers from Stationary Troops and the 1960 Law for Employment Promotion of the Disabled. Gradually selective policies began to replace general employment policies.

The First Oil Crisis and the Period of Low Growth (1973–85)

The first oil crisis at the end of 1973 pushed up the prices of commodities and raw materials (mainly oil), severely damaging oil-importing economies

BOX 11.1
Assisting Displaced Coal Mine Workers

As Japan has virtually no oil resources, coal was the main source of energy during industrialization. But in 1950 the country began to shift to oil as its primary fuel. Demand for coal fell rapidly, resulting in a chronic recession in the coal industry. From 1960 to 1970 the number of coal miners fell by 230,000, or around 80 percent (see table).

Changes in the Number of Coal Miners

	Existing coal miners	Number of workers	Average age
1955	750	349,578	34.5
1960	622	302,768	36.1
1965	222	151,455	38.5
1970	74	70,565	41.2
1975	35	36,073	42.3
1980	25	30,070	42.4
1985	26	24,082	41.2
1990	21	7,977	42.4
1995	13	4,629	43.0

Source: Ministry of International Trade and Industry, Annual Report on Energy Production and Supply/Demand.

In 1959 the Displaced Coal Mine Workers Temporary Measures Law was established to fundamentally rationalize the coal mining industry. This law was revised in 1962 to integrate and downsize the industry and assist coal miners in finding other jobs. The law had several key elements designed to help the displaced workers.

First, all coal miners received job application "pocketbooks" designating the holders as displaced coal miners. Employers hiring pocketbook holders received incentives and housing allowances. Miners who started their own businesses received incentives or debt guarantees to help in borrowing start-up funds. This method of subsidizing the employment of a targeted group of workers became an important pillar of Japan's employment policy.

Second, the government implemented a method of introducing jobs available in other areas to displaced coal miners. Under Japan's Employment Security Law,

(Box continues on the following page)

BOX 11.1   *(continued)*

job seekers were to be matched with local jobs. Finding employment opportunities for displaced coal mine workers in the same locale was difficult, however. The result was a plan that provided workers with information about jobs in other areas in order to encourage geographic mobility and promote reemployment. Relocating workers received funds for moving and housing.

Third, the government provided various educational and training programs to make job transfers easier. Unemployed miners remained eligible for job-brokering services and vocational training longer than for other unemployment benefits.

Fourth, public works projects were specifically designed for displaced miners. Initially, most displaced coal workers were absorbed into existing projects, including (among others) river development, erosion control, and land development. If 85 percent or more of employees in any one project were displaced coal miners, their wages were heavily subsidized (80 percent of a separately set unit price).

These measures highlight the shift in Japanese employment policy from absorbing unemployment by providing jobs directly to subsidizing employment in other sectors. This approach dominated employment policy in and after the 1960s. Coal mining companies cofinanced these measures when miners were involved (55 yen per ton of coal produced), setting an important precedent for future policy.

---

such as Japan. Conserving resources and changing the industrial structure became important policy issues in Japan as this scenario unfolded.

The Labor Market Situation

Rapid price increases attributable to the oil price shock dampened economic growth and employment expansion during this period. Energy-intensive, large-scale heavy industries such as steel and shipbuilding, which had previously taken the lead in the Japanese economy, faced a crisis. Companies responded by reducing their workforces. As the industries most seriously hit by the recession were geographically concentrated in company towns, local unemployment emerged as a key problem.

Although Japan's unemployment rate had remained at the 1 percent level for 20 years, it reached 2 percent in 1976. This decline marked the beginning of permanent unemployment due to structural rather than merely cyclical influences. The unemployment rate has not dipped below 2 percent since this time. Another key labor market trend became visible during this period as well—the aging of the workforce.[11] The growth rate of the senior population was perceived to require specifically targeted programs (box 11-2).

Employment Policies during the Low-Growth Period

The rapid escalation of unemployment and underemployment forced the government to reassess the Second Employment Measures Basic Plan after only two years. In December 1975 the Ministry of Labor's Employment Policy Research Institute proposed an employment policy for the decade beginning in 1975 that focused on full employment amid slow economic growth. This proposal took note of the country's success in reaching levels close to full employment during the period of economic growth. This achievement allowed the government to join the governments of other industrial economies in using monetary and fiscal policies to smooth fluctuations in the business cycle.

The Third Employment Measures Basic Plan, drawn up in June 1976, was based on these ideas. This plan's basic concepts included employment measures appropriate to an environment of slow economic growth. These measures had two objectives. First, they were designed to promote changes in the structure of both the labor force supply and the country's industries. But the second objective—balancing supply and demand in the labor force—was the more important, addressing as it did the question of how to lower the unemployment rate.

UNEMPLOYMENT INSURANCE AND ADJUSTMENT SUBSIDIES. A comprehensive employment insurance scheme was implemented in 1975, replacing the 1947 system that guaranteed livelihoods during periods of unemployment. In addition to providing income support, the new system established a fund for "active" labor market programs such as vocational training and employment subsidies. Employers and employees would each pay 50 percent of the costs of unemployment insurance.

The research group that designed the insurance scheme also created an employment adjustment subsidy scheme. The Ministry of Labor had established the group in May 1973 to develop an active manpower policy under the assumption that Japan's economic growth would continue. Early in its deliberations, however, the group realized that a national economic slowdown or recession might soon create an unemployment situation that

BOX 11.2
Employment Measures for Older Workers

Employment measures for older workers began in earnest in 1975 with discussions surrounding the extension of the mandatory retirement age. In the mid-1970s the most common retirement age at large companies was 55, clearly too young in terms of working capabilities. By the mid-1980s the retirement age had risen to 60 (see table 1). The extension of the mandatory retirement age ignored individual differences among older workers. Depending on the situation and the choices available, older people have different ambitions, possibilities, and needs with regard to continuing employment.

Extending the retirement age to 60 did not solve the employment issues surrounding older workers. In August 1979 the Fourth Employment Measures Basic Plan was drawn up with the goal of expanding employment opportunities for people in their early 60s who have a strong desire to work. The plan had three basic goals:

- To extend employment by raising the retirement age again, with consideration for the conditions of individual companies;
- To promote reemployment after formal retirement or extend the working period by providing employment subsidies and other benefits to companies willing to hire retired and older workers (see table 2); and
- To promote self-employment, part-time employment, and various other forms of employment utilizing older workers' experience and abilities, with consideration for individual preferences.

In 1986 the government enacted a law that prohibited companies from setting the retirement age lower than 60. But this prohibition did not automatically guarantee employment until the age of 60. According to a 1992 government survey,

BOX TABLE 1 Changes in the Mandatory Retirement Age
(% of company surveyed)

	55 years or younger	56 to 59 years	60 years or older
1980	39.7	20.1	39.7
1985	27.1	17.4	53.3
1990	19.8	16.1	63.9
1995	7.6	6.5	85.9
1999	0.5	0.4	99.2

Source: Ministry of Labor, Employment Management Survey.

BOX TABLE 2 Allowances Provided for Elderly Employment

	1991	1992	1993	1994	1995	1996	1997	1998
Continual employment system implementation incentive								
(1,000 yen)[a]	8,330,400	9,939,200	10,421,200	11,437,200	11,371,600	22,377,200	5,601,000	14,910,280
(Number of companies)	1,591	1,894	2,008	2,133	2,226	4,371	4,542	11,279
Elderly employment environment development incentive								
(1,000 yen)				24,000	139,500	207,500	323,500	268,000
(Number of companies)				6	32	66	114	99
Special job seekers' employment development subsidy								
(1,000 yen)	31,331,327	30,500,582	29,937,076	40,946,946	73,869,654	48,913,556	40,083,306	
(Number of people)		91,428	89,007	93,239	113,961	112,774	114,923	
Elderly employment continuation subsidy (100 million yen)					120	370	570	770
(Number of people)					75,416	84,447	89,487	100,174

Source: Ministry of Labor Statistics.

[a] Owing to a revision of the system in 1987, the numbers for continual employment system implementation incentives are not directly comparable to those prior to 1987.

[b] Only the amount paid with regard to employment of the elderly has been included.

(Box continues on the following page)

BOX 11.2   *(continued)*

people in the age group 60–64 who were employed at the age of 55 and who worked until the mandatory retirement age constituted only 37.7 percent of all workers that age.

Employing older workers became even more urgent when the minimum age to begin receiving an old-age pension was raised from 60 to 65. The easiest way to way to maintain income for workers between the ages of 60 to 65 would be to secure continued employment at the same company. Maintaining older workers on the job would also be an effective way of utilizing job skills accumulated over a long career. Recognizing that skill levels are not always enhanced as workers age, however, the government chose to establish a system of subsidies for continued employment (or reemployment) rather than mandating another increase in the retirement age to 65.

The plan established a "continual employment system" that would provide subsidies for five years to companies setting the retirement at age 60 or older that employed workers continuously until the age of 64. The subsidies amounted to between 1 million and 2.5 million yen each year, depending on the size of the company. In addition, eligible companies where workers ages 60 and older made up at least 10 percent of the workforce could receive 30,000–40,000 yen per month for each elderly worker for a maximum of five years.

These subsidy systems have repeatedly been revised and expanded. Companies have used the subsidies as a vehicle to establish and improve a proper environment for retaining and hiring senior workers. In addition these subsidies have facilitated the development of measures to expand employment overall. These measures require an established employment insurance with ample funds and therefore cannot be used as a model for every country. However, the idea behind the subsidy system may be applicable to active labor market programs in many countries.

Japan is also taking a unique approach to elderly employment with its Elderly Employment Centers. Local governments in areas with more than 6,000 workers are eligible for a center, but they must prove that there is substantial need for one. As many as 1,417 centers had been set up as of the end of September 1999. The volunteer-run centers, which receive government subsidies to cover some management expenses, offer temporary, short-term jobs in areas that support the local community, including professional services such as editing and translation, simple clerical work, and supervisory services for local parks and parking lots. Workers at the centers may have specialized skills, or they may provide basic household services. Revenues are distributed among member workers. The centers not only help find jobs but also offer members something fulfilling to do during the transition from work to full retirement.

simple adjustment measures could not handle. Such a scenario would require measures aimed at preventing unemployment as well as assistance for companies that needed help adjusting their employment levels.

The result of this thinking was the Employment Adjustment Subsidy Scheme. It was designed to intervene before companies were forced to lay off workers rather than to support workers after they had been laid off. The program provides subsidies to companies that use temporary layoffs or retraining rather than permanent layoffs during times of economic crisis. Employers pay the costs of the program, and any subsidies the companies receive cover a portion of workers' wages. In effect the system supports employment maintenance in the internal labor market by subsidizing a company's efforts to retain its workers. Recognizing the importance of the scheme, the Diet implemented it before the rest of the unemployment insurance program in order to prevent large-scale retrenchments. Such subsidies soon became an integral part of Japan's employment policy.

PUBLIC EMPLOYMENT SERVICES. In order to handle the deteriorating employment situation after the first oil crisis, the government enhanced the functions of the PESOs. In 1974 it began requiring companies contemplating substantial layoffs to notify the local employment office in advance. This regulation was designed both to provide the local office with timely and accurate information about the employment situation in its area and to facilitate ability to provide needed services. In addition the unemployment insurance payment system was automated and the PESOs reorganized. The staff's level of expertise was enhanced through training. Finally, job-matching services were revamped to include a classification system that speeded up the process of referring job seekers to appropriate jobs.

The Current Recession (1992–2000)

Japan's "bubble economy" collapsed in 1990. Because this period lasted so long, the subsequent recession has been the most serious since the end of World War II. The proximate cause of the recession is generally viewed as the accumulation of too many bad debts by financial institutions. The subsequent tight financial market has led to stagnation in investment and individual consumption. At the same time the Japanese economy has lost its relative advantages in mass production and certain "low-cost" industries.

In 2000 Japan is still struggling to escape from the recession, and the employment and unemployment situations are more difficult than ever.

The unemployment rate reached 4 percent in 1998 and 4.9 percent in June 1999—very close to the 5 percent level.

The Current Labor Market Situation

Several scenarios are being played out on the personnel front. Some workers have been discharged on a nonvoluntary basis from failing companies. Others have applied for early retirement and have left their jobs voluntarily, only to experience difficulties in finding new employment. The number of workers who have left their jobs voluntarily is about the same as the number who have been discharged (table 11.2). Three groups in particular have been unable to find employment: new graduates, those trying to enter the labor market to maintain their standard of living, and seniors reentering the market after a year or more.

With so many challenges to address in the labor market, many observers are beginning to realize that the conventional employment measures taken in the past may not be sufficient in the current situation. The situation Japanese society faces is the result of structural change, and the view that a drastic change in employment policy is necessary is becoming dominant. Concern is growing that the current employment policy framework functions merely as a collection of individual employment policy measures and that what is required is a complete reassessment and reorganization of the country's employment policy at the macro level. As a result, although the eighth version of the Employment Measures Basic Plan was designed to cover six years (1995–2000), it has had to be reassessed during that period. A ninth Employment Measures Basic Plan has been developed to cover the years from 1999 to the early part of the 21st century.

Employment Policies

The diverse populations of unemployed workers that characterize the current recession complicate employment policymaking. Conventional policies for the unemployed, which primarily emphasize maintaining employment in the in-house labor market, are being rethought. The idea of lifetime employment that has long permeated the Japanese labor market is one of the most important issues. It has long been believed that once people enter a company in Japan, they work for that company for their entire career.[12] As a result, labor mobility among companies is very low. If the government develops policies that take this employment relationship as the norm, the primary emphasis is naturally on in-house measures. However, lifetime em-

TABLE 11.2
Why Unemployed Workers Had Left Their Jobs
(percent)

	15–24 years	25–34 years	35–44 years	45–54 years	55 years and older
Office closure, corporate bankruptcy, closure of a self-employed person's business	1.9	5.4	12.8	7.0	8.8
Dismissal, restructuring	5.7	8.1	15.4	25.6	19.1
Mandatory retirement, termination of the employment contract period	5.7	5.4	5.1	4.7	44.1
Potential future instability in the workplace	3.8	5.4	5.1	4.7	1.5
Deterioration of working conditions	13.2	9.5	12.8	7.0	4.4
Working conditions that differ from those expected prior to obtaining the job	11.3	9.5	5.1	4.7	0.0
Want to try some other job	18.9	12.2	7.7	4.7	1.5
Marriage, childbirth, childcare	3.8	9.5	5.1	2.3	0.0
Nursing care, housework, commuting, illness, etc.	5.7	9.5	7.7	9.3	4.4
Other	30.2	25.7	23.1	30.2	16.2

Source: Bureau of Statistics, Special Labor Force Survey, August 1999.

ployment arrangements are changing. In 1998 Japanese companies hired 5.4 million workers, nearly 60 percent of them from other industries and companies (MOL 1998). This trend is not just a recent phenomenon but one that has developed slowly over the past 30 years.

Clearly the current recession demands a different kind of thinking. The industrial structure needs substantial restructuring, and the labor force needs to be reallocated among different industries. New growth areas must be supported in an effort to create and expand employment opportunities. In addition, workers must be able to develop occupational skills that match the new employment opportunities. And finally, the government needs to develop measures to shorten the duration of unemployment.

The latest employment policy envelope is depicted in figure 11-1. The new agenda reflects a policy shift from employment protection to job creation and support for job transfers. Policy initiatives announced by the Ministry of Labor in January 2000 divide policies into three categories. The highest priority is employment development, which encompasses the following four initiatives: subsidies to promote employment creation among small and medium-scale enterprises (SMEs), a program targeting middle-age and senior workers, support for infant industries, and public works projects for local communities.

The first initiative is the Special Subsidy System for Regional Employment Creation by SMEs. The Ministry of Labor and prefectural governments work together to choose promising companies from among SME start-ups to serve as models for the program. The program provides wage subsidies and allowances for employee benefits, human resource development, and the development of an employment management system. While past subsidies have been used to target particular groups of workers such as the elderly, this system targets particular *companies* that could be important employers. According to Ministry of Labor statistics, the program provided companies with subsidies for over 60,000 workers in 1999.

The second measure, the Special Subsidies for the Emergency Creation of Employment, targets unemployed middle-aged people or seniors who leave their jobs on a nonvoluntary basis in regions where employment conditions have deteriorated badly (see table 2, box 11-2). A subsidy of 300,000 yen per person is available to companies that hire such workers. In 1999 this system was implemented in Okinawa, the Kinki district, and the southern Kanto district. To date the program has received subsidy applications for 932 people.

The third measure is the New Growth Area Employment Production Special Incentive, which provides financial support to companies in 15

FIGURE 11.1
Changes in Employment Policy

Measures to support employers' efforts to maintain employment

- Employment Adjustment Subsidy (financial assistance to employers that retain employees through such methods as temporary leave, transfers, and training rather than dismissing workers).

Measures to support the upgrading of human resources

Efforts to foster high-level and creative human resources to help companies develop new business areas and produce goods with higher value added.

- Promotion of the upgrading of public vocational training.
- Support for the upgrading of training in private companies.
- Promotion of vocational skills development for white-collar workers.
- Promotion of individual vocational skills development.

Measures to support the creation of jobs

Support for business ventures, new business development (small and medium-sized companies), and job creation in districts with severe employment conditions.

- Assistance with personnel expenses for workers engaged in establishing or developing new business areas; assistance for expenses and wages relating to in-house and outside training; and wage subsidies for districts with severe employment conditions.
- Special matching system for venture businesses, human resources, and consulting.

Measures to support labor shifts without unemployment

Support for shifts in labor among companies and industries brought about by changes in the industrial structure.

- Subsidies for companies that make efforts to reassign workers, transfer workers to other companies, introduce places of reemployment, conduct training, and make capital investments.
- Implementation of consulting, seminars, and so forth for companies transferring or receiving workers.

growing industries such as information and communications. The Ministry of Labor expects to create employment opportunities for 150,000 people through this measure.

The fourth measure is the Emergency Local Employment Special Subsidy, under which each prefectural government provides a portion of the funds required to develop public works projects around the needs of local communities. Owing to the problems associated with public works projects implemented just after World War II, the Japanese government has long held negative views about work relief projects designed to absorb the unemployed directly. However, as high unemployment continues, the government has decided to implement measures to absorb some unemployed workers (but within certain time limits). The Ministry of Labor expects to create employment opportunities for about 290,000 people through this measure.

It is too soon to comment on the effectiveness of these measures, but the shift in focus this new policy represents—from employment maintenance to job creation—is significant. We can demonstrate this point even more clearly by assessing the employment adjustment subsidy that has been provided since October 1999. As stated earlier, supplementing and enhancing the employment maintenance function with employment adjustment subsidies has been the main pillar of employment policy in Japan since the late 1970s. But given the risk of hindering labor mobility by subsidizing stagnant industries, the government has revised its criteria for targeting industries. The primary focus is now on providing support for "temporary employment adjustments in response to economic fluctuations" (MOL 1999). By excluding industries that are stagnant for structural reasons, the government sets the stage for transferring workers from these industries to growing industries.

In addition to measures that address the specific concerns of the current recession, the government continues to rely on the services of the PESOs. The PESOs play an important role in adjusting the balance between supply and demand in the labor market. As of 1999 Japan had 478 PESOs (26 main offices and 111 branch offices) with a total staff of 13,000 people. The labor force adjustment system for supply and demand is currently being restructured in order to determine which types of information and methods of job placement are most effective in the current employment situation. And in 1999 the Worker Dispatching Law and the Employment Security Law were revised to liberalize the types of jobs that employment agencies are allowed to handle. The revision has made it possible for private employment exchange services to broker jobs, and as a result private employment agencies are becoming increasingly active. It is too soon to judge the impact of either the restructuring or the new laws, however.

Directions for the Future

Japan is at a major turning point in terms of its employment policies. The problem is not just that previous policies have lost their effectiveness and that new policies need to be drawn up. Rather, the policy structure itself must be reconceptualized. Lessons from history are essential to this endeavor. The situation requires analyzing the objectives of previous employment measures, the effectiveness of the methods applied, and the targets of such measures. To this end this chapter has analyzed employment policies through four phases of Japan's economy since World War II.

During the initial postwar period, employment policy focused on direct job provision to absorb the masses of unemployed workers. The programs functioned essentially as government transfer programs, providing primarily simple low-wage jobs to anyone in need of income. While such policies may be appropriate for short-term relief, they do little to stimulate productive, long-term employment. In Japan workers remained in these jobs for long periods, and the government itself became responsible for having created employment opportunities with poor labor conditions. The key to job creation programs lies in appropriately targeting a pool of unemployed workers with certain attributes and providing jobs that allow these workers to display their abilities. Policies designed to alleviate short periods of unemployment resulting from economic downturns must build in incentives for workers to seek jobs outside of the public works projects as the economy recovers. As the Japanese experience proves, a system without such incentives tends to fall victim to social inertia and becomes extremely difficult to discontinue.

Employment policy during the period of economic growth in the 1960s, as initiated under the National Income Doubling Plan, sought to provide a continuous supply of labor for growing industries and a smooth transition for workers retrenched from sunset industries. The First Employment Measures Basic Plan played an important role in promoting a balanced supply of labor to meet demand. The shift to introducing employment opportunities from a wider geographic area in order to encourage labor mobility promoted flexibility in the labor market and improved the ability of the labor force to respond to structural changes. The adaptability encouraged by such labor market policies supported the remarkable economic growth of this period.

During the 1970s the focus of Japanese employment policy shifted to internal labor markets. The centerpiece was the employment adjustment subsidy scheme, which was based on the belief that unemployment could be prevented as long as employers received the right incentives and subsidies at the right time. This and similar assumptions underpinned many of the measures initiated at the time, including the extension of the retirement age and other initiatives directed at older workers. But such policies, which are based on encouraging employment maintenance, ultimately tend to hinder labor mobility. Subsidies may be workable when the industrial structure is relatively stable and excesses in the labor supply are temporary. But employment policies based on the internal labor market and typified by employment adjustment subsidies are best introduced only after such conditions are verified.

The serious long-term recession that has affected Japan since the disintegration of the bubble economy in 1992 proves the importance of considering both the industrial structure and the macroeconomic conditions of an economy in developing employment policies. Currently, the government is promoting new management strategies that jettison conventional management methods in an effort to speed recovery. Attention has turned to the promotion of businesses in nontraditional fields, and the growth of such companies in this sector has been striking. The government is also once again considering policies to facilitate the smooth reallocation of labor. The success of these strategies remains to be seen. They draw on Japan's experience and are specifically geared toward meeting the country's current employment challenges. Policymakers from other Asian economies may find Japan's experience in developing employment policies useful in designing strategies to address their own employment issues.

Notes

1. We do not offer encyclopedic information about Japanese employment policy, nor do we offer actual technical support for implementing employment policies. Policymakers who plan to apply the lessons from the Japanese experience must determine how best to use them.

2. In order to focus more clearly on the impact of employment policies during recession and recovery, we do not cover the bubble economy in depth.

3. There are no reference materials available that we can use to compare the employment situation prior to 1953 with the current situation. The most comprehensive data available on Japanese employment conditions is the Labor Force Survey conducted every month by the Statistics Bureau of the Management and Coordination Agency. However, the size of the respondent pool and the methods

used to analyze the results have been revised a number of times. The revisions made in 1961 were particularly substantial, creating a considerable gap between the new results and those from earlier years. The survey group was able to recalculate previous years' indicators only back to 1953.

4. According to the Bureau of Statistics, of the total workforce of 25.66 million, the number of self-employed people and their family workers earning annual incomes of 25,000 yen or less came to 5.14 million (20.0 percent). At the same time the number of employees (including those under the age of 20 earning monthly salaries of 3,000 yen or less and those ages 20 and older earning 4,000 yen or more per month) was 1.82 million (7.1 percent). The number of people, including the unemployed, whose income could not be determined came to 3.96 million.

5. The first Economic Recovery Plan, released in January 1946, was titled "Urgent Issues to Be Tackled to Resolve the Employment Problem."

6. In accordance with Article 19 of the 1947 Employment Security Law.

7. Under the dual structure, the labor force was divided into two groups: those who worked in large concerns, and those who worked in small- to medium size enterprises.

8. In 1981, in order to help seniors and the infirm become independent and leave public jobs, the government offered a lump-sum payment of 1 million yen to those who withdrew from public works programs. This plan led 18,000 people to leave their jobs. In addition the government abolished or downsized a number of extremely inefficient or uneconomical public works, and in March 1996 the Congress passed a law abolishing public works projects intended to absorb the unemployed. The difficulty of moving workers off the projects underscores the importance of learning from past mistakes.

9. Known as "Golden Eggs," these graduates were generally 15 or 16 years old.

10. Clause 2 of Article 19 in the Employment Security Law stipulates that efforts be made to direct job seekers to jobs that do not require them to move. However, in 1960 the law was amended to allow Public Employment Service staff to direct workers to other regions when appropriate work cannot be found locally.

11. Japan's senior population (65 years old and older) was only 9.0 percent in 1980, the lowest rate among advanced industrial nations. However, the rate was projected to rise to 16.4 percent in 2000, the same level seen in other advanced nations, and to reach 25.2 percent in 2020. This increase would make one of every four Japanese a senior citizen by 2025.

12. One of the first books on Japanese employment customs widely read outside Japan was *The Japanese Factory* (Abegglen 1958), which offers this description of lifetime employment:

At whatever level of the organization in the Japanese factory, the worker commits himself on entrance to the company for the remainder of his working career. The company will not discharge him even temporarily except in the most extreme circumstances. He will not quit the company for industrial employment elsewhere. He is a member of the company in a way resembling that in which people are members of families, fraternal organizations, and other intimate and personal groups in the United States.

References

Abegglen, James C. 1958. *The Japanese Factory.* Cambridge, Mass.: MIT Press.
Bureau of Statistics. Various years. *Labor Force Survey.* Tokyo.
ILO (International Labour Organization). *Action against Unemployment.* Paris.
MOL (Ministry of Labor). 1960. "Special Survey on Workers in the Work Relief Projects." Tokyo.
_____. 1966. First Employment Measures Basic Plan (March 1966).
_____. 1973. Second Employment Measures Basic Plan (January 1973).
_____. 1998. *Survey of Employment Trends.* Tokyo.
_____. 1999. "Emergency package of Measures to Increase Job Security and Strengthen Industrial Competitiveness." Tokyo.